Women's Writing in Exile

. . . .

Edited by Mary Lynn Broe and Angela Ingram

. . . .

Women's

Writing in Exile

The University of North Carolina Press   .   Chapel Hill and London

© 1989 The University of North Carolina Press
All rights reserved
Manufactured in the United States of America

Library of Congress Cataloging-in-Publication Data

Women's writing in exile / edited by Mary Lynn Broe and Angela Ingram.
    p. cm.
    Essays, most of which were presented at the 1986 Modern Language
Association convention.
    ISBN 0-8078-1849-6 (alk. paper). — ISBN 0-8078-4251-6 (pbk. :
alk. paper)
    1. English literature—Women authors—History and criticism. 2. Exiles'
writings, English—History and criticism. 3. Women and literature. 4. English
literature—Foreign countries—History and criticism. I. Broe, Mary
Lynn. II. Ingram, Angela J. C. III. Modern Language Association of America.
Meeting (1986 : New York, N.Y.)
PR111.W655 1989   88-39308
820'.9'9287—dc19   CIP

The paper in this book meets the guidelines for permanence and durability of
the Committee on Production Guidelines for Book Longevity of the Council on
Library Resources.

93 92 91 90 89   5 4 3 2 1

This book is for Jane Marcus,

without whom it wouldn't have started.

. . . .

Again if one is a woman one is often surprised by a sudden splitting off of consciousness, say in walking down Whitehall, when from being the natural inheritor of that civilisation, she becomes, on the contrary, outside of it, alien and critical. Clearly the mind is always altering its focus, and bringing the world into different perspectives.
—Virginia Woolf, *A Room of One's Own*

On June 18, 1986, news coverage of the State of Emergency in South Africa included a report that the Government Censor had ordered the editor of the *Sowetan* to stop "printing" blank spaces (which indicated the enforced omission of news) "because the spaces themselves could be considered subversive."
—ABC "World News Tonight," June 19, 1986

Contents

. . . .

Acknowledgments

. . . .

Versions of most of these essays were presented at the 1986 Modern Language Association convention, in three sessions on twentieth-century English literature arranged by Jane Marcus. For probably the first time, sessions in that division were integrated to constitute a forum for feminist scholars, and we are grateful to the people in the audiences whose comments and discussions in the corridor benefited us all. We are grateful, too, to Hana Wirth-Nesher of Tel Aviv University and to Ann Larabee and Christine Conti of the State University of New York-Binghamton for working with us. The contributions from Susan Hardy Aiken, Trudier Harris, and Louise Yelin, and from Annette Kolodny and Esther Fuchs, were written in response to editorial importunities—and we are very glad indeed that they were.

Susan Stanford Friedman's essay was presented in various forms at the H.D. Centennial Symposium in Bethlehem, Pennsylvania, and the Emily Dickinson–H.D. Symposium at San Jose State University, as well as at the MLA; a version also appears in *Agenda* (Winter 1987). A different version of Bradford Mudge's essay appeared in *Tulsa Studies in Women's Literature* (Fall 1986). The dialogue between Sneja Gunew and Gayatri Chakravorty Spivak, first heard in "The Minders" on Australian Broadcasting Commission Radio National, appeared in print in *Hecate: An Interdisciplinary Journal of Women's Liberation* in 1986. We are very pleased to have permission to reprint the piece in the Northern Hemisphere.

The insights, the strictures, and the suggestions of Linda Kauffman and Rachel Blau DuPlessis have been enormously constructive with regard to the book as a whole and to individual essays. We are happy to be able to acknowledge their helpfulness, and we hope they like the book. We are also very grateful to our copyeditor, Trudie Calvert, who, at the same time that she understood many of our insistent, individual, and shared eccentricities, very swiftly and smoothly cleaned up our collective presentation.

We couldn't have invented a better editor than Sandy Eisdorfer if we'd tried. From the first (a breakfast at the MLA), she has been unfailingly generous with her time, her professional guidance, and her understanding of the difficulties of coediting over a distance of a thousand or so miles. We hope that she knows how grateful we are for her faith in and enthusiasm for this project, as well as for her patience—and, not at *all* least, for her sense of humor.

We are pleased to know and to share a book with the makers of this collection. We are, of course, indebted to them for their scholarly contributions and for their willingness to write about varieties of exile, and we have been grateful for—and amazed at—everyone's patience and promptness in responding to an extraordinary variety of editorial suggestions and requests. Perhaps even more important, we have for two years appreciated the cooperative work that has gone into making this book: the exchanges, the dialogues, the collective energies that have made *Women's Writing in Exile* a result of—if we may take yet another phrase from Virginia Woolf—"thinking in common." (We *do* understand that "in common" raises innumerable questions.) And we also thank each other.

Our greatest debt is happily acknowledged in the dedication.

. . . .

On the Contrary, Outside of It

Angela Ingram

At present we have only theories about writers—a great many theories, but they all differ. . . . We are in the dark about writers; anybody can make a theory; the germ of the theory is almost always the wish to prove what the theorist wishes to believe.

Theories then are dangerous things. All the same we must risk making one . . . since we are going to discuss modern tendencies. Directly we speak of tendencies or movements we commit ourselves to the belief that there is some force, influence, outer pressure which is strong enough to stamp itself upon a whole group of different writers so that all their writing has a certain common likeness. We must then have a theory as to what this influence is. But let us always remember—influences are infinitely numerous; writers are infinitely sensitive; each writer has a different sensibility. That is why literature is always changing.
—Virginia Woolf, "The Leaning Tower"

If one would assign the life of an exiled writer a genre, it would have to be tragicomedy. Because of his previous incarnation, he is capable of appreciating the social and material advantages of democracy far more intensely than its natives are. Yet for precisely the same reason (whose main byproduct is the linguistic barrier) he finds himself totally unable to play any meaningful role in his new society. The democracy into which he has arrived provides him with physical safety but renders him socially insignificant. And the lack of significance is what no writer, exile or not, can take.
—Joseph Brodsky, "The Condition We Call Exile"

Virginia Woolf, talking to the Workers' Educational Association in 1940, and Professor Joseph Brodsky, addressing a conference on exiles in 1987, share a concern with "modern tendencies" and an assumption that it is possible to discuss "a whole group of different writers" whose work reflects "some force, influence, outer pressure." Once we have acceded to these premises, and to Joseph Brodsky's contention that there is a "condition we call exile," we face startling discrepancies between the positions of an "uneducated" middle-class Englishwoman in wartime Sussex and an exiled Nobel Prize–winning Russian poet teaching at an elite women's college in the United States. Such discrepancies can usefully stand for the variance between what male Western culture has commonly found noteworthy in the condition of exile and what the essays collected here suggest about women's writing in exile. The complexities of what might constitute exile are suggested, too, by the radical differences between Virginia Woolf's local, working-class audience in Brighton and Brodsky's international, and obviously internationally mobile, audience in Vienna. The relationships between exile and who commands the lectern, who, "socially insignificant" or not, is paid to speak and who is silenced, who may come to listen and who has to stay at home, pose some of the questions we have, in writing these essays, begun to ask.

At the intersections of historical and critical practice, of geographic place and gendered proprieties, in the margins of contradictory discourses and political systems, we each came to some momentary conclusions. But if these essays have "a certain common likeness," it is in their refusal to be confined, to keep within bounds; individually and collectively they question historical modes of categorizing, challenge theoretical formulations, and test assumptions about cultural value. There are no final words here. And, to "risk" a theory, so it is with exile: the center is always shifting, or, rather, being redefined, re-placed. Yesterday's place of exile can be tomorrow's center, and perhaps only in the today of moving from one place to another can conclusions, momentarily, be drawn.

To risk drawing conclusions about exile is to risk romanticizing and, perhaps inevitably, privileging the exiled subject, hauling her up to the lectern of the dominant culture as a spectacle or, worse, a savior. Such a maneuver, which naturally—if briefly—gives the microphone to whoever undertakes it, defines the new center, concomitantly placing the recently exiled and silenced subject at that (desirable) center. The existence of millions of exiles and refugees in what he terms a century of "displacement and misplacement" prompted Professor Brodsky to suggest that it was "very difficult to talk about the plight of the writer in exile with a straight face." He did, however, tell his international and well-funded audience in Kurt Waldheim's Vienna that "literature is the only form of moral insurance a society has." It is some such notion of "moral insurance," perhaps, that leads critics to make claims like these: "With the exception of D. H. Lawrence, the heights of modern English literature have been dominated by foreigners and émigrés. . . . The outstanding art . . . has been, on the whole, the product of the exile and the alien"; or "[the outsider] becomes . . . a symbolic container of elemental humanness [whose] life, paradoxically extraordinary, nevertheless makes grand statements about the nature of human experience"; or "the great strength of modern writing in English lies much more in its exiles than in its metropolitan writers."[1]

One's unease with regard to such claims stems not so much from their grandness or their finality as from their placement of both the exiled writer and the critic making the claim. Lecturing at Middlesex Polytechnic in 1987, Igor Pomerantsev made such unease healthily explicit in a lovely satire upon Western/English canonization procedures:

I am a bad poet from a distant country. . . . In my life and in my conversation I give the impression of being much more talented than I really am.

The key to my recognition . . . is otherness, my foreign birth and language. But . . . it happens to be the case that [this culture] only accepts those . . . poets who have had their finger nails pulled out at home. The vulnerability of finger nails, or their absence, is—like it or not—somehow connected with poetry. The possibility cannot be excluded that the reader, in order to justify his own creative passivity, will recognize talent only in those poets who have paid for their celebrity with their finger nails. But this means he, the reader, retains the possibility of developing some talent himself. Fate, pain, finger nails, like music, do not need translation. You believe them.

We would not attempt to claim that gender, like fate, pain, and fingernails, needs no translation. The culture, however, the civilization that equates missing fingernails with the creative and the heroic is predominantly that gendered "civilisation"—with Whitehall its emblem—which Virginia Woolf feels "outside of": hierarchical and patriarchal, militarist and imperialist. Regarding *that* civilization, all the contributors to this collection are, necessarily, "alien and critical."

Leaving his wife behind to publish his prewritten prison poems, Pomerantsev will go home to be incarcerated and have his fingernails pulled out, to become, thereby, a good poet and martyr. His wickedly funny analysis of what is crucial to the lionization of literate political exiles suggests, as does Brodsky's disquisition, that "the exile" almost always has a wife.[2] Although it may characterize much of what the media allow us to know of twentieth-century exile, such genderizing leaves us with innumerable questions about the marginalized and differently manicured wives, daughters, sisters, and mothers—about women. Asked recently about the "sacrifices" of being in exile, Miriam Makeba, banned from South Africa for half of her fifty-six years, said, "The first sacrifice is not being able to go home to my country where I was born and to not see the grave where my mother was laid to rest is very painful." And when the black American interviewer—a woman—asked if there were any "consolations" for being in exile, she said, "Just my song. I am very happy when I sing; even when I sing a sad song."[3]

These essays explore varieties of exile women have experienced over the last hundred years—exile in some instances as much metaphor as it is material circumstance. Some writers discussed here exiled themselves (leaped out) from places that were not home to find places where they could write freely; such writers renounced the creative, intellectual, and emotional expatriation that defined citizenship in their countries, their families of origin. Others are exiled less by geography than according to received literary criteria, which, in obscuring the complex interactions of race, class, and sexuality, in delineating hierarchies in matters of genre, arbitrarily determine canons and canonicity. And then, in a century and in a world disrupted by clashing armies and ideologies, destabilized by monumental stupidity and violence, women frequently excluded from what is considered significant action by immobilizing notions of "protection" have produced exilic texts which, in reflecting the master discourses, subvert them.

Geographical exile is often more a *getting away from* than *going to* a place. This is probably true in varying degrees for most exiles, expatriates, leavers of countries (including a few of the essayists here); it is particularly true for women whose home environments, once we actually look at them, are never quite "home." As Susan Friedman says of H.D., "It was . . . where she wasn't, not where she was, that mattered," and one could say as much, though differently, of Gertrude Stein and Ingeborg Bachmann, of

Isak Dinesen and Anna Wickham. Deciding, or having, in Trudier Harris's phrase, "to *be* in the world" somewhere other than a familiarly and familially defined home can have profoundly disturbing effects for writers who simply "leave home" as well as for colonials like Doris Lessing and Jean Rhys for whom the starting place is no more—nor less—home than is the Mother England to which they exile themselves. But even this rather facile generalization is subverted by, for instance, Isak Dinesen, whose *matria*, her "heart's home," was Africa and whose Denmark was a "living death."

Voluntary exile, something of a luxury when we consider it closely, constitutes for a number of writers an escape from the entrapping domain of the silenced mother-under-patriarchy, the manifestation of women's internalized exile/estrangement: a "matricidal" intent is writ large through some of the texts of exile. Such an escape into the world of the apparently liberating Word, the world of culture, of adulthood, though, often means entry into the confines of patriarchal languages and heterosexual and heterosexist imperatives. Enabled, on one hand, to write, to create new worlds and to recreate what should have been home, many writers find the other hand shackled by the expectations and rules of the world of words they have chosen to inhabit. For some, however, the ambiguities and paradoxes inherent in finding a place to write are at least partly resolved by finding a "home" in writing itself.[4] Such writing, even by white women, is often sharply perceptive of dissonances in the dominant culture, as Judith Kegan Gardiner suggests; further, it interrogates the gendered nature of those dissonances, building from them literary structures that conflate inside and outside, margin and center.

The matter of exile, however, extends beyond physical or geographical definitions. The writers discussed in Part I identify, in some ways, communities of women and of writers, their "common likeness" being to make and sometimes question new connections between physical place and home, between familiar and alien social hierarchies. The essays in Part II identify an exile that is more abstract and for that reason somehow more invidious, certainly in the contexts of the feminisms we variously inhabit and from which we speak. Women's writing is often displaced, exiled by the very people who are trying to "re-vise" the canon to include writers excluded by earlier generations and older ideologies. Unexamined, such revisioning risks perpetuating a hierarchy of genre, different, perhaps, from older, more established hierarchies, but nonetheless restrictive in, for example, its ascription of value to formal experimentation but not to radically new content. Even more disturbing are the continuing failures of white liberal feminist scholarship to confront racism, ethnocentrism, elitism, heterosexism—"isms" that if ignored replicate patriarchal and canonical methods and often merely rephrase the languages of exiling and exclusion.

So far, women have had to deal differently from men with the specific workings of political systems designed to oppress and incapacitate those who cannot, or will not, subscribe to the central "home" ideology. Writers confronting those systems, the focus of Part III, are driven into exile, literally or metaphorically, by imperialism, by fascism, by the militarism that informs those ideologies, and by the concomitant demand that women produce children to serve the fathers, to serve in the wars. Displaced by official politics as well as by the political codes, both written and unwritten, of patriarchy, these writers exile themselves in ways that constitute subversion of political norms and of official versions of reality. In the process, they decenter notions of genre and text and consequently challenge and destabilize the reader's political certainties. These exiled writers' own estrangement from the "center" often frees them to dissect oppressive institutions, of which the family and fascism are but the two most obvious tools.

Shari Benstock's essay aptly begins this collection by questioning traditional definitions of Modernism and by exploring notions of exile and expatriation in relation to women. She argues that because women are "ex*patria*ted *in patria*," their writing in exile is necessarily different from that of men; tracing an "internal seam" within Modernism, such writing cannot be subsumed under the conventional criteria. Living in Europe enabled numerous white American women to externalize in their writing the internalized exile they had felt "at home." That externalization is manifest in a great variety of ways—from subject matter to punctuation— in texts written "on the cultural rim," of which the essay gives us an exciting sense before offering a reading of Gertrude Stein—a woman "made to represent for Modernism all that is . . . ex-centric to culture."

Three "ex-centric" women who left home to escape the polarizing and paralyzing dictates of family are the focus of Mary Lynn Broe's discussion of the interrupted texts and interrupted lives of Djuna Barnes, Antonia White, and Emily Coleman. The baleful effect of the family in which the fathers use and abuse the daughters is to consign the daughters to "exile within the family"; the flight into exile is a cultural and personal response to that familial situation, which at its most violent constitutes incest. The isolation and silencing integral to their victimization, Broe suggests, compelled these writers to displace their family exile by constructing an alternative family at Peggy Guggenheim's Hayford Hall. Here they tried to work through the exile of incest in texts that mark powerfully the transgressions and extravagances of women's (Modernist) writing at the same time as they insist that the fathers' incestuous abuses force the daughters into multiple silences which they seem never to have been able completely to break.

It was not what the fathers but what the "suitors" represented, Susan Stanford Friedman shows, that placed H.D. in a particular kind of exile—"exile in the American grain." To escape the "immediate suffocation of America," apparently inescapably placed in her poetry and her life between William Carlos Williams and Ezra Pound—the "regional" and the "international"—H.D. exiled herself to London, finding creative space in her poetry and a more personally expressive space in her prose. The dichotomy of exclusive, cosmopolitan Modernism and "the parochial and provincial" is radically questioned as Susan Friedman charts H.D.'s wanderings and writings to their creative source, an exile that was "a perpetual marginality rooted in both H.D.'s heritage as a Moravian-American and her wanderings as a woman in a man's world."

For American women who, fleeing "femininity," exiled themselves to the cultural capitals of Europe, exile betokened among other things a foreign space redolent of possibilities America did not offer. For white women from the colonies, however, Europe, or, more particularly, England, presented a profoundly different experience. The colonial's position is anomalous precisely because "Home" isn't. Home, for Jean Rhys, Christina Stead, and Doris Lessing, as Judith Kegan Gardiner makes clear, is no place, and thus exile is both at home (Dominica, Australia, "Rhodesia") and at "Home" (the mother country). A white girl growing up "at the periphery of the . . . empire" has home defined for her by her mother, who, herself in exile, teaches her daughter both to think of England as Home (a desirable place) and to be a proper little English lady at home (in the colony). "The Exhilaration of Exile" focuses on several works that address the complexities inherent in the confusion of "home" and "exile" for the writer, who, exiling herself in the home country, is both exhilarated by the freedom it offers and critically aware that it is the locus of those patriarchal, heterosexist, middle-class norms that dominate life in the colony and at the colonizing center.

Colonial writers, like many Americans, made a home in writing. For Isak Dinesen the enormously difficult negotiation of the shift from Kenya back to Denmark threatened her creativity, that voice she had found in Africa. *Exmatriation* to the "living death" of Europe, however, paradoxically gave Dinesen the words to create a brilliantly "transgressive art," which, Susan Hardy Aiken shows in a wonderful reading of "The Dreamers," doubles and redoubles exile and distance. In her own name(s) and writing practice Dinesen blurred and blended gender and language and in this story writes an "exilic aesthetic" in which words are ultimately the "very stuff of resurrection."

Being in exile or finding a community in which the pain of exile might heal does not, clearly, necessitate moving from one country to another. Trudier Harris discusses contemporary Afro-American writers, whose characters, exiled by the demands and rules of men and men's God within their traditional community, the black church, find asylum in communities characterized by women's healing powers and by ways of being in the world which transcend the limitations of Christianity. Those communities are, indeed, at once global and intensely individual. Trudier Harris suggests, however, that many writers—including Ntozake Shange and Gloria Naylor, Ann Allen Shockley and Alice Walker—depict these woman-defined, often lesbian asylums as "a new form of exile." Despite their drawing on ways of thinking and on images "that unite suffering women across history, races, and cultures," such asylums exclude men and children and are in danger of isolation from the larger black community, and it is only Toni Cade Bambara, in *The Salt Eaters*, who "envisions a world where asylum cannot be equated to exile."

There are other kinds of exile than that occasioned by the need to leap out from the land or community of one's birth in order to write or live freely. As countries have written and unwritten laws that impose exile both internal and political, so the world of readers and publishers and writers has laws that effectively exclude writers on the bases of race and gender, subject and genre, which determine a writer's major or minor status, pronounce upon what should be taken seriously. The essays in Part II, testing the integrity of such laws, propose revisionary criteria which are at once more flexible and more precise.

Discussing Gertrude Stein's *Three Lives*, Sonia Saldívar-Hull criticizes the exclusion of Chicanas and other women of color from even revised feminist canons and points to the contortions that result when white liberal feminists assume that only they can speak *for* and theorize *for*

Chicana and "Third World" writers. In the critical enthusiasm attendant upon claiming Stein for our Modernist canon, in the concern for Stein's linguistic experimentation and her encoded depiction of lesbian experience, Stein's racism (notably in "Melanctha") and class bias (notably in "The Good Anna") are frequently sidestepped. Such evasions further exile women of color and working-class women, doubly displacing them from an often unexamined white, middle-class "center" and recolonizing their voices.

The double exiling that can result from unexamined critical practice is central, too, in Bradford Mudge's analysis of Virginia Woolf's subscription to an "autonomy aesthetic" which distinguishes literary from nonliterary, "major" from "minor," critical activity from cultural studies. Ever conscious of her own exiled status, Woolf wanted to revise history by writing the lives of the obscure, but in consigning those lives and their works (here, specifically, those of Sara Coleridge) to the "minor" echelon, she could not avoid barring them from the house of literature she was intent upon rearranging.

Such evaluative distinctions between and within different genres allow and often encourage the exclusion of voices that seem not to meet canonical criteria. Access to the lectern is limited. Celeste Schenck shows how poets who employed traditional meters were "exiled by genre" from the "high Modernist" canon and continue to be excluded from revisionary feminist canons by scholars who have reclaimed, for example, H.D. and Gertrude Stein. She argues that the conventional forms used by such poets as Charlotte Mew, Anna Wickham, and Edith Sitwell not only make some splendid poetry but speak the politics of sexual radicalism, of class analysis, of "cultural criticism." Excluding such poets not only diminishes and homogenizes the multiplicity of modernisms but reinforces the "aesthetic Aryanism" of the male Modernist canon, refencing its boundaries and keeping its gates.

Boundary lines are patrolled not only by canon-makers, of course. Hilary Radner formulates a theory of reading practice which examines texts whose authors and readers exist both inside and outside the academic enclave. Her analysis focuses on the novel, a genre itself forced to jump boundaries, being both "a good read" and "literature" depending upon how it is read. Beyond Roland Barthes's opposition of "readerly" and "writerly" texts, she identifies the exilic character of the woman's novel and, more wonderfully, of its subgenre, the dissertation novel, written in "response to the inadequacy of a purely professional and academic discourse" by and for intellectual women whose citizenship within the academy is determined by how we read what we read.

Any boundary, Jane Marcus has said, keeps somebody out. Her essay here is concerned in part with the ethics and politics of mapping boundaries and of "placing" writers and texts in relation to each other on the margins. It is concerned, too, with the dangers—addressed in different ways by Gayatri Chakravorty Spivak and Sneja Gunew, by Esther Fuchs and by Sonia Saldívar-Hull—of ascribing a "more authentic" exilic voice to some than to others. That danger is manifest when the critic (the cartographer/scientific observer) determines the criteria governing which group or person or species, which life or activity or language, is worth saving from exile. Reading a variety of texts, Jane Marcus explores the ethics of appropriation, practiced often in isolation from communal experience and determined by the limitations of class, race, education, species; she ends with a reading of Sylvia Townsend Warner which undermines any alibis we might want to construct for failing consciously to observe the ethical considerations implicit in any treatment of any exilic subject.

The explicitly political nature of exile and exclusion is the focus of the last five essays, which move from imperialist British India to Nationalist Suid Afrika. In between are discussions of variations on the reality of fascism, Spanish and German as well as British.

We might expect white women writing in British India to have taken the opportunity of their own exile to dismantle some of the stereotypes that bound both Indian and British women. But Rebecca Saunders shows the extent to which Flora Annie Steel, in her fiction at least, remained culture-bound, race-bound, class-bound, despite her access to Indian society/ies—an exemplar of that "psychic split" which almost inevitably characterized the memsahib. A woman "more exiled" than Steel might begin to analyze the disastrous effects of what Virginia Woolf scathingly designated "our splendid empire" and in the Canadian Sara Jeannette Duncan, Rebecca Saunders suggests, we might have one. A colonial herself, Duncan began to identify not only the ethnocentric arrogance of well-meaning British socialists but also, in ways however limited by her time and place, the almost unbearable position of high-caste Indian women, who, trapped between cultures and classes under the polite violence of imperialist politics, "lost [their] voice[s]."

The silencing fostered by the empire provided a ready-made methodology for British fascism. That women were naturally excluded from any place but the church, the kitchen, and the nursery was an imperial imperative which the 1914–18 war questioned only to confirm officially in overplus. Burgeoning abroad, fascism was also abroad in the land, insisting that women mutely but cheerfully produce sons to fight in the next war. "Un/Reproductions" shows how challenges to fascist ideology, suggested by favorable representations of lesbians, homosexual men, pacifists, and women disinclined to produce children were silenced by censorship in the years following the war. The expression of any view that apparently valorized things "unpopular in Whitehall" was banned, its exile prescribed for the defense of the realm, in the name of patriotism/ paternity.

Antifascism was a little more vociferous by the 1930s, of course, but women whose writing was informed by radical left-wing politics were, as Barbara Brothers shows, in "double jeopardy," where they remain, ghettoized or emblematized in literary accounts of the Spanish Civil War, all but erased from even the revised Modernist canon. Sylvia Townsend Warner, probably the best of those critics of Spanish fascism and its supporters, is still "an exile from the pages of literary history." Anatomizing fascism, her essays, poetry, and fiction repeatedly demonstrate the "different" view women have of history. The threat that "different" view embodies is clear in the way her condemnation of the collusion of state, church, and business in supporting fascism abroad and the powerful rich at home practically guaranteed her exile and erasure from the canons of 1930s writing.

Sylvia Townsend Warner dissected fascism even as it tested its strength in Europe; Virginia Woolf, in *Three Guineas* and elsewhere, located the "germ" of fascism in the patriarchal family. Ingeborg Bachmann, whose adolescence was invaded by Hitler's annexation of Austria, spoke even more plainly: "Fascism is the first thing in the relationship between a man and woman and I have tried to say in [*Malina*] that in this society there is always war." *Malina* and Marguerite Yourcenar's *Coup de Grâce* are the focus of Ingeborg Majer O'Sickey's analysis of women's linguistic and literal exile by the fathers' law and by men's control of the symbolic— control that makes language itself an instrument of murder, the ultimate exile. In *Malina* such murderousness is explicit in linguistic and syntactical disruptions created in part by Bachmann's naming her character "I"; such disruptions ultimately suggest, for the reader, a creative space beyond exile and murder. Yourcenar's 1938 novel might be read as an indictment of fascist brutality, but the 1957 preface, denying that fascism, racism, misogyny, and anti-Semitism are what the novel is "really" about, forces the reader to a profoundly disturbing realization that the murdered protagonist is twice exiled and silenced—once by her fascist narrator/murderer and again by her (and her narrator's) creator.

The last essay begins where we began—in an analysis of the quotation from *A Room of One's Own* which is the primary epigraph of this collection. Louise Yelin locates her subjects—Nadine Gordimer and *Burger's Daughter*—in "places" other essays have questioned and tests those questionings: the influence of the father and of "family" is not necessarily pernicious; the mother does not always, paradoxically, hinder the daughter's sexual maturation; European centers of culture are not always the loci of aesthetic freedom, and aesthetic freedom that facilitates the realization of individual autonomy is not necessarily the better part of exile. Destabilizing the political/personal dichotomy, Gordimer implicitly questions the practical value of feminism, an interrogation necessary, Louise Yelin suggests, because in Gordimer's "reverse" *bildung* gender is not the controlling condition of exile. Nadine Gordimer and her protagonist, white women born in a country whose indigenous people have been exiled and enslaved for over three hundred years, are inescapably born into a triple political state of emergency. Prison begins Gordimer's tale; the censor's deletion of part of a letter ends it. Rosa Burger, "taking the place" of her father and her mother in prison, is "simultaneously inside and outside the 'civilization' she inhabits, exiled in the prison (inside) and exiled from the Afrikaner regime against which she struggles, alien and critical, a victim and an opponent." The censor's deletions in this fictive account simultaneously reflect the historical reality of long-standing practice and foreshadow the 1986 censor who provides the second epigraph for this book: in the most effectively oppressive regimes, fascist, militaristic, patriarchal, and academic, even "the spaces themselves can be considered subversive." In our attempts to dismantle those regimes we recognize, as does Gordimer's protagonist, that "no one can defect."

In the academic and literary discourses that constitute this book the spaces *are* subversive. They disrupt the possibly comfortable assumption that to talk about women's writing in exile is to construct a safe place where such discussion may occur. As feminists choosing some attachment to the academy, we need, as Esther Fuchs reminds us, to foster the option of being suspicious when contexts become "congenial." Our professional selves "speaking for" exiles are in danger (it is far more than a "risk") of creating an alibi for those Gayatri Chakravorty Spivak calls "the hegemonic people." That danger compels us to look at the spaces between the politics of the profession and the politics of people in even so small a world as the profession. At these interstices are voices that insist that in conceptualizing exile we may too easily devise ways to contain it, to assume that there are no questions left to ask, to ignore the fact that, from anyone's point of view, there are always people who are, in Annette Kolodny's words, "too something."

Annette Kolodny, confronting her self of ten years ago and herself now, suggests that the communities we think we have are not necessarily the communities we have; there may be little comfort or support in those homes we have been wont to depend on. People *do* "defect"; institutional centrism is a powerful magnet. Esther Fuchs, meditating on the power of the many places she inhabits—feminism, Oriental studies, Israel, Arizona, a family of survivors of the Holocaust—ends, on the page here, with more questions than she or we can begin to answer. Presuming to answer questions about marginalities is too easily transformed into a homogenizing maneuver that can effortlessly be used on anyone outside the dominant culture who, for survival, needs to resist assimilation. Gayatri Chakravorty Spivak and Sneja Gunew, analyzing such maneuvers, emphasize how necessary it is to be suspicious whenever it is "possible to speak in certain circles" whose members, immaculately credentialed, liberally accept "difference"—and thereby refuse the specificity of individual women's lives.

Abstract definitions of marginality and exile, almost unavoidable in discussions of "other people's" texts, are, in these interstitial commentaries, collapsed, transgressed. They are transgressed by the experience of Annette Kolodny, when she avoids former colleagues who thought they were being neutral in the matter of her exile as a woman, as a Jew, and as a feminist in academia. They are transgressed in Esther Fuchs's questioning who and what make some forms of exile "trivial"; in Sneja Gunew's account of a Turkish friend who hangs poems in a shop window to make them accessible "to whoever is passing by." They are transgressed in Gayatri Spivak's account of herself, a "colored woman wearing a sari" negotiating the bureaucratic idiocies of officialdom at London's Heathrow Airport. That under the rubrics of Modernism and of post-Modernism and of feminism such questions and negotiations are "infinitely numerous" tells us that there are messy questions left over. Outside of it.

In the presence of so many nonanswers, we are enormously pleased to illustrate the book with reproductions of Karin Connelly's sculptures, translucent, defined by their nondefinition, all of their spaces subversive.

We are just as pleased that when she sent us the original photograph of *Mail* its inscription was "Untitled at the Moment."

Notes

To Jane Marcus goes all the credit for bringing Joseph Brodsky's article, quoted in the epigraph, to my attention and for discovering Igor Pomerantsev. In the course of revising this introduction I have been very grateful, too, to Louise Yelin, for her suggestions and her persistent American blue pencil, and to Linda Kauffman and Rachel Blau DuPlessis for so severely and so constructively taxing the text.

1. Eagleton, 9–10; Gornick, 127; Gurr, 9.

2. The first, and, so far as one knows, only discussion of the wives of "famous men" in exile (from Nazi Germany) is Gabrielle Kreis's *Frauen im Exil* (Düsseldorf, 1984). I thank Ingeborg Majer O'Sickey for this reference.

3. Interview by Charlayne Hunter-Gault, "MacNeil/Lehrer Newshour," WNET, New York, March 4, 1988.

4. This is certainly true of some male writers, as Gurr and Eagleton point out. Michael Seidel says, "So many writers, whatever their personal or political traumas, have gained imaginative sustenance from exile—Ovid, Dante, Swift, Rousseau, Madame de Staël, Hugo, Lawrence, Mann, Brecht—that experiences native to the life of the exile seem almost activated in the life of the artist: separation as desire, perspective as witness, alienation as new being" (x). Male exiles/expatriates, however, are almost always at home in their Word, and the countries they leave are *their* countries/*patriae*.

Works Cited

Brodsky, Joseph. "The Condition We Call Exile." *New York Review of Books*, January 21, 1988, pp. 16, 18, 20.

Eagleton, Terry. *Exiles and Émigrés: Studies in Modern Literature*. New York: Schocken Books, 1970.

Gornick, Vivian. "Woman as Outsider." In *Woman in Sexist Society*, edited by Vivian Gornick and Barbara K. Moran, 126–44. New York: New American Library, 1971.

Gurr, Andrew. *Writers in Exile: The Identity of Home in Modern Literature*. Brighton: Harvester Press, 1981.

"MacNeil/Lehrer Newshour," March 4, 1988, WNET, New York, interview by Charlayne Hunter-Gault.

Pomerantsev, Igor. "Lost in a Strange City." *Times Literary Supplement*, June 26, 1987, p. 695.

Seidel, Michael. *Exile and the Narrative Imagination*. New Haven: Yale University Press, 1986.

Woolf, Virginia. "The Leaning Tower." In *The Moment and Other Essays*, 128–54. New York: Harcourt Brace Jovanovich, 1948.

. . . .

Part 1

Communities of Exile

Home and Away

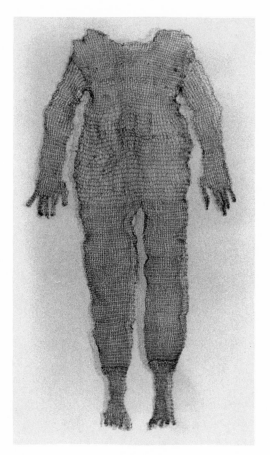

Mail
Sculpture by Karin Connelly

Chapter 1

. . . .

Expatriate Modernism

Writing on the Cultural Rim

Shari Benstock

At the outset I will sketch briefly a network of associations that link women writers in exile and the impact of Modernism, the movement that developed in Europe between 1900 and 1940. Briefly, the thesis of this essay is that the development of literary Modernism in this century encompassed both the notion of "exile" and the "expatriate"—indeed, addressed these not only in its subject matter but revealed them as elements in what we call the "stylistics" of Modernism. Further, the roles played by exile and expatriation in Modernist writing are often not the same for men and women Modernists. For women, the definition of patriarchy already assumes the reality of expatriate *in patria*; for women, this expatriation is internalized, experienced as an exclusion imposed from the outside and lived from the inside in such a way that the separation of outside from inside, patriarchal dicta from female decorum, cannot be easily distinguished. This coincidence of the expatriate and the Modernist as it is written in female experience is only now beginning to be fully explored by feminist critics, whose interest in this subject is, I think, not separate from our own feelings of marginalism within the academy. In looking at female Modernists in exile, therefore, I am also looking at myself and at feminist colleagues whose "writing on the rim" of modern culture is providing a powerful rewriting of female Modernism.

Modernist Definitions

> I am as awful as my brother War,
> I am the sudden silence after clamour
> I am the face that shows the seamy scar
> When blood has lost its frenzy and its glamour.
> —Eleanor Farjeon, "Peace"

> After all everybody, that is everybody who writes is interested in living inside themselves in order to tell what is inside themselves. That is why writers have to have two countries, the one where they belong and the one in which they live really.
> —Gertrude Stein, *Paris France*

Traditional descriptions of the evolution of Modernism as a European-based artistic movement centered in Paris, London, and Berlin argue that for Americans the desire to live and work abroad was brought about by three major historical factors: the crisis of faith in social values that was a primary effect of World War I; the reinforcement of powerful puritanic values in American life following the war (Prohibition, renewed religious fervor, and cultural bankruptcy that wrote itself in isolationism and provincialism); and the economic advantages offered by countries whose currency had been devalued as a result of the war. The effects of the Great War are implicit in each item of this litany we learned in graduate school, and the central place of the war in our understanding of the exodus to Europe following the armistice also suggests that the European-American alliance forged through the experimental writings we now call Modernist was a male bonding, forged either as an effect of or a reaction against the cultural-social-political power structures that caused the war. When the war ended, when the trenches—with their collections of bones, battle implements, and buried hopes—were plowed under and returned to France and Belgium as farm fields, the cultural-social-political power structures in support of which the war had stalemated itself were still in place, bruised but not beaten.[1] According to certain literary historians of the period, the former line of trenches that extended no-man's land from Mons in Belgium to Péronne in France served as an imaginary creative field nurturing texts by major Modernists (e. e. cummings, Ernest Hemingway, T. S. Eliot, for example), the terrors and treasons of its landscape obsessing the male Modernist mind.[2] Out of this nightmare emerged a dawn of renewed faith, but not in God, country, or political systems. Such naive notions had been put aside by this holocaust that served up the brightest and best-educated men of the classes of 1914 to 1918 to support the economic and political appetites of the war machine. Rather, Modernist faith was placed in the Word, specifically the literary Word, that could, perhaps, change the world.[3]

What is wrong with this description of the founding moments of Modernism? Almost everything, I would argue. In arbitrary order, these are its most grievous misconceptions and oversights: (1) It restricts the definition of literary Modernism to Anglo-American centrism, eliminating a crucial defining element of Modernism—its internationalism. (2) It situates literary Modernism in a psychology of *reaction against* the reigning cultural-social-political-religious-economic practices of the day, eliminating altogether those aspects of Modernist practice that overtly or covertly supported the status quo: a Modernism of conservation such as was lived and practiced by Eliot, Pound, and Wyndham Lewis, for instance. (3) It assumes Modernism to be a war-related phenomenon, so that early Modernist texts anticipate the war and later Modernist texts live in its wake.

The roots of Modernism in the nineteenth century and its extension into post–World War II literary practices are overlooked, even denied. (4) It implies a single definition of Modernism, erasing subtle but very important distinctions between Modernist practices in the different cities that supported Modernism or among practitioners whose work constitutes a single thread in a large, diverse, and complex textual pattern. This definition homogenizes Modernism. (5) It tacitly sets aside the complex set of responses to and articulations of the Word in Modernist texts, disallowing a range of literary practices that developed through the various stages of Modernism. (6) This set of defining prerequisites to the Modernist experience eliminates women from the historical canvas because women's experiences differed from those of men in two crucial ways: women were often not directly involved in the war; women usually did not have the classical education that provided them access to the Word in the Modernist sense—in the sense of knowing Latin and Greek.

In reaction against the claims made by this definition, Susan Stanford Friedman has argued that certain women writers, exiled to the margins of Modernist practice (or excluded altogether by Modernist definitions), constructed their own definitions of Modernism—what she terms a "Modernism of the margins." She writes that H.D., for instance, stands in the middle between the expatriatism of Ezra Pound and the nationalism of William Carlos Williams, "a woman between two men, an exile in the American grain, a form of exile both American and gendered. . . . Its inner dialectic suggests ways of moving beyond the parochial definitions of Modernism that either prescribe or condemn so-called internationalism" ("Exile in the American Grain"). Jane Marcus asserts—and has accumulated the historical evidence to prove the point—that World War I "wiped out women's culture." Marcus reminds us that "at the height of the suffrage movement in 1911 there were twenty-one regular feminist periodicals in England, a women's press, a feminist bookshop, the Fawcett Library and a bank run by and for women" ("Asylums of Antaeus"). This "women's culture" defined itself differently from its male Modernist counterpart, and it was not only World War I that led to its erasure, as the history of the magazine *New Freewoman* makes clear, but also the efforts by Modernist entrepreneurs to find a means for marketing the new literature. Thus the feminist *New Freewoman* became the Modernist *Egoist* (see Marcus's Introduction to *The Young Rebecca*). I have suggested that World War II eliminated the communities of women in Paris that throughout the interwar years had fostered a female literary Modernist practice and supported the work of male Modernists: "Hitler closed the door on the communal life of literary Paris" (*Women of the Left Bank*, 454). In describing the classical roots of Modernist language, Sandra Gilbert and Susan Gubar have argued that the interplay of allusions, puns, and linguistic experimentation characteristic of Modernism was born out of an effort to "imagine a kind of language that would have the kind of power, the kind of masculine authority, that Latin and Greek had until women started usurping them" early in the twentieth century (Paul, 8).[4]

Feminist literary history has discovered forms of female Modernism distinctly different from those canonized by male Modernists. The following cultural distinctions are different for male and female Modernism(s): (1) Women's relation to the Word differed from that of men and not only, or merely, because women's educational patterns were radically different from those of men in these years. (2) Female Modernist practices were less in *reaction against* the ruling authority of historical, political, social, and cultural experience than *different from* a (primarily patriarchal) hegemony. (3) Women banded together, their writings often overtly demonstrating various modes of female bonding, but the sense of community among women Modernists was entirely different from what is termed "male bonding." (4) Female Modernists were expatriated (if this term is even applicable) differently than their male counterparts. (5) The notion of exile was internalized by women in ways remarkably like the internalization of cultural misogyny, homophobia, or the assumption that women suffered an intellectual and creative deficiency.

This last distinction marks a crucial difference between the experience of men and women Modernists. The definitions of *exile* and *expatriate* were different for men and women, were experienced differently by them, and the coming together of expatriation and female literary practice traces an internal seam in the Modernist fabric. The standard definitions of the terms *expatriate* and *exile* suggest the cultural assumptions of coextensive self-identity, of coherent subjectivity, of the singular "I" that Modernism so ruthlessly questions. What Modernist writing has so often bypassed— the degree to which the pronoun "he" incorporates the experience of "she" or the tensions between *fatherland* and *mother tongue*—emerges in the historical efforts to distinguish *expatriate* from *exile*. The *Oxford English Dictionary* lists as the primary definition of *expatriate*: "to drive (a person) away from (his) country: to banish"; "to withdraw from one's native country, to renounce one's citizenship or allegiance." The semantic scale of *exile* is narrower, its boundaries more determined, its effects more painful:

"enforced removal from one's native land according to an edict or sentence; penal expatriation or banishment"; "expatriation; prolonged absence from one's native land, endured by compulsion of circumstances or undergone for any purpose." From these definitions we learn that (1) the term *expatriation* is etymologically conjoined to the patriarchal, incorporating the father/ruler whose law effects and enforces expatriating: (2) *expatriation* is defined in terms of the male—"to drive (a person) away from (his) country"—that is, the definition is gendered (or, rather, it assumes gender into a singular form); (3) *exile* is defined in terms of expatriation; (4) in both cases, inherent in the act is an enforcement of the law ("banishment" or "edict," which suggests the law of the land), a force that drives one away from one's native soil; (5) the definition of *native land* is taken for granted, but in this discussion, I suggest that we not pass so easily over this and other "givens" of the definitions.

Sandra Gilbert takes up these issues in her essay "From *Patria* to *Matria*: Elizabeth Barrett Browning's Risorgimento." This essay provides a good starting place for the investigation of the links between gender, the law, native land, and banishment that are knit together in the definitions of *expatriate* and *exile*. I found in Gilbert's essay the link between the political and the poetic in the instance of expatriation. She writes:

> Specifically, I will suggest that through her involvement with the revolutionary struggle for political identity that marked Italy's famous risorgimento, Barrett Browning enacted and reenacted her own personal and artistic struggle for identity, a risorgimento that was, like Italy's, both an insurrection and a resurrection. In addition, I will suggest that, by using metaphors of the healing and making whole of a wounded woman/land to articulate both the reality and fantasy of her own female/poetic revitalization, Barrett Browning figuratively located herself in a re-creative female poetic tradition that descends from Sappho and Christine de Pizan through the Brontës, Christina Rossetti, Margaret Fuller, and Emily Dickinson to Renée Vivien, Charlotte Perkins Gilman, H.D., and Adrienne Rich. In fusing supposedly asexual poetics with the dreams and desires of a distinctively sexual politics, these women imagined nothing less than the transformation of *patria* into *matria* and thus the risorgimento of the lost community of women that Rossetti called the "mother country"—the shadowy land, perhaps, that Freud identified with the mysterious "Minoan-Mycenaean civilization behind that of Greece." In resur-

recting the *matria*, moreover, these women fantasized resurrecting and restoring both the *madre*, the forgotten impossible dead mother, and the *matrice*, the originary womb or matrix, the mother-matter whose very memory, says Freud, is "lost in a past so dim . . . so hard to resuscitate that it [seems to have] undergone some specially inexorable repression" ("Female Sexuality"). ("From *Patria* to *Matria*," 194–95)

Gilbert describes what might well be the opposite of that implied in the definitions of *expatriate* and *exile*. She is not defining a situation of enforced expatriation or exile from the fatherland, but rather a "dream" of "a land of free women, a female aesthetic utopia," a rediscovery of the "*langue maternelle*" (197), associated for Barrett Browning, and others, with Italy. She is not discussing the "native land" of Italy as a "fatherland." Rather, this native land is a "trope . . . a living, palpable, and often abandoned woman" (196). Gilbert lists five distinct aspects of this tropology of Italy-as-woman that appear in the work of Christina Rossetti, Barrett Browning, and Emily Dickinson: "(1) Italy as a nurturing mother—a land that feeds, (2) Italy as an impassioned sister—a land that feels, (3) Italy as a home of art—a land that creates, (4) Italy as a magic paradise—a land that transforms or integrates, and (5) Italy as a dead, denied, and denying woman—a land that has been rejected or is rejecting" (196). *Matria*, then, is that which is repressed, rejected, colonized, written over, subjected, erased, silenced. The woman writer must discover her by peeling back the layers of patriarchy. The desire for this mother country is compelling, its discovery renewing, life-giving, passionate, transforming, and integrative. *Matria*, as Gilbert describes it, is the underside of *patria*, that which requires a *risorgimento*, a resurrection, a resurging, and a rising again up from under.

I would argue, however, that *matria* is not the underside of *patria* or a shadowy lost civilization that might be uncovered through a stripping away of patriarchy, but rather an "internal exclusion" within the entire conceptual and definitional framework, the "other" by and through which *patria* is defined. *Patria* can exist only by excluding, banishing *matria*; *matria* is always ex*patria*ted. She is driven away under penalty of the law that supports the patriarchal; by definition—that is, by genre and in her gender—she exists outside the law, beyond the reaches to which that law has driven her.[5] And yet the law cannot state its claims or effect its legalistic measures without recourse to her: she is the excluded other within the law that ensures the law's operation. Her very body is the "native land" on which patriarchy stakes its claims. Thus *matria* need not leave home to be exiled and expatriated; indeed, the effects of this outsidership within the definitional confines are most painfully felt at home, when the separation from language, body, identity, creativity, passion, and love have been so thoroughly internalized that one under sentence of banishment is complicit in her exile or expatriation. A related definition of *exile* is relevant here: it is the "waste or devastation of property, utter impoverishment; to ravage (a country) or ruin (a person)."

Gilbert's argument is relevant to mine in that it serves as an essential negative element, as *matria* is the implicit negative element of *patria* without which *patria* cannot be defined. In fact, the notions of *exile* and *expatriation* can work only within the movement of the negative. The dream of *matria*—motherland and mother *langue*—can work only within the frame of the ex*patria*ted. This dream of identity, of making whole that which is severed and divided, of *risorgimento*, of utopia, works better for some periods of history than others. As a trope for women's experience across time and space and as a metaphor for *all* women's experience, it is open to question. For my purposes, however, the movement from *patria* to *matria* opens the question for at least those women who in the early years of this century were literally expatriated from the United States to France. Their experiences and their reasons for leaving America and choosing France were different, of course, from those of the men who also chose expatriation. But these two sets of experiences cannot be separated from each other; each mirrors the other and carries the other within it.

For instance, a reading that genderizes the landscapes could argue that men abandoned America and fled to France to follow a circuit of female interdiction and desire. I have argued elsewhere that at the turn of the twentieth century, men felt the effects of what Ann Douglas, in a somewhat different context, called the "feminization of America"; they had retreated to a childish phase of development because their natural urges and desires had been tamed by women (and men associated with institutions that women controlled) so that the dominant structure of American life was not paternal, not masculine, hearty, daring, or aggressive but domesticated, feminine, passive, and constricting (*Women of the Left Bank*, 29–30, 78–79). America had become a mother to her men. One such man, Alex Small, lists his major reasons for expatriation:

The inordinate influence in American life of public spirited women. Of course, the individual who is not poor and helpless may escape their pernicious benevolence, but the spectacle is always there and it is sickening. It is to be dreaded, too, for no one knows what forms it is going to take. These managing women (who may be of any sex) have no respect for liberty. They defend their tyrannies with the claim that all living in society is a restriction on liberty, which is perfectly true, but it is a sophistical excuse for their mischief making. (*Paris Tribune*, July 10, 1930)

The American frontier mentality, that cliché of male experience in the New World, seems to have been replaced by its dread opposite: a flight from a tyrannical feminine.[6] To what were these men running? If we are to believe a good deal of Modernist poetry of this period, they were running to the arms of a French lover, Paris as prostitute. This particular city has consistently been imaged as female, a perfumed *putain* who raised her skirts, kicked her legs, and provided the thrills that tempted the male literary imagination. e. e. cummings called Paris "the putain with the ivory throat," a whore who sold her wares in the streets: "bon dos, bon cul de Paris" ("little ladies more," *Collected Poems*). In the heterosexual scopic male economy, Paris is eroticized and adulterated.

Female expatriates, too, were victims of this "feminized" puritanic culture that denied women access both to their sexuality and to their creativity and constrained their bodies by stays and bustles. They resented having things taken away from them, de facto, because they were women. Gertrude Stein wrote that it wasn't what France gave her that was so important but what it did not take away. It is significant that expatriate women writers did not eroticize Paris or maternalize France, nor did they necessarily genderize their conceptions of America (two evident exceptions to this claim are Willa Cather, who genderized American landscape, and Anaïs Nin, who eroticized urban landscapes). That is, in general France did not serve (as Italy presumably did) as nurturing mother, impassioned sister, a magic paradise or a dead, denied, and denying woman. Unlike the "ruin-haunted Italian landscape," France did not serve as "a symbolic text, a hieroglyph, or perhaps more accurately, a palimpsest of Western history" (Gilbert, "From *Patria* to *Matria*," 195).[7] Paris did become a "home of art" (to borrow once more from Gilbert's description of late nineteenth-century Italy), but Modernist women redefined both components of this safeguarded space—both "home" and "art."

What seemed oppressive to many of these women—to H.D., Gertrude Stein, Sylvia Beach, Djuna Barnes, and Natalie Barney—was the family, especially as it polarized (and paralyzed) the masculine and feminine. For these women the flight to freedom often meant a flight from the implicit expectation of marriage and motherhood; very frequently it meant a journey toward a sexual orientation other than heterosexual. (And for homosexual women the dream of a female paradise located itself not in France but in Greece, with Sappho on the island of Lesbos.) Driven by a need to escape cultural definitions, these women dreamed of rewriting cultural scripts. France opened up a landscape across which the imagination might follow its own lead, its psychic space free of predetermined expectations. France was certainly not, however, a blank space across which male and female Modernists could write their experimental scripts: from Edith Wharton to Anaïs Nin, expatriate women commented that French notions of the feminine and the masculine, of interactions between females and males, allowed for exceptions to both patriarchal laws and matriarchal legacies. Women were freed to write out the internalized expatriation against which they had always defined themselves. The coming together of an internalized and a lived expatriation gave rise to very special forms of writing that both do and do not share the basic premises assumed to be common to Modernism. One common denominator among women's writing of this period is the mark not only of gender but of female sexuality. Heterosexual and homosexual women expatriates, for instance, discovered *sexualized* writing identities in expatriation—and in doing so they changed the history of modern women's writing, charting the terrain of female sexuality from female perspectives. This new kind of writing may have been the single most important gift Paris gave them. It may also be a primary reason why they have been overlooked in the literary histories of the period, histories written by men and supporting androcentric values. The internal seam that women's writing traces in the Modernist fabric is the mark of an internalized condition that expatriation allowed to be externalized *through writing*.

Modernist Practices

Those foreigners
before whom   the soul
of the new Motherland
stands nakedly incognito
in so many ciphers
—Mina Loy, "Exodus"

Guido had lived as all Jews do, who, cut off from their people by accident or choice, find that they must inhabit a world whose constituents, being alien, force the mind to succumb to an imaginary populace.
—Djuna Barnes, *Nightwood*

What are the constituent elements of female Modernist writing, and how does it define itself according to its own (gendered) law? We know it best, of course, by the ways in which it has traditionally *not* fit the law of Modernist writing; or rather, by the ways in which it has seemed second-rate to acknowledged great Modernist texts—*Ulysses, The Waste Land, The Cantos*. It does not, like some male Modernist writing, enforce patriarchal privilege in a feminized, colonized, foreign setting, imaging the landscape as a female (m)other. Also, it does not necessarily take expatriation or exile as subject matter. The internalization of female exclusion provides, rather, the psychic and literary space out of which women Modernists write, even when their subject matter is home, family, and America—as it often is with Edith Wharton, Gertrude Stein, Djuna Barnes, and H.D. This Modernist writing is not a form of *écriture féminine* that can be practiced by either males or females because its common denominator is linguistic experimentation. Instead, it is a genderized writing that situates itself creatively, politically, and psychologically within a certain space and time. Women writers of this period and place both mimed and undermined Modernist principles, and we have yet to discover whether the "Modernist Mime" constituted an enforcement of the patriarchal poetic law or a skillful subversion of it.[8] We do know, however, that those women who, like Gertrude Stein, exposed the politics of patriarchal poetry were also banished from the Modernist canon—they were exiled and expatriated.

What I describe here is not a transhistorical phenomenon, nor does it constitute a common denominator of writing shared among all women of this time period just because they were women. The expression of an internal exile or an expatriation of internal exclusion that meets relief in a foreign land is highly varied. In Djuna Barnes's *Nightwood*, for example, it reveals itself through what might be called a stylistics of inversion that approximates a subject matter of inversion, traced through sexual orientation, religious preferences, political attitudes, landscape—Vienna and Paris—and sets of oppositional forces—night/day, death/life, and so on. In Gertrude Stein's writing the hidden seam of female writing is traced against the formal logic of grammar, syntactic structures, and philosophic categories, not merely resisting the grammatical law but writing itself in, around, against, and through that law. Similar traces of female Modernism appear in the spacings of Mina Loy's texts, in H.D.'s use of time, in Jean Rhys's use of pronouns, in Virginia Woolf's use of dashes and ellipses. These tracings—existing as effects of the female Modernist experience— have often been read as a textual *subsultus* symptomatic of failures of Modernist forms. Thus the narrative perspective of Djuna Barnes's *Nightwood* has consistently been misread, interpreted as an expression of homophobia and a condemnation of homosexuality or a pathological self-indulgence in these subjects. Gertrude Stein's theoretical writings on the nature of linguistic expression under the laws of grammar and logic have been taken as evidence of her lack of understanding of syntax and structure and her inability to conceive of logical arguments. Modernist innovation in poetic punctuation and capitalization, evident from the earliest examples of Mina Loy's poetry, has been attributed to e. e. cummings, making Loy's contributions derivative rather than originary. H.D.'s restatement of temporal functions in both poetry and prose has been thought to be a falling away from Modernist norms, a confusion of Imagist clarity rather than a reconceiving of textual temporality. Jean Rhys's use of pronouns has been overlooked and Virginia Woolf's use of dashes and ellipses has most often been thought to mark moments in her texts when language failed her.[9]

Such oversights, misreadings, and inverted interpretations occur with remarkable consistency in the history of Modernist criticism, suggesting that the effects of the female Modernist experience must be denied, not only by male readers wearing patriarchal blinders, but by women readers as well, even by feminist readers, whose interpretive efforts have them looking for signs of the female Modernist experience in all the wrong places.[10] Something about these Modernist texts is blinded—and blinding—the record of expatriation dispersed and displaced throughout the text, often appearing to be something else calling attention to itself as a presumed gap, a loss, a failure, a silence, a formal fault. Sometimes, of course, the trace of female experience announces itself as that which we have taken to be Modernist, but which has never been taken to have anything to do with the condition of expatriation or exile. Often, such traces do not openly call attention to their gendered condition. Collectively, these traces are precisely that which has been overlooked in literary histories of Modernism and in standard readings of Modernism—overlooked as female Modernists themselves have been overlooked.

It is not enough, of course, merely to suggest that what has been interpreted as a rhetorical tic or a textual symptom is really part of the theory, practice—even the psychology—of female Modernism. It remains to be proven that these tics or symptoms are not what they have always been assumed to be—Modernist failures. What is needed is a critical practice that combines close textual analysis with a renewed and revised literary and cultural history of Modernism. Female Modernism (like male Modernist practice, which has also been consistently misread, I think) requires *both* elements—textual analysis and historical contextualization—because these texts are products of the historical situation of certain women whose writing was itself an effect of expatriation.[11]

Apart from a few comments on Gertrude Stein, however, I will resist the desire to systematize, categorize, analyze, and prove through judicious examples the truth of the foregoing suggestions, not because I think my claims cannot be proven but because I want to put into question the very methods of that proof. This desire to "put into question" is not mine alone but is demanded by the very texts and lives we are here examining. In important ways Modernist feminist criticism has overlooked the gaping holes in its interpretive logic and the impassable obstacles to its own efforts. For the most part, this critique continues to read Modernism through traditional norms of literary history and forms of Modernist writing. As Modernist feminist critics we substitute "female" for "male" on the literary canvas, calling much needed attention to contributions by women Modernists, and we distinguish female Modernism from male Modernism, thus reversing conventional interpretive hierarchies, but we have not yet drawn enough attention to the androcentric premises of interpretation (including canon formation, genre definitions, and questions of literary value), reading (including the politics and economics of printing and publication), historicism (including the analysis of literary production and the politics of literary reputation) with particular attention to sexuality and representation in Modernist writing, on subjectivity and narrative methods, on Modernist formalism, on the connections between women's lives and women's texts. Our project needs to be carried far-ther.[12] I believe, for example, that the traditional analytic method that relies on exemplary texts and selected evidence to "prove" a theoretical claim is part of what Modernism questions. We know that the old notion of Modernism as a monolithic entity circumscribing the interests and literary methods of a few writers whose activities spanned the years 1900–1940 is an *idée reçue* that feminist Modernist criticism cannot accept. Modernism has been opened to Modernisms, and the differences among Modernist practices include differences of gender, but not only. How many Modern-isms are there in it? Gertrude Stein might ask. And what are the differ-ences among them?

> Patriarchal Poetry.
> Their origin and their history.
> —Gertrude Stein, "Patriarchal Poetry," 115

Certain forms of Modernism—those that are in some places now being called post-Modernist, as though to suggest their existence both inside and outside the historical boundaries of Modernism—unsettle the found-ing assumptions of literary practice. These assumptions include the lin-earity of narrative movement, the sanctity of authorial control over the text, generic definitions and limits, the security of textual boundaries, the relation of theme or content to narrative form—to name only a few. One of the lessons of Modernism is that interpretation cannot ignore literary forms or frames, either the linguistic or the textual, by reading "through" these conventions to extract the content or meaning of the work. But to suggest expatriation or exile as conditions of Modernist literary produc-tion experienced differently by men and women writers and apparent textually not as subject matter but as "stylistics" puts great stress on interpretation, even post-Modernist interpretation. We feel lag time be-tween Modernist practices and interpretive modes brought to bear on Modernist texts: Modernism outdistanced criticism, leading, I would ar-gue, to a crisis of criticism that T. S. Eliot, the spokesman for High Modernism, could not have imagined in his wildest dreams. (And it is significant, I think, that Eliot's poetic texts are not among those that generated post-Modernism, with its confusion of reading and writing practices.)

Gertrude Stein felt the effects of this lag time, just as she felt the effects of expatriation, and she commented on them frequently, claiming that real geniuses were always ahead of their time and consequently misunderstood. But Stein felt a sense of outsidership, experienced a form of internalized exile, not only because she was an artist and self-defined genius but because she was a woman (and tried to deny her womanhood for the sake of her art) and a lesbian, whose early emotional experiences had taught her that she was a "lonely outsider." That is, Stein was both temporally and spatially outside her society, expatriated. Her undergraduate work in philosophy encouraged her interest in numerical relationships; her presumed inability to master the basic rules of grammar and syntax made her question the logic and operations of those rules; her distaste for certain aspects of her medical school training at Johns Hopkins led, by a circuitous route, to a literary interest in the body—especially the female body. Gertrude Stein's writings question poetic principles, examine in detail the laws of grammar, and experiment with various numerical combinations in discussions of characters and relationships. As she writes in "Patriarchal Poetry," her interest is in "rearrangement," which is always "nearly rearrangement"—that is, it is never complete, whole, assembled, and appropriate to itself. The title of this text, "Patriarchal Poetry," questions both the patriarchal and the poetic and their internal arrangements: "Patriarchal" announces itself not merely as a subject of the poem—a theme, or significant content—but as the movement of ontogeny ("their origin and their history") and the conceptual scope of ontology ("to be we"). The subject of this text may be poetry, but the text resembles prose, and it asks questions of narrative conventions ("Was it a fish was heard was it a bird . . ."), examines the formal logic of the grammatical copula ("To be we to be"), plays with poetic forms ("Able sweet and in a seat"), questions conclusions ("What is the result. The result is that they know the difference between instead and instead and made and made and said and said") and appearances: "Patriarchal poetry is the same as Patriotic poetry is the same as patriarchal poetry is the same as Patriotic poetry is the same as patriarchal poetry is the same" (115).

What is the relation, then, between "patriarchal," "poetry," and "patriotic"; or between "difference" and "sameness"; between the verb *to be* and the announced topic of "their origin and their history"; between poetry and prose? And might these relations and rearrangements have something to do with "*expatriation*"? "Patriarchal Poetry" is defined and redefined hundreds of times in this text, but no definition is "definitive." The text refuses to stop, changing subjects, changing methods, changing terminology and disciplines, repeating itself, inverting its premises, circling around itself, until it stops, apparently arbitrarily. "Patriarchal poetry and twice patriarchal poetry"—a statement that combines the elements of Steinian numerics: $1 + 1 = 2$; $1 + 2 = 3$; 1 stands alone in relation to 2. At issue here is a concern with patriarchal logic, its definitions of unities and doubles (which, according to Platonic logic complement each other), totalities, divisions, closure, quiddity, quid pro quo. This logic of totalization, of truth, of resolution with no remainders, no leftovers, no outsiders, is patriarchal: "Patriarchal poetry is what is what is what is what is what" (146).

Against this "whatness" of patriarchal poetry, this substantial block on which Western civilization has written its metaphysic, stands Stein, outside its boundaries, expatriated, yet nonetheless implicated in this logic because she has been made to represent for Modernism all that is a-logical, all that cannot be tolerated within its definitions, all that is ex-centric to culture. The evidence of this truth is to be found everywhere and at all times in Stein's work, its positioning and import changing with the development of her writing project and alterations in her personal and professional history. It suggests itself in Stein's refusal of punctuation, in her distrust of storytelling conventions, in Melanctha's "wandering," or in the hyphen of Ida's double name, "Ida-Ida." This intuition of something at work otherwise in Stein cannot find confirmation by means of the old interpretive logic that presents a thesis proven through analysis of exemplary texts. Everything about Stein—her looks, her life, her writings—thwarted that logic and was thwarted by it, which is not to say that we can escape logic or that there is nothing to be done with Stein's writings except to reiterate their a-logicality. But our feminist rereadings of Modernism cannot remain comfortably within the limits of the old logic, within the boundaries of the old definitions, within the conventions of the old strategies. Certain Modernists and certain Modernist texts can show us surprising alliances between expatriation, literary creativity, and gender—alliances that are denied by the old logic, excluded by the old definitions, and overlooked by the old reading strategies. The discovery of such alliances requires a sensitivity to history, to language, to logic, to gender—a Steinian sensitivity: "It could be a puzzle why the intellectuals in every country are always wanting a form of government which would inevitably treat them badly, purge them so to speak before anybody else is purged. It has always happened from the French revolution to to-day. It would be a puzzle this if it were not that it is true that the world is round and that space is illimitable unlimited. I suppose it is that that makes the intellectual so anxious for a regimenting government which they could so ill endure" (*Paris France*, 65).

Notes

1. On how the war sustained the values it hoped to overturn, see my *Women of the Left Bank*, 26–28, 71–72, 117–18. See also Cobb, Fussell, Kedward, and Stephenson.

2. I would include among such critics Paul Fussell, Malcolm Cowley, Hugh Kenner, Sandra Gilbert, especially her "Soldier's Heart," and Susan Gubar, especially in "Sexual Linguistics" (coauthored with Sandra Gilbert). I would also include the traditional definition of Modernism given by Susan Stanford Friedman in *Psyche Reborn* (97), a definition revised from a feminist Modernist perspective in "Modernism of the 'Scattered Remnant.'" Jane Marcus takes issue with Sandra Gilbert's reading of the relation between World War I and female Modernist experience in "Asylums of Antaeus." See also my analysis of the roots of Modernism in *Women of the Left Bank*, 24–30.

3. Kenner articulates his definition in *The Pound Era* and Friedman in "Modernism of the 'Scattered Remnant.'" See my analysis of these two positions in *Women of the Left Bank*, 26–28, 30–34.

As we have traditionally thought of it, Modernism is (like all "isms") a historically bound, totalizing construct. Thus to revise our notions of its ethics and effects, we must first follow carefully its totalitarian, coercive, and threatening practices. We might begin by looking at its manifestos, which were not merely calls to artistic arms but calls to aesthetic and political order. The exclusionary ethics of Modernism were felt by those who always feel them: women, minorities, homosexuals, and the economically and politically disadvantaged. Because the methods of Modernism were disruptive—especially in what were thought to be its "stylistic excesses"—we have been mistakenly led to think that Modernism was revolutionary, an overturning and subverting of the old order, when more accurately we might say that Modernism imposed a new, and thoroughly authoritarian, order. For a discussion of the ideological assumptions that underwrote Modernism, see my *Modernism Made Manifest*; forms of Modernist writing on the margins of this new order are suggested in *Textualizing the Feminine*.

4. The question of the classical roots of Modernist language has been addressed by various critics. See Marcus, "Liberty, Sorority, Misogyny"; Gilbert and Gubar, "Sexual Linguistics"; and Baym. On the destruction of female communities by World War II, see Bernikow, Bryher, Colette, Cook, Monnier, and Nin.

5. I explore the links between generic and gender definitions and the workings of their law in literary texts, with special reference to the female signature, in "From Letters to Literature," "Reading the Signs of Women's Writing," and "The Letter of the Law."

6. Exploring an earlier relationship between the frontier and the feminine, especially through a pastoral vocabulary, Annette Kolodny writes: "At its core lay a yearning to know and to respond to the landscape as feminine, a yearning that I

have labeled as the uniquely American 'pastoral impulse.' . . . In a sense, to make the new continent Woman was already to civilize it a bit, casting the stamp of human relations upon what was otherwise unknown and untamed. . . . If the American continent was to become the birthplace of a new culture and, with it, new and improved human possibilities, then it was, in fact as well as in metaphor, a womb of generation and a provider of sustenance" (*Lay of the Land*, 8, 9). For many men—and women too—this link between feminizing and civilizing the new continent was enormously threatening.

7. For a questioning of France as a palimpsestic Modernist text, see my "Beyond the Reaches of Feminist Criticism." For a different interpretation of the palimpsest from Susan Gubar's "The Echoing Spell," see *Women of the Left Bank* (349–51).

8. Naomi Schor discusses the feminist uses of mimesis, following theoretical suggestions in Luce Irigaray's writing, in "This Essentialism Which Is Not One."

9. For an analysis of some of these traces, see Kolodny; Friedman, *Psyche Reborn* and "'Woman Is Perfect'" (coauthored with Rachel Blau duPlessis); Marcus, "Laughing at Leviticus"; Benstock, *Women of the Left Bank*, 158–61, 184–87, 336–49, 383–89, 438–41; and Benstock, "Beyond the Reaches of Feminist Criticism," for a discussion of Gertrude Stein's theoretical practices and essays on H.D., Stein, and Woolf in *Textualizing the Feminine*.

10. It is essential to produce collective work that reads Modernism against and with current feminist critical practice. As feminist critics of Modernism we must be brave enough to expose "oversights" and interpretive blindness in the work of others and to accept gratefully such exposing light on our own blindnesses. We must be constantly attentive to our own theories and practices, examining the conclusions to which these processes lead us, exposing the underpinnings of our own thinking—most especially our "feminist" thinking.

11. The essays in this volume represent an effort by feminist critics to examine the supporting structures of the Modernist feminist critique. Of particular interest is Celeste Schenck's "Exiled by Genre," which pays attention to the ways in which feminists have called for the canonization of women poets whose writing fit Modernist modes but who had been exiled by androcentric histories of Modernism (good examples are H.D., Mina Loy, Gertrude Stein, and Djuna Barnes). In making claims for *female* Modernism (against the canonized *male* Modernism) feminist critics have—unwittingly, I think—played into the hands of a conservative critical establishment that has rewarded the revolution in poetic language, overlooking contributions by women whose writings stayed within traditional genre boundaries. As Schenck argues, we have overlooked differences among women Modernists, seeing genre "as a pure, hypostasized, aesthetic category" rather than "a highly textured, overdetermined site of political contention, a literary space constructed often ex post facto from the conflicting materials of critical, political, racial, and sexual bias" ("Exiled by Genre").

And genre, of course, is only one example of the effects of "feminist blinding" to implicit differences within and among women. When I examined the ways in which Sandra Gilbert and Susan Gubar overlooked differences among lesbian life-styles, attitudes toward lesbianism, internalized homophobia, and the writings these cultural conflicts produced in women of the Paris Left Bank, I was calling attention to precisely such oversights in contemporary feminist criticism. (See Gilbert's "Costumes of the Mind" and Gubar's "Sapphistries" and "Blessings in Disguise"; see my *Women of the Left Bank*, 173–84.) I admit to a blindness to the question of genre as Celeste Schenck has analyzed it among Modernist women poets, and I appreciate her demonstration of the political and ideological in poetic form. Susan Stanford Friedman's exposition of a "Modernism of the margins," which links gender, sexual preference, race, and poetic practice, makes a similar effort, as does Sonia Saldívar-Hull's essay on Gertrude Stein, racism, and feminist critical practice, and Jane Marcus's analysis of women's responses to World War I, "Asylums of Antaeus." Marcus poses the question of critical and political ethics in her "Alibis and Legends" in this volume. What is called for, I think, is collective work on the ideological premises of Modernist practice in which the ideologies and ethics of both Modernism and feminist critical practices would be jointly exposed. A beginning is proposed by my *Modernism Made Manifest*.

12. As Celeste Schenck points out in her essay in this volume, feminist revisionary histories of the 1900–1940 period in Europe have focused on Modernist experiments with form, privileging narrative over poetry (perhaps because American New Criticism developed its critique through poetry rather than fiction). What of women writers who did not pursue Modernist experiments? What motivated Natalie Barney and Renée Vivien to adopt archaic poetic forms? Or Radclyffe Hall to employ outdated didactic narrative forms? Or Winifred Bryher to write children's narratives? Or Janet Flanner to adapt architectural forms to her novel *The Cubical City*? Much more work on these, and other, women writers is needed before we can graph the varieties of women's literary contributions to "Modernism." In particular, we need to examine the ways in which women's sexual politics informed literary poetics, looking carefully at the literary effects of sexual, racial, religious, and economic exclusions that were associated with primary gender expatriation within both American and European culture in these years.

Works Cited

Barnes, Djuna. *Nightwood*. New York: New Directions, 1937.

Baym, Nina. "The Madwoman and Her Languages: Why I Don't Do Theory." *Tulsa Studies in Women's Literature* 3 (1984): 45–60. Reprinted in *Feminist Issues in Literary Scholarship*, edited by Shari Benstock, 46–61. Bloomington: Indiana University Press, 1987.

Benstock, Shari. "Beyond the Reaches of Feminist Criticism: A Letter from Paris." In *Feminist Issues in Literary Scholarship*, edited by Shari Benstock, 7–29. Bloomington: Indiana University Press, 1987.

―――. "From Letters to Literature: *La Carte Postale* in the Epistolary Genre." *Genre* 18 (1985): 257–95.

―――. "The Letter of the Law: *La Carte Postale* in *Finnegans Wake*." *Philological Quarterly* 63 (1984): 163–86.

―――. *Modernism Made Manifest: The Politics of Periodical Publication, 1900–1940*. Forthcoming.

―――. "Reading the Signs of Women's Writing." *Tulsa Studies in Women's Literature* 4 (1985): 5–15.

―――. *Textualizing the Feminine: Essays on the Limits of Genre*. Norman: University of Oklahoma Press, forthcoming.

―――. *Women of the Left Bank: Paris, 1900–1940*. Austin: University of Texas Press, 1986.

―――. *Feminist Issues in Literary Scholarship*. Bloomington: Indiana University Press, 1987.

―――, ed. *The Private Self: Theory and Practice in Women's Autobiographical Writings*. Chapel Hill: University of North Carolina Press, 1988.

Bernikow, Louise. *Among Women*. New York: Crown, 1980.

Broe, Mary Lynn, ed. *Silence and Power: A Reevaluation of Djuna Barnes*. Carbondale: Southern Illinois University Press, forthcoming.

Bryher. "For Sylvia." *Mercure de France*, no. 349 (August–September 1963): 17–21.

Cobb, Richard. *French and Germans, Germans and French: A Personal Interpretation of France under Two Occupations, 1914–1918/1940–1944*. Hanover, N.H.: University Press of New England, 1983.

Colette. *Looking Backwards*. Translated by David le Vay. Bloomington: Indiana University Press, 1975.

Cook, Blanche Wiesen. "Women and Politics: The Obscured Dimension." In *Women, the Arts, and the 1920s in Paris and New York*, edited by Kenneth W. Wheeler and Virginia Lee Lussier, 147–52. New Brunswick: Transaction Books, 1982.

Cowley, Malcolm. *Exile's Return: A Literary Odyssey of the 1920's*. New York: Viking, 1951.

―――. *A Second Flowering: Works and Days of the Lost Generation*. New York: Viking, 1973.

cummings, e.e. *Poems, 1923–1954*. New York: Harcourt, Brace, 1954.

DuPlessis, Rachel Blau, and Susan Stanford Friedman. " 'Woman Is Perfect': H.D.'s Debate with Freud." *Feminist Studies* 7 (1981): 417–29.

Farjeon, Eleanor. "Peace." In *Scars upon My Heart: Women's Poetry and Verse of the First World War*, edited by Catherine Reilly, 36. London: Virago, 1981.

Friedman, Susan Stanford. "Exile in the American Grain: H.D.'s Diaspora," in this volume.

———. "Modernism of the 'Scattered Remnant': Race and Politics in the Development of H.D.'s Modernist Vision." In *Woman and Poet*, edited by Michael King, 91–116, reprinted in *The Private Self: Theory and Practice in Women's Autobiographical Writings*, edited by Shari Benstock, 34–62. Chapel Hill: University of North Carolina Press, 1988.

———. *Psyche Reborn: The Emergence of H.D.* Bloomington: Indiana University Press, 1981.

———, and Rachel Blau duPlessis. " 'I Had Two Loves Separate': The Sexualities of H.D.'s *Her*." *Montemora* 8 (1981): 7–30.

Fussell, Paul. *The Great War and Modern Memory*. New York: Oxford University Press, 1975.

Gilbert, Sandra M. "Costumes of the Mind: Transvestism as Metaphor in Modern Literature." *Critical Inquiry* 7 (1980): 391–418.

———. "From *Patria* to *Matria*: Elizabeth Barrett Browning's Risorgimento." *PMLA* 99 (1984): 194–211.

———. "Soldier's Heart: Literary Men, Literary Women, and the Great War." *Signs: Journal of Women in Culture and Society* 8 (1983): 422–50.

Gilbert, Sandra M., and Susan Gubar. *The Madwoman in the Attic: The Woman Writer and the Nineteenth-Century Literary Imagination*. New Haven: Yale University Press, 1979.

———. *No Man's Land: The Place of the Woman Writer in the Twentieth Century*. New Haven: Yale University Press, 1987.

———. "Sexual Linguistics." *New Literary History* 16 (1985): 11–43.

Gubar, Susan. "Blessings in Disguise: Cross-Dressing as Re-Dressing for Female Modernists." *Massachusetts Review* 22 (1981): 477–508.

———. "The Echoing Spell of H.D.'s *Trilogy*." *Contemporary Literature* 19 (1978): 196–218.

———. "Sapphistries." *Signs: Journal of Women in Culture and Society* 10 (1984): 43–62.

Heilbrun, Carolyn G., and Margaret R. Higonnet, eds. *The Representation of Women in Fiction*. Baltimore: Johns Hopkins University Press, 1983.

Kedward, H. R. *Fascism in Western Europe, 1900–45*. New York: New York University Press, 1971.

Kenner, Hugh. *The Pound Era*. Berkeley and Los Angeles: University of California Press, 1971.

King, Michael, ed. *H.D.: Woman and Poet*. Orono, Maine: National Poetry Foundation, 1986.

Kolodny, Annette. "Dancing through the Minefield: Some Observations on the Theory, Practice and Politics of a Feminist Literary Criticism." *Feminist Studies* 6 (1980): 1–25.

———. *The Lay of the Land: Metaphor as Experience and History in American Life and Letters*. Chapel Hill: University of North Carolina Press, 1975.

Kostelanetz, Richard, ed. *The Yale Gertrude Stein*. New Haven: Yale University Press, 1980.

Loy, Mina. "Exodus," in "Anglo-Mongrels and the Rose: 1923–1925." In *The Last Lunar Baedeker*, edited by Roger L. Conover. Highlands, N.J.: Jargon Society, 1982.

Marcus, Jane. "Asylums of Antaeus: Women, War and Madness." In *The Differences Within: Feminism and Critical Theory*, edited by Elizabeth Meese and Alice Parker, 49–81. Amsterdam: John Benjamins, 1989.

———. "Laughing at Leviticus: *Nightwood* as Woman's Circus Epic." In *Silence and Power: A Reevaluation of Djuna Barnes*, edited by Mary Lynn Broe. Carbondale: Southern Illinois University Press, forthcoming.

———. "Liberty, Sorority, Misogyny." In *The Representation of Women in Fiction*, edited by Carolyn G. Heilbrun and Margaret R. Higonnet, 60–97. Baltimore: Johns Hopkins University Press, 1983.

———. *The Young Rebecca: Writings of Rebecca West, 1911–17*. London: Macmillan, 1982.

Monnier, Adrienne. *The Very Rich Hours of Adrienne Monnier*. Translated by Richard McDougall. New York: Scribners, 1976.

Nin, Anaïs. *The Diary of Anaïs Nin, 1939–1944*. Edited by Gunther Stuhlmann. New York: Harcourt, Brace, and World, 1969.

Paul, Angus. "Writing by Twentieth-Century Women Reflects Era's Female-Male Conflict." *Chronicle of Higher Education*, November 20, 1986, pp. 6–8.

Reilly, Catherine, ed. *Scars upon My Heart: Women's Poetry and Verse of the First World War*. London: Virago, 1981.

Schenck, Celeste M. "Exiled by Genre: Modernism, Canonicity, and the Politics of Exclusion," in this volume.

Schor, Naomi. "This Essentialism Which Is Not One: Coming to Grips with Irigaray." Unpublished essay.

Stein, Gertrude. *Paris France*. New York: Liveright, 1940.

———. "Patriarchal Poetry." In *The Yale Gertrude Stein*, edited by Richard Kostelanetz, 106–46. New Haven: Yale University Press, 1980.

Stephenson, Jill. *The Nazi Organization of Women*. London: Croom Helm, 1981.

. . . .

Chapter 2

My Art Belongs to Daddy

Incest as Exile, The Textual Economics of Hayford Hall

Mary Lynn Broe

I have a daughter—have while she is mine.
—*Hamlet*, II, ii, 106

No form of family violence has eluded a gendered analysis as successfully as
child abuse and neglect.
—Elizabeth Lunbeck, "Centuries of Cruelty"

I have somewhat forgotten who I am; my family have completed the
estrangement.
—Djuna Barnes to Emily Coleman, March 30, 1940

The Sexual/Textual Order

On December 21, 1909, Zadel Gustafson Barnes, Djuna Barnes's paternal grandmother, wrote a letter to Percy Faulkner, Djuna's husband-to-be. She addressed this fifty-two-year-old man as if he were a small, slightly dim boy (*"remember as you read*, that I do not write with any hidden meaning, any obscure underthought"). She directed him to read over her letter "two or three times to be sure you get my meaning." She claimed she spoke for an ill and absent Djuna, his eighteen-year-old "betrothed." Djuna had been, according to Zadel, "plainly unhappy yet unwilling to reveal the cause." Zadel would speak for her. A remarkable text, more powerful for its gaps and indirections than for what it says, the letter continues by telling Percy that all young Djuna needs is plenty of "outward sign as well as inward assurance" of his affection. The letter, however, must be read in the granddaughter's absence: her stark silence, a silence used to write a subtext of pain, resistance, and difference not only at her impending "arranged" marriage but at what the grandmother terms "the adverse condition" within her family.[1]

For nine months before Zadel wrote this letter, Djuna, who was frequently left in charge of the six children of her father's mistress and wife, who shared the same household, had received letters from Zadel, a journalist and woman of letters who was often away from the Long Island farm on business. Much of each letter inscribed a sexual code language complete with drawings—"pink pebblums," nicknames like "Flitch" and "Starbits." Unmistakably sexual, the drawings figured the eroticism of the grandmother and granddaughter: "Oh, Misriss! When I sees your sweet hands a huggin your own P.T.'s [the drawing is a set of breasts]—I is just crazy and I jumps on oo. Like dis. Wiv dis wesult." [The drawing is of two women in bed, breasts together, one overpowered by the other. Another drawing is of two breasts reaching to meet, nipple to nipple.] The letter is signed, "ownest lishous grandmother." "Flitch," Zadel Gustafson Barnes, claims she is eager to get home to the bed they share.[2]

Djuna was seventeen when she received this letter. Like so many of Zadel's letters that inscribed the grandmother into a privileged role in her "nanocracy," this playfully intimate note was accompanied by the grandmother's bribes of special gourmet treats that were not to be shared with the rest of the children in the families of Fanny Faulkner and Elizabeth Chappell, the mistress and wife, respectively, in the household of Wald Barnes.[3]

Djuna is writing of aging, of her fears of being too old to love, and of the men of Hayford Hall, who seemed reticent lovers, when she says to Emily Holmes Coleman on December 14, 1935: "I always thought I *was* my grandmother, and *now* I am almost right, but fancy being right almost forty odd years ahead of time. But I never did have the idea that no one would love me, that's one form of inferiority complex I never got. I was always blissfully sure that anything I wanted, I would have, and I was right." Two years later, and nearly twenty years after Zadel Barnes's letter to Percy Faulkner, Djuna wrote another letter to Emily, revealing but also concealing "it," what Coleman called her "secret life": "my innate dislike of parading, or 'telling on' the innermost secret, feeling that it should only be exposed by the best artist—when it is done for money it becomes (for me) a brothel of the spirit. In exposing it in art, it is lifted back into its own place again, *given back to itself, though also given to the reader, the eye. Only the best reader will understand it, like initiation which is not for everyone*" (November 30, 1937). "Is not anyone with a childhood like yours justified in being bitter?" Coleman wrote Barnes that same year.

On August 27, 1936, Emily Coleman wrote to Djuna Barnes that her father, John Holmes, visited with considerable frequency during her first summers at Hayford Hall, Peggy Guggenheim's manor in Devonshire: "It is a dreadful fact about parenthood that after maturity the child does not need the parent, but the parent continues to need the child—I ought to live with him, but I never will."[4]

A year later, Emily sent a letter to Djuna from her father's home in West Hartford:

I was writing in my diary about "blood relationship" which I told you I suddenly have begun dimly to understand, for the first time in my life . . . the words seemed to write themselves—as they so often do when I think in writing—and I began writing about you and Scudder [Middleton; Barnes's friend and lover in the mid-1930s]. Why did you say he was a "relative"—does relative mean SEX? If not, why should you have felt such a sex-passion for Scudder, and also for Thelma [Wood; Barnes's one great passion, with whom she lived for nine years in the 1920s] who was also "your family." FAMILY MEANS SEX. I SUDDENLY KNEW IT. (October 30, 1937)

Three years later, Coleman wrote Barnes: "Regarding father, he'll do anything for me, when I'm docile. He's so jealous—he's in LOVE with me" (April 25, 1940).

According to Antonia White, the only "unsafe subject" was her relationship with her father. In attempting to write about her life in her autobiographies (*As Once in May*, 1983; *The Hound and the Falcon: The Story of a Reconversion to the Catholic Faith*, 1983), White never got past age four. Three moments in her life suggest an unfinished text for this writer's block.

One day when she was four and returning home with her father from a visit to the British Museum, the father paused, pointed to two peeling stucco pillars of the porch: "Let's see if you remember what you learnt this afternoon. What kind of pillars are they?" "Concentrating with all my might, I said . . . 'Doric.' . . . 'I wish all my pupils were as good as you.' And bending down he kissed me" (*As Once in May*, 275–76).

When she was fifteen, the fictional form masking the "unsafe subject," we witness another embrace after a visit to Covent Garden. White writes: "By the yellow tiled umbrella stand he kissed her goodnight, more lingeringly than he had done for many months, stroking her hair while she tried to tell him what a wonderful evening it had been" (*The Lost Traveller*, 115).

Finally, in *The Lost Traveller* (1950), the father makes an overtly sexual approach to his daughter's friend, Patsy: "He fell on his knees and leant over her, his face close to hers. . . . His breath, smelling of tobacco, came in gusts against her cheek. . . . He pulled her fur coat open and kissed her neck, almost groaning: 'So white, so soft' " (277–78). The friend, Antonia White later admitted, was pure invention "*to explain things in Daddy*" (emphasis mine).

Explaining Daddy. By 1937, although Antonia White had begun six novels (including two written at school), the only one she had actually completed was *Frost in May* (1933). A series of breakdowns, marriage annulments, divorces, conversions, reconversions, bouts with psychoanalysis, and severe writer's blocks punctuated her life. Although she could write over eighty thousand words to an anonymous correspondent in 1940–41—a "safe" form of intimacy to a fellow traveler in her father's faith; and another twenty-one thousand in notebooks about Ian Henderson; and yet another thirty-one thousand about Basil Nicholson; during the last twenty-five years of her life she sat at a desk, failing to produce a fifth novel.[5]

A Painful, Multiple Exile

I interviewed sixty women and asked them if they had ever experienced a number of forms of sexual violence . . . respecting the definitions that women themselves used. . . . Eighty-nine percent of the women recalled at least one such incident, which is substantially higher than one in four. Moreover, almost two-thirds of the group had experienced two or more forms of sexual abuse.
—Liz Kelly, "What's in a Name: Defining Child Sexual Abuse"

Naturally, recovery from sexual abuse depends on the undoing of this child-hood seduction, which brought the child prematurely to a real, instead of an imaginary, sexual life, and spoiled the child's perquisite unlimited play.
—D. W. Winnicott, *Home Is Where We Start From*

—*I no longer believe in my neurotica.*
—Freud to William Fliess, September 21, 1897

My opening collage figures a radical interruption of the sexual/textual order. The series of textual excerpts forms a painful and multiple exile. For the textual disruptions and jagged form circumscribe the daughter's silence, a silence that not only threatens the closed boundaries of the family but, in turn, is threatened by the universalizing theories of incest currently put forward by lawmakers, clinicians, social scientists, and re-formers. Family dysfunction, infantile sexuality, individual psychopathology, the drive theory, the seduction theory, the cycle of abuse theory, and Lévi-Strauss's elementary kinship exchange theory are just a few of the classifications that obscure a whole spectrum of behaviors and shifting perspectives within families and societies.[6] Often there are modes of sexuality or intrafamilial tensions distinctive to sibling incest, female incest, sex between various relatives of the same age or sex, or multigenerational intimacies which are simply not considered in orthodox psychoanalytic or anthropological interpretations. Many such theories—those of Freud and Lévi-Strauss, for example—have a vested interest in suggesting that the incest taboo is vital to the development of sexual maturity, the family, language, or society.

Not only incest survivors, but survivors of all admixtures of family intimacy become exiled *within* the discourse of incest. Personal experience bows to a category; gender relations are lost to either intra- or extrafamilial distinctions. It is not that actual incest cases can be denied but that the abstract categories within the various disciplines—what Alice Miller calls "poisonous pedagogies"—help explain away specific nuances of case studies and power factors in different contexts. The voices of exiled survivors are frequently not heard. Many of them point to ways in which limited definitions of incest and shifting public policy work to exclude—in fact, to exile—what women experience as a continuum of intimacy and abuse. Such silencing is complicated by our sketchy and elliptical sense of the inequalities of power and the function of "gender relations" within our sacred institutions of home and family, thus rendering the incest survivor invisible and mute.[7]

The exile represented by the interrupted texts of Barnes and White, as well as by the distorting theories of incest, also extends to me. When I first read an early draft of this essay at the 1986 Modern Language Association conference, I had only a very cursory idea of the range of biological, sociological, and psychological approaches to incest. I knew even less about how they constrained the ways we talked, thought and read about incest. I was becoming familiar with challenges to the orthodox interpretations of incest through feminist critiques and sociocultural analyses. Florence Rush (*The Best Kept Secret*) discusses the lively history of the incest taboo common to Greek, Hebrew, Christian, and Roman cultures. Judith Herman (*Father-Daughter Incest*), according to James Twitchell, "extrapolates role behavior from socioeconomic theory": "The father protects his rights to the mother by denying her to the son, the mother maintains her relationship with her husband by excluding her daughter, and they both forbid sibling incest to solidify their positions. But their positions are not equal" (257).

It would be an understatement to say that my literary encounters with incest lacked empirical validity: a few chapters from Faulkner; some brief acquaintance with Lord Byron and his sister Augusta; the sexual subversion of the American family in *Lolita*; some variant readings of "Little Red Riding Hood"; and a stray thought or two cast toward the meaning of vampire myths. On the more theoretical side, I had followed the sensational Malcolm-Masson controversy about Freud's seduction theory. Thanks to Gayle Rubin's classic essay "The Traffic in Women," I knew a bit about women's bodies becoming units of trade in Lévi-Strauss's theory of incest.

Yet what I had done was construct a mythology of incest through the lens of a male incest paradigm, looking for a single cause or determinant: the collusive mother, a betrayal of trust, the social failure to nurture, or just the fact of dominance. So I read the Zadel-Djuna correspondence first as a violation, not a protection, of the daughter; an abuse, not a potential "gesture of care."[8] I failed to see the complicating processes of a historically specific family, often a concealed set of family gender relations at work creating powerful ambivalences.[9]

My closer look at the texts and myths of incest discourse suggested the infinitely elastic "service capacity" of daughters, the intellectual housework they perform through their so-called "traffic" or mediation. Their role stretches from Leviticus and the Garden of Eden, through the Anglo-Saxon epic and Shakespeare's plays, to the spatial configurations of the modern-day wedding ceremony.[10] Claude Lévi-Strauss's notion of how communities are created, for example—alliances of men forged through the mediation of "things" ("things" usually means words, money, and women)—exiles the daughter into a category, as Gayle Rubin demonstrates, which operates across cultures and history for the benefit of male social synthesis.[11] Such a masculine perspective further exiles the daughter from her own needs and desires, from her capacity for producing signs, and especially from her own voice. In addition, Lévi-Strauss's anthropological construction of the family ignores the fact that most mythic or literary fathers—in Jane Austen's and Virginia Woolf's novels, for instance—are not indifferent or disinterested, but, to meet various psychological needs, are set on *retaining* their daughters, who are the most dispensable family members (Boose and Flowers, eds., 60–61).

I was alerted in another way to a "state of exile" for the researcher as well as for the survivor of incest. Linda Gordon reminds us that a "historical amnesia" attends the theorizing of incest and its many interpretive transformations over the last hundred years (56ff.). From the feminist movement's antiviolence campaigns of the 1870s; to the nineteenth-century view that dismissed incest as a problem of the working classes and poor whose housing conditions were said to foster immorality; to the 1920s notion that child abuse was not considered a family problem but a matter of "sex delinquents" in the streets; to the 1970s "gender neutral" studies, which are now being revised by feminist interventionists of the 1980s, incest has always existed on the shifting borderline of interpretation, of social policy, and of public discourse.[12]

To return to the opening letter, Zadel Barnes, the paternal grandmother, speaks for Djuna. In doing so, she suggests two complex and conflicted ideologies: the romantic one is an ideology of childhood with which she protects the granddaughter, who is presumed to be "vulnerable" and "innocent";[13] the other is an ideology of control in which protection—here a code language—masks the structural power imbalance between grandmother and granddaughter, diverting attention from the larger social construction of oppression. Such an ideology of control can be used to deny Djuna access to knowledge, to power, and to her own voice. Both ideologies echo throughout the mythical world which Zadel invents, a deceptive code rather like the Brontës' imaginary Angria or the realm of Pixerina/Witcherina invented by Angelica Garnett and her aunt, Virginia Woolf. At work is a seduction into the family fantasies (in Barnes's case, the father's omnocratic power, the grandmother's matriarchate). Boundaries are transgressed; the duty to protect and the right to use get irrevocably confused.[14]

In the contexts established by such myths, my opening collage is an act of political intervention. It inscribes the struggle of the feminist critic less toward a fully theorized literary discourse on incest than toward a better understanding of the textual struggle of daughter-survivors of incest who must wrest a sense of agency from oversimplifying theorists. For in incest discourse, we are left with a kind of Daddy Warbucks essentialism, a fixed male hegemony over the powerless woman who lacks agency, maturity, or voice. All too often, the daughter is absent from discussion, even from simple regard. Psychoanalytic theory has focused on the triadic "holy family" of father, mother, son and has figured the daughter's role as inheritor of the mother's "empty space."[15] As feminist researchers begin to explore an emotional economics (that is, the freedoms and imprisonments) of the daughter in the literary texts of Djuna Barnes, Emily Holmes Coleman, and Antonia White, it may be useful to keep in mind Eve as "pioneer disobedient." Eve challenged Eden's enclosure, appropriating it as a "room of her own":

The Father's paradise was never an exogamous space, nor does the Father who created the woman ever give her as a sexual gift to Adam in prelapsarian Eden. It is Eve herself who sexualizes this enclosure, Eve who sexually gives herself away from the father, and Eve who compels the proto-exogamy of the movement away from family domain. Like every daughter within her father's house, Eve as daughter is the inevitable traitor within, the breach in enclosure. Though patriarchal history obviously depends on daughters enacting this very role, Eve does not earn patriarchal affirmation for playing her part. Her part dispossesses the father; and thus, for performing it, she becomes the unacknowledged locus for a patriarchal history of women's "disobedience" (Boose and Flowers, eds., 61).

Perhaps the most powerful discovery of recent feminist psychologists and researchers is the function of *multiple silencing* that often passes as cultural normalization in incest discourse. Bounded by the most extreme secrecy both inside and outside the family, the daughter-survivor knows that her voice can topple the family structure. She is, at once, the most exchangeable, yet the most seldom represented, commodity in anthropologists' and psychologists' scripts. The collusive mother, typically estranged from the daughter before the incest pattern develops, is all the more so after; she chooses the patriarchal figure first and, with him, the *appearance* of family structure. The daughter figures last, or more likely not at all, in the many invariable judgments of guilt and innocence that abound in incest discourse.

The daughter-survivor is multiply exiled: from the triadic "holy family" of anthropological studies (mother-son-father); from Western ideology of the family (even the Freudian family romance); from the realm of childhood, where, as the child bride of the father, the mother's husband, she must now act as an adult woman; from her mother, whose silent collusion with the father removes her as protector of the child; from those "facts" which she knows but which are now termed "fantasy"; from naming her continual state of emotional repression; from the realm of adult women with whose power and work she would *seem* to be privileged; from the emotional economics of the nuclear family which now treats her with indifference, erasing her script; and from popularized accounts of mother-daughter nurturance and bonding which simplify maternal relations, as they prescribe a certain responsibility toward the daughter's moral development.

The daughter's exile, literally and culturally scripted, is described by powerful confusions and conflicts. As we begin to theorize the complexities of incest, we find that the daughter is devalued by both parents yet harbors conflicted emotions of warmth and forgiveness toward the father, on whom she remains socially and psychologically dependent. Through incest—a continuous series of events, usually not a onetime occurrence, and not always actualized—the daughter comes to understand the power granted the abuser by the authority of age, gender, culture, and access. Her deceptively elevated social status, yet carefully conscripted power within the family, further binds her. The very matrix of her world—power mixed with dependency so as to maintain order in the family—is contingent upon her unnatural silence. For the incest taboo, as presented to us by clinicians and researchers, is asymmetrical, with incest between mother and son thought to be far more abhorrent because of its assault on the father's power, and sex behavior among peers often missing altogether. Father-daughter incest, on the other hand, is more common because "there is not the punishing father to avenge the father-daughter incest" (Herman and Hirschman, "Father-Daughter Incest," 262).

From Cordelia in *King Lear*, Pecola in *The Bluest Eye*, Ritie in *I Know Why the Caged Bird Sings*, to the ironies and subversions of Lolita, one point becomes clear: the daughter is exiled *within* the community of family, just as she is inscribed as absent in most psychoanalytic discussions of social development. Her text is virtually erased from cultural consciousness. As an actress in a contemporary Eleusinian mystery, the daughter is once again the bargaining tool in a pact which the mother covertly makes with the father. Child bride of the father, the mother's husband, the daughter is the hierophant into the underworld of adult womanhood. She is privy to the full gamut of sexual deception circumscribed in the politics of family. "Home" for her is a stark, threatening prison of intimates in power over her. She is a commodity, an object, a prisoner of silence. She is a tool for the father's silent "traffic in women," a fact of Barnes family history that is represented in Djuna's writing from the earliest poems and stories through *The Antiphon*, a late play.

In the case of Djuna Barnes, such multiple exile is particularly prominent and problematic, since incest theorists' assumptions would seem to dislocate, simplify, or even erase her. The erotic liaison evident in the correspondence with the grandmother is merely a gap in their text, a text that privileges the male figure who has power over the daughter. Their theories relegate to a truly exiled status the woman survivor of female incest, as well as the woman researcher who seeks a language with which to relate the sexual and textual (dis)orders.

With this preface to both the strengths and omissions of incest discourse, I will explore in the final two sections of the essay the enabling affective economy of Hayford Hall in the lives and work of Djuna Barnes, Emily Holmes Coleman, and Antonia White; Hayford Hall's radical departure from the salon and expatriate cultures which we have come to know in the history of Modernism; and last, through a close reading of selected parts of each writer's major novel, an interrogation of the sexual and textual orders. For at stake in at least Barnes's and White's novels is each woman's authority over two texts: the story of *incest survival* and the *incest story* itself.[16] The first story is described by silence, a practiced repression that results in reenactment throughout the life script. The other story is a painful body memory. Both require a control, a spatial logic, peculiar to incest survivors. As Alice Miller points out, dreams or dramas of incest survivors involve taking command of small, tight spaces: a "freeing the self from someone else's power," where one has previously been made an object, denied a subject position (125–26). Each novel contains a narrative of enclosure and then enacts the transgression of that enclosure. Whether control is exerted in mental asylums (Marthe), in convent school infirmaries or ecclesiastical texts (Nanda), or against imprisoning psychoanalytic discourse (Nora), the various enclosures are transformed into embodied forms for dis-closure, for re-membering and releasing the woman's body. In case study after case study, we are told that such release cannot be forced, for it has its own tempo of resolution. In each woman's novel, we find acts that re-create the appropriation of space, the taking control. In fact, transgression becomes a paradox for the incest survivor, a permission of sorts, where it is often a matter of the story of the daughter's survival challenging the "memory" story of the actual incest.

My work, I trust, will begin to open these texts to new and challenging feminist interpretations by scholars who will elaborate an economics of incest.

Nanophilia and the Palimpsest of Power

Suffering for love is how I have learned practically everything I know, love of grandmother up and on.
—Djuna Barnes to Emily Coleman, February 2, 1934

I suppose one lives by the lack of ability to hold the memory too close—otherwise, none of us would reach maturity.
—Djuna Barnes to Emily Coleman, September 20, 1935

There is always more surface to a shattered object than a whole.
—Djuna Barnes to Emily Coleman, November 8, 1935

Djuna Barnes was beautiful, irreverent, sharp-tongued, and intelligent. In the 1920s and 1930s, her quips were legendary in Paris, Berlin, and London and on the streets of Greenwich Village. For over seventy years, Djuna Barnes wrote in a melange of genres and styles, work after work, inscribing an emotional economics of incest. Like the published text of *Nightwood* (1936), which consists of only a third of the original manuscript, or the twenty-nine previous drafts of the 1958 play *The Antiphon*, Barnes's published work is but a small part of her oeuvre. Her talents ranged widely over hundreds of years of cultural history—street ballads of Montmartre, medieval allegories, nineteenth-century French engraving books, eugenics texts, broadsides, and Tudor verse dramas. Though she wrote poems, plays, a chapbook, newspaper journalism, novels, short stories, plays, and an almanac, she was praised—even so, in a limited way—for her one novel, *Nightwood*. The more the experimental and technical aspects of this difficult novel were celebrated ("a kind of literary immaculate conception"), the less political and cultural visibility she gained.[17] As a New York journalist in the teens, she recreated a force-feeding of the suffragists as a rape, a violation of the collective body politic as well as of the literal body of woman. In three early incest stories, formerly part of *A Book* (1923), Barnes explores the interrelation of age, gender, and power.[18] In *Ryder* (1928), she surrounds the nearly suppressed voice of daughter Julie with Wendell Ryder's escapades told in layers of tantalizing prose ("high panache of English on a rampage"). In this way Barnes gives the reader a tangible sense of what it means to conceal the painful events, which are, from Julie's perception, labor pains, childbirth, and death.[19] In *Nightwood*, Barnes turns the entire social order upside down, privileging the resistance of all outsiders (Jews, blacks, lesbians, circus people, transvestites). She makes "modernism of marginality."[20] The dream sequences affirm—as they also interrogate—the erotic control and authority of the grandmother who cross-dresses so as to redress the wounds of incest from the father's house. Finally, *The Antiphon* tells the story of the father's "virginal sacrifice" of the daughter and, in the animal mask scene, of her violation by the brothers. In Act II of this play, the father, Titus, unable to have his daughter sexually, hangs her on a hay hook in the barn. He barters her virginity to a man three times her age for the price of a goat. One might read this play as the father attempting to acquire power, prestige, and revenge through the bestowal of the "gift" of the daughter. Thus the play encodes this "bride price" bestowed by the father, reproducing the paternal script of the father's primacy, and only thinly masks his way of retaining hold on the daughter. As Barnes went through twenty-nine drafts of *The Antiphon* T. S. Eliot advised drastic cuts in Act II, the sexual violation and betrayal of the daughter. When considered together, the cuts form a "textual masquerade" of the daughter's painful violation, her "difference" a subtext of pain within the play. Also, by the authority of his pen, Eliot reproduces the incestuous desires of the violating father by his intrusion in the daughter's script.[21]

If the mother is the vehicle for continued lineage between the son and the father, then the grandmother—in Barnes's case, the mother of the authoritative father—is at the same time *within* yet *outside* the family. She has the power to break into this intimate paternal design because she is absent from the basic kinship triad that guarantees paternal authority by necessary mediation between father and son. Yet she is also the mother of the violating son/father. In Barnes's story, Zadel Gustafson could act collusively with the father, her son, guaranteeing not only the paternal transmission but his primacy by advocating the "bride price" of the civil "wedding" to Percy Faulkner.[22]

At the same time, Zadel's own obvious erotic involvement with Djuna—the letters lavishly illustrated in the margins, encoded with a private mythical world of "Flitch" and "Starbits"—may well have proved an antidote to the actual isolation and pain of Djuna's natal household. The children were not even permitted public schooling. Some of the most prominent visitors to this Long Island farmhouse were the "Eaches" or spirits, who used Zadel's body to come through the dead (Jack London, Franz Liszt, Ludwig von Beethoven, and Chopin were among the more noteworthy).[23] In the private, female discourse with Djuna, Zadel invaded and subverted what was then the new scientific discourse of male sexologists.[24] The correspondence with Djuna also reimagined the entire exogamic incest dialectic in which the mother is mere guardian ("empty vessel") of the father's authority. During the Huntington, Long Island, years, Zadel redrew (quite literally) the hierarchies of gender and power outside the space of male authority. Viewed simply as texts, these letters form a purification ritual of sorts within the family, a matriarchal text in the margins outside time. Their only syntax is that of the eternal present where a mythical world of breasts merges with breasts in the fullness of *puissance féminine*. Zadel and Djuna are empowered to triumph imaginatively over all outside threats. Temporarily safe from the violations of the patriarchal household, Zadel and Djuna played in their symbolic, marginalized world, a queendom of "nanophilia." Zadel, the brilliant psycho-—

or grapho——therapist, did not permit Djuna to repress the sexual trauma of rape, deny it, or blame herself. Instead, the loving exchanges with her granddaughter created a law and a vocabulary of female desire, a "nanerotogeneity" of Flitch and Starbits, corps à corps, admiring their breasts and their bodies, swinging an imaginary invading Chinaman by his braid when he came too near, and privileging, always, female sensuality and desire.

The mythical world Zadel created was a matriarchate similar to that of the original fairy legends, those old wives' tales that celebrated matriarchal societies before the DWEMS (Dead White European Male Scholars) got hold of them, altering them so radically that Florence Rush could claim that these tales were "made, not born," and Simone de Beauvoir could insist that these children's legends were merely "one long exhalation of men ... born of pride and desires of men." Zadel authorized a new, creative space for the granddaughter through her erotic discourse of mutuality, giving Djuna permission "to play." By constructing a healing fictional world, a child-exclusive world like the Brontës' Angria, she culled Djuna back through tenderness to an acceptance of her own body—"our own lovin' lishus P.T.'s" (Zadel Barnes to Djuna Barnes, April 14, 1909).

Yet there may have been another aspect to this unique discourse, this dual langauge, one that not only empowered but also restrained agency in Djuna. Not only does the complex cross-generational legacy from the paternal grandmother guarantee the granddaughter's survival (all the drafts of *The Antiphon* tell of the ruptured bond with the mother), but it also signifies a new sort of *exile* for the granddaughter. Certainly the complexity of the Zadel-Djuna relationship sets it apart from the much heralded model of moral differences specific to women's development, as well as from the French feminists' privileging the female voice as it originates in the primordial voice and body of the mother. What the Djuna-Zadel relationship most closely approaches is an ethic of care as a model of female moral development.[25]

Djuna's early journalistic career was possibly a way of extending her bond with Zadel beyond the boundaries of the repressive Barnes household in which Wald Barnes's two wives and two families mirrored—and exaggerated—the fearful symmetry of the patriarchal family. Djuna and Zadel radically subverted this structure in their correspondence and in the syntax of their professional careers. According to the story told throughout the many drafts of *The Antiphon*, the bond with the mother was severed as the father demanded collusion and complicity in the "sacrifice" of his daughter (see DeSalvo and Curry). Nevertheless, empowered by her grandmother's words, that textual legacy, Djuna entered Pratt Institute and took her first job as illustrator and freelance journalist with the *Brooklyn Daily Eagle* (1912) and later with the *Morning Telegraph* and the *New York Herald*. Her radical portrait of suffragists being force-fed is an elaborate analysis of the politics of rape enacted against Becky Edelman and other militant British women. Djuna visited the headquarters of the International Workers of the World, talked to Piccadilly chorus girls and Brooklyn street people, as well as to the Broadway celebrities whom she is famous for interviewing.[26] For Barnes, there were two classes of people, no more: "those who wear caps and badges, and those who wear hats and canes."[27]

Djuna's activist newspaper work—an example of the woman citizen inhabiting a new public space—is a brilliant logical and moral extension of the purity and temperance crusades her grandmother covered in her late 1880s journalism for *Harper's Monthly*. As Zadel became increasingly involved with the evangelical crusades for moral reform, temperance, and various social movements of the late nineteenth century, like so many "new women" of her generation, she began making connections among those involved in the purity crusade, the vote for women, and feminism. Zadel's challenging *Harper's* articles featured such people as Ellice Hopkins, Frances Willard (founder of the Women's Christian Temperance Union), and William Noble (founder of the English Blue Ribbon Movement). In her long, chatty articles, Zadel linked the welfare of prostitutes with both the double standard of morality and the relations of men and women at the time, displaying a strong feminist consciousness not particularly evident in her Dickensian novel *Can the Old Love?* (1871) or in her poetry, which was clearly influenced by her friend John Greenleaf Whittier.[28]

Our researches are only beginning to explore the Barnes household, a complex palimpsest of power, gender relations, and authority which assured the daughter's exile. The Barnes "nanocracy," complex and ambivalent in its own right, was, we must remember, circumscribed by the patriarchal household, conscripted as it were into the structural hierarchy of the father, who controlled not only the exchange of daughter Djuna but the lives of Muriel, Djuna's half-sister, and all the other children. Whatever Zadel might have done to restore to Djuna a sense of pleasure in her own body, there remains the question of how to interpret Zadel's words and actions. How might we *name* that area, that relation, where abuse and protection intersect with the daughter's trust and vulnerability? Was

Zadel's intervention self-serving? If not, in what other ways did she protect the children from the father, her son? If her attentions were meant to restore to the daughter an appreciation of her body, thereby assuring her emotional survival, what did Djuna perceive as supportive, what abusive? (Recall her opening letter to Emily Coleman in 1935, "I always thought I *was* my grandmother," and Djuna's repeated claims throughout her life about her affection for Zadel.) With what emotional literacy can we begin to answer some of these questions which require of us a far better understanding of family violence, which we have exiled to the files of psychiatrists or social workers, as we have "crimes against women"; or what the survivor-victim experiences and labels "incest." In what ways was the powerful ideology of the patriarchal family supported, in what ways was it challenged by such a relationship as that of Zadel and Djuna Barnes? Read as a text of patriarchal authority, the daughter's violation and Zadel's efforts to restore her were bounded on one side by the story of the father's attempted rape, his "virginal sacrifice" of the daughter, then his brutal barter of his daughter-bride. Reproducing the patriarchal cycle of violation, T. S. Eliot repeatedly attempted suppression, silencing, of the daughter's story in *The Antiphon*, violations that for twenty-nine drafts met with her resistance to his authorial pen and his masquerading "quantitative" language ("I feel sure that there are pages in the middle which can be disposed of"). As Zadel and Djuna broke off their emotional epistolary exchange with Djuna's marriage to Percy Faulkner, Djuna, then at Pratt Institute, battled still another form of patriarchal control in "Uncle Reon," who apparently drew the pursestrings tightly over the family.[29]

Nearly two decades later (1932–38), through the friendships and reconfigured "family" of Peggy Guggenheim's Hayford Hall, Djuna began to revise the brutal, affective economy that had threatened to silence her in childhood.

Hayford Hall: A New Affective Economy

Mother-child incest is extremely rare and, in my findings, more often than father-child incest, associated with adult mental illness; by contrast incestuous fathers have extremely "normal" profiles.
—Linda Gordon, "The Politics of Child Sexual Abuse: Notes from American History"

A child's right to her own body, autonomy and privacy is still a radical concept
which would require the transformation of family power relations.
—Liz, "Too Afraid to Speak."

Hayford Hall was a version of Boccaccio, written for an all female cast.
—Susan Chitty, *Now to My Mother*

For six to seven years after that first summer of 1932, Peggy Guggenheim, using American dollars in a devastated European economy, brought
together a new "kinship" of British and American writers and artists at
Hayford Hall, her baronial castle in the English countryside.[30] The manor
in Devonshire would become a haven for intellectual talk and companionate comfort, as well as a "woman's space" for three brilliant Modernist
writers, each in exile from a difficult family of origin and each at work on
some of her most pathbreaking modern fiction.

Emily Holmes Coleman, a former secretary to Emma Goldman, had
just written *Shutter of Snow* (1930), her brilliant daughter's response to
psychiatric modernism and its complicity with husbands and fathers. She
was writing religious poetry, painting, and working on a second novel,
Tygon, which she completed in 1937. Antonia White had just finished *Frost
in May* (1933), her first novel, set in a girls' school that is a subversive
response to the father's conversion to the patriarchal world of Roman
Catholicism. (Appropriately, White was writing in a liminal "woman's
space," at a time in her life when she had lapsed from the father's faith,
Catholicism, but just before she entered Freudian analysis.) At the convent Nanda attends, the ethic is that "the will must be broken so as to be
reset." The daughter's act of writing, her subversive discourse in the
company of women, challenges the boundaries not only of convent rule
and "mother superior," but of the father's sadospiritual silencing and
denial of will which he forces on daughter, Nanda. Antonia White's
daughter, Susan Chitty, recalls her saying later that the summer of 1933 at
Hayford Hall was "one of the only truly happy times of her adult life"
(Chitty, 61). Together with Emily Coleman and Antonia White, Djuna
Barnes was in residence at Hayford Hall off and on during these years
1932–38. In the old rococo bedroom of the castle, Barnes wrote *Nightwood*, her political novel that privileges the communal resistances of all
marginalized peoples, in particular, the wanderings of her lover of nine
years, Thelma Wood. (After seven rejections, and thanks to Emily Coleman's maverick lobby with T. S. Eliot, Djuna published *Nightwood* with

Faber and Faber.)[31] By the summer of 1938, Emily insisted in a letter to Djuna, "I want to hear about you, Silas, Peter, Phyllis, Peggy and Tony," all Hayford Hallians. They referred to each other as "devoted friends," doubted that there would ever be another Hayford Hall.

In a 1935 letter to Emily Coleman, Djuna Barnes describes the men who were occasional residents of Hayford Hall as "God's innocents . . . bewildered, terribly sad because they are *old children*" (December 14, 1935). William Gerhardie, John Ferrar Holms, Douglas Garman, Peter Hoare, Silas Glossup, Humphrey Jennings, and George Barker seemed an innocuous enough mix of raconteurs, fledgling writers, editors, and sociable political exegetes who mingled with the women, challenging the old lines of demarcation between trust, affection, passion, and companionship.[32] Their most visible professional identity was their brief appearance in print with a poem or review published in Edgell Rickword and Douglas Garman's short-lived *Calendar of Modern Letters* (March 1925 through July 1927).[33] A few years before *Scrutiny*, the *Calendar* essays and politics began defining a cultural sociology in literary criticism, paving the way for scholars and critics of the next decade to challenge the English Tripos and the narrow notion of "belles lettres," social privilege, and academicism that informed the world of British letters. Great debunkers of Britain's "age of idols" and "age of herds" in the mid-1920s, the diverse *Calendar* critics and editors were united by their zeal for subverting the liaisons of social privilege, political conservatism, and the mode of consumption called "literary taste" practiced by the academic English clubs. Men such as John Holms, William Gerhardie, and Douglas Garman—the last, reader and adviser to Wishart and Company, the largest Marxist publisher outside Russia—came out of a moment in Britain when the social and cultural character of the British intelligentsia was being altered. And in their fairly mobile social and sexual roles, their avid interest in what we today call the "talking cure,"[34] the men of Hayford Hall reconfigured "family" for the three women writers, offering them both a challenge and a refuge in their deliberately sustained life of intellect and affection.

In a number of ways—geographic, national, cultural, and sexual— Peggy Guggenheim and her artist and writer residents transgressed boundaries, creating in their alternate family structure a revision of both "expatriatism" and "exile." The usual (male) expatriate movement was from Hoosier schoolrooms of the provincial Midwest to international centers such as Paris, London, and Berlin, to a world Ezra Pound proclaimed was "an old bitch gone in the teeth / . . . a botched civilization" that was also a new, polyglot world where Stephen Daedalus assured us the emphasis was shifting to "silence, exile and cunning." But bold Peggy refused the niche—usually a corner of a bookshop or setting type over a handpress—assigned the women muses and enablers of male Modernists (cf. Sylvia Beach, Adrienne Monnier, Caresse Crosby, Nancy Cunard, et al.). Peggy was her own sort of sexual and social renegade, exile from an upper-crust New York Jewish society ("lysol and hygiene," she called it). With their candor and gossip, her memoirs, *Out of This Century*, subvert the literary canon of academic genres, just as they decenter the power of the class-conscious. Peggy revised the Modernist stereotype of the mild, slightly antiquated bookwoman whose motto seemed to be "They also serve who only stand and wait" by bringing together (then) little-known British men (Djuna Barnes called them "sweet sprigs of sassafras") with outspoken and iconoclastic anarchists such as Americans Emily Coleman and Djuna Barnes.[35] With money from her smelting fortune trust, she brought them *not* to an urban center but to the vernal English countryside, where her structuring of power relationships and her social mobility gave her different credentials than those baronial lords who once inhabited the great houses of Devonshire and displayed their trophies in the halls, the coats of arms over the chimneys, and the temples in the park.

Even as a salon, Hayford Hall had no precedent. It was wholly unlike the Bloomsbury world of the Cambridge Apostles, or Gertrude Stein's rue de Fleurus retreat for the male lions of the art world. Nor was Hayford Hall a frolic in the Burgundian garden of Sido and Colette, or a feminist bal masque in the Doric garden "Temple l'Amitié" of Natalie Barney, where hermaphrodites played music in the bushes to ladies of the livery.[36] Rather, the verbal playfulness of Hayford Hall assumed a cultural and emotional authority which cut across social values and revised the stark silencings and denials in each woman's family of origin. Intellectual authority of talk reshaped a "baronial" space, an alternate culture where women—particularly American women—could act as lovers, mothers, and siblings to British men. In its departure from external restrictions ("completely cut off from the world," Peggy wrote), Hayford Hall elevated a language of affective support and intellectual exchange to a norm.

Unlike those handmaidens to James Joyce, Henry Miller, and other male Modernists, Peggy Guggenheim reclaimed baronial space for the Great Erotic Mother. Hayford Hall became a country space for women, not for the great lord. In their intellectual and personal escapades, they "rewrote" the aristocratic patriarchal "country house" poem, continuing and elaborating the female revision of a genre that began in Jane Austen's *Mansfield Park* and was later criticized in Virginia Woolf's *Between the Acts*. Hayford Hall's shy and weak-ankled heiress invaded and subverted the model great households of the Middle Ages with their diverse classes gathered under the power of a baron or an earl; households whose monopoly of power through pure force, not law, through ownership of land, not ambition, could provide mutual protection (Girouard, 5–12). In an odd way, Guggenheim's country retreat *was* that haven of "protection" against the past for the women writers in residence. The relationship between household and productive resources at Hayford Hall lay in the hands of this Great Erotic Mother, Peggy, whose caveat to the other members of this family was a "hands-off" John Holms policy: "If you rise," she warned Holms one night as he toyed with Djuna's red hair, "the dollar will fall" (Guggenheim, 116). She restructured dependency and reward *not* on sexual exchange, as one might surmise from reading *Out of This Century*, but on cash stipends, revising the domestic metaphor, or at least changing its demands.

Guggenheim was, at best, capricious in the distribution of her wealth. Barnes tells of the time she was promised money to visit Gogarty in Ireland, but Peggy then grew so niggardly about the pledge that she walked to the American Express office to see what third-class passage might be (it was three pounds). Barnes remarked, "You cannot travel to Ireland on three pounds, so here I shall sit until either a hearse or an ambulance or a madman calls for me" (Barnes to Emily Coleman, June 11, 1942). In 1942, when Barnes was living in a single room on Guggenheim's stipend of $100 a month, her patron quipped: "She [Barnes] doesn't need more. She has an inner life" (Barnes to Coleman, June 11, 1942), a comment revealing Guggenheim's intense jealousy of the writers and artists she supported. The money she distributed was always such a small amount, slightly short of adequate, that it merely created desire in its apparent attempt to meet need. Barnes's monthly stipend—$40 in 1940, $300 a month in 1979 when Guggenheim died—was small, regular, and regularly late. It made it necessary for Barnes to appeal to other donors (Helen Westley, Eleanor Fitzgerald, Arlie Lewin, Janet Flanner, and many others) for small gifts, bequests, advances, and supplementary monies. Barnes's response to this "nourishing mother" was an oil painting (*The Unhappy Vixen*) which she never managed to finish. She could never get the "small mean mouth" quite correct. And when Guggenheim asked Barnes if she thought her a witch, hard and cruel, Barnes responded:

"Your mouth is, but then there are your eyes" (Barnes to Coleman, August 19, 1938).

It would seem that at times Guggenheim used her money to "fetishize" art and artistic labor. She bought Berenice Abbott her first camera; the editors of the *Little Review*, Margaret Anderson and Jane Heap, their first typewriter; Mina Loy her lampshop franchise; in addition to the small monthly stipend, she provided Djuna with some elegant, but used, teddies! Barnes lost her beloved Paris flat at 9 rue St. Romain not simply because crooked attorneys mismanaged a series of rentals but because Peggy, who gave Barnes $125 for one year, refused to guarantee that sum beyond the year. Barnes grieved, felt "my house dying, and the past [nine years with Thelma] with it" (Barnes to Coleman, February 14, 1937).

Guggenheim was, however, the first to offer marginalized and little-known modern artists such as Jackson Pollock contracts for their canvases. In a comment on the smugness of high culture, she hung the work of Gypsy Rose Lee and her daughter Pegeen with the art of children and the insane. Perhaps most important, in the final days before Hitler's invasion, she bought up and smuggled out of Europe a pathbreaking collection of modern art, convincing authorities that it was all merely household goods. Nevertheless, Guggenheim elicits strongly skeptical, if not outright conflictual, attitudes from scholars of Modernism.

At Hayford Hall, the new domestic economy Peggy Guggenheim practiced was a wry comment on the eighteenth-century conduct books for women, books that changed the ideal of what "country life" must be, as they replaced the "forms of sumptuary display" of aristocratic life with a new household economy—the "frugal and private practices of the modern gentleman [*sic*]," (Armstrong, 108–14, passim). Hayford Hall legend tells of Peggy discovering a butler eating a leftover piece of overripe fruit; she deducted it from his weekly wages. Surely Guggenheim's openly erotic liaisons revolutionized the "droit du seigneur," with John Holms her lover until his death in 1934, then Douglas Garman, then William Gerhardie, followed by many others.[37]

If Guggenheim defined and controlled the material relations of baronial space at Hayford Hall, the men in residence provided for these singularly brilliant women, all at the peak of their writing careers, the opportunity to revise, often by reenacting, the affective economy that had informed, if not damaged, their early lives. The men made possible a way to reconstruct an initiation into the sexual order, but this time with each woman in authoritative control of both her sexual and literary scripts. "It's why I like weak men," Barnes explained in a letter to Coleman. "I want to be the boss covered with treacle" (February 4, 1939). "God come down for the weekend," Barnes jibed about Holms; or "he was like a Rolls Royce on the blink," Emily wrote about his stifled literary production, "perfectly remarkable, but not quite making it" (Weld, 75). In the letters Barnes and Coleman exchanged between Holms's death in 1934 and Coleman's death in the 1970s, their language everywhere betrays the fact that these men offered an antidote to that power of the father. Barnes and Coleman wrote themselves into positions of power, describing men who were not—or not for long—their lovers, but to whom they were faithful precisely for their "kindnesses." These men enabled them to create a new emotional economics; as Barnes wrote of one of them, he had "the courage of his cowardice." "Little men, good in a clear, simple way," Barnes described, they were "sweet children" for whom these two women had an enduring "gentle affection." Describing Peter Hoare, Coleman's lover of several years, Barnes said he "sits on himself as if he were a doorknob instead of an egg." Barnes described "Muffin," Peter Neagoe, as "a quiet sweet man," saying "I've just dusted two months off his slippers" (Barnes to Coleman, December 14, 1935); the language continues through 1938.

The men's talk and, equally important, their willingness to listen, as well as their mild and companionate presences, created for the women a space in which to negotiate—and renegotiate—the social, political, and personal realms mastered by the father. Edwin Muir has written at length about John Holms's genius in this and other respects: "He had all sorts of odd accomplishments—he could scuttle along on all fours at a great speed without bending his knees; walking, on the other hand, bored him" (Muir, 211). Writing was indeed an obstacle to John Holms, but talking was not:

> There was a strange contrast between his instinctive certainty as a physical being and the lethargy and awkwardness of his will . . . his mind had power, clarity, and order, and turned on any subject, was like a spell which made things assume their true shapes and appear in their original relation to one another, as on the first day . . . his talk gave the same impression . . . through it walked and lumbered the original ideas of things, with their first dark or radiant lineaments. His talk had an extraordinary solidity which made even the best serious talk seem flimsy or commonplace. (Muir, 212)

Conversations with Holms and other men in residence at Hayford Hall created a special province of verbal freedom for Coleman, Barnes, and

White, at once a transgression of conventional family norms yet a playful departure from secrecy. With reason, then, John Holms was a constant point of reference in the Barnes-Coleman correspondence from the time of his sudden death in 1934. Barnes wrote: "The death of John Holms struck me a stronger blow than any of my deaths [both her father, Wald, and his wife, Fanny Faulkner, died in 1934]—as if the one ear that had heard the best of me were closed forever" (Barnes to Coleman, February 8, 1934). And of Peggy Guggenheim, Barnes wrote that it was "through John that she got to like me again, making me a work of John—a part of his life for a time last summer" (Barnes to Coleman, February 8, 1934).

It was with some perception that Susan Chitty, Antonia White's daughter, wrote, "Hayford Hall was a version of Boccaccio, written for an all female cast" (Chitty, 61). The reimagined family that described Hayford Hall's household authority subverted the monolithic family as we know it, in both the roles it enabled and in the brief, but parodic, family history. It all began in the summer of 1928, when Peggy Guggenheim, Emily Coleman (Emma Goldman's secretary at the time), and John Holms met in St. Tropez. Guggenheim fell for Holms, although she did not divorce Laurence Vail until 1930. In St. Tropez, Emily had taken an interest in John Holms, but it was Guggenheim who became his lover in 1929. She brought Holms and his companion, Dorothy, to Pramousquier, near the Vail home, for her convenience. After Guggenheim and Holms had been living together for six months, Holms agreed to marry Dorothy so that, in deference to Dorothy's family, who had, over the years, been told lies about her relationship with Holms, she could file for a proper divorce. Guggenheim, then pregnant by Holms, acted as bridesmaid in this subversion of the conventional family romance. By mocking the social relations and ideologies of the patriarchal family, Peggy Guggenheim challenged the notion of private property and contractual exchanges (wryly, of course) by insisting that her lover marry another woman for the purpose of divorce.

The intersection of Hayford Hall lives would continue in future decades, imprinting and reimprinting the "empty space" of the patriarchal family and its absent daughter with the new cultural markings of a very heterodox kinship. Silas Glossup fathered Antonia White's child, Susan Chitty, but was Barnes's lover after their first meeting in 1937. Antonia White's friend Dylan Thomas became Coleman's pub-crawling lover later in the 1930s. White's relationship with David Gascoyne, George Barker's special friend, mirrored Coleman's intrigue with Barker. Eight months after beginning an affair with Silas Glossup, Barnes wrote that he, Glossup, considered her his sister, someone with whom he could no longer sleep (he nevertheless still did). Barnes, in turn, thought of Glossup as "the perfect relative." She wrote to Coleman to reconsider Peter Hoare's similar response: "His very resistance is a sort of faithfulness" (September 2, 1938). And in the 1940s, largely through the enabling friendship and epistolary exchanges of Barnes and Coleman, Silas Glossup and Peter Hoare became intimates; Barnes referred to them as "bride and bride," claiming that they "should get married and be done with it" (Barnes to Coleman, September 2, 1938).

If the revised ideology of family at Hayford Hall was indeed so heterodox, then the mock-baronial "coat of arms" that represents the clan was a game the residents played each evening called "Truth." The game was a canny one for these survivors of violating families, daughters who were robbed of agency and voice. "Truth" transgressed a number of old boundaries, one between public and private space, another between what we call "realist" and what "post-Modern." In its startling interrogation of voice and silence, presence and anonymity, "Truth" was more than a game, surely, to the Hayford Hall women who knew the politics of both the incest *story*, and the story of *incest*, as well as the codes necessary for protecting what Barnes called "that innermost secret" (see Barnes to Coleman, November 30, 1937). In the game, participants read aloud epigrams and paragraphs that *anonymously* described a particular feature of some other resident. The character sketches were savage, pointed, acerbic. Emily Coleman, however, was not content with this post-Modern condition of the disappearing author. Ever the expressive realist who seeks verisimilitude, Emily Coleman tried to restore to this game, "Truth," a realistic Modernist text. Fiction and its codes were a poor "second" to the culpable, vulnerable author. Late each night Emily could be found going through the wastebasket for the assorted scraps of paper that contained the savage portraits: she was trying to match handwriting with author (Field, 199).

If the coat of arms proclaiming "Truth" was the canny insignia of Hayford Hall, the family register, at least for Coleman, White, and Barnes, was a popular eugenics text, *Man the Unknown* by Alexis Carrel. If we can trust Barnes's letters from this time and her well-annotated copy of the text, the women seriously misread Carrel's "call to intellectual revolution" against the ills of modern society, in general, and against a sterile and mechanistic science, in particular. To them, he championed less an inte-grated "science of man" than a female superiority and the revolution of all women artists through their bodies, "thought being an offspring of the endocrine glands as well as of the cerebral cortex" (Malinin, 119). All three women must have loved the passage "In general, great poets, artists, and saints, as well as conquerors, were strongly sexed" (Malinin, 118). One suspects, too, that the women were profoundly interested in his theories of sex because of his idea that *sexual deprivation* was a strong intellectual stimulus. He used Dante as an example of the mind most stimulated by the unattained object and wrote: "A workingman's wife can request the services of her husband every day. But the wife of an artist or of a philosopher has not the right to do so as often" (Malinin, 119). It is curious, perhaps fitting, that Coleman and Barnes, children of Zadel's generation, that "golden age of scientific determinism, Social Darwinism and eugenics," subverted all those nineteenth-century taxonomies and gender-specific examples by *rereading* Carrel's male eugenics message, believing that the "integration of mind and body in a nurturing environ-ment" *was* Hayford Hall (Smith-Rosenberg, 267).

I have not meant to suggest the myth/script that a community of writing women depends upon enabling "wifelike" men (a notion challenged, surely, by the careers of Virginia Woolf and George Eliot), or that Hayford Hall's reimagined "family" was based on the talking cure alone. I do, however, want to suggest that the breaking of silence within the re-configured family—what Alice Miller calls the challenge to the "impover-ished personality"—and the creation of a supportive community that served as a structure for articulation of a variety of kinship reconfigu-rations, if not of each woman's original trauma, was a powerful experience in the life of each writer.[38] Likewise, the women's texts that were "en-abled" by the kinship of Hayford Hall were, paradoxically, tributes to the repression upon which their survivals were based and which reinforced the consequences of the original trauma. Central to each woman's writing was the ability to articulate experience *beyond* the "repetition compulsion" of the original trauma, in the "double story" of each text, and, in particu-lar, through the appropriation of enclosures.

In 1937, by the time the group had moved up from the baronial manor to Yew Tree Cottage, Petersfield, Djuna wrote to Antonia White: "It's getting the awful rust off the spirit that is almost insurmountable. It's why working every day is important—one may write the most lamentable balls but in the end one has a page or two that might not otherwise have been done. Keep writing. It's a woman's only hope, except for lace-making" (Chitty, 94).

Textual Economics: A Challenge to Incest Discourse

In psychoanalysis, however, all events *become* invested with fantasy, conscious and unconscious, and may on occasion be potentiated *by* fantasy.
—Ann Scott, "Feminism and the Seductiveness of the 'Real Event' "

I loved her most, and thought to set my rest
On her kind nursery.
—*Lear*, I, i, 123–24

Time shall unfold what plighted cunning hides,
Who covers faults, at last with shame derides.
—*Lear*, I, i, 280–81

The position of the father vis-à-vis the daughters' life scripts of each Hayford Hall woman is not fixed or stable, though in none is he simply the anthropologists' "disinterested father." In contrast to Djuna Barnes's powerful story, the story of John Holmes, the father of Emily Coleman, suggests a different emotional economics, for the father *avoids* loss of the daughter. As we learn from Peggy Guggenheim's memoirs, he was frequently present at Hayford Hall. Challenging the anthropologists' notion of "daughter exchange," Emily assigns him the place of "sibling" in the cultural story of family being rewritten by the men and women of Hayford Hall. She thereby privileges the law of brother-sister desire over the threat of the phallus, much as Antigone challenges the fundamental law of patriarchy (marriage; Creon's rule) by affirming a bond with her brother (see Abel). Emily, John Holmes's thirty-four-year-old daughter, romped, climbed trees, hiked, and rode horses. In a startling coincidence of mirroring, she reconstructed an alternate experience of being a "daughter" in the triadic configuration with John Holms and Peggy Guggenheim. Emily challenged the role of traditional daughter, the ignored and exchangeable figure, for one who overturned the carefully proportioned family in Western ideology. As Lynda Boose writes in her Introduction to *Daughters and Fathers*:

The relative absence of father-daughter discussion has something to do with a cultural metrics that assigns value almost by literal poundage. In the four-cornered nuclear enclosure which is the source for Western ideologies about the family, the father weighs most and the daughter least. To consider the daughter and father in relationship means juxtaposing the two figures most asymmetrically proportioned in terms of gender, age, authority, and cultural privilege. All of these asymmetries are ones which are controlled by the idiom of presence, which defines the father, and absence, which identifies the daughter. (20)

Surely the mirroring of the names—the literal and reimagined father-lover, *Holmes* and *Holms*; the father as brother and brother as father—only emphasizes the fact that Emily closed the gap between father and daughter in the therapeutic family of Hayford Hall. We might even go so far as to say that just as incest collapses the defined scripts or roles, "father" becoming "lover," Emily Holmes Coleman appropriates the power of collapsing terminology and confounding ideologies. She turns *Holms* into father and becomes daughter to her sibling "parents" (Peggy-Mother). She makes *Holmes* her brother in a brilliantly transgressive life script in which the ironic nom du père is "Homes"—Hayford Hall.[39]

Keeping in mind the life scripts of both Emily Coleman and Djuna Barnes, what follows is an attempt to look beyond the cultural authority of the reconfigured family of Hayford Hall to some ways in which such a community empowered the women writers to interrogate the sexual/ textual order. Close readings, though of only select parts of each woman's novel, are not meant to foreclose future interpretations but rather to invite a more extensive reading of the relationship between the disruptions in the text and the sexual experiences in each of the three novels. At stake is the writer's authority over two texts: the survival story and the incest story, both of which require control to break the denial of the subject position that has described the women's lives. Transgressions or transformation of enclosures in dreams or dramas manifest a peculiar spatial logic that testifies to the women's new-found authority.

In Emily Coleman's 1930 novel *Shutter of Snow*, Marthe is incarcerated for "post-puerperal madness" after the birth of a baby. The novel, however, actually tells a *Lear* story, but in terms of modern psychiatry and a woman's transgressions. Rejected by a child she tries to nurse (it is unclear from the text if the child is stillborn), aware always of her dead mother who in her dreams "rustles in and out in a carcass of black silk" (30), Marthe returns, again and again, to the repressed scenes of childhood with her father: "Always she had kept telling of it, not one word of it must be forgotten. It must all be recorded in sound and after that she could sleep. . . . When the last itemized syllable was told it would all be over. No one would understand until that had happened" (5–6). When later she is told to "stop talking," she responds, "No one can make me stop until I am through" (28). The art of writing and telling is urgently important to her: she fashions a bold retort to the emotionally needy father.

Marthe challenges the various imprisoning structures in the world of the asylum. She appropriates the space such structures release—the shroudlike sheets into which patients are sewn, the corridors of the building.[40] But just as Cordelia must solace Lear, suckling him, Marthe must first nurture the father. She says: "*Her father must be taken care of first.* He was the one Yahweh had trifled with. She would make him smile his whistling smile, he would whistle for her bright in the new morning, whistle the mill song and strop his razor. She loved his hands. . . . She would make him a blue handkerchief with a great J which would be like life springs to him. . . . *Her father, with chocolate almonds in the hay*" (13–14; emphasis mine).

At the same time Marthe assumes the mother's role by feeding/nurturing the father, she nevertheless privileges by reproducing the absent mother's aggressive madness against the father. Marthe's scripted freedom—"swinging in yards of green space"—is obtained by her imaginatively *impregnating the father*: "It was this that was to be again, he was to have this again and in his heart was growing a stern and ruddy pear that he would take and offer for them both. He would make of his heart a stolen marrow bone and clutch snow crystals in the night to his liking. He came by her bed and she told into his hand the whole of what it had been. *She knows him they said. . . . Now she knew what had happened now she could see. It had been this it had been this very thing*" (30–31; emphasis mine).

One view of this painful daughter's story is that Marthe impregnates the father, and, in doing so, suggests the ambiguity of her response to the death of the mother by substituting herself in the mother's role. But the language here is curious. Taken together with the syntax and rhythm, it suggests terrible strain and conflict, the urge to reveal run up against the need to repress and conceal. The language here is both blunted and halting, yet continuous. Where "it" should be named, time after time the image does not yield, yet the passage is cadenced so that what "would be" declared is sustained in its secrecy ("was to be again," "was to have . . . again"). There is a hint of a religious communion here, but an ambiguous one: the hierophant permitted a glimpse of the forbidden ("Now she could see") yet a communion of sinner and saint offering up some terrible black sacrament of the body ("stolen marrow bone"). But the offering is unilateral ("he would take and offer for them both"). The phrasal repetitions in the last lines ("It had been this it had been this") race to communicate a pressing perception, and the definite past tense now ("It had been") suggests that the event(s) will at last be named. But no. Repression reigns. So does restraint: "It had been it had been *this very thing.*"

To find a way to write this story of father-daughter dynamics is to tell of the father's desires, his need to be suckled. To invent a discourse, to construct a text that violates the closed boundaries of the family—paradoxically *repressing what it must reenact*—is to place the father's house, here the asylum with its various forms of enclosure, *under siege.* Emily Holmes Coleman has done just that: "The words unfolded and came out on the paper. They slid up and floated and came down and stood in line. She was making them, she was saying things with a pencil on a small piece of yellow paper. It was a letter to her father and there were the words, the words that she was capturing out of the red lights and pinning under her pencil like squirming moths. The moths had yellow tails and pulled desperately away from the pencil" (20).

Throughout the novel, Marthe names herself "god," the ultimate patriarch, but we soon learn that *this* god is housed in an asylum that figures the female body as invaded, entered, stifled, appropriated, or kept locked up. In appropriating the Christological myth, she frees herself to various alternative discourses: the scarf dance, imitation of Christ from the sermons, "reading" patterns of oranges in the snow. Now she "leads orchestras she for so long understood," her own discourse empowered at last. Against all these obstacles, she releases herself to the power of her own words, her narrative, and her telling: "Her voice penetrated the bars and drew out their metal marrow" (23).

As we turn to *Nightwood* (1936), a novel that Djuna Barnes wrote in large part while at Hayford Hall, the two grandmother incest dreams suggest another subversive new construction of the daughter's story. One way of looking at dreams is to consider them active reenactments of things passively endured in childhood (Miller). In this novel, then, Nora the daughter struggles to discover a discourse for the modes of the "differently" erotic within the violating patriarchal family.

Jane Marcus claims that *Nightwood* is the representative modern text, "a prose poem of abjection, tracing the political unconscious of the rise of fascism, as lesbians, Blacks, circus people, Jews and transvestites—outsiders all—*bow down* as the text repeats, before the truly perverted levitical prescriptions for racial purity of Hitler" ("Laughing at Leviticus"). More specifically, if the novel is, as Marcus claims, a book of "communal resistances of underworld outsiders to domination," then we need to look specifically at the grandmother dreams, reading them as transgressions of age, power, gender, and female desire in the context of *Nightwood*'s catalog of *other* transgressions (transgressions of genre, style, sequential perception, even referential meaning).

The first dream in the novel occurs just before Nora observes Robin's betrayal with Jenny in the garden. In her essay "The Sweetest Lie," Judith Lee claims that the Robin-Nora relationship embodies Julia Kristeva's mother-child dialectic, and the "symbiotic bond" that Nora experiences is a "split within herself that allows her double identity of both mother and child." Lee observes an elaborate shift in the novel from the cultural differences between the old dualities "masculine" and "feminine" to the more intimate difference between thinking of self as subject and self as object. (Here we must recall Barnes's 1935 letter to Emily Coleman in which she said, "I always thought I *was* my grandmother, and *now* I am almost right.") In the first dream, Nora is alone in the empty grandmother's room at the top of the house. Cannily, she is enveloped in the grandmother's nourishing and protective "text": the walls surrounding her are papered with her grandmother's journalism. All around, patriarchal history and the generations of family memorabilia are decaying, falling into broken disarray. The structure of the house is an embodied enclosure. What seems to be interrogated here is whether the power of identity is separate or interchangeable: Nora looks down into the "body" of the house but only to find Robin receding from her.

Challenged here, too, is the notion of control, of empowerment, and—in the case of Nora's gesture toward Robin—of the need to respect difference: that fragile notion of self as subject in distinction from self as other. Both relations are important concerns in same-sex, cross-generational incest. It is also worth noting that a central aspect of the emotional survival story in nearly every form of sexual violence is the survivor's recovery of the *control* she has lost (MacLeod and Saraga, 48). The dream also marks the grandmother's influence as powerful yet imperiled. We are told that the "architecture of dream had built her everlasting and continuous" (63), that is, out of time and in that marginal space of the mythical world constructed in the Zadel-Djuna letters. We also learn that the grandmother's voice, the speaking subject, enables Nora, as her light illuminates her perception. Yet the grandmother is continually in the process of leaving the dream, her presence in continual jeopardy, tenuous, imperiled somehow. Not unrelated, the interchange of love and power between the lovers Robin and Nora in *Nightwood* is equally fragile and imperiled, as the following scene demonstrates.

The grandmother appears in two images, both suggesting a masquerade of the body in cross-gendered clothing: the images of transgression here are those of *both* age and gender. In one image, her aging body is covered in "soft folds and chin laces, the pinched gatherings that composed the train taking an upward line over the back and hips in a curve that not only bent age but fear of bent age demands" (63). In the other, the grandmother is dressed as a man, wearing a billycock, corked mustache, looking plump and ridiculous in tight trousers. Her arms are spread and she leers, "My little sweetheart" (63).

In both images of the grandmother, the reader is invited to "see through" both the performance and the gendered clothing—the dream offering the tools of its own deconstruction—to the "spine curved with fear." The dream would seem to refute the nineteenth-century sexologists' fixation with biological determinism and their obsession with cross-dressing by exposing the *contingency* of both images of woman as mere gender conventions, but nevertheless conventions that were dictated to women as "natural" (Smith-Rosenberg, 289). Just as *Nightwood*'s verbal excesses construct a "strategy of disguise" (Lee), this dream passage interrogates both disguise and revelation in all their ambivalences. (Elsewhere in the novel, Matthew-the-Mighty O'Connor, the garrulous transvestite doctor, fills the book with a lavish syntax that promises, but never really delivers, coherence; Nikka the Nigger's back encodes all of Modernism, thwarting in its lavish archaeology of styles and genres "essential" or referential meaning.)

The feminist reader-critic is invited to make sense of all this symbolism, the critical gesture itself under scrutiny, for the grandmother is " 'drawn upon' as a prehistoric ruin is drawn upon, symbolizing her life out of her life" (63). Even as this occurs, its strategy noted, the influence of the grandmother and her double-engendered legacy makes *permissible* Nora's desire for Robin: The dream "now appeared to Nora as something being done to Robin." What is scripted here is the mutuality of female desire,

Nora's attempt *to control* that desire, and the fragile shape of that desire. Significant, too, is the dreamer's *power over* her dream, her need as she remains on the *margins of the dream* (marginalized; ex-centric) to construct an authority of interpretation over conflicting family imagery: "The dream will not be dreamed again" (62), Nora says from within the dream. Barnes's Nora, it seems, is not susceptible to the appeal of ideologies, and the dream consciously reenacts the defiance of intellectual and ideological enclosures.

The second grandmother dream occurs in a late section of *Nightwood*, where, as Jane Marcus has shown, the Freudian psychoanalytic collaboration with fascism is exposed, and where the whole misshapen history of treating female hysteria ("womb disease") is overturned. Nora is the archetypal Dora; O'Connor the parodic Freud; O'Connor's womb envy exposes penis envy, the psychoanalyst's office is a filthy bedroom with a reeking chamberpot, the instruments of his trade, some rusty abortionist's tools, and so on (Marcus, "Laughing at Leviticus"). Learned with his mock case histories, Matthew O'Connor, the novel's brilliant transvestite psychoanalyst got up as Irish washerwoman taking in the dirty laundry of the world, deconstructs Nora's dream. His advice? His prescription? According to Jane Marcus, Dr. O'Connor tells Nora to get out of herself through carnival, invert high and low cultures, and reckon with the animal that she is (Marcus, "Laughing at Leviticus"). Barnes debunks the therapeutic model here as an unequal power relation, one that merely reproduces the dynamics of the daughter-survivor's initial sexual violation. Barnes was always wickedly irreverent about analysis: "You might get well, but what might you lose in the doctoring?" She continued, claiming that the only change she believed in was wrought out of self-struggle, in desperate circumstances: "Any other change is aseptic. I believe in self-contamination" (to Emily Coleman; November 22, 1935).

To return to a close reading of the dream, the grandmother here is cast as Snow White in a glass coffin somewhere out in the forest. But instead of being awakened from her passivity by a kiss, what is privileged in the dream is her power to compel her son to join her in the "tight glass space" of the coffin. He is under her control, it would seem, though her control is figured only as a state of waking death. The law of the phallus, the violating father, is neutralized here, though the dreamer is still tentative about her power *to read* the dream ("me, stepping about its edges [of the dream] . . . weeping and unable to do anything or take myself out of it," *Nightwood*, 149). Powerlessness. Lack of control. Denial of agency. Denial of subject position. The dream exhibits considerable aggression toward the father and grandmother, who would seem to be in collusion, since Nora, the dreamer, exerts the authority of control by assigning them to the tight space of the coffin. Again, what concerns Nora is the protocol of dream analysis: how one constructs a discourse to express the subversive family collusion and the cruel disregard that leaves the daughter silenced yet with the task of engendering her script, her story.[41]

Antonia White published *Frost in May* (1933) four years after the death of her father. She recreates the sadospiritual rule of order, conflating the military and the ecclesiastical in her description of the patriarchal family during the last decade before World War I.[42] Nanda Grey (significantly, Non-d*a, nada*, and no, da) is enrolled at the Convent of the Five Wounds, a boarding school. Born a Protestant and middle class, Nanda is forced into the father's text of "convert," a term meaning exile in the midst of the "old great Catholic families, the frontierless aristocracy of Europe." In the novel, Mother Superior attempts to obliterate, both physically and fictively, the text of Nanda: "I am God's instrument to break your will" (24). Antonia White's script, however, discloses the daughter's struggle to reveal her father's secret, even though he is armored and protected by the props of his male world: Roman Catholicism, patriarchal privilege, the ascetic military rule of having "the scantiest possible belongings stored in the smallest space." In a courtship ritual held late one night in the drawing room, the father says: " 'Once upon a time, I used to wish I had a son. But a daughter's a much better thing to have.' . . . He did not look at Nanda, but she saw that his hands were shaking so that it took even more matches than usual to get the pipe going again" (177). And two pages later, the dynamics of exiling the daughter *within* the family and *against* the mother, continue: " 'for goodness' sake, don't tell your mother I kept you up so late.' He held her longer than usual as she kissed him good night, smoothing back her hair from her forehead and looking into her eyes" (179).

Boldly, yet secretly, Nanda has begun writing her own novel about a conversion. The father's and daughter's texts, a quasi-military, quasi-ecclesiastical antiphon and response, are locked in struggle in this novel. They reproduce the incest survivor's embattled discourse in and on textuality. In fact, it is *Frost in May*'s textual warfare within both the natal and convent families that underscores the daughter's exiled position. First, Mr. Grey is a textual minimalist. He is a note-collector for an "important but not yet written" pamphlet called *A Catalogue of Ships in the Iliad* (174). He is a devotee of order, rules, "scrubbed boards and whitened walls and shining brasses," formalities, taxonomies, litanies (190). In contrast to his pamphlet, Nanda's text has grown organically, from "labored little lyrics about spring and the sea" to a full-length novel about a "brilliant wicked worldly society" in which one wallows in sin and carnal delights (158). (We never really learn just how objectionable her writing is, though we do know her heroine receives "a kiss of burning passion on a scarlet mouth.")

With their lively oral legends, the nuns of Five Wounds also write stories; they bear the suspiciously military mark. Their texts, like the girl who mistakenly got a communion veil fastened by a safety pin goring her ear, are full of lively brutalities that valorize the silent endurance of the daughter: "The poor little girl . . . thought it part of the ceremony, and . . . never uttered a word of complaint" until she fainted at breakfast (86). And Nanda writes her text in secrecy in a wing of the college infirmary, surrounded by a "family" of renegade schoolgirls.

At Five Wounds, the nuns' oral legends subvert the dry, ecclesiastical stories derived from the official *Lives of the English Martyrs*, just as the schoolgirls' texts—*Candide* in a plain brown paper wrapper, Shelley tossed into the lake to avoid discovery, and a novel called *Dream Days*—all subvert the dull etchings, long advisory letters, and boring transcriptions of papal bulls which comprise the official life of the founder, Mother Guillemin. (Again the military metaphor of embattled textuality is not lost on the witting reader.) Elsewhere in the novel, the girls' curiosity about Paolo and Francesca challenges the school's wish to begin their Dante pageant *not* with the vaguely erotic but with the long-suffering: the *Purgatorio*, not the *Inferno*.

In *Frost in May*, thirteen-year-old Nanda never successfully negotiates the two embattled forms of discourse, no more than the girls' final staging of a carnival of creative debauchery ever transcends *their* stage, the convent infirmary. What is significant, however, is that Antonia White has brought the embattled textualities to the foreground, creating an entire novel about the contest. (One thinks of the incest survivor's paradoxical stories.)

It might be argued that Nanda Grey inscribes the father's story of conversion—a literal convert and the converter of daughter to a mastery of his patriarchal order—within her own novel. But her seized text, one in which she also inscribes her difference (her love of Léonie) remains a fragment, unfinished. The violation of the daughter, the incest survivor, and her compromised family situation, but most important, her battle for a textuality not yet infiltrated, is reenacted in *Frost in May* as the absolute sovereign silencing by the father. When Nanda writes her erotic tale of "conversion"—though she never gets beyond "perversion" and "inversion"—she offers it as a gift of love to her school chum and inamorata, Léonie, a Catholic aristocrat at Five Wounds. Nanda's work is seized by Mother Superior, the ecclesio-military collusive mother, who presents the "gift" to the father, thereby forging her alliance through the trade of the daughter's words. This action in White's novel occurs precisely at the point at which Nanda was about to disrupt the father's power and authority. She would have subverted the sadospiritual economy by giving her text to Léonie, another girl whom she both admires and desires, thereby inscribing her words in another affective economy than that of the father: female desire.

But Nanda's transgressive text never manages to get beyond the "per" and "in" versions to "conversion"—neither her own, nor her father's. Her text is reappropriated, seized, disapproved, subsumed to patriarchal will. Nanda's status as daughter is also jeopardized, as her father says: "If a young girl's mind is such a sink of filth and impurity, I wish to God that I had never had a daughter" (216).

Like all daughter-survivors, it would seem that Antonia White, at last, still interrogates the daughter's text: is it a subversive subtext? a counter-text? or a nontext? (that is, one that simply reproduces the father's conversion story, as it reenacts the daughter's violation within the father's power). White exiles her reader to this state of critical indeterminacy, but not without suggesting that the hazardous textual negotiation for a clear-cut discourse of the incest survivor is no less than a state of exile. As such, it must be challenged by the woman writer both critically and theoretically. The recognition of this state of exile places new demands, as well, on the feminist reader and critic.

For the textual politics of survival/exile argues for a whole continuum of readings, as it does for a better understanding of a spectrum of sexual violences both within and outside the family. In literary discourse, as in other disciplines, it is unwise to presume certain theoretical givens, abstract theories, universal categories, and the "entrenched power" of the psychoanalytic societies whose goal it is, according to Alice Miller, to "uphold the defense mechanisms of generations of fathers" (147). Daughter-survivors write out of that paradoxical link between survival and exile, between bodily memory and repression of that memory. Thus the textuality of incest discourse falls outside the boundaries of conventional

disciplinary frameworks, pushing the margins of sociological, psychological, and anthropological research, challenging multiple silences. The texts
of Barnes, Coleman, and White alert us to the power structures within
families, as they mark those disabling ideologies of "family," "childhood,"
even "incest" itself. In their scripts we are invited to entertain transgressions of boundaries whether those imprisoning spaces be the discourse of
Freudian analysis, the psychic architecture of the mental asylum, or the
sadospiritual rigors of a convent school.

Although space has not permitted the rendering of full interpretations
of each of the three novels—what I call exilic "daughter-scripts" which
break the silence and the stereotypes of incest discourse—I have begun
exploring some of the most controversial and subversive parts of each
novel. It is here in each novel that the daughter's challenge to the myths of
incest discourse, to the fictions of the patriarchal family and its hierarchical modes of power, and to the struggle for a new authority of space is most
apparent. The affective economy of the Hayford Hall experience, that
"domestic haven," enabled Djuna Barnes, Emily Holmes Coleman, and
Antonia White to seize their various stories as they rewrote the cultural
scripts of the two well-loved daughters.

Notes

Special thanks to Louise Yelin, Elizabeth Meese, Jane Marcus, and Angela
Ingram for their lively, critical responses to the first draft of this essay; also to
Lynda Koolish and Paula Bennett whose vocal presences and encouragement at a
session on Exile arranged by the Division on Twentieth-Century English Literature at the Modern Language Association in 1986 proved to be enabling in the
completion of this essay.

1. Zadel Gustafson Barnes to Percy Faulkner, December 21, 1909, Djuna
Barnes Papers, McKeldin Library, Special Collections, University of Maryland,
College Park.

2. Zadel Barnes to Djuna Barnes, March 4, 1909. In another letter, November
14, 1909, Zadel praises Djuna: "You are a dear good girl to be cheerful when
cheerfulness is needed so much, and in being bright and pleasant and patient you
are doing good to the children who are very sensitive to moral conditions." "I'm
huggin' you close to the Pinknesses, and they is chortlin' tremendous." Zadel
continues with drawings of breasts ("Pink Tops") that are laughing, writing, "Wot
yer think of them little wed mouths open?" She speaks of the nipples on her
drawings. The rest of the letter is full of the imagery of mothering.

3. While there are many gaps and omissions in the history of the "double household," the following information, derived from research at the McKeldin Library, was confirmed by Duane Barnes, Djuna's half-brother. Brian [Wald] Barnes was married to Djuna's mother, Elizabeth Chappell, from July 3, 1889, through November 6, 1912. On February 22, 1912, Elizabeth Chappell issued a summons to Wald, forcing him to respond within twenty days. On August 2, 1912, divorce papers were filed. The marriage was dissolved three months later. On November 13, 1912, a marriage certificate was issued to Fanny Faulkner and Wald Barnes.

I am grateful to various members of the Barnes family for their generosities: Duane; his son, Kerron; Djuna's brother, Saxon, and his wife, Eleanor. *Cold Comfort: The Selected Letters of Djuna Barnes*, coedited by Mary Lynn Broe and Frances McCullough, now in preparation (Random House, forthcoming), will present to scholars new materials to help explain many puzzling gaps and omissions in the chronology of Barnes's first twenty years. This biographical portrait through letters will also correct errors in the only biography now available.

4. The Coleman-Barnes letters were opened to the public at the McKeldin Library, University of Maryland, in January 1985. In 1988 the University of Delaware-Newark acquired another 225 letters from Barnes to Coleman, 1934–74. As we go to press, 36,000 pages of writing—diaries, eleven drafts of a novel, "Tygon," literary correspondence, poetry, and short stories—have been acquired in the Emily Coleman Papers, Special Collections, University of Delaware-Newark Library, Newark. Examination of this material will obviously add immensely to our understanding of Emily Coleman and of other writers at Hayford Hall.

5. See Introductory material, *The Hound and the Falcon* and *As Once in May*.

6. The MacLeod-Saraga essay in *Feminist Review* details various theories of incest, such as the "mother blaming" or "systems" theories. These authors are excellent interpreters of the theoretical and social policy flip-flops in reigning influential theories of incest. They offer a feminist critique of three: the libertarian view, psychoanalysis, and family dysfunction. See also Herman, "Considering Sex Offenders," for a detailed summary of the various conflicting incest discourses. The last section of Twitchell's *Forbidden Partners* also offers an excellent synopsis of the biological, sociological, and psychological approaches to incest.

Most of the theoretical information synthesized in my essay derives from the feminist approaches of Butler, Russell, Rush, Herman and Hirschman, and Miller. The Boose-Flowers introduction proved invaluable for its rich rereading of Deuteronomy and Genesis myths as well as classical and contemporary literary texts. The list here cited is by no means a complete representation of the excellent feminist work being done on incest theory, ranging from recovery of survivors' voices to socioeconomic analysis of role behavior.

Other useful works are: the evolutionary anthropology of Fox, who synthesizes cross-disciplinary materials from primatology, psychology, and brain functions with other disciplines; Gordon's new work, which argues that the changing visibility of family violence, particularly its historical and political construction, cannot be understood outside of a historical context; the voices of survivors; Toni McNaron and Yarrow Morgan; and Twitchell's study, which weaves together art, myth, and popular culture to explore the development of incest theory in the early modern world.

7. Gordon, Kitzinger, and Smith-Rosenberg offer excellent criticisms of the ideologies of home and family. This article was in preparation before either Elizabeth Pleck's *Domestic Tyranny: The Making of American Social Policy against Family Violence from Colonial Times to the Present* (New York: Oxford University Press, 1988) or Linda Gordon's *Heroes of Their Own Lives: The Politics and History of Family Violence, Boston, 1880–1960* (New York: Viking, 1988) was available. See Lunbeck.

8. See Tronto, "Beyond Gender Difference," as well as Carol Gilligan, *In a Different Voice*, and Nancy Chodorow, *The Reproduction of Mothering*, for now controversial theories of moral development and ethics of caring.

9. Jane Flax warns, " 'Gender relations' is a category meant to capture a complex set of social relations, to refer to a changing set of historically variable social processes. Gender, both as an analytic category and a social process, is relational . . . constituted by and through interrelated parts. These parts are interdependent, that is, each part can have no meaning or existence without the others" (628).

10. Stories of daughter exchanges in the Anglo-Saxon epic, for example, may be intended as mediations between the two cultures of male blood kinship and the hoarding of treasure, but in fact they function to erode such conjunctions: the daughter "both determines and exposes the dangerously paradoxical linkage between the culture's two defining systems of value" (Boose and Flowers, eds., 28).

11. See Hartsock for a critique of both Lévi-Strauss's exchange theory and Gayle Rubin's use of Lévi-Strauss.

12. The MacLeod-Saraga essay informs us that recently social workers and psychologists have suggested three approaches which they claim to be most responsible for constraining the way we think and talk about sex abuse: the libertarian view, psychoanalysis, and family dysfunction. Reduction of incest discourse to "family dysfunction" or to a focus on intrapsychic or interpersonal formulations has characterized analysis of incest in the last ten years, according to Sandra Butler (210).

13. See Gordon, "Politics of Child Sexual Abuse," and *Heroes of Their Own Lives*; also Ariès.

14. See Kitzinger and Garnett.

15. Boose writes: "Daughterhood is, in fact, inseparable from absence in the psychoanalytic definition of social development, for it is the daughter's recognition of her 'castration,' her renunciation of the active, phallic state, and her acquies-

cence to passivity that, in Freud's assessment, constitutes the prerequisite step backward that sets her on the pathway to 'normal femininity' " (21).

16. I am grateful to Elizabeth Meese for recommending Elly Danica's book to me and for her opening comments at the May 6–12, 1988, conference in Dubrovnik, "The Politics and Poetics of Women's Writing." There she warned against the "little drummer girls of theory" as the new polemicists.

17. The eighteen essays in *Silence and Power: A Reevaluation of Djuna Barnes* (Carbondale: Southern Illinois University Press, forthcoming) include radical feminist, cultural, and sociopolitical readings of the complete range of Barnes's writings, restoring her as an influential critic of Modernism, a brilliant parodist and social critic, and an incest survivor. See also Shari Benstock's chapter on Djuna Barnes in *Women of the Left Bank*.

18. See "Mother," "Oscar," and "Indian Summer." In the forthcoming *Gender of Modernism*, edited by Bonnie Kime Scott, in my chapter on Barnes I use one of these stories, a play, early drawings, and journalism to discuss the relation of verbal and visual image in her work particularly in the context of a feminist revision of Modernism.

19. See Marie Ponsot's moving essay, "A Reader's *Ryder*," in *Silence and Power*.

20. See Jane Marcus's pathbreaking essay, "Laughing at Leviticus: *Nightwood* as Woman's Circus Epic," in *Silence and Power*. Marcus reads *Nightwood* as the "representative modern text, a prose poem of abjection, tracing the political unconscious of the rise of fascism, as lesbians, Blacks, circus people, Jews and transvestites—outsiders all—*bow down* as the text repeats, before the truly perverted levitical prescriptions for the racial purity of Hitler."

21. Both Louise DeSalvo's "To Make Her Mutton at Sixteen: Rape, Incest and Child Abuse in *The Antiphon*" and Lynda Curry's " 'Tom, Take Mercy' " on Barnes's 1950s play are forthcoming in *Silence and Power*. Each offers a far more detailed analysis of "the story behind the story" (Field, 194) in *The Antiphon*.

22. See the opening letter, Zadel to Percy Faulkner, December 21, 1909. Saxon Barnes, the author's brother, has made available at the McKeldin Library, University of Maryland letters and a statement about this event.

23. In two private conversations with Duane Barnes over the past two years, his discussion of "visitors" to the farm (that is, Zadel as a practicing medium and spiritualist) confirmed the information in a document given me this summer: that the "Eaches" or spirits who used Zadel's body to "come through the dead" always seemed to be public men, mostly musicians or writers of note, who urged diligence on the children. As late as 1988, Duane Barnes still felt the power and accuracy of the visitors and *never* felt that there was a "rigged" session.

24. See Smith-Rosenberg.

25. Tronto, 648. The now controversial work of Carol Gilligan on female moral development and its "different voice" for expression from the male ethic of justice

comes very close to describing Tronto's proposed "ethic of care": "In this conception, the moral problem arises from conflicting responsibilities rather than from competing rights and requires for its resolution a mode of thinking that is contextual and narrative rather than formal and abstract. This conception of morality as concerned with the activity of care centers moral development around the understanding of responsibility and relationships, just as the conception of morality as fairness ties moral development to the understanding of rights and rules." In addition to addressing different moral concepts, the ethic of care is "tied to concrete circumstances rather than being formal and abstract" and bears a morality "best expressed not as a set of principles but as an activity, the 'activity of care'" (648).

26. See my review "Gunga Duhl, the Pen Performer," for an analysis of Barnes's deconstructive interview techniques and for an analysis of the Alyce Berry–Douglas Messerli collection, *Djuna Barnes Interviews*.

27. Barnes has, in some circles, gained the reputation (which is, I suspect, part of her legendary haughtiness) for being apolitical and elitist. The Coleman-Barnes letters at the University of Delaware indicate that Barnes worked for the WPA in the 1930s, covering furriers and jewelers for a WPA "Cultural Baedeker" Guide to New York City. In 1940 she was thrown out of the mental asylum, Tratjela, for spending time talking and drinking with the working staff and not the inmates and doctors.

28. My thanks to Kerron Barnes for sharing Zadel's poems with me during the summer of 1988. See my forthcoming article "Word Made Fresh: The Journalism Careers of Zadel Gustafson and Djuna Barnes."

29. Reon Barnes to Djuna Barnes, October 3, 1912. By 1916, Zadel, too, was in the care of Uncle Reon and financially dependent on him. Reon's letter scolds Djuna for seeming to deceive him regarding $23 tuition costs. He recommends she take gym.

30. There are a number of accounts that describe the life at Hayford Hall: see Weld and Field, for example; also Susan Chitty's *Now to My Mother* and her half-sister, Lyndall Passerini Hopkinson's *Nothing to Forgive*. By far the liveliest accounts of "Hangover Hall" are Peggy's own in *Out of This Century*, as well as the candid commentary in the Coleman-Barnes letters, University of Maryland, and both letters and diaries at the University of Delaware-Newark. The Weld disappoints because she discusses *Nightwood* but omits many of the group exchanges at Hayford Hall.

31. Emily Coleman's curiously backhanded lobby with T. S. Eliot on behalf of *Nightwood* continues in letters from October 25, 1935, and October 31, 1935. She tells Eliot of Barnes's two previously published books ("both of which seem to me quite worthless"), then launches into a litany of the faults of Barnes's novel: "Of course, it is not a book which would have a wide sale—except that (as is known, I believe, even to American publishers) genius seems eventually to make itself

known. . . . It is strange, to me, that anyone of such great unconscious intelligence should be as wanting in a kind of intellect as the writer of this book seems to be. She cannot create character. She has no sense of dramatic action; she can only describe people." Coleman ends up by arguing for the book's illumination of good and evil, and for its brilliant style of writing. In the October 31, 1935, response to Eliot's letter to her, Coleman delightfully, if unwittingly, commingles sexual and religious arguments, eventually justifying *Nightwood* on the basis that in it "something new has been said about the very heart of sex, going beyond sex, to that world where there is no marriage or giving in marriage, where no modern writer ever goes."

32. William Gerhardie was a Russian émigré who had authored a number of experimental novels and the first English study of Chekhov. In the years immediately following Hayford Hall, both George Barker and Humphrey Jennings gained reputations as poet and documentary filmmaker. John Holms, in the several years before his accidental death while having a broken wrist reset, carried around with him a five-page short story, "Death," a kind of textual passport to verify that he was published. His literary distinction ended there, for in the occasional review he did write for *Calendar of Modern Letters*, he merely quoted quips by other writers such as Wyndham Lewis, who called Gertrude Stein "the best known exponent of a literary system that consists of a gargantuan mental stutter" (Vol. 3, 330).

33. See accounts in Mulhern and Muir; see also Terry Eagleton, "The Rise of English," in *Literary Theory*.

34. See Chapter 8 in Showalter; also Hunter.

35. Guggenheim once, for a brief time, worked in her cousin Harold Loeb's bookstore, the Sunwise Turn, where she startled the customers by insisting on sweeping the floor while wearing her mink coat.

36. See Jay, *The Amazon and the Page*. Hugh Ford's *Published in Paris* also discusses salon culture in Paris and environs during these years. Readers should of course be familiar with Benstock, *Women of the Left Bank*, and George Wickes's *Americans in Paris*.

37. The Barnes-Coleman letters (800 pages, 225 letters) at the University of Delaware-Newark are a rich resource for women's ideas of art and aesthetics, economics, family and sexual politics, and writing in progress. This correspondence figures centrally in *Cold Comfort: The Selected Letters of Djuna Barnes*, co-edited by Mary Lynn Broe and Frances McCullough.

38. See Alice Miller's brilliant work, esp. chaps. 12, 13, and 14.

39. Thanks to Louise Yelin for her purposeful critical reading of this essay and, in particular, for pointing out the significance of the Holmes/Holms/Homes coincidence.

40. See Jane Marcus's review of *Shutter of Snow*.

41. Returning to Paris in 1936, Barnes laments her "melancholy and loved white elephant of an apartment," which she can no longer afford to keep, as she cele-

Lynn Broe

brates café life where she claims that one does not have to be intimate. In a passage that complements the dream sequences in *Nightwood*, Barnes writes to Emily Coleman (May 24, 1936) about her "lost life—Thelma and Thelma only—and my youth—way back in the beginning when she had no part in it and yet she is the cause of my remembrance of it." She writes to Emily of her nightmares: "Thelma is dead in them and being buried in a blue china coffin (queer thought) as big over as a child's, but when she is laid in it it becomes the right proportion. I am screaming, then crying with difficult sleeping tears, and in my sleep saying to myself, "You are over dramatizing this, now—you know you are—Henriette [Metcalfe] running out of a crowd of mourners at me as organ grinders move forward, sad but seeming to be asking me for a *pour bois*—My God!"

42. My thanks to Christine Conti, a graduate student in my English 333 class at SUNY-Binghamton in spring 1986, for alerting me to the appropriateness of the term "sado-spiritual" with regards to the White novel.

Works Cited

Abel, Elizabeth. "Resisting the Exchange: Brother-Sister Incest in Fiction by Women." In *Doris Lessing: The Alchemy of Survival*, edited by Ellen Rose and Lucy Kaplan. Columbus: Ohio University Press, forthcoming.

Ariès, Philippe. *Centuries of Childhood: A Social History of Family Life.* Translated by Robert Baldick. New York: Knopf, 1962.

Armstrong, Nancy. "The Rise of the Domestic Woman." In *The Ideology of Conduct*, edited by Nancy Armstrong and Leonard Tennenhouse, 96–141. New York: Methuen, 1987.

Banks, Olive. *Faces of Feminism*. Oxford: Basil Blackwell, 1986.

Barnes, Djuna. *The Antiphon*. New York: Farrar, Straus and Giroux, 1958.

———. *A Book*. New York: Boni and Liveright, 1923.

———. Collection. Special Collections, University of Delaware Library, Newark.

———. *Nightwood*. New York: New Directions, 1937.

———. Papers. McKeldin Library, Special Collections, University of Maryland, College Park.

———. *Ryder*. New York: Horace Liveright, 1928.

Benstock, Shari. *Women of the Left Bank*. Austin: University of Texas Press, 1986.

Boose, Lynda E., and Betty S. Flowers, eds. *Daughters and Fathers*. Baltimore: Johns Hopkins University Press, 1988.

Broe, Mary Lynn. "Gunga Duhl, the Pen Performer." Review of *Djuna Barnes Interviews*, edited by Alyce Barry, foreword and commentary by Douglas Messerli. *Belles Lettres* 1 (September–October 1985): 2–4.

————, ed. *Silence and Power: A Reevaluation of Djuna Barnes*. Carbondale: Southern Illinois University Press, forthcoming.

Buddington, Zadel Barnes. *Can the Old Love?* Boston: James R. Osgood and Co., 1871.

Butler, Sandra. *Conspiracy of Silence: The Trauma of Incest*. San Francisco: Volcano Press, 1985.

Carrel, Alexis. *Man the Unknown*. New York: Harper and Brothers, 1935.

Chitty, Susan. *Now to My Mother: A Very Personal Memoir of Antonia White*. London: Weidenfeld and Nicholson, 1985.

Chodorow, Nancy. *The Reproduction of Mothering: Psychoanalysis and the Sociology of Gender*. Berkeley and Los Angeles: University of California Press, 1978.

Coleman, Emily Holmes. *The Shutter of Snow*. 1930. Reprint. New York: Penguin Books, 1986.

Cunningham, Valentine. *British Writers of the Thirties*. Oxford: Oxford University Press, 1988.

Curry, Lynda. " 'Tom, Take Mercy': Djuna Barnes's Drafts of *The Antiphon*." In *Silence and Power: A Reevaluation of Djuna Barnes*, edited by Mary Lynn Broe. Carbondale: Southern Illinois University Press, forthcoming.

Danica, Elly. *Don't: A Woman's Word*. Toronto: Gynergy Books, 1988.

DeSalvo, Louise. "To Make Her Mutton at Sixteen: Rape, Incest and Child Abuse in *The Antiphon*." In *Silence and Power: A Reevaluation of Djuna Barnes*, edited by Mary Lynn Broe. Carbondale: Southern Illinois University Press, forthcoming.

DuBois, Ellen. "The Radicalism of the Women's Suffrage Movement." In *Feminism and Equality*, edited by Anne Phillips, 127–38. New York: New York University Press, 1987.

Eagleton, Terry. *Literary Theory*. Minneapolis: University of Minnesota Press, 1983.

Family Secrets/Child Sexual Abuse. Special issue of *Feminist Review* 28 (Spring 1988).

Field, Andrew. *Djuna: The Formidable Miss Barnes*. Austin: University of Texas Press, 1985.

Flax, Jane. "Postmodernism and Gender Relations in Feminist Theory." *Signs* 12 (Summer 1987): 621–43.

Ford, Hugh Douglas. *Published in Paris*. New York: Macmillan, 1975.

Fox, Robin. *The Red Lamp of Incest*. New York: Dutton, 1980.

Garnett, Angelica. *Deceived with Kindness*. New York: Harcourt Brace Jovanovich, 1985.

Gilbert, Lucy, and Paula Webster. *Bound by Love: The Sweet Trap of Daughterhood*. Boston: Beacon Press, 1982.

Gilligan, Carol. *In a Different Voice: Psychological Theory and Women's Development*. Cambridge, Mass.: Harvard University Press, 1982.

Girouard, Mark. *Life in the English Country House*. New York: Penguin, 1980.

Gordon, Linda. "The Politics of Child Sexual Abuse: Notes from American History." *Feminist Review* 28 (Spring 1988): 56–64.

Guggenheim, Peggy. *Out of This Century: Confessions of an Art Addict*. 1946. Reprint. New York: Universe Books, 1979.

Hartsock, Nancy C. M. *Money, Sex and Power: Toward a Feminist Historical Materialism*. Boston: Northeastern University Press, 1983.

Herman, Judith Lewis. "Considering Sex Offenders: A Model of Addiction." *Signs* 13 (Summer 1988): 695–724.

———. *Father-Daughter Incest*. Cambridge, Mass.: Harvard University Press, 1981.

Herman, Judith Lewis, and Lisa Hirschman. "Father-Daughter Incest." In *The Signs Reader on Gender and Scholarship*, edited by Elizabeth Abel and Emily K. Abel, 257–78. Chicago: University of Chicago Press, 1983.

Holroyd, Michael. *Unreceived Opinions*. New York: Holt, Rinehart and Winston, 1974.

Hopkinson, Lyndall Passerini. *Nothing to Forgive: A Daughter's Life of Antonia White*. London: Chatto and Windus, 1988.

Hunter, Diane O. "Hysteria, Psychoanalysis and Feminism: The Case of Anna O." In *The (M)Other Tongue*, edited by Sheila Nelson Garner, Claire Kahane, and Madelon Sprengnether, 89–115. Ithaca: Cornell University Press, 1985.

Jay, Karla. *The Amazon and the Page*. Bloomington: Indiana University Press, 1988.

Jeffreys, Sheila. *The Spinster and Her Enemies: Feminism and Sexuality, 1880–1930*. London: Pandora Press, 1985.

Kelly, Liz. "What's in a Name? Defining Child Sexual Abuse." *Feminist Review* 28 (Spring 1988): 65–73.

Kitzinger, Jenny. "Defending Innocence: Ideologies of Childhood." *Feminist Review* 28 (Spring 1988): 77–87.

Lee, Judith. "The Sweetest Lie." In *Silence and Power: A Reevaluation of Djuna Barnes*, edited by Mary Lynn Broe. Carbondale: Southern Illinois University Press, forthcoming.

Lévi-Strauss, Claude. *The Elementary Structures of Kinship*. Translated by James Harle Bell. Edited by John Richard von Stormer and Rodney Weedham. Boston: Beacon Press, 1969.

Lewis, Jane. *Women in England, 1870–1950: Sexual Divisions and Social Change*. Sussex: Wheatsheaf Books, 1984.

Liz. "Too Afraid to Speak." *Leveller*, April 12–17, 1982, pp. 18–21.

Lunbeck, Elizabeth. "Centuries of Cruelty." Review of *Domestic Tyranny: The Making of American Social Policy against Family Violence from Colonial Times to the Present* by Elizabeth Pleck, and *Heroes of Their Own Lives: The Politics and His-

tory of Family Violence, Boston, 1880–1960 by Linda Gordon. In *Women's Review of Books* 12 (September 1988): 1, 3.

Lurie, Alison. "Fairy Tale Liberation." *New York Review of Books*, December 17, 1970, p. 42.

McIntosh, Mary. "Introduction to an Issue: Family Secrets as Public Drama." *Feminist Review* 28 (Spring 1988): 6–15.

MacLeod, Mary, and Esther Saraga. "Challenging the Orthodoxy: Toward a Feminist Theory and Practise." *Feminist Review* 28 (Spring 1988): 16–55.

Malinin, Theodore I. *Surgery and Life: The Extraordinary Career of Alexis Carrel.* New York: Harcourt Brace Jovanovich, 1979.

Marcus, Jane. "Laughing at Leviticus: *Nightwood* as Woman's Circus Epic." In *Silence and Power: A Reevaluation of Djuna Barnes*, edited by Mary Lynn Broe. Carbondale: Southern Illinois University Press, forthcoming.

————. "Of Madness and Method." Review of *The Shutter of Snow* by Emily Holmes Coleman. In *Women's Review of Books* 3 (August 1986): 1, 3–4.

Miller, Alice. *Thou Shalt Not Be Aware.* New York: Farrar, Straus and Giroux, 1983.

Muir, Edwin. *The Story and the Fable.* London: George G. Harrap, 1940.

Mulhern, Francis. *The Moment of Scrutiny.* London: Verso Press, 1981.

Newton, Judith. "Making—and Remaking—History: Another Look at 'Patriarchy.' " In *Feminist Issues in Literary Scholarship*, edited by Shari Benstock, 124–40. Bloomington: Indiana University Press, 1987.

Ponsot, Marie. "A Reader's *Ryder.*" In *Silence and Power: A Reevaluation of Djuna Barnes*, edited by Mary Lynn Broe. Carbondale: Southern Illinois University Press, forthcoming.

Rubin, Gayle. "The Traffic in Women." In *Toward an Anthropology of Women*, edited by Rayna Reiter, 157–210. New York: Monthly Review Press, 1975.

Rush, Florence. *The Best Kept Secret.* New York: McGraw-Hill, 1980.

Russell, Diana E. H. *The Secret Trauma: Incest in the Lives of Girls and Women.* New York: Basic Books, 1986.

Scharf, Lois, and Joan M. Jensen, eds. *Decades of Discontent: The Women's Movement, 1920–1940.* Boston: Northeastern University Press, 1987.

Scott, Ann. "Feminism and the Seductiveness of 'The Real Event.' " *Feminist Review* 28 (Spring 1988): 88–102.

Scott, Bonnie Kime, ed. *The Gender of Modernism.* Bloomington: Indiana University Press, forthcoming.

Showalter, Elaine. *The Female Malady: Women, Madness and English Culture, 1830–1980.* New York: Random House, 1985.

Smith-Rosenberg, Carroll. *Disorderly Conduct: Visions of Gender in Victorian America.* New York: Knopf, 1985.

Tronto, Joan C. "Beyond Gender Difference to a Theory of Care." *Signs* 12 (Summer 1987): 644–63.

Twitchell, James B. *Forbidden Partners: The Incest Taboo in Modern Culture.* New York: Columbia University Press, 1987.

Ward, Elizabeth. *Father-Daughter Rape.* New York: Grove Press, 1985.

Weld, Jacqueline Bograd. *Peggy: The Wayward Guggenheim.* New York: Dutton, 1986.

White, Antonia. *As Once in May.* Edited by Susan Chitty. London: Virago Press, 1983.

————. *Frost in May.* New York: Dial Press, 1933.

————. *The Hound and the Falcon.* London: Virago Press, 1983.

————. *The Lost Traveller.* New York: Dial Press, 1950.

Wickes, George. *Americans in Paris.* New York: Doubleday, 1969.

Zipes, Jack. *Fairy Tales and the Art of Subversion.* New York: Methuen, 1983.

Chapter 3

. . . .

Exile in the American Grain

H.D.'s Diaspora

Susan Stanford Friedman

I can't write unless I am an outcast.
—H.D. to Marianne Moore, 1921

But I am very much an American. . . . Anyway, I feel one. Sometimes by living
away one grows closer.
—H.D., Interview, 1960

The prerequisite to adulthood is leaving home. The founding gesture of American Modernism seems to have been expatriatism, a self-imposed exile from the parochial and provincial for the cosmopolitan and international. The two are not so unrelated, for Victorianism in both its English and American forms is akin to parentalism, a cultural dominance, a parental superego prescribing duty over pleasure, obligation over freedom, social order over personal rebellion: a wet blanket over the fire and ice of desire. The young moderns growing up in the Victorian era had to leave home. Alienation from family, religion, and nation was the precondition of their art. Or so at least we have been led to believe by the archetypal weight of Stephen Dedalus's ringing *Non Serviam* at the end of James Joyce's *Portrait of the Artist*: "I will not serve that in which I no longer believe whether it call itself my home, my fatherland or my church: and I will try to express myself in some mode of life or art as freely as I can . . . using for my defence the only arms I allow myself to use—silence, exile, and cunning" (246–47). Joyce borrowed from the meaning of externally imposed exile to suggest that an artist's survival depends upon an internally imposed exile—upon, in other words, alienation—the state of being alien, that is, foreign, outside, exiled from belonging to the larger *communitas* of family, religion, and nation—to which we might add class, sex, and race. Exile is flight—a double-word evoking both fleeing from oppression and flying in freedom. On a flight from the Victorian past, the moderns sought freedom to "make it new," as Ezra Pound proclaimed.

Drawn by the magnetism of Europe's culture capitals, the aspiring artists for whom Stephen is an exemplum established their own *communitas* of aliens in the intellectual cross-currents of international urban centers—London, Paris, Berlin, Rome, Vienna. For the Americans in particular, Henry James was their precursor—a "crusader" against "provincialism" and for "internationalism," the "modern enlightenment," as Pound wrote in his 1917 essay "Provincialism the Enemy" (*Selected Prose*, 189). Leaving behind the American Renaissance with its odd prophets of an original, indigenous American genius, James paved the way for Pound, T. S. Eliot, H.D., Gertrude Stein, and many others for whom leaving home did not mean striking out for the territories, as it did for Huck Finn, but rather leaving the United States to be nourished at the fountains of Western culture, as true innocents abroad.

Modernism, many critics tell us, is like the cities in which it developed—eclectic, innovative, assimilationist, pluralist, multifaceted, in flux, and above all international—the opposite, in short, of regionalism.[1] As cultural grafts, the expatriate moderns produced hybrid texts that might graft the Provençal lyric with the Japanese haiku, the Greek fragment with French *vers libre*, the Japanese Noh drama with the Celtic saga. The flight from home freed the writer to explore the art of any time, any place, to re-fuse the shards of history into something new, to define a poetics of potpourri—the poem as mixture of cultural fragments and fragrances.

In "Patria Mia," an essay first published in 1913, Pound expounded on the importance of expatriatism for Americans who would become serious writers. The American genius, he believed, could not develop in the cultural "Dark Ages" of the United States, but would flourish only in London or Paris (*Selected Prose*, 111). "If you have any vital interest in art and letters," he wrote, "you sooner or later leave the country" and go to a metropolis like London, which he called "the capital of the US so far as art and letters . . . were concerned" (122). As early as 1909, Pound had claimed "world citizenship" for himself (145), thereby anticipating the term "international hero" that Delmore Schwartz applied to Eliot: he was "cosmopolitan and expatriated," the true "international hero" whose ex-perience and words transcended the national, as symbolized by *The Waste Land*, which ends with lines in five languages (Howe, 279).

William Carlos Williams was appalled and hurt by the example of Pound, Eliot, and H.D. in whose expatriatism he saw a Eurocentric bias against things American and an elitist privileging of the erudite and learned. "Pound," he wrote in his 1918 Prologue for *Kora in Hell: Improvi-sations* (1920), "is the best enemy United States verse has" (*Imaginations*, 26). Eliot's "Prufrock" was nothing but "a rehash" and "repetition." De-fensively, Williams blasted all those "who run to London," rejecting America, turning backward instead of forward. To write the new, Ameri-cans needed to look to American culture and history, not to "desolation of a flat Hellenic perfection of style," a phrase that deliberately evoked H.D. (13). To emphasize his own genuine American "newness," he mockingly quoted a letter she wrote him suggesting that the flip tone in one of his poems betrayed his sacred gift, to which he responded: "I'll write what-ever I damn please" (13). Williams's Prologue is a defiant attack on American expatriatism that calls for an American Modernism based in idigenous American culture—the "little tradition," not the "great tradi-tion" of Europe. His examples are telling; he celebrated the imagination of his mother, whom he called a true "castaway," along with Afro-American work songs, women's folk art, and the cigar box trimmings of a hermit—

the art, that is, of the marginalized (4–9). As a defiant celebration of things American, *In the American Grain* (1925) is his imaginative recreation of American heroes from Eric the Red to Lincoln. For Williams and many others, this volume served as a counterweight against the anti-American scorn of those "who run to London."[2]

The opposition seems clear—the expatriatism of Pound and the nationalism of Williams; the learned internationalism of Pound's *Cantos*, an epic that celebrates the culture heroes of the great civilizations, and the democratic nationalism of Williams's *Paterson*, an epic in which an obscure man and his city are inseparable from each other and their history. Williams, inheritor of Whitman, became in the eyes of many the paradigmatic Modernist bard of twentieth-century American poetry. But not to everyone. To Hugh Kenner, whose prototypical American Modernist is Pound, internationalism is mandatory for Modernism—so much so that he dismissed Williams, Virginia Woolf, and William Faulkner as "provincial writers," mere "regionalists."[3]

But where does H.D. fit in this tug-of-war between two American giants? Where does she fit when we consider that the place of woman in the *Cantos* and *Paterson* is as silent muse and that H.D.'s place in Kenner's influential *Pound Era* is nearly invisible? Curiously, H.D. stands right where she did when the two young men courted her in the fields and forests of Upper Darby, Pennsylvania and right where she stands today in the masthead of the journal *Sagetrieb*'s subtitle: "A Journal Devoted to Poets in the Pound-H.D.-Williams Tradition"—in the proverbial middle, a woman between two men, an exile in the American grain, a form of exile both American and gendered. This middle position is not a passive one, however. It is defiantly dynamic and revisionary. Its inner dialectic suggests ways of moving beyond the parochial definitions of Modernism that either prescribe or condemn so-called internationalism. It thereby points to a revisioning and an (en)gendering of Modernism.

On one hand, H.D. was undeniably an expatriate like Pound. As she recalled in 1929 for Margaret Anderson in the *Little Review*, "The happiest moment in my life was when I stood on the deck of a second class boat called the Floride . . . free, my first trip to . . . 'Europe' in 1911, going with a friend I loved [Frances Josepha Gregg]" (365). Leaving home in 1911, she only returned to the United States six times. At her marriage to Richard Aldington in 1913, she took on British citizenship with his name and returned to her American citizenship only after her daughter Perdita led the way by taking American papers in 1956. Offered refuge by American family and friends during both wars, she refused both times. To flee the war would be desertion, betrayal of the city that had set her free.[4] London was the scene of her flight, in both senses of the word—her escape from the confinement of Upper Darby and her soaring success as the most perfect of the Imagists. Exhilarated in spite of the war, she impulsively invited Marianne Moore to London in 1915 as soon as she saw Moore's first poems: "I know, more or less what you are up against, though I escaped some five years ago! . . . I felt so terribly when I was in U.S.A., the putty that met my whetted lance!" (August 21, 1915). "Can you see," she once asked Bryher (her intimate British friend and companion), "how London at least left me *free*? Will you *ever* realize what it meant?" (August 23, 1924).

On the other hand, H.D. continued to feel very American, in spite of or maybe because of her British passport, her loyalty to London, and her later residences in Switzerland and Italy. " 'But I am very much an American,' " she told her interviewer just before the awards ceremony of the American Academy of Arts and Letters. "Anyway, I feel one. Sometimes by living away one grows closer" (Stix). The imagery of her early poems, she told Norman H. Pearson, was not Greek at all but drawn from her memories of the North Atlantic shores in New Jersey, Rhode Island, and Maine.[5] London was the scene of her escape, as she told Moore, but she was nonetheless always a foreigner in England. Owing much to James's novels of Americans abroad, *Paint It To-Day*, H.D.'s first novel, completed in 1921, explores the psychic borderlines of expatriatism in London. Her persona in the roman à clef, the young Midget DeFreddie, senses her isolation: "Yes, she was an American. In time, in space, a thousand, thousand years separated from this English woman, pretty, civilized, of her own world, sympathetic, well-dressed who was pattering of grape-blossoms and a house-party in the south of France" (455). Sophisticated and civilized, the Englishwoman is like domesticated grapevines; the two American girls, Midget and her friend Josepha, modeled on Frances Josepha Gregg, the woman H.D. loved, are in tune with the "roughness and the power of that wilderness" of America (452). H.D.'s early poetry, Harriet Monroe speculated, might owe a great deal "to the pioneers . . . [who] took a shut-in race out of doors, exposed it to nature's harsh activities, and then restored a certain lost fibre to its very blood and bones" (93). Symbolically, America is the untamed, the wilderness.

No wonder, then, that H.D. would later lament to Bryher, "I miss something now of the American timbre in almost all English writing." She loved the "drive and velocity and the depth and the art" of American prose, especially Faulkner's: "He seems so oddly at times, complete James, . . . then bursts off into sky-rockets of prose. . . . And one thinks and wonders of the language, itself. How the Americans do put drive and push and punch into it" (August 30, 1935). As an expatriate, she kept in close touch with American literature both past and current. It is no accident, but part of a lifelong identification, that she liked the "beatnik" poets of the 1950s and established warm friendships with such American poets as Robert Duncan and the British expatriate Denise Levertov.[6]

H.D.'s position in the middle between Pound and Williams—exile in the American grain—was not static, however. It was deeply conflictual. Like all the other "two's and two's and two's in my life," as she wrote in *Tribute to Freud*, "There were two countries, America and England as it happened, separated by a wide gap in consciousness and a very wide stretch of sea" (32). Pulled both ways, she was fully at home in neither world. As Madelon, her persona in the sketch "Pontikonisi" muses about the source of her pain: "Was it that [the] break toward re-birth, artificial psychic caesarian, America-Europe, [was] beginning to tell now? The place where the graft was, rubbed raw. She hadn't felt it till this letting go London, where her graft-bandages still were" (4).

The graft rubbed raw forever. The gap in consciousness remained. That is the central point about H.D.'s expatriatism. She needed to be an outsider to write, as she told Moore: "I am beginning to feel as if the world approved of me—and I can't write unless I am an outcast" (January 17, 1921). To feel fully at home, to be harmoniously integrated into the *communitas* of family and nation—whether America or England—was to be domesticated and tamed. As a woman in particular, home meant a web of conventional feminine obligations, a domesticity that was incompatible with her creativity.

Not that she did not at times long for the harmony of home, a home. But she understood that her homelessness, with all its pain of dislocation and alienation, was fundamental to the psychodynamics of her creativity. Being foreign was an externalization of an interior difference, the very difference that fueled her writing. Being expatriate was a spatial metaphor, a geographic manifestation of a more fundamental exile from convention—all kinds of convention. She felt different as the only girl to survive in a family of five brothers; she felt different as a Moravian in a predominantly Christian world that considered the Moravians an exotic sect; she felt different as a woman nearly six feet tall; she felt different as a woman who "had two loves separate," as she wrote, who was bisexual (*Collected Poems*, 453); she felt different as the mother of a child whose parentage she had to hide; she felt different as an artist in a materialistic world; she felt different as a woman born with a powerful gift, driven by a daemon that compelled her to write; she felt different as a woman poet in a male world of letters. Being an American in Europe was both symptom and sign of these other differences. Expatriatism was a living symbol of her own marginality—particularly, but not exclusively, her marginality as a woman.

And marginality was essential to H.D.'s concept of modernity. The movie *Borderline*, in which she and Paul Robeson starred as white and black expatriates, embodies this modernism of marginality, as the pamphlet she wrote to accompany the film makes abundantly clear. A geographic borderline serves as a spatial metaphor for racial and psychological marginality, the state of being perpetually alien, decentered at the fringes of the mainstream like the women, Jews, and commoners in Virginia Woolf's "Society of Outsiders" in *Three Guineas*.[7] H.D.'s description of the film's characters underlines the link between expatriatism, modernity, and marginality. The white man and woman, Astrid and Thorne, "are borderline social cases, not out of life, not in life. . . . Astrid, the white-cerebral is and is not outcast, is and is not a social alien, is and is not a normal human being, she is borderline. These two are specifically chosen to offset another borderline couple of more dominant integrity. These last, Pete and his sweetheart Adah, . . . dwell on the cosmic racial borderline. They are black people among white people" (*Borderline*, 29–30).

As I have argued elsewhere, H.D.'s extensive involvement in the Afro-American Renaissance—centered in Harlem and extending into London and Paris through expatriate communities—played an important part in the development of her own Modernism—a Modernism not of an alienated elite but of what she variously called the "dispersed," the "scattered remnant," the "wandering," the "reviled," and the "lost."[8] In "Two Americans," the sketch she wrote in 1930 about herself and Robeson, she recognizes the bond between them as two Americans in exile. She feels regenerated by her identification with the spiritual power of Robeson, the uncrowned king who had so brilliantly countered the heritage of slavery by bringing Afro-American spirituals, an ur-tradition of the American folk, to Europe. Even more radically than Williams's *In the American Grain*, "Two Americans" celebrates an indigenous American heritage and culture. Soon after, in the 1930s, she was deeply moved by the diaspora of the Jews, especially under the rise of Nazism. She made connections between the wanderings of the Jews and the persecutions of her own Moravian ancestors, who borrowed the term *diaspora* to name their own homelessness. As a Jew born in Moravia, Freud became a father figure for H.D., tying her irrevocably to the "scattered remnant" of history—a phrase she absorbed from Isaiah, who foresaw the survival of a mere remnant in the desolation of cities burned in fire (Isa. 1:7, 9; 10:20–22).

So it was not London per se that set H.D. free, any more than Zurich freed Joyce. No doubt the particular artists in London's prewar heyday as the axis of English-language Modernism were important influences on her imagist work, as they were for Pound and Eliot. But being at an international center of Modernist ferment was not the only precondition of H.D.'s Modernism. It was the *break* from home, the absence of America, not just the presence of London, where she wasn't, not where she was, that mattered. In contrast with Kenner's Eurocentric view of Modernist expatriatism, in contrast also with Williams's suspicion of Anglophilism, geographic location was not nearly so important for H.D. as the break from America. Nothing illustrates this more clearly than the paradoxical debate between Bryher and H.D. on where they should live—England or the United States. Ironically, the very place H.D. had to flee was the center of Bryher's dreams of freedom. Conversely, the city that was the setting of H.D.'s awakening was the scene of Bryher's suffocation. "I had to GET AWAY to make good," H.D. once explained to Bryher. "London was MY OWN, just as Berlin is your own" (June 24, 1931). This conflict led over the years not only to much dispute about where they would live—Switzerland was the compromise—but also to an awareness that freedom did not reside in any one location. In 1918, H.D. urged Bryher to go to the United States but warned her that it was the break from her family that would free her, not America: "Don't go with the false idea that America will give you *anything* that you don't already possess. But the break from England may give you a spiritual impulse that will carry you on. . . . *Go to America!* . . . Forgive my preach—but your mind and your surroundings, and your problems (though in some ways so different) are also very similar to my own early ones. There is no help for it! You must have freedom of mind and spirit soon, or things will close over you & it will be too late" (December 31, 1918).[9]

Expatriatism provided freedom of mind and spirit. Freedom from what, we might ask. From convention, from the pressure to conform, to do the respectable, the proper, the expected. For women, the pressure to conform centered on the question of gender. Freedom of mind and spirit meant above all freedom from family pressure to conform to conventional feminine norms. Marrying an artist was unconventional enough for H.D.'s parents; they were deeply opposed to her engagement to Pound. But being an artist—going to Europe to live and travel, first with a woman she loved and then alone—was scandalous. Probably even more disturbing than their open disapproval, however, was the example of her mother, who was artistically gifted but "morbidly self-effacing" and all too willing to sacrifice everything to the needs of her brilliant husband (*Tribute to Freud*, 164).

Paint It To-Day vividly explores the connection between the expatriate flight from home and alienation from a conventional feminine destiny. As Midget and Josepha arrive on the London art scene, they discover that they are exiled even from the exiles—separate as women in love with each other from both American and European norms. Nothing could be further from Pound's celebration of London as the capital of international culture in "Patria Mia": "She and Josepha and such as she and Josepha were separated, irreparably, from the masses of their own country people. . . . from the great mass of the people of the nations of the world. They were separated from the separated too; how can we make that clear? They were separated from the elite, from the artist, the musician, at least from all the artists and literary specimens it had been their privilege so far to encounter, in the art circles of the mid-layers of so called bohemia" (*Paint It To-Day*, 456–57).

The expatriatism of "She and Josepha and such as she and Josepha" meant separation from the social order, the kind of total break from conventional femininity that Woolf envisioned when she observed: "Across the broad continent of a woman's life falls the shadow of a sword. On one side all is correct, definite, orderly; the paths are strait, the trees regular, the sun shaded; escorted by clergymen, she has only to walk demurely from cradle to grave and no one will touch a hair of her head. But on the other side all is confusion. Nothing follows a regular course. The paths wind between bogs and precipices. The trees roar and rock and fall in ruin" ("Harriette Wilson," 179). H.D.'s expatriatism also anticipates Sheila Rowbotham's formulation of women's perpetual exile in patriarchy, one that echoes W. E. B. Du Bois in *Souls of Black Folk*: "But always we were split in two, straddling silence, not sure where we would begin to find ourselves or one another. From this division, our material dislocation, came the experience of one part of ourselves as strange, foreign and cut off from the other which we encountered as tongue-tied paralysis about our own identity. We were never all together in one place, we were always in transit, immigrants into alien territory" (Rowbotham, 31).[10]

For H.D., then, expatriation was a flight from femininity, not from womanhood but from the conventional norms of Victorian femininity that clashed with the demands of creativity. In this respect, her journey to London functioned much like Emily Dickinson's retreat to reclusivity, which Susan Howe has called a "self-imposed exile" (13), and Woolf's move from fashionable Hyde Park Gate, under the control of her socially conscious half-brother, to the less reputable Bloomsbury with her sister Vanessa.[11] Because H.D.'s parents, like Woolf's, so embodied the Victorian polarity of masculine and feminine, her expatriatism even incorporated a psychological matricide and patricide, a "killing" of the motherland and fatherland embedded in the psyche of the fleeing artist, for which she felt perpetually guilty. Perhaps this symbolic conflation of nation and family helps to explain why H.D. was so angry with Bryher in 1935 after Bryher apparently told her it was her duty to live in the United States. The matricidal aspect of expatriatism and its consequent guilt is a theme in both *Paint It To-Day* and the roman à clef *HER*. To break free in these novels means—terrifyingly—to "kill" the mother. In *Paint It To-Day*, Midget likens her refusal to return to the States as her mother asks to the matricide of Orestes: " 'Your mother, your mother, your mother,' the present said to Midget, 'has betrayed, or would betray, through the clutch and the tyranny of the emotion, the mind in you. . . . Look,' said the present, 'and choose. Here is a knife, slay your mother. She has betrayed or would betray your gift' " (473).

H.D.'s expatriatism, then, was not based primarily on flight from the so-called provincialism of America to the international cultural centers of Western civilization nor on a search for a new aristocracy of artists. Rather, her dynamic middle position between the internationalism of Pound and the nationalism of Williams combined the physical and imaginative wanderings of Pound with the democratic alienation of Williams. Mediating between the two poles was her situation as a woman. Like Pound, she found freedom in the homelessness of belonging to all times and all places. Like Williams, she identified with the "drive and punch" of American energy, with the "little tradition," the history and art of the marginalized. Like Pound, she could not live in America. But like Williams, she was very disturbed by Eliot's conversion to Anglican Toryism. As she wrote to Bryher on the subject of expatriatism, "T. S. Eliot is so, so terribly wrong—yet is saving his skin, I suppose simply. . . . H.D. tries to remain in the balance between these two vibrations" (August 30, 1935).[12] This balance made her akin to Joyce, whose removal from Dublin allowed him to be Irish from that position of exile. Away from the immediate suffocations of America, H.D. could be American and use Afro-Americans, Indians, and women as prototypes of modern humanity, as Joyce used Bloom, the Wandering Jew, in *Ulysses*.

H.D.'s expatriatism not only affected her freedom to work but also shaped the evolving nature of that work—her Imagist lyric, her experimental prose, her epics of the 1940s and 1950s. As the scene of her break from her family, London is inseparable from the creation of "H.D., Imagiste," the poet whose musical cadence and crystalline image led her to be called the "perfect imagist," even the "most perfect or nearly perfect of all American poets" (Kreymborg, 347).[13] But her poems were not set in London, not even in the unspecified metropolis of poems like Eliot's "The Love Song of J. Alfred Prufrock." Instead, they create an alternate world, a fourth dimension seemingly outside historical time and geographical space. Expatriatism—being perpetually foreign—helped free her from the weight of history, remove her from the social order with its web of obligation, to create a lyric, fourth dimension.

Theocritus, the Hellenist poet and father of the pastoral, was significantly one of her earliest models. As a genre, the pastoral suggests a binary opposition between nature and culture in which the poet is located in an imaginary realm temporarily removed from the confinements of the social order—a space and time traditionally connected with the Golden Age. The pastoral posits a temporary expatriatism from the oppression of the real world. *Sea Garden*, her first volume, published in 1916, is a sequence of modern pastorals set in a symbolic green world removed from conventional space and time. A stone, a pool, a cliff, a shore, a flower designate space. The cycle of night and day, the ripeness of the fruit, and the heat of the sun signify time. It is a landscape of the imagination in which nature is an exteriorization of the poet's consciousness.

Listen for a moment to the first part of "Mid-day."

The light beats upon me.
I am startled—
a split leaf crackles on the paved floor—

A slight wind shakes the seed-pods—
my thoughts are spent

as the black seeds.
My thoughts tear me,
I dread their fever.
I am scattered in its whirl.
I am scattered
like the hot shrivelled seeds.
(*Collected Poems*, 10)

There are many absences in this poem. There is no place or time more
specific than a windy, fall, hot midday anywhere, anytime. Like the disembodied initials of the poet's signature, "H.D.," the speaker may be man
or woman—we cannot tell. Clearly, there is a story behind the speaker's
anguish, but the poem has no narrative—we never learn the cause or
consequence of the intense emotion frozen forever into the lyric present of
the poem. As a poem whose autobiographical origin has been erased, it
anticipates Eliot's theory of impersonalism.[14] The text denies its context,
refuses a reference to its autobiographical and historical origins. The
living woman's emotion has been transmuted into a seemingly timeless,
universal realm of the imagination.

How does this emotion relate to H.D.'s expatriatism? Barbara Guest has
said it well in speaking generally about the effect of perpetual dislocation
for expatriates: "Suddenly you have this luminous realization that you are
going to be in another country—the real country, that of your dreams. A
place where your poetry begins, within you" ("Exile," 2). The sprinkling of
unnamed shrines and temples, daemons and dryads in *Sea Garden* evokes
Greece, but the landscape of the volume is never anchored in human
geography because, as Guest suggests, the "country" is imaginary and
symbolic. The poet in this realm is "depersonalized," to echo Eliot. As she
later reflected, the "early H.D." was not "personal," "intimate," or "narrative." Instead, she was "clairvoyant," "transcendental." Seemingly removed from history, she was disembodied, like a psychic medium or
Delphic sybil, a conduit for the sacred in an animistic realm.[15] Not that
this realm has the static harmony of a Golden Age; there is a sense of
tremendous conflict in the polarities of *Sea Garden*. But this natural world
seems to exist outside the time-bound world of the modern city.

It was exactly this otherworldliness in H.D. that Williams mocked and
connected ultimately to the expatriate rejection of America in his Prologue
to *Kora in Hell*. "When I was with her," he wrote, "my feet always seemed
to be sticking to the ground while she would be walking on the tips of the

grass stems" (*Imaginations*, 12). What he and many others did not realize was that the landscape of *Sea Garden* originated in America and that her use of nature as objective correlative for spirit attested to her American literary heritage—the Transcendentalism of Emerson and Thoreau. But Williams was correct in seeing that her Imagist lyric did not directly root itself in American culture. Influenced as they were by Greek lyrics, Troubadour songs, and Japanese haiku, her poems constitute her version of Pound's internationalist potpourri.

The pastorals of *Sea Garden* also reflect the gendered dimension of H.D.'s expatriatism—her flight from conventional femininity into the relative freedom of a foreigner to be "different." The imaginary realm of the poems is not overtly gendered, but read in the context of her expatriatism the pastoral space covertly constitutes the poet's womanhood in opposition to the confining social order. The poem "Sheltered Garden" serves as a touchstone for the volume, with its desire for escape from the domestic garden into the wild. I quote it in part:

I have had enough.
I gasp for breath.

. . . .

I have had enough—
border-pinks, clove-pinks, wax-lilies,

. . . .

O for some sharp swish of a branch—
there is no scent of resin
in this place,
no taste of bark, of coarse weeds,

. . . .

only border on border of scented pinks.

. . . .

O to blot out this garden
to forget, to find a new beauty
in some terrible
wind-tortured place.
(*Collected Poems*, 19–21)

H.D.'s "wind-tortured place," imaginatively constructed in her Imagist lyrics, represents her first solution to the problem Victorian femininity posed for her creativity. Externalizing her alienation, her status as outcast, this wild space on the borderline accomplishes what Woolf said women

writers must do—kill the Angel in the House, the phantom of the unselfish, intensely sympathetic, delicately pure Victorian lady who casts her
shadow on the woman writer's page. H.D.'s lyric wilderness also represents a flight from the stereotype of the "poetess," the sentimental versifier
of soft love and sweet sighs from whom women poets often felt they had to
separate themselves to establish their own poetic authority in the male
world of letters. The popular versifier and illustrator Kate Greenaway
wrote: "Twist and twine Roses and Lilies / And little leaves green, / Fit for
a queen" (85). But H.D. opens *Sea Garden* with her language of flowers in
"Sea Rose," which encodes her own vulnerability and defiant difference in
an austere eroticism reminiscent of Georgia O'Keeffe's flower paintings:

> Rose, harsh rose,
> marred and with stint of petals,
> meagre flower, thin,
> sparse of leaf,
>
> more precious
> than a wet rose,
> single on a stem—
> you are caught in the drift.
> (*Collected Poems*, 5)

Like most solutions, however, H.D.'s lyric flight became its own problem. The perfection of an impersonal, timeless discourse created a pastoral realm that she successfully used to counter first conventional feminine norms and cultural parochialism and then, later, the increasing
horror of the war. But it left her no discourse to tell her personal story, the
embodied narrative of a woman whose life was being shattered by the
intersecting public and private catastrophes caused by the Great War. The
biographical outline is familiar: the baby born dead in May 1915 just after
H.D. heard about the sinking of the *Lusitania*; her husband's enlistment
and consequent despair, which led to a series of affairs; her escape from
London's bombs in Cornwall with Cecil Gray, which provided consolation
but left her pregnant with a child she refused to abort; the loss of D. H.
Lawrence's vitally important friendship; the related deaths of her soldier
brother and father; the devotion of Bryher, who was herself suicidally in
need of support; the deadly influenza in the final days of pregnancy;
Pound's anger that the child was not his; the birth of Perdita and the
miraculous survival of mother and babe; Aldington's final, brutal rejec-

tion; emotional breakdown and recovery with Bryher on an idyllic trip to the Scilly Isles; the series of visionary experiences she had in her travels with Bryher, especially in Corfu in 1920. Love and war, birth and death, betrayal and loss were inseparably woven into her psyche.

Writing about these experiences and their roots in her earlier life seemed to H.D. the only way to "work through the wood," as she wrote to John Cournos, to get past the "tangle of bushes and bracken out to a clearing, where I can see again" (July 9, 1918). Before she could be the "clairvoyant" poet, she explained to Cournos, she needed to write about her personal self, anchored clearly in human space and time, human history. The transcendental "H.D.," disembodied poet of a timeless space, could not clear these tangles so she invented a series of alternate noms de plume or noms de guerre, as she sometimes called them—personae born of the war to reconstitute her shattered self in fictional form—for example, Helga Dart, Helga Doorn, D. A. Hill, Rhoda Peter, Delia Alton, each with a distinct personality but all more "intimate," more "narrative" than "H.D., Imagiste."

H.D.'s expatriatism was as significant for her prose as it was for her early poetry in seemingly contradictory ways that incorporate both the nationalism of Williams and the internationalism of Pound. First, because the novel was for H.D. the discourse of the "personal self," she could write directly about herself as an American woman in her prose, touching subjects she did not overtly explore in her pastoral lyrics. The symbolic landscapes of her poems, for example, are explicitly Americanized in her roman à clef *HER*, about her youth in Upper Darby. I have already mentioned how she explored her Americanness and the Americanness of her expatriatism in *Paint It To-Day* and "Two Americans." These themes remain central to her prose of the 1920s and 1930s and show that, contrary to Williams's fear, H.D. continued to identify herself as American.

Second, expatriatism fostered the development of international, geographic metaphors for psychic states of mind. As Susan Willis wrote, "The notion of traveling through space is integral to the unfolding of history and the development of the individual's consciousness with regard to the past. The voyage over geographic space is an expanded metaphor for the process of one person's coming to know who she is" (220).[16] In the 1920s H.D. became interested in telling her own story in different historical settings, especially ancient Greece, Rome, and Egypt, where each locale symbolized a specific ambience. Movement back in time and horizontally in space led H.D. to another kind of fourth dimension—not the one removed from history in her lyric pastorals but one anchored in history. This fourth dimension, in which the imagination wanders freely throughout human space and time, is a palimpsest of superimposed layers. Adapting Einstein, H.D. increasingly regarded space and time as interdependent and inseparable, meeting most strikingly in the unconscious. In her novel *Palimpsest*, two refrains recur that signal this conflation of space and time in the "interweaving realms of consciousness": "James Joyce was right" and "Einstein was right"—"The present and the actual past and the future were (Einstein was right) one. All planes were going on, on, on together" (166).[17] As palimpsests, H.D.'s novels were archaeological and syncretist, that is, they drew parallels between different historical moments and cultures. They embodied Pound's view of space and time in *The Spirit of Romance* in which he wrote, "All ages are contemporaneous. . . . especially [in] literature" (6). The experience of the Greek exile Hipparchia, mistress of a Roman soldier in the first triptych of *Palimpsest*, parallels the story of Raymonde Ransome in postwar London in the second part. Prewar and postwar London are transposed to Greece and Rome. The trip to Egypt in the last triptych is an externalization of an inner journey through space and time to a sacred revelation in a birth house in the ancient valley of the kings. These three stories in turn repeat the story of exile in H.D.'s other history novels of the period: the displacement of the aging Athenian Hedyle to an obscure Aegean island in the novel *Hedylus*; the exile of Veronica, an Etruscan, in Palestine as the wife of Pontius Pilate in the unpublished novel "Pilate's Wife." Exile is a theme in all these archaeological novels. They "unnerved" her, as she reflected about them in *H.D. by Delia Alton*: "They are all set in antiquity, not strictly of the classic period but of the so-called dispersion. Perhaps dispersion is the key-word. We were dispersed and scattered after War I" (184).

The two strands of H.D.'s expatriatism—the national and the international; the American and the syncretist; the historical and the transcendental; the narrative and the lyric—came together brilliantly in a pair of works she wrote in London during World War II. In *Trilogy*, the epic poem of the clairvoyant poet-prophet who wanders through the bombed-out city of ruin for signs of apocalyptic renewal, the place is London, but it could be anytime, anywhere, as the poet fuses the syncretist shards of many cultures into a new vision of birth. And in *The Gift*, her personal memoir of her Moravian childhood in Bethlehem, her fragmentary memories contain the Moravian Secret, a gift that means survival for the adult woman caught in world war. Each seems to represent one strand of her expatriatism; but in fact, each incorporates both sides of the dialectic, thus embodying together and separately the delicate balance H.D. sought between Pound and Williams.

I will turn in conclusion to *The Gift* to sketch how her memories of Bethlehem weave together the different strands of her expatriatism. *The Gift* is a testament to survival, a textual talisman against the bombs.[18] In the midst of war, she would think of peace; in the midst of death, she would think of birth. So she returned in the "dark room" of memory to the place of her birth, to the American Bethlehem. Being far away allowed her to get close, to "feel American." There she found not dispersion and chaos but a Moravian *communitas*, the *Unitas Fratrum*—a large family circle, the "sisters" and "brothers" of the seminary and church, a religious tradition to which she belonged, a rich heritage of intellect and art. She was not exiled in Bethlehem. Memories of a Moravian Christmas—her grandfather carving the clay sheep for the *putz*, the tree, the beeswax candles, the treasured ornaments carefully unpacked each year—become the emblem of the child's belonging. There was death in this garden, however. The opening line of the memoir immediately avoids the rosy light of sweet sentiment by initiating the key leitmotiv of the text—death by fire: "There was a girl who was burnt to death at the seminary. . . . The Christmas tree was lighted at the end of one of the long halls and the girl's ruffles or ribbons caught fire and she was in a great hoop" (1). And there are snakes, and shooting stars, and stories of massacres, and all the dead girls in the family cemetery to frighten the child Hilda, whose consciousness is rendered in near-Steinian prose. But exile, the experience of being alien, comes with the move—sudden and frightening to Hilda—to Upper Darby when she was about ten. H.D.'s first exile, we learn from *The Gift*, was not her chosen flight to freedom in 1911 but her forced removal from Bethlehem in 1894.

Bethlehem, not London, was the scene of her artistic awakening. What H.D. chose to highlight as her own initiation into the magic realm of the imagination significantly recalls Williams's catalog of indigenous forms of American culture. Chapter 1 focuses on the impact a local performance of Harriet Beecher Stowe's *Uncle Tom's Cabin* has on the little girl, who like Huck Finn at the circus cannot understand why everyone is laughing when the dogs chase little Eva. She is influenced not by Shakespeare or Dante or Villon, whom Pound once called his "congenial ancestors" (*Selected Prose*, 145), but by Harriet Beecher Stowe—a woman, a radical, an

American, whose popular and didactic novel inspired the outrage against slavery that helped start the Civil War. As H.D. interprets her own life story, the young Hilda's identification with the suffering and flight of the black slave awakens her creative "Gift."

As her memories of Bethlehem and researches into its history deepened, she discovered that her American heritage contained a message of peace, brotherhood, and sisterhood of great relevance to the world caught in a cycle of violence. The peace-loving Moravians, she learned, founded communities with the Indians, received their gifts, and gave gifts in return. Moravian Bethlehem had a nearby sister community of Indians called Friedenshuetten. The Moravians and Indians met frequently and celebrated love-feasts on Wunden Eiland, Isle of Wounds, a little island in the Monacacy Creek at the foot of the Ladies Seminary. Pyrlaeus, a refugee from Bohemia, made a dictionary of Indian dialects and a notation system for their music. Paxnous, a great Delaware chief, convinced many related tribes to leave the Moravians in peace. After a distant tribe burned alive the whites in the biracial Moravian community of nearby Gnadenhuetten, David Zeisberger, one of the founders of Bethlehem, helped some Indians establish New Gnadenhuetten, which became a peaceful and prosperous village in the Midwest. This heritage, H.D. was horrified to discover, was betrayed by a "band of 'soldiers,' gangsters of the then new west, toughs, flotsam and jetsam, washed up on the shores of the Indian continent" (MSS "Notes," 86). These men, whom H.D. calls white "savages," killed every single Indian in the town. This betrayal of peace made between Indians and Moravians is emblematic, she concludes, of America's heritage, a mix of peace and violence, gift and theft, freedom and oppression.

Although H.D.'s writing about her personal American roots in *The Gift* parallels Williams's epic of an American city in *Paterson*, it also embodies Pound's internationalism, as well as the overt syncretism and transcendentalism of her own *Trilogy*. The Moravians were able to live with the Indians in peace because they were themselves persecuted exiles, "political and religious refugees," whose history went back at least to a Greek church in ninth-century Constantinople, after which they were dispersed in a diaspora that carried them across Europe and into the New World. As H.D. reflects in the "Notes" for *The Gift*, "I have felt all along a deep gratitude for the place of my birth and for my people—but my people . . . are not parochial, not conditioned by small boundaries, not shut-in by provincial barriers" (MSS "Notes," 51–52).

H.D.'s own expatriatism mirrored that of her ancestors—to fulfill the promise of her gift, she had to wander as they had wandered. Like them, she would not be parochial. The Moravians who founded Bethlehem came from all over Europe, brought a love for learning and music with them, and looked even to the cultures of Asia, Africa, and Arabia, as well as the native Americans, she discovered. Like Pound, she found the healing qualities she admired in a great leader—Count Zinzendorf, who offered safe haven for Moravians all over Europe on his estate in Bohemia before he helped them journey to the New World. But unlike Pound's leaders, patriarchs and proto-fascists, H.D.'s Zinzendorf represented the outcast and the marginal. She wrote: "He was a dreamer, a poet, a reformer, a man-of-the-world, a mystic, a great gentleman and an intimate friend of carpenters, wood-cutters, farmers, itinerant preachers and all women" (MSS "Notes," 92). His enemies believed his great "Plan" was a conspiracy for world dictatorship, but she learned that his "Plan" was for the peaceful organization of democratic communities wherever the persecuted could find freedom.[19]

The internationalism of the Moravians was also syncretist, H.D. writes in *The Gift*. Sensitive to persecution, tolerant of difference, themselves a heterodox sect of Christianity, the early Moravians were not fundamentalist in their religion. This is the great Secret that Mamalie passes on to young Hilda. Surrounded by Nazi bombs as she writes *The Gift*, H.D. remembers her grandmother's mysterious story of deciphering the tattered papers her first husband found in the Moravian archives. Written by Pyrlaeus and the Indian priest Shooting Star, they contained Greek, Hebrew, and Indian script; Moravian and Indian symbols; and notations for Indian music. They were about a meeting between a few Moravians and Indians on Wunden Eiland, about a promise made, about the ritual exchange of names made by the European Anna von Pahlen and the Indian woman Morning Star, all in the name of peace. The meeting led to scandal; more literal-minded Moravians feared Indian magic and a pact with the devil. They did not understand what the few initiates had learned—that the Great Spirit of the Indians and the Holy Spirit of the Moravians were one; that human beings could transcend sectarian hate and racial distrust through the inner, esoteric teachings of all religions.[20]

This Secret, H.D. writes from the perspective of World War II, could save civilization. It is the "Gift" of her hidden heritage that she must pass on through her Modernist writing. The family conduit is matrilineal. It is her mother's family who is Moravian, not her father's. It is her grandmother who passes on the mystic laughter of peace, who tells of the kiss of peace and offers feasts of love to her granddaughter. Cozy and somewhat senile in *The Gift*, she is a dear old lady, a wise woman who is both like and not like the hieratic Lady of *Trilogy*, the poet's muse and savior. Mamalie's Gift to the child is personal, but also transcendental, American, but also international in spirit. It is like the city of Bethlehem—American in its history of religious refugees and commerce, international in its analog to the first Bethlehem, like Helen, the name of H.D.'s mother, the name that shares its root with Hellas—Greece. *The Gift*, which so effectively weaves together the different strands of H.D.'s Americanness and expatriatism, is dedicated:

HELEN
who has
brought me home
for Bethlehem Pennsylvania 1741
from Chelsea London 1941

From London, *for* Bethlehem, H.D.—to borrow Howe's description of Dickinson—"built a new poetic form from her fractured sense of being eternally on intellectual borders" (21). Exile did not mean the formation of an international elite, a new center made up of those superior "world citizens" and "international heroes" disgusted with the philistinism of "regional" people. Rather, exile meant a permanent diaspora, a refusal to move to the center, a perpetual marginality rooted in both H.D.'s heritage as a Moravian-American and her wanderings as a woman in a man's world.

Notes

This essay was presented at the H.D. Centennial Symposium at Moravian College, Bethlehem, Pennsylvania, in September 1986; the Emily Dickinson–H.D. Symposium at San José State University in November 1986; and the MLA in December 1986. It also appeared in a special H.D. issue of *Agenda* 25 (Winter 1987). I am indebted to Jane Marcus for her suggestion that I write the essay, which was completed before the publication of Shari Benstock's *Women of the Left Bank: Paris, 1900–1940*. For sparking the general direction of this essay, I also want to thank Barbara Guest for her paper "Exile and Expatriatism: An Influence on the Life of H.D." (1980) and Louis Martz for his discussion of H.D.'s "border-lines" as spatial metaphor in his Introduction to the *Collected Poems of H.D.* I am indebted to H.D.'s daughter and literary executor Perdita Schaffner, Beinecke Rare Book and Manuscript Library at Yale University, the Rosenbach Foundation, and Houghton Library at Harvard University for permission to quote from H.D.'s manuscripts and correspondence. H.D.'s letters to Marianne Moore are at the Rosenbach Foundation; her letters to John Cournos are at Houghton Library; all other letters and manuscripts quoted in the essay are from the Beinecke collection. The first epigraph is from a letter from H.D. to Moore, January 17, 1921. The second is in Harriet Stix, "Prize-Winning 'H.D.' Is Returning Native" (May 25, 1960), from an unidentified newspaper clipping at Beinecke.

1. See especially Malcolm Bradbury's "The Cities of Modernism" in Bradbury and McFarlane, 96–104.

2. In spite of his identification of his mother as primary artist in the Prologue to *Kora in Hell*, Williams was quick to dismiss women from the ranks of poetic genius in *In the American Grain*, where American heroism is entirely masculine. He wrote in the Introduction: "It is the women above all—there never have been women. . . . Poets? Where? They are the test. But a true woman in flower, never. . . . Never a woman: never a poet. That's an axiom. Never a poet saw sun here" (quoted as epigraph in Howe).

3. Kenner, "The Origins of Modernism." See also "The Modernist Canon" in which he uses the formal title "International Modernism" for the movement he had previously called "modernism" and for his statement that Woolf "is an English novelist of manners, writing village gossip from a village called Bloomsbury for her English readers" (371). His internationalist bias is further evident in a comment about Wallace Stevens: "Like Virginia Woolf of Bloomsbury or Faulkner of Oxford, he seems a voice from a province, quirkily enabled by the International Modernism of which he was never a part, no more than they" (373).

4. See Wolle, who wrote that H.D. refused safe haven in the United States because "as an English citizen she could not run out on them in an emergency" (59).

5. See H.D.'s first letter to Pearson (December 12, 1937), which he printed in Benet and Pearson, 504. In her review, Bryher also noted that "to people born in England H.D.'s work is peculiarly American" (334).

6. See H.D.'s letters to Duncan and Levertov; "Life in a Hothouse"; and Friedman, "Modernism of the 'Scattered Remnant,'" which discusses H.D.'s interest in the literature and music of the Harlem Renaissance. Guest's contention in *Herself Defined* that H.D. "never much cared for the work of others," especially her contemporaries, is inaccurate (150). H.D.'s American friend Mary Herr frequently sent H.D. the latest American publications, and H.D.'s letters to a wide circle of people demonstrate her voracious reading habits, which included the best contemporary literature as well as "potboilers" and the classics.

7. This image of marginality appears frequently in H.D.'s prose of the 1920s. Hermione in *HER*, for example, thinks, "Bastards like herself, alien to either

continent had yet no signposts" (47); the Hermione of the unpublished novel "Asphodel" (1921–22) asks, "What is this family that seeks its own, brothers and sisters, lost people" and makes the connection between herself and a Jewish sculptor—"Isaac was gone. Jews loving beauty. No country. Like Hermione no country. But she had a country. She had a husband" (Part II, 125, 62). Although neither H.D. nor Woolf would have sympathized with Bersani's attraction to violence and sadomasochism, his description of marginality in *A Future for Astyanax* is applicable to their stance. He wrote, "The dismissal of the marginal is in itself an ideologically significant gesture which uses the notion of centrality as a criterion of value in its attempts to classify and to judge experience. . . . I will be looking at alternatives to a psychology of stable centers of desire, centers which allow us to construct an intelligible self. What is the appeal, the power, and the danger of a psychology of the marginal or the peripheral—which would also be a psychology (if the word still applies) of the deconstructed self?" (59).

8. See Friedman, "Modernism of the 'Scattered Remnant.'"

9. H.D. understood that her daughter Perdita might continue the paradoxical process. She wrote Bryher, who had taken Perdita to the United States: "Tell Puss that I love her but not les Etas so much and that really she must have a good time and lick off the cream—but come back to Britinnia Rules the Waves. Of course, I have licked the cream off that, so naturally Puss wants to reverse—and she is right. But don't let her get swamped" (January 28, 1935).

10. For additional discussion of women's "double consciousness" as exiles in patriarchy, see DuPlessis, *Writing*, 33–44, 108–17, 179–83, and Friedman, "Women's Autobiographical Selves." See also Du Bois, 45.

11. The anecdote that Adrienne Rich makes the motif of "Vesuvius at Home" evokes the link between H.D. and Dickinson, for whom H.D. felt a strong affinity. Pretending to lock herself and her niece into her room, Dickinson said, "Matty, here's freedom" (Rich, 162).

12. In the spring of 1936, H.D. was considering a permanent move back to the United States, and her letters to Bryher contain scattered references to American writers and her attempt to maintain a balance. Her letter of May 11, 1936, is particularly important: "Funny, he [Kenneth Macpherson] does not write me [from New York], but does not even mention me in letters. I suppose he thinks I am a menace, as against the U.S.A. vibration, but that is quite wrong. I have to stabalize [*sic*] myself with the old war-muck, in my writing, but my whole novel is planned, in a wild crescendo, sort of Angel-River style, to get me BACK to the States. . . . I have been going on with Wolf [Woolf, *To the Lighthouse?*] and there really IS nothing here [London] to match up with the States thing . . . only, what Rvr. [Rover, i.e., Macpherson] will not see is that *we* have had to fight so hard, *we* have to get away from the Sattes [*sic*] and all that WE had to fight . . . then get back in some psychic way, and are after all, the half-way-house, or sort of light-house and that *we* in a sense, have got *him there*."

13. For examples of the label "perfect," which in itself tended to fetishize H.D., see also Lowell, 279; Sinclair, 88; Untermeyer, 307; and Bryher, 333.

14. See Eliot, "Tradition and the Individual Talent" (1919) in *Selected Prose*, 34–45, and Kenner, *Invisible Poet*. For discussion of H.D.'s impersonalism, see Friedman, "Hilda Doolittle (H.D.)," 124–26.

15. See *H.D. by Delia Alton* for H.D.'s repeated references to "the early H.D." as a specific identity, style, and discourse. See p. 199 for her designation of "the early H.D." as not "narrative." For her distinction between her "personal" prose persona and her "clairvoyant," impersonal poetic persona, see her letter to John Cournos, July 9, 1918.

16. I am indebted to Lisa Marcus for bringing this statement to my attention in "Moving Forward," 45.

17. See also *Palimpsest*, 138, 155, 157, 162, 165. Science metaphors pervade all of H.D.'s work, demonstrating no doubt the importance of her father's and grandfather's science to her thinking. H.D. may have become particularly interested in Einstein after seeing Sullivan's "A Sketch of Einstein's Theory" in the same issue of the *Adelphi* as the one in which her poem "At Athens" appeared, at about the same time that she was writing *Palimpsest* (1924). See also Morris, "Einstein Was Right." In *Tribute to Freud*, H.D. used the term "the fourth dimension" to define the unconscious, with its other "time-element" fusing past, present, and future (23).

18. I have worked with the manuscript of *The Gift* because the version published by New Directions is so severely altered by cutting and editing that it is no longer the text H.D. sent, fully corrected, to Pearson for publication. Where the published version coincides with the manuscript, I will refer to it; where the published version deviates from the text, I will refer to the manuscript. The manuscript has seven chapters and a section entitled "Notes" (94 pages). New Directions dropped Chapter 2 and the Notes entirely and cut portions from other chapters. For a discussion of this editing, see DuPlessis, "A Note." For a discussion of *The Gift* in relationship to H.D.'s "gift economy," see Morris, "Relay of Power." For a discussion of H.D.'s Moravian background, see Robinson, 3–9, 81–90.

19. H.D. wrote about the eighteenth-century European Moravians in "The Mystery" (1949–51), an unpublished novel at Beinecke Library.

20. The New Directions edition deleted some thirty-five manuscript pages from "The Secret" (Chapter 5 of the manuscript, Chapter 4 of the published version). These pages, which detail the Secret Mamalie passed down to Hilda, and the "Notes" contain detailed material on Moravian history, particularly the period of theological disruption known as the "Sifting Period."

110   .   Susan Stanford Friedman

Works Cited

Anderson, Margaret. *Literary Review Anthology*. New York: Hermitage House, 1953.

Benet, William Rose, and Norman Holmes Pearson, eds. *Oxford Anthology of American Literature*, Vol. 2. New York: Oxford University Press, 1938.

Benstock, Shari. *Women of the Left Bank: Paris, 1900–1940*. Austin: University of Texas Press, 1986.

Bersani, Leo. *A Future for Astyanax: Character and Desire in Literature*. New York: Columbia University Press, 1984.

Bradbury, Malcolm, and James McFarlane, eds. *Modernism, 1890–1930*. New York: Penguin, 1976.

Bryher. "Spear-Shaft and Cyclamen-Flower." *Poetry* 19 (March 1922): 333–37.

Du Bois, W. E. B. *The Souls of Black Folk*. 1903. Reprint. New York: Signet, 1963.

DuPlessis, Rachel Blau. "A Note on the State of H.D.'s *The Gift*." *Sulphur* 9 (1984): 178–82.

———. *Writing Beyond the Ending: Narrative Strategies of Twentieth-Century Women Writers*. Bloomington: Indiana University Press, 1985.

Eliot, T. S. "Tradition and the Individual Talent" (1919). In *Selected Prose of T. S. Eliot*, edited by Frank Kermode, 37–44. New York: Harcourt Brace Jovanovich, 1975.

Friedman, Susan Stanford. "Hilda Doolittle (H.D.)." *Dictionary of Literary Biography*, Vol. 45: *American Poets, 1880–1940*. 1st ser., edited by Peter Quartermain, 115–49. Detroit: Gale Research, 1986.

———. "Modernism of the 'Scattered Remnant': Race and Politics in H.D.'s Development." In *Feminist Issues in Literary Scholarship*, edited by Shari Benstock, 208–32. Bloomington: Indiana University Press, 1987.

———. "Theories of Autobiography and Fictions of the Self in H.D.'s Canon." Paper presented at the Modern Language Association, New York, New York, 1983.

———. "Women's Autobiographical Selves: Theory and Practice." In *The Private Self: Theory and Practice in Women's Autobiographical Writings*, edited by Shari Benstock. Chapel Hill: University of North Carolina Press, 1988.

Greenaway, Kate. *The Kate Greenaway Book*. Edited by Bryan Holme. New York: Viking, 1976.

Guest, Barbara. "Exile and Expatriatism: An Influence on the Life of H.D." Paper presented at the Modern Language Association, Houston, Texas, 1980.

———. *Herself Defined: The Poet H.D. and Her World*. Garden City, N.Y.: Doubleday, 1984.

H.D. "Asphodel" (1921–22). Manuscript at Beinecke Rare Book and Manuscript Library, Yale University.

———. *Borderline—A Pool Film with Paul Robeson*. 1930. Reprint as "The Borderline Pamphlet." *Sagetrieb* 6 (Fall 1987): 29–50.

———. *Collected Poems, 1912–1944*. Edited by Louis Martz. New York: New Directions, 1983.

———. "The Gift" (Manuscript). Beinecke Rare Book and Manuscript Library, Yale University.

———. *The Gift* (Edited version). New York: New Directions, 1982.

———. *H.D. by Delia Alton* (1949–50). *Iowa Review* 16 (Fall 1986): 174–221.

———. *Hedylus*. 1928. Rev. ed. Redding Ridge, Conn.: Black Swan Books, 1980.

———. *HER* (1927). Published with title *HERmione*. New York: New Directions, 1981.

———. Letters to Bryher, Robert Duncan, and Denise Levertov. Beinecke Rare Book and Manuscript Library, Yale University.

———. Letters to John Cournos. Houghton Library, Harvard University.

———. *Paint It To-Day* (1921). Chapters 1–4 in *H.D.: Centennial Issue*, edited by Susan Stanford Friedman and Rachel Blau DuPlessis. *Contemporary Literature* 27 (Winter 1986): 444–74. Complete manuscript (Chapters 1–8) at Beinecke Rare Book and Manuscript Library, Yale University.

———. *Palimpsest*. 1926. Rev. ed. Carbondale: Southern Illinois University Press, 1968.

———. "Pilate's Wife" (1924, 1929, 1934). Manuscript at Beinecke Rare Book and Manuscript Library, Yale University.

———. "Pontikonisi (Mouse Island)." Published under name Rhoda Peter. *Pagany* 3 (July–September 1932): 1–9.

———. *Tribute to Freud*. 1945–46, 1965. Rev. ed. Boston: David R. Godine, 1974.

———. *Trilogy*. 1944–46. Reprint. New York: New Directions, 1973.

———. "Two Americans" (1930). In H.D., *The Usual Star*, 93–116. Dijon: Imprimerie Darantere, 1934.

Howe, Susan. *My Emily Dickinson*. Berkeley: North Atlantic Books, 1985.

Joyce, James. *Portrait of the Artist as a Young Man*. 1916. Reprint. New York: Viking Press, 1973.

Kenner, Hugh. *The Invisible Poet*. 1959. Reprint. New York: Citadel, 1964.

———. "The Making of the Modernist Canon." In *Canons*, edited by Robert von Hallberg, 363–76. Chicago: University of Chicago Press, 1984.

———. "The Origins of Modernism." Lecture at University of Wisconsin-Madison, October 1983.

———. *The Pound Era*. Berkeley and Los Angeles: University of California Press, 1973.

Kreymborg, Alfred. *Our Singing Strength: An Outline of American Poetry (1620–1930)*. New York: Coward-McCann, 1929.

"Life in a Hothouse." Review of *Bid Me to Live (A Madrigal)*. *Newsweek* 55 (May 2, 1960): 92–93.

Lowell, Amy. *Tendencies in American Poetry*. New York: Macmillan, 1917.

Marcus, Lisa. "Moving Forward by Thinking Back through Our Mothers." Senior thesis, University of Wisconsin-Madison, 1986.

Monroe, Harriet. *Poets and Their Art*. Rev. ed. New York: Macmillan, 1938.

Morris, Adalaide. "Einstein Was Right—H.D.'s Astronomical Observations." Paper delivered at the H.D. Centennial Conference, Orono, Maine, June 1986.

_____. "A Relay of Power and of Peace: H.D. and the Spirit of the Gift." *Contemporary Literature* 27 (Winter 1986): 493–524.

Pound, Ezra. *Make It New*. London: Faber and Faber, 1934.

_____. *Selected Prose, 1909–1965*. Edited by William Cookson. New York: New Directions, 1973.

_____. *The Spirit of Romance*. 1910. Reprint. New York: New Directions, 1968.

Rich, Adrienne. "Vesuvius at Home: The Power of Emily Dickinson" (1975). In *On Lies, Secrets and Silence: Selected Prose, 1966–1978*, 157–84. New York: Norton, 1979.

Robinson, Janice S. *H.D.: The Life and Work of an American Poet*. Boston: Houghton Mifflin, 1982.

Rowbotham, Sheila. *Woman's Consciousness, Man's World*. London: Penguin, 1973.

Schwartz, Delmore. "T. S. Eliot as the International Hero." In *The Idea of the Modern in Literature and the Arts*, edited by Irving Howe, 277–85. New York: Horizon, 1967.

Sinclair, May. "Two Notes." *Egoist* 2 (June 1, 1915): 88–89.

Stix, Harriet. "Prize-Winning 'H.D.' Is Returning Native." May 25, 1960. Newsclipping at Beinecke Rare Book and Manuscript Library, Yale University.

Sullivan, J. W. N. "A Sketch of Einstein's Theory." *Adelphi* 2 (December 1924): 597–605.

Untermeyer, Louis. *American Poetry since 1900*. New York: Henry Holt, 1923.

Williams, William Carlos. *Imaginations*. Edited by Webster Schott. New York: New Directions, 1970.

_____. *In the American Grain*. New York: New Directions, 1925.

Willis, Susan. "Black Women Writers: Taking a Critical Perspective." In *Making a Difference: Feminist Literary Criticism*, edited by Gayle Greene and Coppélia Kahn, 211–37. New York: Methuen, 1985.

Wolle, Francis. *A Moravian Heritage*. Boulder, Colo.: Empire Reproductions, 1972.

Woolf, Virginia. "Harriette Wilson" (1925). In *The Moment and Other Essays*, 179–85. New York: Harcourt Brace Jovanovich, 1948.

_____. "Professions for Women" (1931). In *Death of the Moth and Other Essays*, 235–42. New York: Harcourt Brace Jovanovich, 1970.

_____. *Three Guineas*. 1938. Reprint. New York: Harcourt, Brace and World, 1963.

Chapter 4

· · · · · · · · · · · · · · · · · · · ·

Writing (in) Exile

Isak Dinesen and the Poetics of Displacement

Susan Hardy Aiken

People who dream . . . know that the real glory of dreams lies in their atmosphere
of unlimited freedom . . . the freedom of the artist.
—Isak Dinesen, *Out of Africa*

The Art of Dreaming

> Day is a space of time without meaning, and . . . it is with the coming of dusk, with the lighting of the first star and the first candle, that things will become what they really are, and will come forth to meet me. . . . During my first months after my return to Denmark from Africa, I had great trouble in seeing anything at all as reality. My African existence had sunk below the horizon, . . . then faded and disappeared. . . . The landscapes, the beasts and the human beings could not possibly mean more to my surroundings in Denmark than did the landscapes, beasts, and human beings of my dreams at night. Their names here were just words. . . . There they were, all of them, nine thousand feet up, safe in the mould of Africa, slowly being turned into mould themselves. And here was I, walking in the fair woods of Denmark, listening to the waves of Öresund. . . . What business had I had ever to set my heart on Africa? (Dinesen, "Echoes from the Hills," 112–14)

Thus Karen Blixen would recall her bereavement on losing the place she called "my heart's land."[1] Paradoxically, going "home" to "the fair woods of Denmark" in 1931, after seventeen years in Kenya, seemed to her tantamount to entering a condition of permanent exile, a forced dwelling in a space—both geographical and psychological—from which she had felt herself estranged since earliest childhood. Inscribing this event in *Out of Africa* and *Shadows on the Grass*, she would repeatedly write repatriation as *exmatriation*: to lose Africa was to lose more than a homeland of the spirit; it was also to lose the place she claimed as the matrix of her creativity, the place where, as she wrote in "Mottoes of My Life," she began at last to speak "freely and without restraint" (7).[2] For it was in Africa that she found her mature voice as a storyteller, creating the earliest versions of the haunting narratives that would become *Seven Gothic Tales*. To leave Africa, then, was not only to enter what she described as a living death but potentially to risk the loss of that authorial voice as well.[3]

Yet it was, after all, the voice alone that remained to her when she returned, bankrupt and bereft, to Denmark, and with it she would make her future as a writer, taking those "words" to which her African existence had been reduced and transforming them into fictive flesh: the body of writing that would bring her worldwide recognition as "Isak

Dinesen." Incipient in the passage above, then, is a poetics of displacement, grounded in a reading of the author's diurnal, living "reality" as a
form of death or dream, an exile in which, like an unquiet spirit, she
becomes a permanent wanderer. In this oneiric realm, words—which
seem at first a ghastly remnant, appalling shreds, the insubstantial traces
of a lost plenitude—paradoxically become the very stuff of resurrection,
strands from which she would fabricate both a persona and a textual
corpus. For Dinesen, writing became at once the sign of wounding, a form
of mourning, and a way to regeneration: words, even while bearing witness
to her permanent loss of what she called "my real life," would also give rise
to the vibrant life of her texts ("Mottoes," 6).[4] It is no accident that the
figure of dreaming, with all it implies of discontinuity and displacement,
would become one of her recurrent metaphors not only for exile but for
narrative itself.

Beginning in geographical alienation, displacement operates in Dinesen's writing at many levels. Consider, for example, her extraordinary
double textual system, her practice of writing virtually every text twice—
once in English, as Isak Dinesen, then in Danish, as Karen Blixen—an
extension of the many names and masks she bore throughout her life.[5] By
choosing English as her primary literary language, she displaced herself
from her native tongue; by rewriting the texts in Danish, she displaced
them from their own ostensible origin(al)s. The gap opened by this two-
fold inscription goes beyond the transatlantic distance between national
borders and literary canons: just as the sexual doubleness of her signature
mystifies the "true" nature of the writer's body, so the textual doubleness
of her literary production calls into question the "true" nature of her
narrative corpus, the body of her writing. In either case, writing marks a
process of dislocation; the place of the author becomes indeterminate.
Moving between two linguistic worlds, locatable in neither, Karen Blixen
both is, and is not, Isak Dinesen.

As her choice of a male pseudonym implies, these enactments of writing
as a form of exile are inseparable from issues of sexual difference. Dinesen's *Letters from Africa* develops an extensive analysis of woman's irrevocable status as a foreigner within androcentric culture and discourse, an
analysis that provides an important perspective on her fiction (e.g., 163,
240–41, 244–51, 258–65, 399). By writing her English texts "as a man,"
in effect displacing herself from herself, Dinesen made the male signature
the sign of alienation, inscribing her own difference from patriarchal
traditions even as she appeared to enact her erasure within them. In the

light of her many reflexive speculations on the power of woman—operating perforce on the margins of the dominant discourse—to challenge, disrupt, and ultimately transform the symbolic order that would enforce her otherness, the signature would become for Dinesen an ironic instrument of resistance, turning apparent subservience into subversiveness (e.g., *Letters*, 240–41, 246; *Out of Africa*, 179–80).[6] It is no coincidence that the Hebrew meaning of *Isak* conflates exile with both woman's laughter and female generativity. As I have shown elsewhere, Dinesen uses those connotations in radical ways, destabilizing the preeminent Judaeo-Christian patriarchal formula—"Abraham, Isaac, and Jacob"—by appropriating and feminizing its central term.[7] Thus she transforms exile into the space for engendering stories suffused with what, describing one of the many subversive female artists in her fiction, she called the "laughter of liberation" (*Seven Gothic Tales*, 21).

This conflation of exile, sexual difference, voice, and writing is elaborated in many of Dinesen's greatest works, most obviously, of course, in her memoirs *Out of Africa* and *Shadows on the Grass*. In this essay, however, I will consider its operations not in one of her fictionalized autobiographies but in one of her most complex autobiographical fictions: an early novella entitled, significantly, "The Dreamers."[8] Just as she blurred the boundaries between names, nationalities, and sexual identities, so Dinesen would put into question traditional generic boundaries separating fiction from fact, story from theory. "The Dreamers," as its linguistic link to the autobiographical meditations quoted above suggests, is an intensely self-reflexive text. In its frame story Dinesen develops a poetics of displacement that, like "Echoes from the Hills," equates dreaming, dis-ease, exile, and loss with the production of narrative.

The character who elaborates that figural conjunction in "The Dreamers" is one of the many tale-tellers who become their author's fictive doubles. Mira Jama, "the inventions of whose mind have been loved by a hundred tribes," is a permanent outcast from his native land, a wanderer, who, having lost the ability to dream up new fictions, now dwells in and on the fictions made up in dreams:

> "In my dreams I . . . carry with me something infinitely dear and precious, such as I know well enough that no real things be, and there it seems to me that I must keep this thing against some dreadful danger. . . . And it also seems to me that I shall be struck down and annihilated if I lose it. . . . The air in my dreams . . . is always very

high, and I generally see myself as a very small figure in a great landscape. . . .

"You know, . . . that if, in planting a coffee tree, you bend the taproot, that tree will start, after a little time, to put out a multitude of small delicate roots near the surface. That tree will never thrive, nor bear fruit, but it will flower more richly than the others.

"Those fine roots are the dreams of the tree. As it puts them out, it need no longer think of its bent taproot. It keeps alive by them—a little, not very long. Or you can say that it dies by them, if you like, for really, dreaming is the well-mannered people's way of committing suicide." ("Dreamers," 276–77)

Dinesen would repeat these figures many years later in "Echoes from the Hills." In "my dreams," she writes there,

I move in a world deeply and sweetly familiar to me, a world which belongs to me and to which I myself belong more intensely than is ever the case in my waking existence. . . . The second characteristic of my dreams is their vastness, their quality of infinite space. I move in mighty landscapes, among tremendous heights, depths, and expanses and with unlimited views to all sides. . . . At times I feel that the fourth dimension is within reach. I fly, in dream, to any altitude, I dive into bottomless, clear, bottle-green waters. It is a weightless world. Its very atmosphere is joy, its crowning happiness, unreasonably or against reason, is that of triumph. For we have in the dream forsaken our allegiance to the organizing, controlling, and rectifying forces of the world, the Universal Conscience. We have sworn fealty to the wild, incalculable, creative forces, the Imagination of the Universe. (108–10)[9]

As its title suggests, this text, juxtaposed with "The Dreamers" and *Out of Africa*, sets up an echoic dialogue across the span of Dinesen's career, illuminating both the text of its author's life and the life of her texts. This exchange is extended in the companion story to "The Dreamers," published in *Last Tales* in 1957, which treats the same protagonist at an earlier moment in her fictive history; its title, "Echoes," suggests the degree to which Dinesen connected it with "The Dreamers," *Out of Africa*, and "Echoes from the Hills"—that reminder and remainder of *Out of Africa*— as elements in a metatext, an extended interactive series of meditations on writing (in) exile. In the poetics of displacement inherent in these conjunctions, Dinesen not only associates exile and death, paradoxically, with creative "triumph," but implicitly genders this figurative nexus. Her description of dreaming/fiction-making as a radical subversion of "the organizing, controlling and rectifying forces of the world," a transgressive place of *jouissance* wherein "the wild, incalculable, creative forces" come into play, anticipates recent theoretical speculations on the "wild space" that women, as a culturally "muted" group, occupy "outside the dominant boundary" of the androcentric symbolic order (Showalter, 200).[10] It is from this "elsewhere," as Luce Irigaray has called it (76), that the possibilities of an other, feminine discourse may be imagined.

Peter Brooks has argued that "deviance is the very condition for life to be 'narratable': the state of normality is devoid of interest, energy, and the possibility for narration. In between a beginning prior to plot and an end beyond plot, the middle—the plotted text—has been in a state of *error*: wandering and misinterpretation" (139). Such a reading of narrativity raises acutely the question of woman, since phallocentric discourses have traditionally represented her as the most extreme example of deviance.[11] In this context, then, an equivalency emerges between narrativity and femininity, each being construed, according to phallocentric law, as the principle of deviation, swerving—literally *extra-vagance*. And if the story of woman is the story of stories, then the greatest storyteller of all, potentially, would be woman herself, she who can both embody and engender the "narratable" by telling her own tale. In "The Dreamers," as in many other texts, Dinesen sets up precisely such a possibility, suggesting that within the confines of patriarchal culture, those "wild, incalculable, creative forces" find their fullest expression in woman.

Consider first the storyteller through whose monologue about his authorial impotence Dinesen constructs a reflexive speculation on her own situation. Mira Jama is not only a permanent exile but a mutilated man— "the nose and ears of his dark head cut clear off." Like "Isak Dinesen," Mira—as the pun on his name suggests—is a reflection of his author, a masculine mask that doubles Karen Blixen's pseudonymy—hence an implicit sign of her multiply alienated status as a woman speaking (through) a masculine discourse. As a symbolic castration, his condition suggests an oblique play on the Freudian model of woman as castrated man. But his wounds also recall Dinesen's figurative dismemberment in another sense: the breakup of the Ngong farm and the severance from Africa that precipitated her own exile. As if to underscore this connection, the frame story takes place in a dhow sailing off the African coast.

Mira's inability to tell stories becomes, paradoxically, the precipitating condition for the story of a woman, a narrative recounted by Mira's companion Lincoln Forsner: "I will tell you a tale tonight, Mira . . . since you have none . . . [of] how I was, twenty years ago, taught . . . to dream, and of the woman who taught me." I shall return to the problematics of the text's several male narrators, but first let us consider the tale of the woman who knew the art of dreaming, the narrative on which "The Dreamers" pivots. Through it, Dinesen obliquely tells not only her own story but the story of her stories as well.[12]

Dreaming Woman

"A woman's (re)discovery of herself can only signify the possibility of not sacrificing any of her pleasures to another, of not identifying with anyone in particular, of never being simply one."
—Luce Irigaray, *This Sex That Is Not One*

Briefly summarized, Forsner's narrative concerns the wanderings of Pellegrina Leoni, a renowned operatic diva—*Prima Donna Assoluta*—who loses her voice through injuries from a fire in the Milan opera house.[13] This event precipitates her lifelong wanderings, a self-imposed exile from her former place and name, and her refusal to become "tied up" in a stable, permanent, unitary identity: "I will not be one person again. . . . I will be always many persons from now. Never again will I have my heart and my whole life bound up with one woman, to suffer so much" ("Dreamers," 345). First fabricating her own "death" by erecting a monument inscribed with her name—literally turning self into text—Pellegrina begins a lifelong play, assuming new names, new personae, each time the old threaten to constrain her. This serial staging of perpetual difference from herself is aided by her loyal "friend" and "shadow" Marcus Cocoza, a wealthy Jew from Amsterdam, whose ambiguous relation to Pellegrina, like the male-authored narrative through which her story unfolds, becomes one of the story's principal interpretive conundrums.[14]

Forsner's narrative emerges as a series of flashbacks, generated from his own recollections and the tales told to him by two other male narrators, whom he had met "one winter night" twenty years before, in an inn "amongst mountains, with snow, storm, great clouds and wild moon outside" (279). Like Forsner himself, each of his companions has fallen in love with, and subsequently lost, an extraordinary, magnetic woman, who turns out, as they discover in conversation, to be the same person in different guises. They are able to read their "different" women as the same because of a mark imprinted on her body like a signature, "a long scar from a burn, which, like a little white snake, ran from her left ear to her collar bone" (285). Paradoxically, this stigma, which serves as proof of her identity, is also the hieroglyphic sign of its absence; emblematizing Pellegrina's lost voice, name and selfhood, it is the trace of the story—as yet untold—of how her wanderings began.

At the very moment their narratives are ending, a veiled woman enters the inn, as if called forth on cue from their discourse. She glances at the three companions and hastily departs but not before being recognized, belatedly, by her former lovers. Strangely desperate to elude them, she takes a coach upward toward an Alpine pass that leads through the otherwise impassable mountains, proceeding afoot after the coach becomes stuck in the snow. They follow, but their own carriage is halted by drifts. Continuing to pursue her in this space of unmarked, impassable terrain, amid "this wildness of the elements," they enter a state like that of dreams or "fairy tale" (318), where time seems suspended and only hunter and hunted exist.

But here I would like to halt my own tracking of the story by raising a question: what do these men seek? What does this dream/woman mean? And what can we in the uncomfortable position as parallels to her fictional pursuers, read in the linguistic traces that represent her even as they mark her disappearance?

Pellegrina's peregrinations may appear picaresque, but the roles she chooses are not random: she becomes, successively, whore, revolutionary, and saint, thereby enacting three of the most overdetermined versions of "woman" available in Western patriarchal culture.[15] But there is a difference, for by playing these roles to the full yet retaining the power to abandon them at will, she can remain at once inside and outside the semiotic systems that would codify woman according to androcentric logic, resisting even as she appears to fulfill traditional patriarchal categorizations of the feminine. In traversing the continuum that would polarize woman as virgin or whore, domesticated object or revolutionary agent, Pellegrina demonstrates the essential interchangeability—hence invalidity—of these oppositions. Exposing the provisionality and instability of masculine conceptions of woman, she threatens the very foundations of patriarchal culture, predicated, as feminist critics have demonstrated, on the control of women as both bodies and signs (see, for example, Beauvoir and Suleiman). Significantly, in role after role, Pellegrina flees involvement with a male lover whose desire would appropriate hers, claiming her permanently as his, writing her into his own script. She eludes these appropriations by flight, literally dropping out of (his) sight, fabricating another self, another script to be enacted elsewhere, hence stealing, in a sense that anticipates Hélène Cixous's play on the double meaning of *voler* (fly/steal), the very identity by which he would construct himself (89; see Herrmann).

Entering perpetual exile, Pellegrina casts herself as a moving signifier in several senses of that term, liberating herself from the domination of male speculations even as she deliberately solicits them. True to her names (pellegrina = wanderer; leoni/*leone* = lion), she is simultaneously rover and devourer, consuming those men who would consume her by fixing her as their object, putting her in her—their—place. Perpetually in flight, she makes exile itself into a source of creative energy. As every man's ideal Woman, she appears to be the ultimate embodiment of "*le sexe*" adored and feared by the masculine imagination that created it; but Dinesen, anticipating the redefinitions of Luce Irigaray (and investing with new meaning the operatic tradition of *la donna mobile*), subverts that masculine conception by representing Pellegrina as the "*sexe qui n'en est pas un*"—a multiple, mobile figure who cannot be encompassed—*cannot be read*—by the appropriative gaze of the other and who therefore escapes masculine hermeneutical control even as she acts as its ever-elusive object. If in this context Pellegrina seems to turn men into dreamers, the text suggests that they are victims not so much of a woman as of their own desire and of the fantasies that are its products: solipsistic mirror images that ultimately focus not on the woman, their putative object, but on themselves.[16] Similarly, insofar as each of these men becomes in effect an author, seeking to inscribe and circumscribe Pellegrina within his own life text, her power as an artist is manifest precisely in the way her fictions, lionlike, swallow up—literally incorporate and thus transform—theirs.[17]

Yet the text never lets us forget that *story* cannot ultimately elude *history*, that it is, finally, a man's world from which Pellegrina seeks liberation, and that given the historical realities of that world for women, the condition of freedom may ultimately be death. Caught at "the pass," Pellegrina faces an *impasse* of androcentric constructions. She is surrounded at last by former lovers whose echoic, relentlessly reiterated demand, "Tell me who you are" (325–26), is in fact a question of *masculine* identity: by being the woman I desire, tell me who *I* am; reflect me to myself.[18]

Overtaken—and potentially taken over—by those who would constrain and own her, Pellegrina answers the question of identity not with words but with a gesture that severs her from the consuming gazes that would hold her permanently as a mere reflection. Having already constituted herself as a signifier, she now puts herself literally *en abîme*, in a gesture that condenses and reenacts all her earlier flights/thefts: "She did not turn, or look at me. But the next moment she did what I always feared that she might do: she spread out her wings and flew away. Below the round white moon she made one great movement, throwing herself away from us all. . . . For one second she seemed to lift herself up with the wind, then running straight across the road, with all her might she threw herself from the earth clear into the abyss, and disappeared from our sight" (327).

Forsner and his companions rescue from this flight no more than what they would have made her from the outset: the shell of a woman, no longer resistant to their manipulations. Lying iconically "immovable" on a stretcher at the monastery to which they carry her, she is surrounded once more by the men who wait, at last, "to get an answer . . . of her" (328–29). Enclosed within a male space whose very name signifies oneness and incarceration (Greek *monasterion* = "hermit's cell," from *monos*, "single"), claustrated within the monological discourse that reiterates the Law of the Same against the multiplicity that she had made the sign of both subjectivity and freedom, Pellegrina dies doubly—not only literally but by becoming the object of a final male narrative. It is the account of Marcus Cocoza, the wandering Jew who, having acted as "her shadow" throughout her exile, now proposes to tell her "true" story, to utter "her real name." At its conclusion,

> "She stirred upon the couch. . . . I looked at the Jew. It was obvious that he was terrified lest she should see him. . . . He shrank back and took shelter behind me. The next second she slowly looked up. . . . In spite of the Jew's move to hide himself, her gaze fell straight upon him. He stood quite still under it. . . . She tried to speak two or three times, without getting a sound out, and again she closed her eyes. But once more she opened them, looking again straight at him. When she spoke it was in her ordinary low voice, a little slowly, but without any effort." (349–50)

Her discourse engenders a fiction that returns her to the opera before
the loss of voice, place, and identity: a dialogue that revives Pellegrina
Leoni as creator, shaping Marcus Cocoza as a character in her script of
desire, making his words the entrée into her own "song"—paradoxically a
scene from *Don Giovanni*, the quintessential script of the phallic appropriation of woman:

> " 'My little star,' said he. . . . 'It is sure to go well with you tonight. It is
> the second act of *Don Giovanni*; it is the letter air. It begins now with
> your recitative.' . . . As she spoke [the] words of the old opera . . . her
> face broke, as the night-old ice on a pool was broken up when, as a
> boy, I threw a stone into it. It became like a constellation of stars,
> quivering in the universe. . . . 'Oh,' she cried, 'look, look here! It is
> Pellegrina Leoni—it is she, it is she herself again,—she is back . . . on
> the stage again.' . . . Of a sudden he took up his little walking stick
> and struck three short strokes on the side of the stretcher. 'Donna
> Pellegrina Leoni,' he cried in a clear voice. *'En scène pour les deux. . . .'*
> She collected herself at his words. Within the next minute she be-
> came quiet in a gallant and deadly calm. . . . In one mighty move-
> ment, like that of a billow rising and sinking, she lifted the middle of
> her body. A strange sound, like the distant roar of a great animal,
> came from her breast. Slowly the flames in her face sank, and an
> ashen gray covered it instead. Her body fell back, stretched itself out
> and lay quite still, and she was dead." (352)

This final scene—like the complex relation of Pellegrina to the wandering
Jew who "shadows" her or the letter on which the reenacted "*scène*"
reflexively turns—invites contradictory readings. It is arguably an enactment of a deceptive and destructive deathbed delusion, born of hysteria,
manipulated by the Mephistophelean character whose words—as seduc-
tive in their way as Don Giovanni's—direct the woman in her final moments, and culminating in a death precipitated by the incoherent "roar"
that concludes her fantasy of return. In this context, she is indeed destroyed by the discourse that beckons her "*en scène*" before the engulfing
masculine gaze, just as, on stage at the opera, "she would have died for"—
indeed in the fire virtually did die for—her audiences (334).

But who, one wonders, controls whom? Who speaks through—and
for—whom? In this discourse on the power of the name, whose name does
Marcus Cocoza invoke? And what of Pellegrina's own voice? Her final
"song" can be heard by the men who surround her only as incoherent

noise—an uninterpretable "distant roar"—but Dinesen implies that for Pellegrina herself, it has an altogether other meaning, a liberatory potential that she herself has created by ventriloquizing her desire through Marcus's words, making him a mimetic means to her own end in both senses of that phrase. "If women are such good mimics," remarks Irigaray, "it is because they are not simply reabsorbed in this function. *They also remain elsewhere*" (76).[19] One might argue that in the final moments of Pellegrina's story, this subversive feminine "mimicry" is doubled, for Pellegrina "speaks" through both Marcus's discourse and her own, giving voice to an "elsewhere" that is hers alone, unfathomable to the men who hear it. That this moment marks the site of another story is reinforced by the echoes Dinesen sets up between the figure of Pellegrina as "star," her face like "the night-old ice on a pool . . . broken up" or "a constellation of stars, quivering in the universe," and Mira Jama's earlier reflections on stories/dreams as emerging from "a deep well" from which "there comes up a spring of water, which runs out in little streamlets to all possible sides, like the rays of a star" ("Dreamers," 277). The text suggests that even as Marcus's story would impose on her his own "truth," freezing her fluidity into some final rigid form, she ultimately shatters those alien(ating) narrative structures with her creative energy, turning him into the instrument for regaining her voice and her self—which is to say, her own fiction(s). Similarly, one might argue, Dinesen's narrative pervades and incorporates all the male-authored narratives in the text, using them at last to ventriloquize her own encompassing self-reflexive story, her own ineluctable "elsewhereness."

But what does it mean to regain "oneself" in this context? The text suggests that *being oneself* is not the same as being *one self*. Paradoxically, Pellegrina Leoni is most herself when she is least herself: she "lives" most intensely as operatic actress, a figure quintessentially *plural*, a *character*, in the several senses of that word, who "sings" in many voices. For her (as for her author after the loss of Africa), "real life" is fiction and vice versa: the very interchangeability of those terms and the irresolvable ambiguity of their statement emblematizes the paradoxes Dinesen plays out in Pellegrina. Whether on the literal stage or in the stagings of life that she has enacted after leaving the opera, the fundamental truth about the self that Pellegrina enacts is that there may be no fundamental truth about the self: what she does, whether as diva or mask-wearing wanderer, in the theater as an imitation of life or in life as an imitation of theater, is to enact the self as a dynamic of displacement, to make literal the internal multiplicity that traditional unitary, monological conceptions of identity would repress. In this sense Pellegrina has never left the theater; hence her affirmation of "return"—"it is she, she herself again"—is inseparable from its qualifying conclusion: "on the stage again."

Even in death, then, Pellegrina—like her author—resists reductive readings that would turn her into a sign "tied up" within another's discourse (347). Ultimately, the question of who is speaking in "The Dreamers" becomes as undecidable as Pellegrina's identity.[20] This elusiveness of both woman and narrative finds a metaphor in the opening scene of the text, in the floating world in which the frame story transpires—a scene that anticipates the climactic conjunction of dreaming, fluidity, multiplicity, and illumination that figure Pellegrina's life and death. From the dhow moving on the midnight ocean, the ordinary, separable positionings of up and down, above and below, are rendered problematic, "bewildering," as sky and sea become indistinguishable, mirroring one another in an infinite series of reflections:

> as if something had happened to the world; as if the soul of it had been, by some magic, turned upside down. . . . The brightness of the moon upon the water was so clear that it seemed as if all the light in the world were in reality radiating from the sea, to be reflected in the skies. The waves looked solid as if one might safely have walked upon them, while it was into the vertiginous sky that one might sink and fall, into the turbulent and unfathomable depths of silvery worlds, forever silver reflected within silver, moving and changing. . . . The heavy waters sang and murmured. (271)

In comparable ways, Dinesen dislocates her readers, sets them afloat as wanderers in the "vertiginous" world of her texts, at once lured and unmoored by the story of woman, which, like Pellegrina or the "heavy waters" beneath the floating dhow, has depths that "sing and murmur" in many voices—voices that from an androcentric perspective may appear indecipherable, "bewildering," even incoherent, but that persistently invite another hearing, rewriting exile as exploration outside the bounds, a form of creative ecstasy.

As a mobile, endlessly inventive figure, Pellegrina inspires an ever-widening process of interpretation. Even after death, she continues to engender narratives:

"I have thought," said Lincoln, "what would have happened to this woman if she had not died then? She might have been with us here tonight. . . . Or she might have gone with us into the highlands . . . and have been honored . . . as a great witch. In the end . . . she might perhaps have decided to become a pretty little jackal, and have made herself a den on the plain. . . . I have imagined that so vividly that on a moonlight night I have believed that I heard her voice amongst the hills. . . ." "Ah la la," said Mira, . . . "I have heard that little jackal too. . . . She barks, 'I am not one little jackal, not one; I am many. . . .' And pat! in a second she really is another, barking just behind you: 'I am not one little jackal. Now I am another.'" (353–54)

Just so, Dinesen herself refuses final placement, proves equally resistant to finalizing readings. The story of the woman as artist and exile both enacts and explicates its author's own transgressive art, quintessentially the product of displacement, which remakes as it transcends the masculine models it appears to serve—a discourse of disclosure that invites yet always eludes interpretations. The name Leoni was also Dinesen's; "Lioness" was one of her many appellations, the sheer profusion of which, like Pellegrina's many names, suggests her refusal to be fixed by any single *logos*.[21] Late in life, Dinesen would repeatedly speak of Pellegrina's lost voice as a figure for her own loss of Africa. Out of Africa, Dinesen conceived of her life as a form of exile, a living death, a "dream." Yet by a great act of courage and imagination she would turn the space of that dream—the dislocations of that life—into the site for the engendering of her narratives. And if, as she ruefully remarked, she also died, figuratively, by turning herself in the process into inert "printed matter" (*Daguerreotypes*, 196), it is paradoxically through the displacements of writing that she continues to live, marking the place of exile as the ever-receding horizon of new readings.

Notes

1. The phrase "my heart's land" comes from Karen Blixen's early poem "Ex Africa," published in the Danish journal *Tilskueren* in 1925. For an English translation, see Gatura, n.p.

2. For her configuration of Africa as mother, see *Letters from Africa*, 416, and *Out of Africa*, 356.

3. "When in the early thirties coffee prices fell, I had to give up my farm. I went back to my own country, at sea-level, out of earshot of the echoes of the plain. . . . During this time my existence was without an answer from anywhere. . . . Under the circumstances I myself grew silent. I had, in every sense of the word, nothing to say. And yet I had to speak. For I had my books to write" ("Mottoes," 10).

4. For an analysis of Dinesen's writing as mourning see Aiken, "Isak Dinesen and Photo/Graphic Recollection," 29–38. See also Langbaum, 119, on *Out of Africa* as a pastoral elegiac version of *Paradise Lost*; and Thurman, 282–84, on *Out of Africa* as a text of loss.

5. On Dinesen's many names and pseudonyms, see Thurman, 6.

6. Her analysis of Portia's use of male disguise in *The Merchant of Venice* obliquely comments on her own situation as a woman writing as a man: "In the performances of *The Merchant of Venice* which I have seen, Portia has, according to my view, been played incorrectly. In the court scene she has been all too solemn and doctrinaire. . . . Just as she sparkles in the entire comedy, . . . quick to laughter, so she should also, I think, sparkle in the closed, severely masculine world of the court. . . . Her magic lies precisely in her duplicity, the pretended deep respect for the paragraphs of the law which overlies her . . . quite fearless heresy" ("Oration at a Bonfire, Fourteen Years Late," in *Daguerreotypes and Other Essays*, 82–83).

7. Isaac ("the one who laughs"), born during his parents' exilic wanderings, occupies a uniquely "feminine" position by virtue of his name, which his mother, Sarah, bestowed on him as a sign of her own laughter. See Genesis 18:10–12, and 21:6. On the subversive implications of Dinesen's pseudonym, see Aiken, "Dinesen's 'Sorrow acre.'"

8. Published as the sixth of *Seven Gothic Tales* (pp. 271–355), the text, like most of the Gothic tales, is perhaps more accurately characterized as a novella than as a short story because of its length. For discussions of how extensively Dinesen fictionalized her "autobiography," see Thurman, 282–85, and Juhl.

9. For an extension of the link between flying, woman's fiction-making, and the underwater world of the unconscious, see "The Diver," in Dinesen's last collection, *Anecdotes of Destiny*, 16–20.

10. Showalter is elaborating on the model proposed by Ardener, 3. See Cixous and Clément, 67–69.

11. See, for example, Aristotle, *Generation*, I, ii; *Politics*, I, xii–xiii; Thomas Aquinas, *Summa Theologiae*, I, Question 92; Rousseau, 109; Kierkegaard, 66–67; Freud, "Femininity."

12. For Dinesen's explicit identification of herself with Pellegrina Leoni, see Bjørnvig, 158–63. See also Thurman, 399–400. Significantly, after Forsner finishes his tale, the storyteller, Mira, Dinesen's double, claims it as his own: "I know all your tale. . . . I have heard it before. Now I believe that I made it myself" ("Dreamers," 354).

13. I am grateful to my student Lynn Gerou for reminding me of the use of the

phrase *Prima Donna Assoluta* to characterize the greatest female singers. The phrase resonates at many levels with Dinesen's representation of woman in the text.

14. Dinesen reinforces the reading of Pellegrina as a figure of and in exile through a complex nexus of literary reference. As Langbaum notes, "In Pellegrina, the allusions are so various and shifting that we cannot identify her with any one of them. . . . In her aspect of penitential pilgrim, she recalls the Wandering Jew; Marcus's presence helps us to make that connection. Marcus calls her a Donna Quixotta de la Mancha: "'the phenomena of life were not great enough for her; they were not in proportion with her own heart.'" This connects her with Faust, still another wanderer; and since the force that makes her so effective in her metamorphoses . . . is an erotic force, she is also a female Don Juan. It is surely to make this connection that Isak Dinesen has the fire break out when Pellegrina is singing Mozart's *Don Giovanni*" (99). As I shall argue below, there are further implications in Dinesen's use of *Don Giovanni*. Space does not allow a thorough exploration of the intertextualities in "The Dreamers," but each of the cases cited by Langbaum illustrates a strategy characteristic of Dinesen throughout her career: the appropriation and consequent revisionist interpretation of male-authored, androcentric texts—here classic texts of exile literally reembodied in woman, their male desire-in-narrative dislocated and replaced.

15. As feminist scholarship has long recognized, the virgin and the whore serve as quintessential polar opposites on the symbolic spectrum representing woman in Western cultural history. See, for example, Warner, 49–67. Woman as the locus of revolution, a threat to the order of the state, is a recurrent topos in masculine discourses from antiquity on. See Pateman, 20–34.

16. Dinesen's insight here has obvious similarities to Woolf's famous observation that "women have served all these centuries as looking-glasses possessing the magic and delicious power of reflecting the figure of man at twice its natural size" (35) and to Irigaray's discussion of the "role of 'femininity'" in Western culture: "The rejection, the exclusion of a female imaginary undoubtedly places woman in a position where she can experience herself only fragmentarily as waste or as excess in the little structured margins of a dominant ideology, this mirror entrusted by the (masculine) 'subject' with the task of reflecting and redoubling himself. The role of 'femininity' is prescribed moreover by this masculine specula(riza)tion and corresponds only slightly to woman's desire" (104).

17. Cf. Cocoza's image of Pellegrina as "a python": "You have no poison whatever in you, and if you kill it is by the force of your embrace. This quality upsets your lovers, who . . . have neither the strength to resist you, nor the wisdom to value the sort of death which they might obtain with you. . . . The sight of you unfolding your great coils to revolve around, impress yourself upon, and finally crush a meadow mouse is enough to split one's sides with laughter" ("Dreamers," 337).

18. The text makes a significant distinction at this point between Lincoln and the two other men who have pursued Pellegrina. Having reached her before them, Lincoln has come close to comprehending the intensity of her need for imaginative freedom. His willingness to participate with her in a new sort of play—in both senses—suggests that he may be capable of creating, with her, a new story in which the two might participate together, in genuine mutuality (322–24). The arrival of the two other lovers shatters the fragile "house" of fiction in which they take shelter (324). Driven by jealousy that has more to do with the other men than with the woman for whom they fight as for a rare trophy, Lincoln betrays Pellegrina: "She turned to me slowly, and looked at me, as if she were confident that I would be on her side. So I should have been, against all the world, ten minutes before, but it is extraordinary how quickly one is corrupted by bad company. When I heard these other people talking of their old acquaintance with her, I myself, who stood so much closer than the others, turned toward her. . . . 'Tell them,' I cried. 'Tell them who you are!' " (326).

19. See Nancy Miller's discussion of this passage in "Emphasis Added," 38–39.

20. On this question and its import for women and feminist criticism, see Foucault, and the debate between Kamuf ("Replacing Feminist Criticism") and Miller ("The Text's Heroine").

21. See *Out of Africa*, 70, where Dinesen conflates this appellation with the figure of herself as text: "After Ismail had gone back to Somaliland, I had a letter from him which was addressed to *Lioness Blixen*, and opened: *Honorable Lioness*."

Works Cited

Aiken, Susan Hardy. "Dinesen's 'Sorrow acre': Tracing the Woman's Line." *Contemporary Literature* 25 (1984): 156–86.

———. "Isak Dinesen and Photo/Graphic Recollection." *exposure* 23 (Winter 1985): 29–38.

Aquinas, Thomas. *Summa Theologiae*. New York: English Dominican Province, 1947.

Ardener, Edwin. "Belief and the Problem of Women." In *Perceiving Women*, edited by Shirley Ardener, 1–17. New York: Halsted Press, 1977.

Aristotle. *Aristotle's Politics and Poetics*. Translated by Benjamin Jowett and T. Twining. New York: Viking Press, 1957.

———. *Generation of Animals*. Translated by A. L. Peck. Cambridge, Mass.: Harvard University Press, 1943.

Beauvoir, Simone de. *The Second Sex*. Translated by H. M. Parshley. New York: Knopf, 1953.

Bjørnvig, Thorkild. *The Pact: My Friendship with Isak Dinesen*. Translated by

Ingvar Schousboe and William Jay Smith. Baton Rouge: Louisiana State University Press, 1983.

Brooks, Peter. *Reading for the Plot*. New York: Knopf, 1984.

Cixous, Hélène, and Catherine Clément. *The Newly Born Woman*. Translated by Betsy Wing. Minneapolis: University of Minnesota Press, 1986.

Dinesen, Isak. *Anecdotes of Destiny*. New York: Random House, 1958.

———. "The Dreamers." In *Seven Gothic Tales*, 271–355. New York: Random House, 1937.

———. "Echoes from the Hills." In *Shadows on the Grass*, 107–49. 1961. Reprint. New York: Vintage Books, 1974.

———. *Letters from Africa*. Chicago: University of Chicago Press, 1978.

———. "On Mottoes of My Life." In *Daguerreotypes and Other Essays*, 1–15. Chicago: University of Chicago Press, 1979.

———. "Oration at a Bonfire, Fourteen Years Late." In *Daguerreotypes and Other Essays*, 64–87. Chicago: University of Chicago Press, 1979.

———. *Out of Africa*. New York: Random House, 1937.

———. "Rungstedlund." In *Daguerreotypes and Other Essays*, 195–218. Chicago: University of Chicago Press, 1979.

———. *Seven Gothic Tales*. New York: Random House, 1937.

Foucault, Michel. "What Is an Author." In *Language, Counter-Memory, Practice*. Translated by Donald F. Bouchard and Sherry Simon, edited by Donald F. Bouchard, 113–38. Ithaca: Cornell University Press, 1977.

Freud, Sigmund. "Femininity." In *New Introductory Lectures on Psychoanalysis*. Translated by James Strachey. New York: Norton, 1965.

Gatura, Kamante. *Longing for Darkness: Kamante's Tales from Out of Africa*. Edited by Peter Beard. New York: Harcourt Brace, 1975.

Herrmann, Claudine. *Les voleuses de lange*. Paris: Editions des femmes, 1976.

Irigaray, Luce. *This Sex That Is Not One*. Translated by Catherine Porter. Ithaca: Cornell University Press, 1985.

Juhl, Marianne. "A Comparison between *Letters from Africa* and *Out of Africa*." In *Karen Blixen/Isak Dinesen: Tradition, Modernity, and Other Ambiguities. Conference Proceedings*, 34–38. Minneapolis: University of Minnesota, 1985.

Kamuf, Peggy. "Replacing Feminist Criticism." *Diacritics* 12 (Summer 1982): 42–47.

Kierkegaard, Søren. *Stages on Life's Way*. Translated by Walter Lowrie. Princeton: Princeton University Press, 1940.

Langbaum, Robert. *Isak Dinesen's Art: The Gayety of Vision*. 1964. Reprint. University of Chicago Press, 1975.

Marks, Elaine, and Isabelle de Courtivron, eds. *New French Feminisms*. New York: Schocken, 1981.

Miller, Nancy K. "Emphasis Added: Plots and Plausibilities in Women's Fiction." *PMLA* 96 (1981): 36–48.

_____. "The Text's Heroine: A Feminist Critic and Her Fictions." *Diacritics* 12 (Summer 1982): 48–53.

Pateman, Carole. " 'The Disorder of Women': Women, Love, and the Sense of Justice." *Ethics* 91 (October 1980): 20–34.

Rousseau, Jean-Jacques. *Politics and the Arts: A Letter to M. d'Alembert on the Theatre.* Translated by A. Bloom. Ithaca: Cornell University Press, 1968.

Schopenhauer, Arthur. *Parerga and Paralipomena.* Translated by T. Bailey Saunders. London: Allen & Unwin, 1890.

Showalter, Elaine. "Feminist Criticism in the Wilderness." *Critical Inquiry* 8 (Winter 1981): 179–205.

Suleiman, Susan Rubin, ed. *The Female Body in Western Culture.* Cambridge, Mass.: Harvard University Press, 1986.

Thurman, Judith. *Isak Dinesen: The Life of a Storyteller.* New York: St. Martin's Press, 1982.

Warner, Marina. *Alone of All Her Sex: The Myth and the Cult of the Virgin Mary.* New York: Knopf, 1976.

Woolf, Virginia. *A Room of One's Own.* 1929. Reprint. New York: Harcourt, Brace and World, 1957.

Chapter 5

. . . .

The Exhilaration of Exile

Rhys, Stead, and Lessing

Judith Kegan Gardiner

For the colonial woman writer of the colonizing race and class, the exile that sends her from the colony to the cultural center must always be profoundly ambiguous. The three women writers with whom I am concerned—Jean Rhys, Christina Stead, and Doris Lessing—were born at the periphery of the British empire—Rhys in 1890 in Dominica, the West Indies; Stead in 1902 in Australia; and Lessing in 1919 in Persia, from which her family moved five years later to Rhodesia, now Zimbabwe. As young women, each of the three left a home that practiced traditional sex roles for England, which provided a freer personal life and the chance to be an artist—Rhys at age sixteen in 1910; Stead at twenty-six in 1928; Lessing at thirty in 1949.[1]

Although the writers' fictions developed from their unique histories, all three were shaped by parallel and paradoxical forces, represented by the words *home* and *exile*. These words signify the profound ambivalence felt by the three writers about their place in culture because they grew up in contexts in which "home," for some purposes, meant England, not the nation in which they were raised. Because England was unknown to them and alien to their immediate experiences, these writers were able to see English culture critically and to feel its domination as arbitrary, unjust, and foreign. They grew up with adults who thought of home as elsewhere, and their own family homes were places of confinement and restraint for them; they were expected to grow up as ladylike participants in white English culture. Home was therefore a trap from which they had to escape as well as an implied goal. Like the conventional hero of the *bildungsroman*, each woman traveled from her provincial backwater to the more appreciative, more cosmopolitan, more diverse center—to London. To be exiled from the periphery to the center of one's culture is not the traditional meaning of exile, yet these writers do not define this center as home either: neither place is home; each is alternately desirable and oppressive. This situation heightens their resistance to the sentimental claims of the home canon, country, and culture. As admiring and resentful foreigners, as colonials, they see English culture as a dominating discourse imposed upon their creativity, at the same time that it enables that creativity by freeing them from the psychological foreclosure of entrapment within home as the family of origin. In short, being a colonial-in-exile for these three women puts into play an oscillation whereby no place is home; home is ambiguous and ambivalent, here and elsewhere, and so there remains always a missing point of origin in their works, a fruitful unsettledness that makes the three women simultaneously inheritors of and antagonists to imperialism rather than self-sufficient local colonists or comfortable, controlling citizens of a communicative global village. For all three, the English literary tradition is both mother tongue and somewhat alien, shadowy, and duplicitous. Moreover, and more simply, their situation between cultures helps them recognize that personal circumstances are inevitably politically charged and that the family is a political institution.[2] They perceive home—in both directions—as periphery and center, as individual colonial family and as dominant culture—as a site of oppression in which they learn to articulate that oppression.

Lessing's parents were English, her father an eager exile, her mother a reluctant one from middle-class English clerical work and social codes. Rhys's father was Welsh although her mother's Creole family dated back for generations in the West Indies, far enough to have been prominent slaveholders before emancipation occurred early in the nineteenth century. Stead's grandfather had emigrated from England, and the family preserved his myth about his travels, in which Dickens's *Great Expectations*, with its suddenly wealthy transported convict, inspired him to set out young and alone to make his fortune in Australia. Thus all three women grew up in homes that paid homage to the home of the dominant culture and literary canon, and they therefore did not identify the familial home that they wanted to escape with the physical place where they lived, but instead with their families' internalization of the values of the home country that seemed factitious to them because they were incongruent with their direct experiences of the resident country, a locale they could romanticize but could not assimilate as truly "home," truly their own.

Short stories by Rhys and Lessing vividly illustrate these ambiguities of home and exile and the psychological tensions created for the white colonial girl living within these ambiguities. Adolescence is the time when girls confront society's expectations for them and its confusions about female sexuality and often the time when girls rebel against their mothers as the enforcers of these social expectations. Writing as mature women in exile, far distant from their childhood families, Rhys and Lessing set some of their richest meditations on the colonial experience as short stories focusing on the period of early adolescence.

The protagonists of both Rhys's "The Day They Burned the Books" (1960) and Lessing's "Flavours of Exile" (1957) are unnamed twelve-year-old girls autobiographically similar to their authors; both stories are told in the first person from the perspective of the young narrator, though the narrative voice occasionally changes to that of a more experienced older woman distanced from her childhood culture. Both stories criticize English culture's dominance over the colonial, its claim to be home, by contrasting the foods and flowers that the English parents romanticize with the sensory plenitude of the children's experience.

The hero of "The Day They Burned the Books" is the narrator's friend Eddie Sawyer, a boy she "loved" and "despised." His father is an Englishman who "detested the moon and everything else about the Caribbean"; his mother, "a decent, respectable, nicely educated coloured woman" from the islands (41–42). "It was Eddie," the narrator tells us, "who first infected me with doubts about 'home,' meaning England." Eddie announces that he doesn't like strawberries and he doesn't "like daffodils either." He tells the other children: "Dad's always going on about them. He says they lick the flowers here into a cocked hat and I bet that's a lie" (43). The narrator admires Eddie for his boldness, which corroborates her own, more timorous thoughts in the same line: "I also was tired of learning and reciting poems in praise of daffodils," she says; "my relations with the few 'real' English boys and girls I had met were awkward. I had discovered that if I called myself English they would snub me haughtily: 'You're not English; you're a horrid colonial,'" they would taunt, and when she replies that it's "much more fun to be French or Spanish or something like that, and as a matter of fact, I am a bit," they find her ridiculous and snub her even more: "Heads I win, tails you lose—that was the English" (43–44).

Lessing's story is set in Africa rather than the West Indies, and its girl narrator is similarly unimpressed with the English tinned foods her parents eat "with a truly religious emotion" and a shared "nostalgia" (576). The adults "agreed that the soil of Africa was unable to grow food that had any taste at all," whereas the narrator finds just the reverse, relishing the local bounty. "Brussels sprouts, cherries, English gooseberries—they were my mother's; they recurred in her talk as often as 'a real London pea-souper,' or 'chestnuts by the fire,' or 'cherry blossom at Kew'" (577). For Lessing's narrator as for Rhys's, the parents' exile is the child's home; the parents' tastes are alien and their love for things English a lie, as the supposed flavorlessness of the local food is a lie that will carry over for the children from fruits and flowers to their judgment of other values their parents seek to impress upon them. "I no longer grudged these to her," Lessing's narrator says of her mother's English enthusiasms, not quite accurately, if we judge from the grudging tone of the story: "I listened and was careful not to show that my thoughts were on my own inheritance of veld and sun" (577).

Both stories associate England or home in this sense of an inauthentic, nostalgic clinging to dominant values that is inappropriate to the colonial setting, with the homes formed by the children's parents and with the patriarchal sex roles found in these homes, even though, unlike the Lessing story, "The Day They Burned the Books" displaces this situation to the narrator's friend's parents rather than her own. In both stories, the oppressive imposition of adult values on children parallels the impositions of the master culture on the colonial one and is complicated by the imposition of male authority on women. In both stories the mothers have had to accommodate to their husbands' wishes. Active, angry women, the mothers in the stories subject their children to surveillance and correction. The fathers are shadowy, barely there. Lessing's narrator's mother regrets being in Africa rather than in England or in Persia, where she had lived as "the wife of a minor official" in "a vast storehouse" "among roses and jasmine, walnut trees and pomegranates. But, unfortunately, for too short a time" (577). Therefore she clings to her English garden, her English vegetables and ways of cooking them, even to "the large china vegetable dishes brought from that old house in London." In contrast, she feels her African garden is, like her unwilling life in Africa, a "defeat" (575).

Whereas Lessing's narrator's father merely grumbles and shouts about his wife's garden, Mr. Sawyer in the Rhys story publicly humiliates his wife as a nonwhite woman. He pulls her hair at a dinner party, announcing that her beautiful, abundant hair is "not a wig." "You damned, long-eyed, gloomy half-caste, you don't smell right to me," he says, while Mrs. Sawyer remains silent under his abuse, trying "to pretend that it was all part of the joke, this mysterious, obscure, sacred English joke," instead of retaliating across their reciprocal cultural differences, as the narrator thinks would be more just and normal, by replying, "You don't smell right to me, either" (42).

Although the parents' marriages are acrimonious, both stories champion heterosexuality, at least insofar as they pose a young adolescent crush that heralds the beginnings of the girls' sexuality as a liberating stage opposed to the restrictions of childhood in the family. If identification with their parents' culturally dominant values represents home for these girls, then their heterosexual desire is a force expelling them from home and freeing them from its values. Both stories begin by setting the colonial scene so as to criticize English "home" values. Both then develop a plot in which each twelve-year-old female protagonist forms an innocent yet erotic couple with a boy whom she says she loves; both stories thus redefine heterosexuality as a kind of exile, breaking the dominant culture of home, encouraging motion away from its closed circuit, and thereby enabling art.

In "Flavours of Exile," Lessing's narrator enjoys an innocent sensuality with her friend William MacGregor. Under the Cape gooseberry bushes, she says, "The smell of the leaves . . . intoxicated us. We would laugh and shout, then quarrel; and William, to make up, shelled a double handful of the fruit and poured it into my skirt and we ate together, pressing the biggest berries on each other" (576). Three years older than she is, William humors the adults by pretending that their bitter brussels sprouts are delicious, and the narrator then emulates this "beautiful lesson in courtesy" by pretending that she, too, likes English foods. Suddenly the narrator becomes infatuated with her childhood chum, feeling that he is the answer to all the emotional deficits of her adolescence. She sees "a promise of warmth and understanding I had never known" in his eyes. "It hurt to be shut out from the world of simple kindness he lived in," she thinks, and she daydreams about him until she dwells perpetually in a "marvellous feverish world" (579).

This sudden infatuation takes place at exactly the same time that she is trying to identify with her mother's tastes by fostering her mother's sickly pomegranate tree. Unlike the English cherries and brussels sprouts, "pomegranates were an exotic for my mother," says the narrator, with the voice not of the child but of the exiled adult woman writer, "and therefore more easily shared with her" (577). The pomegranate tree gathers multiple symbolic freight. It not only represents the narrator's effort to unite with her mother but also her adolescent self on the verge of sexual awakening: the tree, she says, "was about my height, a tough, obstinate-looking thing" (578). As its fruit matures, its sexual connotations become more pressing, and she wants her friend William to be present when the fruit bursts: "It seemed as if my whole life was concentrated and ripening with that single fruit" (579). At the same time, the pomegranate becomes associated with the mother, with maternity, and with female sexuality: "The fruit looked lumpy and veined, like a nursing breast" (580). The fruit cracks while it is still on the stalk, and black ants invade the oozing red flesh. When the narrator thinks the pomegranate is finally ripe, she persuades her mother to invite the MacGregors for the occasion. William arrives, looking a bit like the cracked pomegranate himself, his lips "full and thin-skinned" with their "blood, dull and dark around the pale groove" (581). Impervious to her romanticizing him or the fruit, he says the fruit is "bad" and she is "mad" for taking it so seriously, and he hits the tree with a stick so that the pomegranate "exploded in a scatter of crimson seeds, fermenting juice, and black ants" (582). Submissive to this gestured lesson in male sexuality, the narrator feigns unconcern, properly returning to the adults and their colonial teatime.

Like the god of the underworld, the boy separates Proserpina the pomegranate-eater from Ceres, her mother, violently breaking the girl's identification with her mother as a sexual, maternal person by breaking her identification with her mother's exotic fruit. At the same time, as in the Proserpina myth, this rupture of the preoedipal mother-daughter bond places the daughter in an oedipal subordination to patriarchal culture and dominant values. Her Eden destroyed, its fruit uneaten, she joins the boy in humoring the adults; she too becomes a grownup, that is, a socially responsible person who hides her feelings and expresses proper clichés. She allows the dominant culture of home and family to define her and her experiences. Although the narrator adapts to her social situation, the author rebels against this conformity by stressing its falseness and the violence needed to bring it about. Moreover, the story idealizes the girl's innocent frolicking with the boy on the veld; that innocent freedom intimates the possibilities for an authentic response to the nature of the colonized country in contrast to the mother's inauthenticity, her inability to perceive her actual surroundings because of her meretricious and blinding nostalgia for the home country.

This story does not mention that all its characters are whites, who impose their culture not merely on a landscape new to them but more seriously on the people displaced from that land. The story does not identify any blacks as such, though a cook and a "garden boy" cater to the mother's desires for English foods (575), but this apparent omission disappears in context. "Flavours of Exile" appears in one of Lessing's collections of African stories, a setting that repeatedly highlights the interracial tensions of that society and thereby clarifies the story's criticism of colonial culture.

Rhys's "The Day They Burned the Books," in contrast, dramatizes the racial as well as gender and national aspects of the colonial predicament by focusing not on the narrator's white family but on her friend's racially mixed one. Unlike the boy in Lessing's story, Rhys's Eddie is a debunker, not a conciliator, of colonial belief in the superiority of all things English. Mrs. Sawyer never articulates such a skepticism of European values. We infer that she hates her abusive husband's tradition because she seeks to destroy it by destroying the texts associated with it. After his death, she divides his library into two piles: one consists of English poetry, glossy encyclopedias, history books, and so on, which she can sell; the other includes less valuable books to be burned. The idea of burning books is a thrilling and wicked one; the Sawyers' servant, presumably a black woman from the islands, is "half hugely delighted, half-shocked, even frightened" at the prospect (45). Eddie resists the destruction of his father's part in his heritage; he flies at his mother shrieking, "Now I've got to hate you too" (46). When he thinks the narrator slights his mother "because she isn't white," however, he immediately shifts ground to attack the narrator and defend his mother, taunting, "She's prettier than your mother" (47). Oscillating between loyalties to both his parents, Eddie thus preserves the stereotypes of the sensuous, hot-tempered island beauty versus the cold English intellectual without staking out a clear ground for himself. Standing outside these stereotypes, the narrator sees them as engendering terrifying conflicts. When Mrs. Sawyer sorts the books, the narrator discerns her hatred for women writers like Christina Rossetti; "by a flicker in Mrs. Sawyer's eyes I knew that worse than men who wrote books were women who wrote books. . . . Men could be mercifully shot; women must be tortured" (46). Subordinated to her husband by national, racial, and gender categories, Mrs. Sawyer thus internalizes the same divisive and oppressive values against which she rebels.

Each child saves a book from the potential pyre. Eddie takes *Kim*, which he was already reading; its hero, an orphaned English boy who lives on the East Indian road as a native, might well appeal to Eddie, despite Rudyard Kipling's role as a stalwart apologist for imperialism. The narrator, however, is disappointed to discover that her volume is "in French, and seemed dull" (48): Guy de Maupassant's *Fort comme la mort*, the story of an artist's fatal obsession for his mistress's daughter. These choices of books from the great Western tradition reinforce gender stereotypes—adventure for the boy, a love story for the girl. And it is through the conventions of romance that she tries to understand her encounter with Eddie's mother and Eddie's books. Away from the furious mother, Eddie and the narrator hold hands and cry together, an experience that convinces the narrator that she and Eddie are now married. This mock wedding alliance defines heterosexuality as mutual suffering, as exile from the garden of innocent identification with parents. Having tasted the fruit of difference and defiance, they are hand in hand under Eddie's mango tree like Adam and Eve outside of paradise, facing a fallen world. Throughout Rhys's and Lessing's work, heterosexuality will retain this ambivalence for the female hero: a necessary and enabling break out of the symbiosis of preoedipal relations but also a contact with someone alien, a potential oppressor analogous to a cultural colonist. For Stead, too, heterosexuality is ambivalent. Although she centered her personal security in her relationship with one man, her fellow in exile, whom she defines as her home, she generally writes about marriage and families as negatively as either Rhys or Lessing.

Unlike Eve, none of these three writers can look back on a paradisal home because the white colonial woman has no secure point of origin. Their birth nation is not the home of their culture; England is not the home of their birth; and the home in which they grow up demeans women and makes it impossible for them to identify with the mothers they yearn for. The children are impatient with parental lies about their origins and their position as colonists. Each of the three authors understands the colonial culture as one riven by race, class, and gender divisions, not as a unified site of origin. Although they are oppressed as women, the authors nonetheless recognize their white privilege and suffer guilt at their family's complicity in colonial racism. Rhys speaks of her shame at having slave-owning ancestors. Lessing rages against white supremacy and has been prohibited at times from reentering both Rhodesia, where she grew up, and the Union of South Africa. Stead, who, unlike Rhys and Lessing, did not grow up in a white minority culture, nonetheless conceptualizes Australia in terms of its displaced indigenous peoples.

The opening sections of her autobiographical novel *For Love Alone* (1944) juxtapose the motifs of cultural exile and the oppressions of home with unusual clarity, setting them out in prologue and text, respectively. Teresa, the hero, is nineteen years old when the novel opens, older than the protagonists of the Rhys and Lessing stories but still an innocent adolescent trying to understand her family relationships and her sexuality. Before the first scene of the novel, a prologue called "Sea People" begins, "In the part of the world Teresa came from, winter is in July, spring brides marry in September, and Christmas" dinners are set "near the tall pine tree loaded with gifts and tinsel as in the old country" (xi). Things are upside down, topsy-turvy, from the English norm, yet, as in the Rhys and Lessing stories, still defined by "the old country": "from a scarcely noticeable island up toward the North Pole the people came." These voyagers head toward "a fruitful island of the sea-world, a great Ithaca," linked with the great Western myths, with an epic tradition into which the female colonial writer will seek to insert herself (xi). But she must leave her colonial home to do so, as the first scene of the novel's action makes clear. The chapter begins: "Naked . . . he stood in the doorway, a tall man with . . . a skin still pale under many summers' tan" (3). This imposing figure turns out to be the hero's father, and his first words are a lesson to his daughters based on comparing them with an aboriginal woman he saw "sitting on the ground nursing her black baby, . . . herself . . . black as a hat, with a strong, supple oily skin, finer than white women's skins" (3). He claims that the black woman admires his white feet; he makes her an object lesson for his daughters on proper womanly behavior. "What do we look for in women—understanding!" he pontificates. "In the rough and tumble of man's world, the law of the jungle is often the only law observed, but in the peace and sanctity of the man's home, he feels the love that is close to angels! . . . Don't forget, Kitty, to clean my boots" (8). He insults Teresa by telling her she has the "face of a little tramp" (6) and that she is "unbending" and unattractive (9). Simply, somewhat crudely, Stead underscores the domineering banality of the father's use of myths that assert white cultural superiority and that treat black people and white women as like the land, nature to be exploited so that it serves, nurtures, and enhances white men. Teresa screams that her father disgusts her, that he is immoral and "ignoble," incapable of understanding her (12). "I'll go away," she announces; "I have suffered too much" (13). It takes her the rest of the novel to fulfill this boast, leaving Australia for England and daughterly subservience for a free female sexuality.

Unlike Rhys and Lessing, Stead managed to make heterosexuality psychologically into home rather than exile while remaining in exile from Australia for forty years. During this period she lived with William J. Blake, an American Marxist writer and economist whom she eventually married. For years they roamed through England, America, and Europe, in political exile from America during the McCarthy years because of Blake's Communist affiliations. They lived in hotels and rented rooms; much of the time they were extremely poor, getting by on translations, reviews, and miscellaneous writing jobs, their two typewriters clacking together: "We never thought of having a home," she wrote; "home was where the other was" (*Ocean of Story*, 512).

She did not return to Australia until after Blake's death, writing a short piece, "Another View of the Homestead" (1970), about this visit. After a lifetime abroad, Stead defines both home and exile retrospectively in terms of time as well as space and of the emotional pulls in both directions. In this essay Stead contrasts her trip to England on shipboard in 1928 with her return by plane in 1969. "Homeward bound on that ship in 1928," she begins the essay, confusingly displacing her own position: she is outward, not homeward, bound in 1928, and homeward bound in 1969, not earlier. But it turns out she is not talking about herself but describing her shipmates; it is a Lithuanian woman who is eagerly "homeward bound" (513). In contrast, an Australian woman, a "redgold girlish ˙mother," "cannot bear to part" from her three unmarried adult daughters; she grows more and more nervous and distracted as the vessel journeys from Sydney along the Australian coast. Finally, before the ship ventures into transcontinental waters, the woman disembarks, willing to face ridicule and give back her going-away presents rather than leave a neurotic symbiosis with her daughters that prevents them and herself from growing up (513–14). Stead thus establishes her long exile as normal maturation, as independence, while she imagines home as a site of perverse self-enclosure, of a preoedipal mother-child union portrayed as monstrous rather than as Edenic.

Thus exile must be defined in terms of time as well as place. We know that we can't go home again, that childhood memories and the families of our youth no longer exist. The Australian mother on Stead's boat shows the ineluctability of this fact by her perversity in not recognizing it. For the geographic exile, the woman away from her native country, this sense of necessary estrangement from a childhood home is exaggerated: all three of these writers remained in exile most of their adult lives. When Stead returns to Australia, she reminisces about her childhood house: "I knew all that was gone; they had driven surveyors' pegs into the gardens" (515). Time, progress, and urbanization are vaguely personified here as "they," as all the forces that make history, the past outside ourselves, ungovernable. In the moment of returning, the former exile sees them all at once by understanding what is no longer there to see; the romantic vision flashes on the mind's eye in the blaze of its cumulative destruction. "In Australia I never lived in suburban or city streets, but with wide waters and skies, and this life expanded was coming home to me" (516), Stead writes, finding that she is more comfortable in the airplane than when she sets foot on Australian land. Whereas the other women from her plane shout to one another, "Isn't it good to be home?" (517), her own ambivalence is acute: in two sentences she worries the word *home* seven times: "Novalis said . . . that you must know many lands to be at home on earth; perhaps it is that you must be at home on earth to know many lands. A child in Australia, in the home of an active naturalist who . . . knew . . . keen stirring men and women who found their home on earth, I hearing of them, felt at home; this was my first, strongest feeling in babyhood. I have had many homes, am easily at home, requiring very little" (517). She requires little, perhaps protests too much: a childhood home that gives and requires very little may make one homeless and restless forever after. She describes an idea for a novel about a wandering man who "marries a stranger" "so that if he should cross the high bridge of air sometimes, going homewards, he is also on the outward path" (518). Such a childhood family and colonial origin, it seems, demagnetize one's inner compasses.

When Stead returns once again to England from Australia, going "outwards," she attends a dinner party at which someone asks her, "What was Australia like?" She answers, "It's the wonderful light." A Texan and an East Indian murmur, "Yes." She explains complacently, "three exiles. No more was said; and the others, Londoners, did not even know what we had understood" (519). Yet the natural splendor of southern climes glitters over a grim heritage to which the nostalgic exiles do not wish to return. "There is the melancholy," Stead says. "I knew as a girl that looking backward was not joy; the people dead of thirst, again the hatred of England. . . . the uneasiness and loneliness felt by Russians, US Americans, Brazilians, who with, at their backs, the spaces and untamed land, seek Paris, the Riviera and New York" (519). The freedom of the "untamed" and "unfinished" land in Australia inspires a melancholy of alienation, a quest to explore places and civilizations unknown. Although Stead blames the "uneasiness and loneliness" of colonials on their geography, her version of her childhood traces the boundless home that is everywhere and nowhere back to her father-dominated family: as "a child in Australia," she came from the "home of an active naturalist," who told her about other people who "found their home on earth" until she "felt at home," not in the cradle of family warmth but in the displacement of story, of "hearing of them." It is both the dislocations of home and the disabilities of exile, Stead implies, that enable her creativity: "Well, let us be discontented then; it has never hurt art," she concludes (520).

Lessing's discontent and alienation, her sense of homelessness, pervade her canon, from the gentle critique of nostalgia in "Flavours of Exile" to the cosmic homelessness of her space fiction. As it is for Stead, this discontent is empowering. Rage against the racist administration of southern Africa is one of the simpler forms that the energies of exile take for Lessing. This direct political attack, however, is complicated and deepened by nostalgia for "her" Africa, an Africa that never belonged to her yet whose loss she regrets. Even in "Flavours of Exile," in which she lampoons her mother for enjoying "the language of nostalgia" (576) and for thinking that nothing in Africa tastes like the food of her English memories because "the soil is no good" (578), the narrator's own nostalgia exactly parallels her mother's, albeit with the poles of Africa and England reversed. The vegetables from the African vegetable garden, she says, tasted "as I have never found vegetables taste since" (575); they form a part of her own "inheritance of veld and sun" (577).

Like Stead, Lessing expresses a nostalgia for the space of the colony as opposed to the civilization of the center, nostalgia not for home but for homelessness, for boundlessness. Returning to Africa by plane in 1956, Lessing records her feelings in a book entitled *Going Home*. Eleven years later, looking back at that trip, she sees herself in 1956 "in the position of someone coming from 'the centre'—which is the romantic way people living in outposts see people who live in London" (249). In 1956 her idealistic Rhodesian friends wanted her to tell them information from this "centre." Ironically, however, it is not news about English fashion or literature that they seek but instead facts about the Soviet Union that will enable them to deny Stalin's atrocities and so retain the faith in the "glories of the Russian revolution" that had sustained them in their isolated campaign against their colony's racism. In this context, the old categories of home and exile make no sense. Political allegiances obliterate them so that one's home is with comrades around the world, and one feels alien in one's native place when it is inhabited by the politically retrograde: "Your local conditions may be primitive—but somewhere is good, the truth, progress. Your neighbours think you are mad and treacherous kaffir lovers—but in other parts of the world you have friends. . . . No one should laugh at this, or think it childish who has not lived in a backwater full of neurotic and bigoted racists" (250). Here simple moral polarizations supersede those of locale. In the essay "Being Prohibited," reflecting on southern Africa after her 1956 visit, she claims that a "fault of the Left was that we continually ascribe our own intelligence and high-mindedness to our opponents." These opponents deserve no such consideration; they are "cynical oafs" even though they have managed to "keep a whole subcontinent in thrall" (156).

In *Going Home*, her vision is somewhat less simple. "Africa belongs to the Africans; the sooner they take it back the better," she pronounces righteously, then adds, "But—a country also belongs to those who feel at home in it" (8). Clearly she is claiming Africa as home, even though, to do so, she must momentarily perform the colonial trick of ignoring the very Africans whose rights she has just defended. She speaks of her ideals for Africa and of its effects on her, looking down from her plane at a "black-maned" landscape as natural and aloof as a beast: "a magnificent country, with all its riches in the future. Because it is so empty we can dream. We can dream of cities and a civilization more beautiful than anything that has been seen in the world before" (11). Her feelings for her childhood territory are proprietary, and, like Stead, she focuses on the light: "This was my air, my landscape, and above all, my sun" (8). She compares the full, hot African sun, "a creature of the same stuff as oneself; powerful and angry, but at least responsive," to the weak, "feminine" English sun (8), a "swollen, misshapen, watery ghost" (7). At least one sun, it seems, is a daughter; the African and English suns stand as alternate self-images implying angry colonial expression on one hand, estranged wandering on the other.

Lessing stops feeling her exile as estrangement, however. Despite her childhood rejection of England as part of her mother's stultifying and dead culture, within a year of her arrival she comes to feel that England is home rather than exile. By coming home to England rather than "going home" to Africa, she succeeds where her mother failed; she both repeats her mother's desire and triumphs over her mother. In a recent essay entitled "Impertinent Daughters," Lessing complains about her mother: "Had she, had my father, not escaped from England? Why, then, was she winding me back into that shroud?" (52–53). "I can't put myself in her place. It was the farm, the veld, that she hated, that trapped her. . . . But the farm, the veld, Africa is to me, quite simply, the luckiest thing that ever happened" (68). Thus Lessing uses her African home as leverage against the unhappy home her mother provided: "My memories of her are all of antagonism, and fighting, and feeling shut out" (61). By returning to England years ahead of her mother, she perhaps succeeds in shutting her mother out at the same time that she writes celebrations of Africa that confute her mother's tastes. Yet her mother is also responsible for enabling her daughter to write, for endowing her with the dominant culture, especially the English literary canon, as her heritage: "It was my mother who introduced me to the world of literature into which I was about to escape from her" (68).

Thus writing becomes both home and exile for these writers, marking their displacement from childhood homes but replacing them with intimate invention, with places of their own. All three authors carried manuscripts around with them for years from country to country. Lessing and Stead brought manuscripts for their first works from the colonies to England; Rhys saved story-filled notebooks for decades. Ford Madox Ford's mistress Stella Bowen reminisced about Rhys, "when we met her she possessed nothing but a cardboard suit-case and the astonishing manuscript," which was "an unpublishably sordid novel of great sensitiveness and persuasiveness" (166). Like children's teddy bears, the women's manuscripts remained extensions of themselves that reassured them about home, that *were* their homes, at the same time enabling them to repeat, reunderstand, and master the experience of exile. Lessing describes her early impressions of England: "During that first year in England, I had a vision of London I cannot recall now. Recently I found some pages I wrote then: it was a nightmare city that I lived in for a year; endless miles of heavy, damp, dead building on a dead, sour earth, inhabited by pale, misshapen, sunless creatures under a low sky of grey vapor. Then, one evening, walking across the park, the light welded buildings, trees and scarlet buses into something familiar and beautiful, and I knew myself to be at home. Now London is to me the pleasantest of cities, full of the most friendly and companionable people" (*Going Home*, 8).

The light, like exile, is what is seen and also what enables perception. Lessing claims that she cannot recall her first impressions of London and then tells them, not as remembered but as written, her own past text mediating between her present self and the reader to create the present text. The derided pale English sun nonetheless wields a magic light, powerful as an acetylene torch to weld "buildings, trees and scarlet buses" and make them "familiar," like a family, and hence both "beautiful" and populated with friendly people, so creating the comfort of "home."

Lessing's notation of exile has been safely acclimated to home in this passage. It is a passage friendly to her readers, non-threatening by claiming to repress everything truly unsettling in the original vision and protective through its double layer of words, those written then put in the service of those written now. Of the three authors discussed here, Rhys is perhaps the most powerful writer about exile precisely because she refuses to transform alienation into familiarity. Whereas Lessing joins us, so to speak, in smoothing over the discomfort of exile, letting us know that she can no longer feel it either, Rhys involves us rhetorically in reexperiencing an oscillation between home and exile that gives us no comfortable textual ground on which to settle, as we can see in the remarkable opening passage of her autobiographical novel, *Voyage in the Dark*.[3]

It was as if a curtain had fallen, hiding everything I had ever known. It was almost like being born again. The colours were different, the smells different, the feeling things gave you right down inside yourself was different. Not just the difference between heat, cold; light, darkness; purple, grey. But a difference in the way I was frightened and the way I was happy. I didn't like England at first. I couldn't get used to the cold. Sometimes I would shut my eyes and pretend . . . I was standing outside the house at home, looking down Market Street to the Bay. . . . (When the black women sell fishcakes. . . . They call out, "Salt fishcakes, all sweet an' charmin', all sweet an' charmin'.")
. . .

Sometimes it was as if I were back there and as if England were a dream. At other times England was the real thing and out there was the dream, but I could never fit them together (7–8).

This passage is considerably more disorienting than Lessing's. Whereas Lessing's "nightmare city" is safely on the other side of a curtain of repression, lost except for written memories, Rhys introduces a drama on a stage but does not reveal for a while which side of it we and the narrative are on: "It was as if a curtain had fallen." There is no waking from this nightmare; instead, both sides are a dream; nothing has become familiar, but all remains strange. Differences between past and present, between "there" and "here," exfoliate richly; difference itself is what matters, moving from visual differences outside the self to intimate differences in smells and feelings. The expected opposition between black and white, the one crucial social difference of life "there" in the West Indies, is temporarily evaded in favor of the more scenic, muted colors purple and gray. On the other side of the fallen "curtain" we see the lost home from which the narrator feels so cut off. Even in nostalgia for her warm, sensual Caribbean past, she places herself and our vicarious gaze not inside, within the family, but outside, where black women sell fishcakes "all sweet and charmin'." "Outside the house at home" may imply that her childhood sense of belonging is so great that it includes her entire island environment: she does not need to be in the house to be at home. Yet the phrase creates a slight jar, as though house and home are too easily separable, a possibility wryly hinted, even in this idyll, by the vision of escape from home past the market, where black and white women sell and are sold, out to the ocean. Much of the rest of the novel will detail Anna's futile efforts to find a home and her inability either to be nurtured by others or to nurture them, culminating in her perhaps fatal abortion.[4]

For these three colonial authors, then, exile can be an exhilarating release from the confines of a restrictive or rejecting home. At the same time, it can involve an alienating empowerment through loneliness, nostalgia, and defamiliarization. For each writer, the universal story of growing up and leaving home acquires political reverberations; the psychological drama of breaking from an idealized imaginary mother-daughter symbiosis into heterosexual adulthood gets conflated with this story of exile, with longings for freedom and yearnings for a maternal home. Each writer's individual psychology differs, as does her colonial placement—the nation of her upbringing, the date she comes to England, and the nature of the circles she sets up there—and so the specific solutions to exile vary, including Lessing's making a home for a while in a political party, Stead's making a home for his lifetime with an unusual man, and Rhys's ultimate internal exile, making herself almost a posthumous hermit in a Devonshire cottage. Yet for all three, for decades of productive literary lives in exile from the countries of their childhood, their writing provides their home, a safe arena from which they can both criticize nostalgia and use their own nostalgia in the service of social criticism.

Notes

1. Stead and Lessing arrived in London wanting to be writers; Rhys trained as an actor.
2. Compare Carolyn Heilbrun's concept of the double outsider (49).
3. An early version was Bowen's "sordid novel."
4. The original unpublished version specifies the hero's death.

Works Cited

Bowen, Stella. *Drawn from Life*. Maidstone, Kent: George Mann, 1974.
Heilbrun, Carolyn. *Reinventing Womanhood*. New York: Norton, 1979.
Lessing, Doris. "Being Prohibited." In *A Small Personal Voice: Essays, Reviews, Interviews*, edited by Paul Schlueter, 55–60. New York: Random House, 1975.
———. "Flavours of Exile." 1957. Reprinted in *African Stories*, 575–82. New York: Popular Library, 1965.

_____. *Going Home*. New York: Fawcett Popular Library, 1968.

_____. "Impertinent Daughters." *Granta*, no. 14 (Winter 1984): 51–68.

Rhys, Jean. "The Day They Burned the Books." 1960. Reprinted in *Tigers Are Better-Looking*, 41–48. New York: Popular Library, 1976.

_____. *Voyage in the Dark*. 1934. Reprint. New York: Popular Library, n.d.

_____. "Voyage in the Dark." Unpublished manuscript used with permission of the McFarlin Library, University of Tulsa, Tulsa, Oklahoma.

Stead, Christina. *For Love Alone*. 1944. Reprint. New York: Harcourt Brace Jovanovich, 1979.

_____. *Ocean of Story*. Edited by R. G. Geering. New York: Viking, 1985. "Les Amoureux," 503–12; "Another View of the Homestead," 513–20.

Chapter 6

. . . .

From Exile to Asylum

Religion and Community in the
Writings of Contemporary Black Women

Trudier Harris

oni Cade Bambara begins *The Salt Eaters* (1980) with a question: "Are you sure, sweetheart, that you want to be well?" The question is addressed to Velma Henry, an emotionally abused wife and community activist who has slit her wrists and stuck her head in a gas oven in an attempt to find a place of safety for herself. Minnie Ransom, a self-styled folk healer who works with the medical doctors of the Southwest Community Infirmary in Claybourne, Georgia, is the person who puts the question to Velma. Velma's aborted attempt at self-destruction has landed her in the infirmary and in a somewhat surrealistic scene. The healer and the young activist sit on stools facing each other, with Minnie holding on to Velma, while a lay prayer circle (representing the signs of the zodiac) surrounds them; a group of doctors observes as Minnie encourages Velma to find deep within herself the will to live. What has brought Velma to that stool and her confrontation/interaction with Minnie is in many ways the history of black women characters in contemporary Afro-American fiction; what will get her off the stool and into health again is one possible future predicted for these women. Minnie has the unenviable responsibility of convincing Velma that life can be good and healthy, that there can be peace even in turmoil, and that only Velma can determine what and how she will *be* in the world.

How to *be* in the world has religious and feminist implications, many of which show Velma's kinship with previous characterizations of black females and how those former categories will not serve to define her. Bambara's vision and philosophy in *The Salt Eaters* are universal and cosmic, as well as individual and communal. She suggests that a variety of forces and beliefs—God, Christianity, the loa, Iching, rootwork, and many, many other systems of thought—should be drawn upon in finding self and in making that self harmonious with the forces around it. She also suggests, in contrast to some of her contemporary sisters, that black women should not isolate themselves from black men in the finding of self. Bambara's vision, therefore, is at once revolutionary and traditional. Velma and Minnie communing on their stools and having out-of-body experiences are unlike anything that black female characters have experienced before in the literature, but what they engage in is also religious and is very much like what many characters have undergone before.

Traditionally, religion has meant devotion to a supreme—frequently invisible though sometimes represented by icons—being or beings in relation to whom human beings recognize an innate inferiority. Humans pray to that being to intercede in the course of their affairs and generally recognize that they are powerless and that the otherworldly force is omnipotent. It would be blasphemous to attribute to the self power equal to the supreme being's or to attempt to reduce that supreme being to a human level. Traditionally, religion presupposes inequity—a supplicant and a Power to grant the wishes of the supplicant. Although Christianity has historically been the form of religion most frequently practiced in black communities, it is not the guiding force for contemporary black women writers. Bambara is the exception in using it along with other beliefs, but generally these writers redefine religion as a means of showing devotion toward and communing with the self, with other women, with nature, and with the expansive forces of the universe. Morality becomes a principle that evolves from the individual rather than from the community; it cannot be superimposed by external strictures. The center is the human being, not a supreme being, and the forms of prayer are as much self-valuing and self-appreciation as they are appreciation for anything or anyone else. Loving the self enough to save the self from destructive social and political forces becomes as religious as praying to God. That is what Velma Henry must discover.

Velma's attempt to find safety in annihilation, which is imaged as a glass jar with a top on it, from which she can see out but into which no disturbances can come, is not unlike the path to safety that was taught to black women historically and mirrored in that institution in which they sought safety: the black church. From the pains of scrubbing white women's floors and the confrontations with husbands who took out their anger at white men on them, black women crawled into the sanctuary of the church, in which they envisioned another way of being. Membership within the Protestant church community meant spiritual death for most black women, however, for they gave their labor and sacrificed to male egos any desires for self-fulfillment they may have had; they were taught to put God, their husbands, and their children before themselves. Their vision of sanctuary, therefore, could be fully realized only in their deaths; only heaven could solve all the problems of the world. As a prelude, they settled for the myth of sanctuary in their numbers in the church.

As many social observers have noted, however, even when black women made up 70 to 90 percent of the congregations, their power was never consonant with their numbers. Indeed, they found themselves within a peculiar exile even in the church. They may have sold fried chicken and fish dinners to support the church financially, or furthered its programs by tending the sick and executing other tasks of various church clubs, but they were essentially powerless, resigned to doing "women's work" for a massive body represented figuratively and literally by a male head. They found it necessary in the early twentieth century to institutionalize a "Woman's Day" to give focus to their concerns. That institution, though, did not win them equal recognition within the church, for frequently their speakers could not ascend the pulpit to deliver their messages and their programs might be relegated to chapels or fellowship halls.

That traditional view of woman's place in the church, of her efforts to find safety where there is none, is no more vividly reflected than in James Baldwin's *Go Tell It on the Mountain* (1953). Elizabeth, Florence, and Deborah Grimes are all women who have cried out to a masculine God to provide some sanctuary for them. What they find is a church tradition that exiles them to the status of sinners or object lessons on the consequences of sin. The voices of male preachers intone the wrath of a masculine God in consigning women to lesser spaces and value in the church because of their assumed innate impurity. The negative position of women is memorialized in a sermon Gabriel Grimes delivers: "For let us remember that the wages of sin is death; that it is written, and cannot fail, the soul that sinneth, it shall die. Let us remember that we are born in sin, in sin did our mothers conceive us—sin reigns in all our members, sin is the foul heart's natural liquid, sin looks out of the eye, amen, and leads to lust, sin is in the hearing of the ear, and leads to folly, sin sits on the tongue, and leads to murder. Yes! Sin is the only heritage of the natural man, sin bequeathed us by our natural father, that fallen Adam, whose apple sickens and will sicken all generations living, and generations yet unborn!" (103–4). Men can be forgiven for their sins through prayer, but women are united by their nature in a movable island of sin; they cannot transcend their exile.

Deborah, gang-raped by a group of white men when she is seventeen, becomes the object of community scorn and Gabriel Grimes's objective correlative for his own piety—he marries the defiled woman who no other man in the community would touch and thereby elevates her into permanent exile in the front pew of his little fundamentalist church (the front pew could be mistaken for a station of honor in this instance, but it is also the site of the traditional "mourners' bench," where sinners cry out before God and the preacher for purification of their unclean states). Deborah has stature only in direct proportion to her willingness to acquiesce in her exile by reading loudly the scriptural passages Gabriel occasionally requests of her. The rape makes the community view her as untouchable and as somehow responsible for her own defilement ("Since she could not be considered a woman, she could only be looked on as a harlot, a source of delight more bestial and mysteries more shaking than any a proper woman could provide" [73]). Elizabeth, Gabriel's second wife, is taught to feel that giving birth before marriage is similarly the sin for which she must make perpetual atonement; her guilt places her squarely in front of the altar, in a permanent stoop between the need to feel guilty and private, stubborn defiance. Such stubborn defiance is also the fate of Florence, Gabriel's sister, who is consigned to hell by her brother and others because she decided to leave her home and a dying mother to pursue some other way of being in the world, some way that would not necessitate bending the self to the will of the men around her. Unfortunately, the guilt that permeates the environment in which she lives eventually claims her, and she ends up being just as exiled from her self as the other women who look to the church for sanctuary. Historically, being in the church meant identifying with a huge circle of women who surrounded but were yet cut off from the small circle of men who controlled things, as well as from the male God to whom they were taught to pray for transformation of the fallen state they had all inherited from Eve. They were guilty by sex and exiled by the power of that guilt to exert its influence upon their lives. Baldwin's women, too guilty and insecure to follow Velma Henry's attempt at suicide, die little deaths every day.

Baldwin's black female characters share religious kinship with Mama Lena Younger in Lorraine Hansberry's *A Raisin in the Sun* (1959). For Mama Lena, God is the center of her being; if doing His Will separates her from her family, so be it, for God offers more sanctuary than they ever can. Certainly she exhibits belief in God when she high-handedly responds to her daughter's atheism, but there is also fear in being unsafe. When Beneatha Younger declares that she is going to be a doctor, Mama Lena retorts: "Course you going to be a doctor, honey, God willing," to which Beneatha replies, "God hasn't got a thing to do with it" (38). She maintains that God is not necessary and that she is sick and tired of hearing about Him: "Mama, you don't understand. It's all a matter of ideas, and God is just one idea I don't accept. It's not important. I am not going out and be immoral or commit crimes because I don't believe in God. I don't even think about it. It's just that I get tired of Him getting credit for all the things the human race achieves through its own stubborn effort. There simply is no blasted God—there is only man and it is he who makes miracles!" (39). The mother, who is now in her sixties, and who has worked throughout her life to make sure her children appreciated God, rises and "powerfully" slaps her daughter's face. But this blasphemy demands more than a mere slap; the mother stands tall before her daughter and forces her to repeat the following sentence: "In my mother's house there is still God" (39). Beneatha dares to suggest another way of being in the world, one predicated upon man's ability to achieve things "through his own stubborn efforts," a view that writers following Hansberry would find particularly appealing; for Mama Lena and other women who have preserved the sanctuary of the church, even when they may have had constant evidence that that sanctuary was a fiction, are unable and unwilling to let go of that image of safety.

These women have to learn what Velma eventually discovers: there is no safety except in the self; there is no savior except the self. But Velma discovers that only after she has been through an extensive period of long-suffering and self-sacrifice that is almost identical in its suicidal tendencies to those exhibited by the earlier characters. Between Elizabeth Grimes and Velma Henry, however, there are a large number of characters who try to expand the way of being in the world, who realize that their communities are both smaller and larger than the traditional church, that if they would be healthy, they must reject Christianity with its masculine God and forge for themselves a new kind of religion, a new kind of communion, with a community of women. Therefore, ideas that would have been blasphemous to Baldwin's and Hansberry's characters become the norm for characters in works by more recent black women writers.

Initially, in a direct violation of traditional edicts to serve, many of these characters put self-fulfillment above self-sacrifice; they do not value husbands, or lovers, or children in the way that traditional conceptions of Christianity and community among black people have dictated. Most important, they nullify the dichotomy of good and evil, and they strongly deny that working in God's vineyard on earth could lead to any reward in heaven. Toni Morrison, Alice Walker, Paule Marshall, Ntozake Shange, and Gloria Naylor all create characters who show clearly that the Elizabeth Grimeses of the world were long-suffering fools. These recent characters are as egocentric as any heathen would be judged to be in the traditional Christian scheme of things, and the communities with which they are concerned may be as small as a single individual.

Self-fulfillment is a major theme in the works of these writers, especially the novelists, and their characters frequently fight their families, friends, and communities in an effort to commune with themselves. For example, Morrison's *Sula* (1973) is concerned with the ways the personality of the title character is stifled by interaction with people in a small-town community. How the community judges her has its basis in Christianity—evil Sula explains the "fourth face of God"—but there is no physical, and ultimately no moral, constraint exerted by a church. When Sula lets Chicken Little slip from her hands to his death in the river, her refusal to share that information with the representatives of the moral forces in her community separates her forever from them; it places that action in the light of her experimental life, her intense curiosity, her understandable desire to explore to the fullest whatever situation she finds herself in. When she puts Eva in an old folks' home, that, too, must be evaluated from a perspective that is more puzzling than dichotomous. Evil actions in *Sula* defy the test of an absolute morality superimposed upon them; and yet possibilities for determining evil do exist. They center upon violation of community and destruction of family trust rather than upon God and the Bible.

Marshall's *Praisesong for the Widow* (1983) also emphasizes the effects of traditional morality and community expectations on a middle-class black woman. Avey Johnson gives up love and laughter for respectability, financial security, and—after her husband's death—extended cruises until she realizes that her pristine existence leaves her waterlogged with the pressure of unfulfillment. She deserts her friends on a cruise and ends up on a Caribbean island where she recovers herself in ceremonies (dances and prayers to African ancestors) that would be judged pagan and immoral. She must reject traditional Western, Christian notions of appropriateness to save herself.

Contemporary black women writers also frequently deal with topics that are not conducive to the traditional worldview as reflected in most black churches. Questionable death—murder or involuntary manslaughter—is one such topic. Sula finds her means of friendship in the bond created between herself and her girlfriend Nel when she kills Chicken Little. Though the drowning is technically an accident, it nevertheless serves as a positive expression of the tie the girls share, one that cannot be broken even in Sula's death. Celie in Alice Walker's *The Color Purple* (1982) and Myrtle Black in Ann Allen Shockley's *Say Jesus and Come to Me* (1982) introduce lesbianism as another one of those taboo subjects for the black church. By allowing women to find fulfillment with other women, rather than with men or with God, Walker and Shockley continue the iconoclasm characteristic of many contemporary black women writers.

In addition to lesbianism, other forms of free love, promiscuity, and traditional infidelity engage the attention of these writers. When Mary Helen Washington advocated the destruction of the "sacred cow" image of black female character in her 1975 introduction to *Black-Eyed Susans*, she might have been envisioning the women in *Sula* as varieties of that welcome change. Eva, Hannah, and Sula all exhibit "manlove" and all are outside the usual confines of marriage. Hannah, who needs "some touching every day" (Morrison, 44), teaches her daughter that sex is casual and uncomplicated; one does not need the commitment of romantic love or marriage to enjoy it. Later, Sula expresses herself, confronts her innermost identity, only after having sexual relationships with married men in her town. This culminates in her having an affair with Jude, Nel's husband. She is unapologetic and unrepentant about her actions, and, ultimately, Morrison does not pass a moral judgment upon her or the other characters. That is perhaps what distinguishes Morrison most clearly from her literary predecessors; although she has commented in interviews that she sees Sula as the personification of evil, she consistently refuses to superimpose a moral vision upon her or other of her characters; they must find one for themselves. Her stance is in marked contrast to Baldwin's in *Go Tell It on the Mountain*, in which the ironic voice of the narrator lets us know that Baldwin disapproves of the actions of Gabriel Grimes and that there is a measure of moral censure being passed on Florence Grimes. Morrison allows her characters to be and to do as they wish; the only consequences they experience are the ones they heap upon themselves (the community may attempt to ostracize them, but they finally decide to "let evil run its course").

Morrison's female characters show that the church is too small to contain them, and the community can only exert the power of gossip over them; it has no means effectively to censure them, and they refuse to respond to any suggested restraints. Indeed, Ann Allen Shockley and Alice Walker picture their characters in the church and either departing from it or violating its strictures. In *Say Jesus and Come to Me*, Shockley portrays Myrtle Black assuming the traditional role usually assigned to males in black churches, that of the spiritual leader. She travels from town to town as an evangelist, selecting ripe young women from each congregation to seduce. She thereby explodes the myth of safety for black women in the church by being explicit about the violation by spiritual leaders that some observers have hinted at historically. Shockley makes it clear that she is not interested in portraying the expected (as early as 1974, when most black writers considered lesbianism taboo in their works, Shockley had been explicit in the treatment of a love affair between a black woman and a white woman in *Loving Her*). She, more directly than Walker, posits that conventional ways of seeing within black churches must be altered. She takes the church environment that created pain for so many of Baldwin's characters and introduces elements into it that Baldwin's women could not begin to imagine. She shows the strictures of the church and ultimately makes her vision much larger than anything it has to offer; for her, women who would commune with each other must not merely imitate men, for by so doing they end up being as exploitive as their male counterparts. They must transform the church environment, not merely step into its traditional posts of power, for God is oppression, not love. Consequently, Shockley ends her story romantically by having Myrtle settle into a monogamous relationship with a famous blues singer and by having her declare her lesbianism from her pulpit.

Walker also portrays Celie as beginning in the church and finding it unsatisfactory; her move is also toward a transforming love relationship. She attends church during her stepfather's sexual abuse of her and during the resulting two pregnancies, but she finds little sympathy there. Like many black women before her, she has gone looking for a haven and found herself in exile not only from the males in the church but from the females as well. She tries to win favors by performing chores—cleaning floors and windows, making communion wine, and washing altar linen. The minister may compliment her on the quality of her work, but it ultimately does not elevate her in the sight of the women or her husband. This early training in rejection may be viewed as one reason Celie has little difficulty leaving the church later on—in becoming a pot smoker and engaging in an atypical love relationship, steps that may initially seem incredible in her progression. But in the absence of the ability to commune with women in the church or in the community, Celie must look for another haven. She finds it in Shug, who acts as the Minnie Ransom figure for her by teaching her how to love herself enough to reach for a nontraditional self-fulfillment. Shug inspires Celie to see that she has within herself the power to save herself; God is distant if not superfluous. From this perspective, then, we might say that Celie moves from the absence of communion in the church to communion in a lesbian, religious relationship, in another one of the contemporary redefinitions or discoveries of the possibilities of being in the world. Celie's twenty years of faithful membership in a church have neither brought her peace nor any closer to God; her brief time with Shug brings her peace and a definition of God as an It that dwells in all of us, the core of potential that Ntozake Shange uncovered in *For Colored Girls*.

Celie has tried in her own way, in the structure of the novel, to redefine that distant God. When she is raped at fourteen, she tells her story by writing letters to God—the traditional white-haired, white male visualization. That act may be viewed as an attempt to redefine what God *should* mean to such an abused human being. God becomes her confidant because there is no one on earth in whom Celie can confide. Her mother is ill and eventually dies, and she is too much the country bumpkin even to think of telling her minister what has happened to her. Therefore, God becomes playmate, sister, mother, friend, and psychiatrist. Certainly He has played those roles to others, notably to Mariah Upshur in Sarah E. Wright's *This Child's Gonna Live* (1969); what is different about Celie casting God in those roles is that she expects Him to sympathize with her when she is raped, but, more important, to approve of her lesbian affair with Shug. God, then, is not the vengeful God of the Old Testament, ever ready to rain down fire and brimstone, or even the One who tempered mercy with justice in the New Testament; rather, He is a mirror to whom Celie holds up things that distress her and with whom she celebrates things that please her. She recreates the traditional God in the image of her own suffering until Shug teaches her how to reconceptualize God within herself. She asks very little of the God to whom she writes other than that He be quiet and let her tell it as it has happened to her. She does not expect Him to come into her life and change her condition; nor does she expect that her life is one that the traditional God would be interested in enough to want to change. She accepts God as one-way communication, from earth to heaven, until Shug teaches her that another possibility exists.

Celie's attitude reflects Walker's and Morrison's to the extent that it focuses on the individual's problems and lets the larger philosophical and religious questions take second place to the plight of the individual trying to find a place and a space to live in this world; this recentering of the individual reflects the very image of Velma and Minnie sitting on their stools communing with each other. Religion evolves out of the personal situation; it is not superimposed upon human experience. If we were to compare, for example, Walker's treatment of the incestuous relationship in *The Color Purple* with the one Baldwin treats in *Just Above My Head* (1979), sharp differences would emerge. While both are depicted as repulsive acts, an aura of censure surrounds the relationship in Baldwin's novel, and the neighbors stand ready to pass moral judgment on Joe Miller and his daughter Julia. Walker, on the other hand, is concerned only with the effect of the relationship on Celie. Julia Miller's incestuous affair with Joel will have meaning for her father, her brother, her extended family, and the neighbors. The abuse of Celie is of interest because it is a step in her claiming her life for herself; how others respond is finally unimportant. Again, the problems of Walker's characters are individual, whereas those painted by Baldwin are the communal ones that reflect the moral values of the persons in that community.

Communion with the self and with other women is the pattern for most black female characters appearing in works after the mid-1970s. This communion becomes devotion, a love that borders upon worship and hence further recovers the meaning of religion. Ntozake Shange destroyed the image of man as god in *For Colored Girls Who Have Considered Suicide When the Rainbow is Enuf* (1976) by making her male characters into perpetrators of evil who beat their wives and girlfriends and kill their children; in reaction to such abuse, the women do not pray to God, whom they align vicariously with their abusers. Instead, they turn to each other in feminine solidarity against the masculine forces of evil. They give up the heterosexual community for a community of women. The comfort they find is located within themselves. At the end of the play, the women stand in a circle with their arms around each others' waists and lament the excessive "laying on of bodies" that has not resulted in salvation for any of them; they insist that they need a "laying on of hands," and those hands can only be female. Together they declare: "i found god in myself & i loved her" (67).

Salvation for black women, Shange and other writers assert, lies within restructuring the process of salvation—out of the church and into the hands of other women, sometimes in lesbian relationships, sometimes in healing relationships that transcend sexuality. The general premise is that black women are abused; more often than not, their abusers are black men. Therefore, they cannot find salvation in anything masculine.

That pattern is equally clear in Gloria Naylor's *The Women of Brewster Place* (1982). The women form a community against the abuses of men, and they find salvation within themselves or mirrored in the inspiration of other women; they survive the physical, spiritual, and emotional isolation of Brewster Place by looking outward to their sisters and inward to their own strengths. Mattie Michael becomes the healing force in the lives of many of the women in the seven sketches in the novel. Having known pain herself, and having discovered that she could turn to no one but herself, Mattie offers her experience in pain and understanding of its consequences to the women who suffer around her. When Mattie's prized son Basil, for whom she had given up her family and any life not including him, disappears rather than face a trial—and thereby causes her to lose the house she has put up for his bond—she sits trembling but resolute in her kitchen when she understands that he is gone for good. There is no howling out to God, no railing about why this had to happen to her, for she finally knows that her son has been dipped from the same vat of irresponsibility as his good-timing father; instead, she moves to Brewster Place and goes on with her life.

Although Mattie goes to church, that part of her life is not extensively dramatized within the novel. We do see her, however, providing the comfort that is so necessary for her fellow sufferers. Her actions are certainly religious, even if we cannot attach Christianity to them. For example, she is devoted, loyal, and understanding of her friend Etta's sometimes promiscuous behavior with men. When Etta uses a trip to church with Mattie as the occasion to form yet another disastrous liaison, Mattie does not criticize her or pass moral judgment on her; rather, she sits like the wise woman of the world as Etta discovers her mistake for herself, and she greets Etta's downtrodden return the next morning with the most soothing sound she can effect: playing the Billie Holiday records that Etta so loves. Without touching and without condemning, Mattie succeeds in being a holy ghost, a comforter, to Etta.

For Ciel, granddaughter of the generous woman who had taken Mattie and Basil in when they desperately needed a shelter, Mattie comforts through touching, and she becomes, thereby, a healer in the tradition of Minnie Ransom. If one of the functions of religion is indeed to comfort, to heal, to help people live with their troubles, then certainly what Mattie does for Ciel is religious. Twice rejected by her husband, Eugene, Ciel helps him pack for yet another departure. While they are out of the room, their young daughter is electrocuted. That experience leaves Ciel numb, anorexic, and tearless, conditions that she hopes will lead eventually to her own death. Like Velma Henry, she seeks the ultimate safety from pain. Mattie enters in a healing, saving role, the god-as-woman idea in a slightly altered form. She, like Minnie Ransom, must save the sufferer from herself and encourage her to want to live again. Mattie does that not by calling on Jesus but by tying Ciel's suffering to some of the most excruciating mother-loss that females have ever suffered. She takes her in her arms (the laying on of hands) and rocks her, as Minnie Ransom does Velma Henry, from death-in-life to a desire to live:

> Mattie rocked her out of that bed, out of that room into a blue vastness just underneath the sun and above time. She rocked her over Aegean seas so clean they shone like crystal, so clear the fresh blood of sacrificed babies torn from their mother's arms and given to Neptune could be seen like pink froth on the water. She rocked on and on, past Dachau, where soul-gutted Jewish mothers swept their children's entrails off laboratory floors. They flew past the spilled brains of Senegalese infants whose mothers had dashed them on the wooden sides of slave ships. And she rocked on.
>
> She rocked her into her childhood and let her see murdered dreams. And she rocked her back, back into the womb, to the nadir of her hurt, and they found it—a slight silver splinter, embedded just below the surface of the skin. And Mattie rocked and pulled—and the splinter gave way, but its roots were deep, gigantic, ragged, and they tore up flesh with bits of fat and muscle tissue clinging to them. They left a huge hole, which was already starting to pus over, but Mattie was satisfied. It would heal. (Naylor, 103–4)

Ciel begins her healing process by regurgitating, getting the physical and emotional poison out of her system—not unlike Velma's growling and grunting when the first stirrings of renewal begin in her. Then Mattie bathes her like a baby. Finally, Ciel begins to cry. This process of rebirth, of transformation, may have its parallel in Christianity, but the impetus is far from that source. Ciel's reclaiming of self after tragedy is comparable to Avey Johnson's transformation in *Praisesong for the Widow* when she finds the strength—through the caring hands of women who help her during a storm and through another who bathes her after she has soiled herself—to overcome the tragedy of having spent years in wasteful activity. For Ciel, Mattie holds the keys to spiritual and physical rebirth. Through her own caring and concern, she encourages Ciel to look within herself for that bit of human desire, no matter how tiny, that makes it possible for people to live in this world in spite of the pain they have suffered.

The images that Naylor uses to describe the healing process are not only outside Christianity but outside black American culture as well. They are images that unite suffering women across history, races, and cultures—the women who, for whatever irrational reason, have seen their children die or have been forced to kill them. The identification with

women, through motherhood, is the means of growing again; that community is thus once again larger than the church and larger than the
Christian God. No male God need tell women how to grieve for their
children or can comfort them in an experience He has never known. The
loss of a child is what ties Ciel and Mattie together, and that is what ties all
of those suffering women of the world together.

Ciel and Mattie, Shug and Celie, the women in *For Colored Girls*, and
Nel and Sula all end up forming their communities and saving themselves
in reaction to something, men in the first three cases and grown-ups in
general in the case of Nel and Sula. Velma Henry also ends up in the
Southwest Infirmary and in Minnie Ransom's hands because of something that has happened to her. Unlike Mattie's healing of Ciel, or Shug's
healing of Celie, which form parts of their stories, Bambara's *The Salt
Eaters* is the story of a healing. Once the doctors have attended to Velma's
physical wounds, Minnie tries to bring her back to a desire for life after
she has been overworked, cheated on, used, abused, and disrespected.
Desire is most important here as earlier; Minnie can do little for Velma
unless she *wants* to be healed. Therefore, a major part of Minnie's role is
convincing Velma of the need to go on living, then helping her as much as
she can once she starts the journey back from her wandering, dreamlike
state.

In their redefinitions of the religious, Minnie and Velma break down the
inequity between natural and supernatural. Velma must uncover the power
within herself to save herself, a power exemplified in her ability to traipse
off through the universe, into the past as well as into the future, in
evaluating her life and what saving it will mean for her community. She has
as much power within herself as that assigned to any traditional God, and
Minnie, similarly empowered, acts as the guide to Velma's uncovery of her
own resources. Together, they form a community of communion that
resembles the prayer circle around them as well as many of the events
going on in the larger community. Velma is the key to the healing of the
community and its many political schisms; when she uncovers the supreme power within herself, she can return to her activist work without the
possibility of it driving her to a gas oven again.

The individual, for Bambara, as for Naylor and Walker, holds the key to
healing or saving herself. Far removed from the likes of Elizabeth Grimes
and her brand of suffering black womanhood, Minnie and Velma advocate
no conversions in the traditional Christian sense; the changes these
women undergo may equal in power some of the traditional conversions,

such as those described in George Rawick's *God Struck Me Dead*, but they are nonetheless based in the individuals' drawing upon their own resources—through the help of those in this world who are immediately available and who care about them—and not upon God.

Some of the techniques used in Bambara's novel, however, might seem as otherworldly as speaking in tongues. Minnie has out-of-body experiences with her supernatural companion/guide, Old Wife, who is invisible to all except Minnie and who seems at best to be a ghost. And even Velma has her own share of extranatural experiences. The community of women being defined in *The Salt Eaters*, therefore, is natural as well as supernatural. Yet none of it is frightening. Bambara has drawn upon beliefs more ancient in black and Third World communities than is Christianity to make her case for a new breed of religious experience. Her incorporation of extensive research into the creation of memorable, fascinating characters makes her story convincing.

Though they may have the universe at their disposal, Bambara's characters search for a way to live on earth; they do not defer the temporal for the extraterrestrial. Nadeen, one of the spectators in the infirmary room where Minnie is communing with Velma, observes at one point a peculiar transformation in Velma's physical appearance and concludes: "Whatever it was that had fallen away was showing her another way to be in the world" (104). Sophie, Velma's godmother, recognizes too that the young people need some way "to be in the world, to move about, to explain things, to make up things to go on living blind. In time [rather than eternity]. And in time Velma would find her way back to the roots of life. And in doing so, be a model" (147). Velma's eventual "conversion" to life, her stepping away from the door that would take her to death, that final haven for Christians, solidifies the argument for *being* in the world. Her rise from the stool at the end of the novel, presaging a healthy future for her, is pictured as emergence from a cocoon, an image that suggests the ability of the confined to effect its/her own birth/freedom. The cocoon image also evokes connotations of the legendary phoenix, which reproduces itself from its own ashes in a two-thousand-year cycle.

Velma, like all her fictional sisters, has clearly found a way to move beyond the traditional meaning of church and religion; she and Minnie can "worship" with the blues or with other forms of music. Clearly, too, these women have found something to alleviate the pain of their lives and to rectify their isolation and punishment within the traditional structure of the church. But in establishing their new—sometimes larger, sometimes smaller—communities, have they reached an asylum and/or created a new form of exile? Is there any room for men in the spaces these women re-create? For children? For women who are still married, with children, and attending church?

The majority of these women would respond that they have created an asylum, but the physical geography and the prospects for the future frequently suggest otherwise. Certainly the women in Brewster Place commune with each other, love each other, help each other, but no men are admitted to the society they finally forge. Ciel's husband, Eugene, is so subdued by the censoring judgment of the women around his wife that he refuses to attend his daughter's funeral. Old Ben has been smashed to death by Lorraine, the lesbian woman he has befriended but who mistakes him for one of the young men who has raped her. Communion with men is not possible on Brewster Place, and even the place itself is deteriorating; as we applaud the survival strategies of the women who live there, we are mindful of Naylor's benediction for it. The place dies, and whatever the women have forged is relegated to memory; their temporary asylum cannot reproduce itself.

Nor can that of the women in *Sula, For Colored Girls,* or *The Color Purple.* Nel has Sula, then for twenty-five years after Sula's death, she is alone, unfulfilled, reduced to seeking a traditional place of service in the church; her realization that she has missed Sula instead of her husband all those years leaves her with "circles and circles of sorrow," a pain that locks her into communion with her dead friend but is ultimately too late to offer a way for her to be in the world. She is permanently exiled to sorrow. The women at the end of Shange's play are alone with their affirmation and their misery, looking toward some unstated fulfillment; they are clear about what is missing from their lives, but they are not equally clear about what menless futures will entail. Shug and Celie may be clear about what the future holds for them, but that future necessarily isolates them from men except on platonic or mothering levels; Celie and Albert may sit and sew together, and Celie may serve as mother to her returned Adam, but the female community, like the one in Shange's play, advocates asylum/exile that presages communal extinction (at least as far as these individuals would be *directly* involved in its continuation).

The same is true of Myrtle Black and her lover in *Say Jesus and Come to Me.* Although Myrtle is much more tolerant of men, especially homosexuals, than the women in *Brewster Place* or *For Colored Girls,* she is also instrumental in creating a new community of acceptability; invariably, some will be included and others will be exiled. The peace she has earned for herself by her heroic announcement of her lesbianism has not been tested in the fire; her lover's fans and her congregation (though initially accepting) could turn upon them, and they will be reduced to a community of two, perhaps more exile than asylum.

What the women in most of these works have discovered is a formula for how *not* to be, how not to live in the world, and, except for Celie and Shug, they spend brief periods on how to live. The being they have sought is envisioned primarily as what they lack; they know that being deserted by sons and lovers or beaten by husbands is not a way to live, and they know that the church has not afforded them any safety or provided any satisfactory model of living to them. Of course, we could say that the progression to a realization of the lack and a rejection of current circumstances are sufficient, that the works only define what is wrong with present states of being, and that that analysis is enough; we could stress process rather than completion. After all, the struggles of these women have been individual, and for the sake of female community, not for the community at large. Certainly women with women can grow in spiritual ways and sustain each other artistically, but once they have reached the stages of bliss and creativity, what new challenges are available to them, either personally or in perpetuating their communities? Will they occasionally allow men into their midst only long enough to donate sperm for the continuation of the female communities? Will they coexist without cohabitation with men? Most of the writers leave the women, as Toni Morrison leaves Milkman Dead in *Song of Solomon*, poised on a precipice of self-growth and self-understanding, uncertain as to exactly what those startling discoveries will mean for the future.

Of all the writers discussed here, only Toni Cade Bambara envisions a world in which asylum cannot be equated with exile and women saving themselves need not sever themselves forever from the society of men or from the larger goals of black communities. Bambara projects Velma into the future so that she envisions clearly what her place in that larger society will be. Community activism is possible without the self-destructive side; equality between the sexes does not mean separation between them; marriage is possible without either partner being diminished thereby; and children are the responsibility of the entire community. Though utopian in some of its particulars, the choice Bambara offers for total community is finally more appealing than the more uncertain, if sometimes more realistic, endings of the other works. Bambara's utopia has a stronger base in the possible, for example, than even Shockley's suggestion that homophobia will pale in the face of true homosexual love.

Paradoxically, Bambara's aggressively innovative worldview reflects the most traditional politics in reference to the writer's place within and commitment to his or her community. Bambara clearly sees her novel as offering a corrective, healing force to a community splintered by the civil rights and black arts movements and stagnating in the wake of their accomplishments. In contrast, Walker, Shange, and Naylor are all concerned with some subset of those larger black communities and do not exhibit concerns that transfer easily to all of them. From this perspective, they create one of the schisms Bambara observes, for they put their energies to work for a fraction of the group rather than for the whole. Such focus separates them from the self-generated cosmic energies and extranatural forces that could inspire them to forge healthy psychic links with all segments of their black communities. Rather than exile herself from the illnesses that would lead husbands to desert or brutalize their wives or stepfathers to violate their daughters, Bambara embraces them all in an effort to encourage the spiritual survival, the survival whole, as Alice Walker once said, of all black people. In effecting such a large vision, black people, Bambara would probably assert, no matter the impetus to such actions, can never afford to exile themselves from other black people.

Works Cited

Baldwin, James. *Go Tell It on the Mountain*. New York: Dell, 1953.

————. *Just Above My Head*. New York: Dial, 1979.

Bambara, Toni Cade. *The Salt Eaters*. 1980. Reprint. New York: Vintage, 1981.

Hansberry, Lorraine. *A Raisin in the Sun*. New York: Signet/New American Library, 1959.

Marshall, Paule. *Praisesong for the Widow*. 1983. Reprint. New York: Dutton, 1984.

Morrison, Toni. *Song of Solomon*. New York: Knopf, 1977.

————. *Sula*. 1973. Reprint. New York: Plume/New American Library, 1982.

Naylor, Gloria. *The Women of Brewster Place*. 1982. Reprint. New York: Penguin, 1983.

Rawick, George. *God Struck Me Dead: Religious Conversion Experiences and Autobiographies of Negro Ex-Slaves*. Nashville: Social Science Institute, Fisk University, 1945.

Shange, Ntozake. *For Colored Girls Who Have Considered Suicide When the Rainbow Is Enuf.* 1976. Reprint. New York: Bantam, 1980.

Shockley, Ann Allen. *Say Jesus and Come to Me.* 1982. Reprint. Tallahassee: Naiad Press, 1987.

Walker, Alice. *The Color Purple.* 1982. Reprint. New York: Washington Square Press, 1983.

Washington, Mary Helen, ed. *Black-Eyed Susans: Classic Stories by and about Black Women.* Garden City, N.Y.: Anchor/Doubleday, 1975.

Wright, Sarah E. *This Child's Gonna Live.* New York: Delacorte, 1969.

"I Dreamed Again That I Was Drowning"

Annette Kolodny

4 A.M., May 9, 1978

The water is cold. My clothes cling to me in layers, weighting me down. Every part of my body is chilled and none of my exertions warm me. Around me the water is dark and choppy, but there is still light—it seems to be early evening—and I can see for some distance. What I see are shores on two sides. On one there is a road where cars pass too quickly for the drivers to catch any glimpse of me. On the other there is a paved walkway, parallel to the water, but no one comes just now. I am trying desperately to swim toward the walkway shore, but a current keeps me in place. Exhausted, I tread water, trying at least to stay afloat. I am not a good swimmer, I remember I have always been afraid of the water, and I am not very strong. I cannot keep this up much longer.

Then I see a woman coming along the footpath. There is something odd about the perspective because, although the shore is some distance away, I can see her distinctly. She wears sensible low-heeled shoes and a tailored paisley print dress in shades of brown. Her improbable red hair is shoulder length with a prominent gray streak on one side. She wears no makeup, and her face is slightly pockmarked, the scars of adolescent acne. At some point, I realize that I know this woman.

For a time, she doesn't see me even though I am shouting and waving my arms, thrusting my body out of the water to catch her attention. Then she does see me, and her face momentarily registers concern. Her mouth opens and her eyes narrow to a squint as she strains against the glare from the water to focus on me. I am trying to shout that there is a life preserver further along the walkway—a white inner tube with a long rope attached. I hadn't noticed it before, but it is there now. If she comes down to the water's edge, she can throw it close to me. She seems to understand, she looks around, she sees the thing lying on the grass up ahead.

But she hesitates and does not go toward it. Instead, she shouts back to me, explaining that if she came any closer to the water, the waves would spray her dress. Apparently, my movements have so agitated the water that it splashes hard against the bank. I am crying and pleading, screaming with all my force; I hear my voice crack with the effort. My movements have become frantic. The woman on the shore watches, her body stiffening. She is indignant that I am demanding so much of her. She has a right to refuse, she feels: I should understand that she cannot get her hems wet. Finally, she turns and continues along the walkway, her back to me.

I am weeping, swallowing large mouthfuls of dark brackish water. I am gulping for air, I am having trouble breathing, I am sinking. . . .

I wake up bathed in sweat, and I am crying.

Thank God, thank God Dan is here beside me. I nudge him and tell him I have had a nightmare. He grunts from somewhere deep in sleep and rolls toward me, putting his arms around me. He says something, but I can't make out the words, they are incoherent. He isn't really awake. But he *is* holding me, slowly running his hand up and down my arm, comforting. In a few minutes he will sink back into deep sleep and roll away again. In the morning he probably won't remember any of this. I could wake him if I wanted, force him to full consciousness and make him listen while I retell the dream. But I won't—he's heard it too many times before. He held me when I was crying, he heard me even from sleep. It is enough.

1 P.M., May 9, 1978

I slept till noon again today, and still I feel exhausted. Last night I dreamed again that I was drowning.

It is now almost three years since I filed a discrimination complaint against the University of New Hampshire. I charged the school with sex discrimination and anti-Semitism. The Department of English had twice denied me promotion to associate rank, eventually promoted me, and subsequently voted not to tenure me. When the New Hampshire Commission for Human Rights found probable cause in my favor, the university refused to attend settlement hearings or to redress any of my grievances. The school again refused to come to the bargaining table when, thirteen months later, the Equal Employment Opportunity Commission made similar findings. This last year I have employed legal counsel, filed suit in federal court, and am in the throes of preparing for trial. My lawyers say it will be a landmark case.

Something else has happened this last year: both the women junior to me in the tenure track have been tenured, and one woman brought in as a full professor—subsequent to my initial discrimination complaint—has also been tenured. One by one, they are turning into people I no longer recognize, except in my dreams. Sheila, my closest friend and confidante when she was still an assistant professor, now says she can't be seen talking to me, on campus or anywhere. "It hurts my credibility," she explains. Amanda arrived last year from a small college in the Midwest where she already held the full professor rank. We had mutual friends from graduate school. From the first week, Amanda told everyone—department colleagues and others—that the denial of my tenure was "a clear case of discrimination." She was sure I'd win. But this year Amanda was given tenure at New Hampshire, and she's now begun blaming it all on my style. "It's your style, Annette," she keeps saying to me, although she never explains what she means. Amanda has shoulder-length red hair with a gray streak on the right and skin scarred by acne. Amanda was the woman in last night's dream.

Like Sheila, Jennifer is the other junior woman who has just been tenured. A week after she learned the good news, she told me she believes people get what they deserve. More recently, she has begun to ask why I don't leave. "You've done all you can here, there's nothing more to be done on this campus. So why don't you just go someplace else?" She seems to think it would be easy, as if the lawsuit and the denial of tenure have not marked me, as though the department has not told prospective employers that I'm "abrasive," the new code word for feminist. Jennifer also has been in my drowning dreams. She didn't throw me the life preserver, either. She was late for an appointment, she said, and hurried along the concrete path.

Now that these women are tenured, I have asked them to speak up for me and for women's issues at department meetings; I have asked them to tell my lawyers if there are breaches of professional procedure in the votes on my various appeals; I have asked them to support me in every way they can. But it's been three years now, and I am becoming a burden to them. "You expect too much," Jennifer tells me. "Don't ask people for anything," advises Amanda, "let them do what they can on their own—and understand if they feel they can't do anything." "I've got to back off where you're concerned," Sheila tells me again and again. "It jeopardizes my standing in the department." The drowning dreams began this year. Always, it is Sheila or Jennifer or Amanda who will not get her hems wet, who cannot be late for an appointment.

I am, of course, the truth too awful to allow. Each woman wants to believe that her tenure and promotion were earned, deserved—not the result of my lawsuit and the department's attempt to prepare itself for trial. And, to be sure, each woman *did* merit her tenure and promotion, as did many women before them whom this department let go. I was the first woman and the first Jew ever reviewed for promotion to associate rank in the department's entire history. Before me, no woman and no member of any ethnic minority group had gotten even that far. But if my women colleagues acknowledge that the department made a mistake in my case, how can they rest comfortably with the department's decision in their own? Adamant, Sheila and Jennifer keep insisting "they hired Amanda McKinney. She does feminist criticism. And they tenured us. So how can you say the department discriminates? They hired Amanda McKinney!" The refrain bludgeons. They have ganged up on me.

The terrible irony is that my women colleagues have invested their self-esteem in the judgments of men whom previously they would ridicule and sneer at in private. At dinner parties, Sheila and Jennifer used to parody one or another of the senior men or make fun of the pretensions of a department chair. But now those men have presumably found each woman worthy, and the approval of others is difficult to dismiss. It is easier to dismiss *me*, to see *me* as the problem.

Sometimes I think maybe I am crazy, maybe I have some other personality I don't know about. I've read the testimony of some of the senior members and don't recognize the person they describe as me. I don't remember saying some of the things they say I said, and I don't believe I've ever held some of the opinions or attitudes they attribute to me. Their versions of certain meetings and encounters bear no resemblance to my memories of those occasions. What's so scary is that their testimony is consistent; they all agree with one another. I seem to be the only one with a different version. My lawyers say not to worry. The university lawyer is simply coaching his witnesses into producing a coherent story to offer the judge. They don't have any professional grounds for the denial of tenure—I've outpublished them all, the department chair concedes that my teaching is "outstanding," and my committee work has always been diligent—so they're building a case based on personality. They're going to characterize me as "uncollegial," whatever that means. The second time I was denied promotion, the reason given was "collegiality." I went to the department chair to ask what it meant. He said he didn't know, wished they wouldn't use the term, called it a "will o' the wisp." But he, too, had voted against me—always has.

My lawyers' assurances do not comfort. These people are inventing a personality for me, forcing me to live inside it or defend against it. How can three men say the same thing about an incident that I remember differently? Am I crazy? I appeal to Dan: "Am I really this person they say I am? Do I ever do or say these things?" I sometimes fear I am losing my grip on my own reality. In department or committee meetings, I take notes frantically, fearful of forgetting, of being convinced by others that something different transpired. "I'm not this person, am I?" I keep asking Dan. I need to hear it from someone who sees me daily. I need to know I am not the monster they say I am.

I am trying to write an essay about the accomplishments of feminist criticism over the last ten years. What I really want to write about is what it feels like to be an outsider, a pariah. I want to write about being angry and scared and how it feels to be abandoned. If it weren't for Dan, I would be crazy now.

I find the essay difficult to work on because I am afraid it may be the last one I'll ever write. Unless this lawsuit is settled quickly, or I can find another job, I'm afraid I won't have any career. I have already been blackballed at several schools—friends have told me about department meetings at which someone fears I'm "too political," "too feminist," "too strident," too something. And my lawyers say a trial will take at least a year, with another three to five years of appeals when the university loses. The essay has become a sort of life preserver: it reminds me of what I'm fighting for. I was going to put "drowning" in the title and use my dream as a metaphor to hold together its disparate sections. But every time I try to use drowning as a symbol, I start crying. Not for fear of drowning so much as for the pain I feel when I remember the woman continuing along the walkway. I cannot bear the desertion. I will title the essay after another dream, one not so awful because I survive it each time. In that dream, I am dancing through a minefield. . . .

May 1987

The preceding is a partial transcription of a 1978 entry from a hand-written journal that I kept erratically from December 1975 through November 1980. It was at the end of December 1975 that I first learned that the Senior Members Committee of the Department of English at the University of New Hampshire had voted 10 to 0 against my promotion to associate professor. Almost five years later, in October 1980, two weeks before trial was to begin, the university opened negotiations for an out-of-court settlement. By late November, the settlement was final. In both its stipulations and its financial terms, the settlement was what my lawyers had all along predicted: a landmark. During the three years of pretrial litigation, we had set important legal precedents from which Title VII complainants after me would benefit.

Unpacking the journal after all these years, I am forced to remember the anguish of that period: the repeated deep depressions, the paralysis of mind that slowed my writing, the endless nights when I could not sleep or when sleep brought only nightmares and the unremitting sense of anger and isolation. Rereading the journal today, I am struck by the rancor and bitterness expressed toward my three women colleagues. In the first two years of journal entries, my anger is directed at the senior men who resolutely tried to keep the tenured ranks a private Christian men's club. As I had recorded in an early entry, one of those men told me, "It *is* a club, Annette; we can keep out anyone we want to." But as the women on whom I depended for emotional support gradually pulled away, they became the focus of my desperation, and, finally, my anger. By the third year of journal entries, I was hardly writing about the men at all. A small clique of tenured men had discriminated against me as a woman and as a Jew. I could understand that, and I could fight it. But the women, I felt, had betrayed me, abandoned me, even used me. That I had not expected, and I knew no way of fighting what I did not even want to admit.

Under these circumstances, I am amazed that I didn't crack—though the journal entries suggest I came close more than once. I did not crack because, although I didn't always recognize it at the time, I had been embraced by extraordinary caring. My lawyers and one paralegal—all women, all committed feminists—negotiated the legal system as my advocates and, in that process, became my friends. A nationwide network of colleagues from both the American literature and women's studies communities responded to my letters of appeal with contributions to my legal fund, letters and phone calls of warmth and encouragement, offers of expert testimony. My students—women and men, graduates and undergraduates—dutifully kept the lawsuit out of the classroom and then organized on my behalf all over campus; they threw parties and fund-raisers to let me know they would share the burden. My colleague Gary Lindberg steadfastly remained independent within the English Department and supported me, without reserve, never letting me know the prices he paid. Judy and Peter Lindberg, his wife and son—together with Gary—were more than friends: talking and listening to music together, often until dawn, they became extended family. And, finally, my husband, Daniel Peters, was always the target of my anger and frustration, the recipient of my grief and depression. In our society, men are rarely trained to nurture or give care, and Dan was certainly no exception. But if he did not always anticipate my needs or divine the depth of my depression, he nonetheless provided the crucial assurance that would see me through. In endless patient responses to my appeal, "I'm not this person, am I?" he helped me hold onto reality. In words, in little gifts, in loving gestures, he let me know that even when I did become irrational, even when my fears overcame me, he would keep loving me and believing in me. All else might fail, but Dan, I knew, would never betray me.

I read the journal now almost as if it were someone else's. I don't quite recognize the person writing those pages, but I want to put my arms around her and tell her it will be all right. Part of the anguish, you see, was that I could never be sure of that.

Happily, in the end it *has* been "all right." After several uncertain years, my career stabilized, and schools competed with one another to hire me. Nowadays, I am quite secure, I teach, write and publish about all the things that are important to me. I no longer have nightmares, I never have dreams of drowning, and I take great pleasure from swimming regularly. Not incidentally, as I write this coda to the journal entry, I approach my forty-sixth birthday. When I look in the mirror, I find I like the person I see there. I know that the woman in the mirror will never abandon another woman because, ten years ago, something irrevocable happened in New Hampshire. Lines were drawn. Sheila, Jennifer, and Amanda believed they could avoid taking sides; they thought they could avoid getting their hems wet. In their view, they were not actively doing anything to harm me; they were simply "not getting involved." What they never understood— but I always will—is that their supposed neutrality gave the men in the department tacit permission to continue refusing me promotion and tenure. The women's silence encouraged the men's recalcitrance. The neutrality of Sheila, Jennifer, and Amanda, in other words, was itself a position. It is a position that leaves *all* women isolated from one another, vulnerable to drowning.

I have never forgiven those women their lack of courage. Even today I avoid seeing or speaking to them at professional conferences. I have never forgiven the University of New Hampshire for trying to exile me from its private "club." For all the loveliness of the New Hampshire countryside which I adored, and for all the friends we left behind there, for me the town of Durham is forever a tainted place. Above all else, however, I can never forgive the mask of institutional decorum that made it impossible for Dan and me to return for the memorial service—held on campus—after Gary Lindberg died in 1986 of Hodgkins disease. I needed that ritual of mourning for a loving friend who had made my own survival possible. And, finally, I will never be reconciled to the fact that the University of New Hampshire mired me in debt and emotional anguish during the last years in which I might reasonably have planned on pregnancy. Forced to concentrate all my energies on professional survival, I watched the biological time clock run out.

I realize as I write these words that the rage I felt ten years ago is still with me. Anger recollected in tranquillity does not transmute; it is still anger. Perhaps it is not as sharp, certainly not the constant companion it was then. But it is there, a familiar vibration, and one I think I've earned a right to. The common wisdom, of course, is that we must let go of our anger, forget our pain, lest they eat away inside and turn us bitter. My trusted friends do not give such advice. They know what is really being asked of us by such so-called "wisdom": that we forget our history. When we can no longer call up the feelings, after all, the events of our past are dead to us, without meaning or motivation. I want my past to remain vital to me because I need to keep learning its lessons.

They are not easy lessons, to be sure, nor have I yet fully comprehended them. But they are lessons that no individual or political movement can safely evade. As a result of what happened to me in New Hampshire, the contradictions in my life open out like a hall of mirrors. I fought, I believed, for principles and for people. Even so, the people who stood to gain the most from what I was doing proved the least helpful. The rabbi assigned to the university said he'd never heard any complaints of anti-Semitism on campus; the more senior faculty women in my department would take no risks on my behalf, instead condemning me for risking all. The two people who stayed with me, ironically, were two WASP males: my husband, Dan, and my friend and colleague, Gary. If the personal is political, then what sort of politics emerges from such truths?

I don't have the answer to that question, but I know it is one I—we—

must pursue beyond the cliché of cognitive dissonance. The question leads, ineluctably, to an examination of the corrosive *professionalization* of identity within patriarchal institutions that constrains women from bonding with one another. So long as I remain within academe, this is something I must strive to understand and overcome. To do that, I must hold firm to my memories—the pain and the anger both—and cherish the challenge they engender. Bitterness, I suspect, comes from trying to bury what will not die. Bitterness is the attempt at repressing anger, refusing contradiction. The woman I see in the mirror is not bitter. She knows that to embrace one's anger is to return from exile from one's self.

Note

With the exception of the Lindberg family and my husband, Daniel Peters, all names are fictitious. Those characterized as departmental colleagues are composites drawn from several persons. Chronology and other details have been altered to protect the privacy of individuals.

In helping me to examine the implications of my journal entries, Susan Koppelman has been a generous friend and loving resource. I am also grateful to Judy Lindberg, Nancy Gertner, Ann Lambert Greenblatt, and Sandy Eisdorfer for their careful readings and valuable suggestions.

. . . .

Part 2

The Canons of Exile

(Dis)Placement and Difference

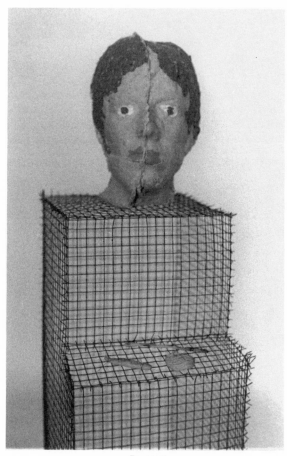

Dementia
Sculpture by Karin Connelly

. . . .

Chapter 7

Wrestling Your Ally

Stein, Racism, and Feminist Critical Practice

Sonia Saldívar-Hull

And this movement that began with a moving evocation of truth, begins to appear fraudulent from the outside, begins to mirror all that it says it opposed, for now it, too, is an oppressor of certain truths, and speakers, and begins, like the old oppressors, to hide from itself.
—Susan Griffin, "The Way of All Ideology"

It is crucial that women participate in the open questioning of the exclusionary project of canonization, in literary theory as well as in literature. Through the pioneering efforts of such feminist scholars as Cherríe Moraga and Gloria Anzaldúa, Gloria T. Hull, Patricia Bell Scott, and Barbara Smith, Paul Lauter, and Jane Tompkins, we could begin to imagine what a truly reconstructed canon would offer. In the spirit of sisterhood we believed that as feminist scholars we were allies, united in our mutual liberation project. As allies we would join forces and assert our authority, concentrate on re-discovering, re-reading women's texts historically suppressed by those in charge of creating literary canons.

In theory, the availability of previously "suppressed" or "lost" texts would unite academic women of diverse races and classes as "mujeres de fuerza" (women of strength) in a political coalition whose immediate goal was restructuring the literary canon which legitimized the social power of male hegemony. In practice, however, women who might have been natural allies in a struggle against exclusionary, patriarchal practices in the academy instead are estranged because the feminist mainstream has not dealt adequately with differences of women on the periphery of the power structure: working-class women, Chicanas, Afro-American women, women of the Third World, for examples.

In 1983 Shari Benstock, as editor of *Tulsa Studies in Women's Literature (TSWL)*, called for a reevaluation of the choices made by women in power to establish a feminist canon ("Feminist Critique," 148). She cautioned us to realize the danger of women's mirroring patriarchal, exclusionary tactics in our own literary project. "Have women writers and women critics," she asked, "successfully set up shop in a separate part of the literary universe, establishing a canon that parallels the established one, defining a gynocentric axis from which radiate the various forms of women's literary imagination?" ("Feminist Critique," 139).

Benstock then cited an example of white feminists who privilege feminist criticism but exclude issues of race and class. She saw that this blindness potentially establishes a literary hierarchy no less exclusionary than the traditional male literary canon. Her example was Joanna Russ's *How to Suppress Women's Writing*.[1] Russ, perhaps unintentionally but significantly, relegates Third World women, women of color, and lesbians to the back of the bus, so to speak. Though Russ discusses her slip at length, nevertheless, Third World women, women of color, and lesbians, the "aliens" of Russ's universe, find it hard not to see the irony in Russ's own form of suppression. Indeed, Russ's exclusionary practice is symptomatic of an almost exclusively white feminist movement and, in turn, of liberal feminist critical theory. These symptoms point to the urgency for us to confront the contradictions of white, middle-class women who fetishize an abstract marginalization, oblivious to the concerns of the alienated women who exist only at the periphery of the women's movement, the contemporary exiles of the feminist literary and critical projects.

As women on the border, we are aware of the dangers inherent in celebrating marginalization. We fear that like those liberal feminists who have made careers out of their own marginalization, we too might diffuse political praxis, thereby defeating the Third World feminist project. Feminism as a critical political stance is a fraud when practiced in a cultural and historical void. To avoid echoing the patriarchal, capitalistic exclusionary agenda, feminist criticism must integrate race and class issues with gender issues.

Questions of difference within feminist projects also must be addressed; we must remember that insidious racism is so ingrained in the ruling-class consciousness that it can emerge even in the most sympathetic discourse. Benstock continued her editorial by urging her colleagues to examine the "authority of our own experience . . . to challenge its assumptions and maneuvers." But she then undermined her own commitment to a feminist liberalism when she called for "essays on women writers in foreign language literatures, essays on women of color, essays on third world women writers" ("Feminist Critique," 147, 148). Even the sympathetic Benstock unconsciously designated as "object," as "other," as "foreign," the study and practice of non-English-speaking, nonwhite women's writing.[2] Surely the editor of one of the leading feminist literary journals did not assume that white feminist critics in the First World must take up the banner for women they perhaps consider to be inarticulate, uneducated Third World sisters. As a Chicana, a member of a group clearly alien to the pages of *TSWL*, I propose to take Benstock's challenge further.

My response is that of a bilingual woman of color whose use of Spanish is not considered foreign in East Austin, Texas, East Los Angeles, the barrios of Chicago, or in many other cities of the United States. Third World women who live at the periphery, within the national borders of the United States, women of color, working-class women, refuse to become objects of theoretical studies by white, liberal feminists or by "mainstream" patriarchal critics. We "other" women insist on decentering the privileged position that liberal feminists have created for themselves as we articulate and examine issues which many feminist theorists apparently have great difficulty in addressing.

Another site of our struggle with the hegemonic tendencies of our white, liberal, U.S. sisters is the literary anthology. Chicana writers have been exiled from the pages of important texts like the *Norton Anthology of Literature by Women* (*NALW*). Editors Sandra M. Gilbert and Susan Gubar express regret for omitting Chicanas and Italian-American women from the collection, citing the same "space-restrictions" excuse the male editors of anthologies have long used. The implication to Chicanas is that our writing is too marginal to be canonized in this mirroring of the male power structure. The implication to those women exiled by their allies is that they are too alien to be included in a female ruling-class tradition that is also part of the white power structure. Compared with the issues that some of our compañeras in the field face, however, the plight of the Chicana writer in academia is one we find painful to face. As daughters of the campesino, women of the working class, we are in danger that our new status as bourgeois academics allows us such self-indulgent rhetoric as "Chicana writers have been exiled from the pages of important texts."

Another way of looking at this problem, however, is through Lorna Dee Cervantes's assertion that theoretical criticism for the Chicana "is not an arbitrary practice, it is a strategic aim. . . . A Chicana critic is one who wants to undermine the system she lives under through a calculated act of intellectual and discursive sabotage" ("Chicana Critics," 8). Through such acts of sabotage we engage in a guerrilla warfare with women who preserve their privileged positions when they merely urge conciliation without actually changing the oppressive system. Liberal feminists express dismay when Chicanas call for a boycott of offending anthologies. When they wonder why women fight other women, why the unquestioned, male-centered anthologies were never subjected to a similar boycott, we answer as second-generation feminists, often trained by white feminist mentors to demand more from women who themselves struggled against exclusionary phallocentric practices.[3] We expect that white, liberal feminists understand that their history is not monolithic. They must remember that history for those of us who are Chicanas is the dual history of oppression as women and exploitation as daughters of the campesino. Our dual history is tied, for example, to the history of farmworker boycotts our parents and grandparents used as acts of sabotage in places like the Rio Grande Valley, an area of Texas where 90 percent of the people who live below the poverty level are Chicanos.

The issues exiled women confront, however, are even more problematic than exile from the canon. In articulating a feminist poetics, scholars point out the dangers of allowing stereotypes of women in literature to stand unchallenged. When we consider which women to include in a women's studies curriculum, we must acknowledge other dangers when we resurrect writers patriarchal academics buried simply on the basis of gender. Gertrude Stein, in many ways an example of the exiled woman writer, is a case in point. The patriarchy banished her from its canon while it privileged the boys she taught to write.

Only one year after Shari Benstock challenged us to include "other" women for publication in *TSWL*, she published an essay on the problem of where to place Gertrude Stein in the feminist alter-canon:

> Do we want the women writers we discover to join the canon of male writers or do we want a separate canon, and if we want a separate literary canon and a separate critical practice—our own—how will these differ from the "enshrined canons of achievement" around which course descriptions, dissertations . . . and academic careers construct themselves? Do we claim the center for ourselves (taking up the Modernist project) or do we redefine the limits of authority by which the center constitutes itself (taking up the post-Modernist project)? Or do we, like Gertrude Stein, try to do both? . . . And such questions poise themselves—and in so doing poise us—on that awkward border between Modernism and post-Modernism, between practice and theory. ("Beyond the Reaches," 10)

I propose that it is that "awkward border" between practice and theory that liberal feminists such as Russ, Benstock, Gilbert, and Gubar neglect to acknowledge as the space where racism can enter and undermine the effectiveness of the feminist project. In theory, Benstock can call for sensitivity toward women of color, but in practice she includes the white supremacist Gertrude Stein in her feminist pantheon of great writers. In theory, women of color can aspire to membership in the feminist critical school; in practice, we find an editorial essay in a leading feminist journal which praises a writer whose racism and class bias I will examine in this essay. I propose that we use the same feminist and deconstructive methodologies in the study of Gertrude Stein as those tools that Benstock sees merged in a "most fortunate marriage of theory and practice" ("Beyond the Reaches," 19) to dismantle and work out the extreme "marital" alienation between liberal, white feminists and feminists of color whose literary and critical discourses have been exiled by their allies. My project, then, is a dual one. As well as drawing attention to the exile of Chicanas from the feminist canon I hope to explore the writing of a woman we are encouraged to consider a literary foremother.

The reader can approach Gertrude Stein's *Three Lives* in the spirit of re-discovery. Imagine the secure comfort of a naive student who "discovers" an allegedly suppressed literary mother. It was in this spirit that I began the first "life," "The Good Anna."

At first, the pathetic character of a German immigrant, Anna seems to be representative of one stereotypical version of an older woman: bitter and alone. As Stein develops her character, however, Anna's attitudes about class and gender become the narrator's assumptions of traits possessed by all "lower-class" servants. The question of whether the good Anna is really "good" becomes irrelevant as statements that I wanted to accept as ironic became suspiciously stated as facts: "Anna had always a firm old world sense of what was the right way for a girl to do" (*Three Lives*, 24), as well as the distinction Anna made between the class of "maid" and that of "servant." Anna's penchant for controlling her employers' lives seemed to be presented as a model of how "good help" should behave. The good Anna would never allow herself to sit down with her superior, Miss Mathilda: "A girl was a girl and should always act like a girl, both as to giving all respect and as to what she had to eat" (24).

At this point in the story, the naive reader could still believe that Stein presented the good Anna's servant credo as idiosyncratic to the unique character in a fiction. Stein's tone is ironic, the reader can argue. Surely Stein is being consciously ambiguous so the reader can see for herself that these are class issues that must be subverted. When we were undergraduates, our professors warned us about the intentional fallacy; as sophisticated readers we are supposed to understand that Anna's situation is a result of her own peculiarities. Readers can comfort themselves with the belief that Stein was creating a portrait of a woman who manipulates those around her by sacrificing her own life for them.[4] Anna is the consummate martyr figure who uses self-sacrifice to gain power over people. Surely that is all Stein is saying.

This naive reader, however, was becoming more uneasy. Was it possible that Gertrude Stein, the writer I was supposed to admire, could not see the obvious class issues that contribute to Anna's character? I began to question phrases like "obedient, happy servant" and "by nature slatternly and careless," which Stein used to describe other working-class women. By now I was being forced to question whether I could ever again read for character and plot and literary technique and ignore more pressing political issues.

"Melanctha," the next "life," had promised to be an avant-garde portrait of a black woman who searches intensely for self-knowledge and seeks an outlet for her sexuality. But for the readers who are of the working class and/or are women of color, the betrayal soon is unmistakable. The more this naive reader read, the more obvious it became that Stein *believed* in the basic "unmorality of the black people," that she *believed* that the "negroes" have a simplicity which is exhibited in their "joyous, earth born, boundless joy" (86).

Clearly, the next step for the naive reader to take is to search the academic sages for published support for a growing disgust with the narrow, prejudiced portrayals of the women in *Three Lives*. We find blindness instead of insight. Issues that seemed to provide the very reasons to undermine Stein's portrayals are hailed by some critics as the reasons to study and include Stein in canon formation.

In his 1973 biography of Stein, Howard Greenfeld discusses intellectual influences on her, the most important one being her relationship with William James, who first introduced the young Stein to the use of language "under unusual circumstances" (13). Her published psychological experiments are relevant to her presentation of the "lower-class" German immigrants and the "half white mulatto girl" in *Three Lives*.[5] But Greenfeld's analysis of the characters' speech in the stories is most disturbing:

> These tales, especially *Melanctha*, are somewhat unconventional in language and style. Gertrude tried to re-create the actual sounds and rhythms of her characters using colloquial speech and a kind of sing song repetition. Her overall desire was to create what she felt Cezanne had created in his paintings, works in which each element was as important as the entire work itself. . . . The author herself never intrudes—the people in these stories speak for themselves, in their own voices. (Greenfeld, 42)

For Greenfeld to claim that these characters speak "in their own voices" is incomprehensible. If we accept his statement, we must ignore the always present, powerful, controlling narrative voice that is Stein. Greenfeld, however, can be explained away as a symptom of the phallocentric disease. His aestheticist, ahistorical, non-class-conscious analysis is typical of the critical approach of many scholars of his school, New Criticism.

Unfortunately, even the poststructuralist feminist critic Marianne De-Koven is not immune to using such an approach. DeKoven is one of those contemporary critics who sidesteps issues of race and class in awarding Stein a place in the feminist canon as an experimental writer whose style is emblematic of antipatriarchal writing. DeKoven claims that she cannot deconstruct Stein's work because it is already deconstructed: "It is the indeterminate, anti-patriarchal (anti-logocentric, anti-phallogo-centric, presymbolic pluridimensional) writing which deconstruction, alias Jacques Derrida, proposes as an antidote to patriarchy" (xvii). Although DeKoven admits that Stein never intended for her writing to be anti-patriarchal, she insists that there is "specifically feminist content" in *Three Lives* (xviii). The feminist content, however, is obscured by more disturbing issues.

DeKoven defeats her own thesis by concentrating on purely patriarchal, theoretical concerns. She addresses only the linguistic structures in Stein's works. DeKoven also forgets the perhaps mundane concerns of the "objects" that Stein portrays in her three studies: the working class, women, and people of color. DeKoven's work is an example of the flaws of deconstruction without the mediation of either class or race analysis.

Undoubtedly it is easier for such a critic to deal with "signifiers" and forget that real people, races, and classes are affected by the stereotypes she never challenges. When DeKoven places Stein's work in opposition to patriarchal linguistic structure because of Stein's "linguistic radicalism," the critic forgets that linguistics are part of a totality—the content, the plot, the theme.

For a deconstructionist like DeKoven to look at the totality of *Three Lives*, particularly "Melanctha," would be to subvert her own thesis, which is, "in theory," valid. She claims to focus her "current French feminist, post-structuralist, and psychoanalytic criticism" on the "interplay of language and culture," yet she accepts the most insidious forms of class and race bias. Liberal feminist critics must address this bias. Her brief analysis of "Melanctha" exposes her ties to the patriarchy as much as it unwittingly unveils Stein's own prejudices. Melanctha is defeated by a "divided self," DeKoven claims (31). In the short novel, "wisdom becomes an emblem of everything in life that is desirable but difficult to attain; excitement, of everything that is alluring but dangerous" (44). DeKoven goes on to assert that "Stein's very success in rendering in language a unique core of personality leads her away from recognizable depiction of character. In *Melanctha*, it is the wavelike cadence and the repetition of a reduced, strangely resonant and at the same time simple, childlike vocabulary that hold our attention most forcefully as we read, beyond our recognition of character, anticipation of plot, or reflection upon theme" (44–45).

When we as feminist critics accept blatant slurs like the claim that black people speak with a "childlike vocabulary," when we do not question Steinian images of "negro sunshine" or assumptions of the "simple promiscuous unmorality of the black people," we are lulled and mesmerized by Stein's cadence and repetitions. Perhaps this is Stein's political agenda. The reader loses consciousness of the racism and classism because s/he is encouraged to think only of an aesthetic category, urged to remember that Stein wrote at a specific time, in a particular culture. But these embarrassments that feminist scholars do not discuss at any depth are at the center of "Melanctha." It is a story that appeals primarily to intellectuals who assume that everyone who reads Stein will accept the slurs in the spirit of linguistic authenticity, of authorial irony, of Stein's exotic depiction of the "primitive." These are the tactics of ruling-class ideology; these are the methods the ruling class employs to retain power over the dominated.

In a more sensitive essay on Stein, Catharine Stimpson discusses the author's disregard for displaying class bias.[6] Stimpson also explores how Stein's need to mask her lesbianism forced her to devise tactics that would allow her to live as a "possibly tainted anomaly." Indeed, Stimpson does address Stein's racism in her treatment of black people as strongly sexual creatures. She points out that "problematic passion among whites is transferred to blacks, as if they might embody that which the dominant culture feared" (501). But she does not seem to believe that the racial issue is of prime importance as she glosses over the unpleasantness of Stein's bigotry: "The facts that Stein disliked raw racial injustice and that a black author, Richard Wright, praised 'Melanctha' in itself must be balanced against the fact that racial stereotypes help to print out the narrative" (501).

I find it disturbing that even a leading feminist like Stimpson turns to Wright, a misogynistic writer, to exhibit her spirit of egalitarianism. Why does Stimpson need to defer to Wright's authority in her attempt to deal with the embarrassing problem of Stein's perhaps unintentional bigotry? Stimpson seems to believe that though she sees the blatant racism in

"Melanctha," a simple footnote stating that white intellectuals in Stein's time overlooked it as a matter of course says enough about the race issue.[7]

In contrast, though Stimpson is content to accept Wright's evaluation as evidence of an Afro-American consensus, John Brinnin includes Claude McKay's response to "Melanctha": "In the telling of the story I found nothing striking and informative about Negro life. Melanctha, the mulattress, might have been a Jewess. And the mulatto Jeff Campbell—he is not typical of mulattoes I have known anywhere. He reminds me more of a type of white lover described by a colored woman" (quoted in Brinnin, 121).

In her essay on the Afro-American female literary tradition Lorraine Bethel reminds us that "Black women writers have consistently rejected the falsification of their Black/female experience, thereby avoiding the negative stereotypes such falsification has often created in the white American female and Black male literary traditions" (177). She cites Wright's *Native Son* as an example of "how the falsification of the Black experience for the purpose of political protest can result in characters that reinforce racist stereotypes" (187).

From the first page of "Melanctha," the racial slurs obscure any sympathetic portrayal of a character in Stein's story. The stereotype begins immediately as two women are introduced. Melanctha Herbert is "patient, submissive, soothing, and untiring"; Rose Johnson is "sullen, childish, cowardly, black Rose," who "grumbled and fussed and howled and made herself to be an abomination and like a simple beast" (*Three Lives*, 85). Stein's always controlling narrator casts Rose into literary infamy as a "careless and negligent and selfish" woman whose baby dies from her neglect, although she had "liked the baby well enough and perhaps she just forgot it for awhile, anyway the child was dead and Rose and Sam her husband were very sorry but then these things came so often in the negro world in Bridgepoint, that they neither of them thought about it very long" (85).

Although Stein's assumption that poor black people care less, feel less pain about a baby's death can be explained away as a sociological reality viewed by the author when she was a Johns Hopkins medical student, the portrait is not just of one black couple who lost a child and soon forgot. It is an indictment of the "negro world in Bridgepoint" and, by association, of the "negro" world in general.

The hierarchical scale that Stein presents is as obvious as it is vicious.

Of course, "white" is the privileged center. Stein takes for granted that her reader will assume that the white race is superior, so she places her characters in opposition, privileging white over black, good over bad, intelligent over simple-minded, sophisticated over childlike vocabulary. Since the world she portrays is the "other" world of black people, the gradations she makes are within the context of an already flawed black world.

Stein wants her reader to remember which "girl" is "good" and which is "bad." Since Melanctha and Rose belong to this alien, primitive race, perhaps Stein feared that her bourgeois readers would not be able to tell them apart so her technique is the "badder" the "girl," the "blacker" the skin. At one end of the spectrum is Rose, a "real black, tall, well built, sullen, stupid, childlike, good looking negress," who was "never joyous with the earth born, boundless joy of negroes," but was instead a "careless and lazy woman brought up by white folks" (85–86). Even Stein cannot decide how ultimately to place the black people in her story. She wants them all to conform to her vision of this foreign race, but she keeps undermining her own project by making exceptions. She stresses that Rose has not taken advantage of her white patrons' kindness when they raised her as their own child but, in the instinctual way of the "lower" orders, has "drifted from her white folks back to the colored people." She is unable to become part of the higher order not only because of skin color but because of the innate depravity of her black soul: "She needed decent comfort. Her white training had only made for habits, not for nature" (86).

Stein is not content to portray the "real black" Rose as inferior because of her unique psychic makeup. The implication is that Rose is deficient because of her genetic composition as well as her skin color. For Stein, color is fate in the same way that character is fate. "Rose had the simple promiscuous unmorality of the black people," the Stein narrator proclaims. The degree of the characters' sexuality is equivalent to the degree of their depravity.[8]

Tied to Rose in a kinship of dark sexuality is Melanctha's father, James. "Melanctha's father was a big black virile negro" (90). As Angela Davis suggests, the stereotype of the hypersexuality of black men seems to fascinate Stein.[9] She describes Melanctha's mother's attraction to this man solely in terms of this myth: "He only came once in a while to where Melanctha and her mother lived, but always that pleasant, sweet appearing, pale yellow woman, mysterious and uncertain and wandering in her ways, was close to sympathy and thinking to her big black virile husband"

(90). James is not within the realm of the "nicer colored folk." On the contrary, this evil presence is described as a "powerful, loose built, hard handed, black angry negro. Herbert was never a joyous negro." Like the black Rose, "he never had the wide abandoned laughter that gives the broad glow to negro sunshine" (92).

Melanctha, on the other hand, "was a graceful, pale yellow, intelligent, attractive negress. She had not been raised like Rose by white folks but then she had been made with real white blood" (86). The reader should be properly impressed and should learn more about this curious specimen, a "mulatto girl," who is half white and half the product of a very black, virile James: "Melanctha was pale yellow and mysterious and a little pleasant like her mother, but the real power in Melanctha's nature came through her robust and unpleasant and very unendurable black father. . . . Melanctha Herbert almost always hated her black father, but she loved very well the power in herself that came through him" (90).

Melanctha's mystery lies in her search for "wisdom" and in her "wandering" in quest for that self-knowledge. But Stein has already informed the reader that even "with her white blood and attraction and her desire for a right position," Melanctha is sexually active but has "not yet really been married" (86). The assumption that black people have a typically "promiscuous unmorality" has been made. The reader is to understand, then, that Melanctha's secret yearning for knowledge is inextricably tied to her sexuality, but only in a negative context: that of a deviant, savage "unmorality" found in its natural state in the inferior races. After all, these are the "colored folks," those childlike creatures Stein likes to compare fondly to nature in her acclaimed "experimental" style: "And the buds and the long earthworms, and the negroes, and all the kinds of children, were coming out every minute farther into the new spring, watery, southern sunshine" (195). The reader who has been mesmerized by Stein's radical writing style may overlook the "negro" next to the earthworm in Stein's great chain of being.[10]

Even in a scene that is supposed to show her heroine's education as a wanderer, Stein cannot resist stereotype as she caricatures the railroad porters from whom Melanctha is to "learn": "As the porters told these stories their round, black, shining faces would grow solemn, and their color would go grey beneath the greasy black, and their eyes would roll white in the fear and wonder of things they could scare themselves by telling" (99).

Stein's class prejudice further intrudes on the Melanctha persona when the wandering girl befriends black dockworkers in the daytime but turns to "upper class" black men for her real lessons. Stein depends upon this same class distinction when she portrays Melanctha's relationship with Jane Hardin, "a roughened woman," who "had much white blood and that made her see clear, she liked drinking and that made her reckless" (104). Jane initiates Melanctha into active sexuality; Stein implies a lesbian relationship along with sex with white men. Significantly, some of the most believable exchanges are between these two women who obviously care about each other as people. Stein needs to mask and code her own lesbianism, but she allows the reader a glimpse of herself as a woman-identified woman whose story might have worked if she had not needed to mask her sexuality and transfer it to an aberrant "other."[11] Jane and Melanctha's sexual wandering is more credible and described less patron-izingly, but both these women have white blood and therefore Stein can deal with them more sympathetically than she does the other black characters.

When Melanctha's major love interest is introduced into the story, it becomes clear that Stein's overt racism frames the central story of Melanctha and Dr. Jefferson Campbell. As Catharine Stimpson states, this love story is a coded autobiographical version of Stein's love affair with May Bookstaver (495–501). Stein suddenly drops the racial generaliza-tions in this subplot that makes up the major part of "Melanctha." Perhaps when Stein was being "personal," she was able to suspend racist ideology.

Unfortunately, once the racism all but disappears, blatant class bias takes its place. Jeff becomes the Stein persona who espouses a bootstrap mentality. He states that his "colored" people do "bad" things because they "want to get excited" (*Three Lives*, 121). As a mouthpiece for Stein, this character has no social or political awareness. Campbell's repressed sexuality emerges in his confused philosophy of correct behavior: "I cer-tainly do only know just two ways of loving. One kind of loving seems to me, is like one has a good quiet feeling in a family when one does his work . . . and then the other way of loving is just like having it like any animal that's low in the streets together, and that don't seem to me very good (124).

Once this love story section is over, Stein returns to her racist frame. She concludes that Melanctha is too much a product of her "very black virile father" to settle for a bland, mulatto, bourgeois domesticity with Dr. Jeff. She drives him away and turns instead to a "lower class" man, a "young buck" who eventually discards the complex Melanctha.

Stein brings her narrative full circle when she returns to the story of Rose and Melanctha and the baby's death and Sam's sympathy for Melanctha in her troubles. With the repetition and the celebrated run-on sentences, Stein drills in racist stereotypical characterizations of these inhabitants of the Afro-American world. The narrator reminds the reader that Rose's baby dies because of her negligence and again that neither Rose nor her husband thinks about it very long. Black Rose begins to feel jealous of her husband's passing attentions to Melanctha, and in a brutal scene, the always "careless, negligent selfish" Rose severs the friendship with the victimized heroine.

Melanctha's deterioration proceeds rapidly. She has driven Jeff away and is now betrayed by Rose. Stein then finishes the job by giving her previously healthy though melancholy heroine a disease, putting her in a home for "poor consumptives," and killing her off with a swift stroke of the pen in one sentence. We are to understand that since "these things [come] so often in the negro world" (85), neither Stein nor her seduced feminist readers think about issues of race and class for very long.

As a woman of color, I will reply to Benstock's question on the direction that feminist criticism is now to take. I cannot presume to be able to answer the opposition between aesthetics and content that writers such as Gertrude Stein force us to confront, but we do need to continue challenging the authority of those who forget that there are differences within the feminist project. We know what can happen when women begin to question their allies. The Chicana writers who are compelled to write what they know sometimes write passionate poetry of wife beating, of rape, of betrayal by their men and culture. These women risk the label of "vendida," sellout.

The poet Lorna Dee Cervantes writes: "Consider the power of wrestling your ally. His will is to kill you. He has nothing against you" (*Emplumada*, 1). We are killing Chicana and Italian-American women's writing when we leave it out of our breakthrough *Norton Anthology of Literature by Women*. We are killing the dignity of women of color and working-class women when we continue to promote authors like Gertrude Stein without acknowledging their race and class prejudice. What are we to conclude when the editors of *NALW* include "The Gentle Lena" portion of *Three Lives* but leave out the more blatantly racist and class-biased "Melanctha" and "The Good Anna"? We must consider the power that we hold when we choose to exile some literatures and canonize others. The women

exiled from the pages of feminist journals, anthologies, and course syllabi
are indeed "alien and critical" as we make ourselves subjects in feminist
literary analysis.

Notes

1. In her Afterword, Russ lumps together all the "other" women she neglected
in the text proper. Black women, Chicanas, Native American women, and lesbians
become a collective "other" and lose their inherent "difference." For further
evaluation of Russ's Afterword as afterthought, see Carol Sternhell's review. In
formulating my ideas while trying to suppress my rage at being designated an
outsider in the women's society of outsiders (feminist scholars) I have been guided
and encouraged by Jane Marcus. I appreciate not only her encouragement but also
her ability to share my anger and teach me how to harness it in my writing. A
version of this essay was first presented at the 1986 Modern Language Association
convention held in New York. The panel was called "Women Writers in Exile I:
Communities of Exile."

2. This is an example of the feminist "theory" versus "practice" that Gayatri
Spivak discusses in the Foreword to her translation of "Draupadi" by Mahasveta
Devi. Shari Benstock is also an example of how committed feminists can begin to
transform theory into practice. At the 1987 South Central MLA Feminist Forum
she included my essay "Chicana Feminism: A Counter Discourse," in which I
suggested that women of the Southwest boycott the *Norton Anthology of Literature
by Women*. As a result of that panel, the 1988 South Central MLA Feminist Forum
had a section called "Women of Color in Academia," and the caucus panel, "The
Politics of Feminism." Benstock continues to show her commitment to Third
World feminisms in coediting with Celeste Schenck a series for Cornell University
Press, *Reading Women Writing*.

3. For a discussion of feminist scholarship in terms of "generations" see Jane
Marcus's "Daughters of Anger."

4. See Steiner, *Exact Resemblance*, and DeKoven, "Gertrude Stein and Modern
Painting," for discussions of Stein as a cubist writer.

5. See Brinnin, *Third Rose*, for a thorough discussion of Stein's undergraduate
psychology experiments.

6. See Stimpson, "The Mind, the Body, and Gertrude Stein," for a complete
analysis of Stein's acceptance of pseudo-scientist Otto Weininger's anti-Semitic,
misogynistic ideology in his 1909 *Sex and Character*. Stimpson posits that Weininger provided some hope for Stein when he claimed that "the homosexual woman
is better than the rest of her sex. Actively partaking of male elements, she may

aspire to those aesthetic and intellectual pursuits that are otherwise a male province" (497). Another important essay is Richard Bridgman's "Melanctha" (1961). I was surprised and further disillusioned with contemporary feminist Stein scholars when I discovered in this essay similar points as mine on the racism in "Melanctha."

7. This opens up the debate on the appropriation of Afro-American experience by white feminists, an issue I cannot adequately address in this essay. For further elaboration, see Bell Hooks in *Ain't I a Woman*, especially her critique of Stimpson's " 'Thy Neighbor's Wife, Thy Neighbor's Servants.' " Richard Wright's position on Stein's representation of the Afro-American dialect was part of another debate among the writers in the Harlem Renaissance. For a discussion of these issues see Wahneema Lubiano's chapter "The Harlem Renaissance and the Roots of Afro-American Literary Modernism," in "Messing with the Machine." Brinnin cites the Wright quotation, which appeared in a review by Wright of Stein's "Wars I Have Seen," first published in *PM Magazine* March 11, 1945. Wright states: "Miss Stein's struggling words made the speech of the people around me vivid. From that moment on, in my attempts at writing, I was able to tap at will the vast pool of living words that swirled around me." In spite of Wright's own political affiliations, the social and political position of Afro-Americans as an internal colony in 1945 are revealed in his implication that it took reading a story written by a white person to make him suddenly value black English. See his 1937 review of Zora Neale Hurston's *Their Eyes Were Watching God* for an example of his misogynism. It is ironic that he in effect destroyed Hurston's literary career when he critiqued her novel yet he admired Stein's depiction of the Afro-American experience.

8. See Stimpson, "The Mind," 497, on Stein's interest in Weininger's pseudo-scientific work. Stein still believed Weininger's claims when she wrote *Three Lives*.

9. See Davis, "Rape, Racism, and the Myth of the Black Rapist." Davis cites Stein's *Three Lives* in her examination of the sexual abuse of black women by white men. She states: "Such assaults have been ideologically sanctioned by politicians, scholars and journalists, and by literary artists who have often portrayed Black women as promiscuous and immoral. Even the outstanding writer Gertrude Stein described one of her Black women characters as possessing 'the simple, promiscuous unmorality of the black people' " (176).

10. For an analysis of the construct of the "mulatta" figure, see Spillers, "Notes on an Alternative Model."

11. For further elaboration of Stein's revision of the autobiographical *Q.E.D.* into the coded "Melanctha," see Stimpson, "The Mind," 498–502; also Ruddick, " 'Melanctha.' "

Works Cited

Benstock, Shari. "Beyond the Reaches of Feminist Criticism: A Letter from Paris." *Tulsa Studies in Women's Literature* 3 (Spring–Fall 1984): 5–27.

———. "Feminist Critique: Mastering Our Monstrosity." *Tulsa Studies in Women's Literature* 2 (Fall 1983): 137–49.

Bethel, Lorraine. " 'This Infinity of Conscious Pain': Zora Neale Hurston and the Black Female Literary Tradition." In *All the Women Are White, All the Blacks Are Men: But Some of Us Are Brave*, edited by Gloria T. Hull, Patricia Bell Scott, and Barbara Smith, 176–88. Old Westbury, N.Y.: Feminist Press, 1982.

Bridgman, Richard. "Melanctha." *American Literature* 33 (November 1961): 350–59.

Brinnin, John Malcolm. *The Third Rose: Gertrude Stein and Her World*. Boston: Atlantic Monthly Press, 1959.

Cervantes, Lorna Dee. "Chicana Critics, ¿Y Que?" Paper presented at Chicano Literary Criticism in a Social Context Conference, Stanford Humanities Center, May 28, 1987. Quoted in review of the conference by Laura Paull, *Campus Report*, June 3, 1987, p. 8.

———. *Emplumada*. Pittsburgh: University of Pittsburgh Press, 1981.

Davis, Angela. "Rape, Racism, and the Myth of the Black Rapist." In *Women, Race, and Class*, 172–201. New York: Vintage, 1983.

DeKoven, Marianne. *A Different Language: Gertrude Stein's Experimental Writing*. Madison: University of Wisconsin Press, 1983.

———. "Gertrude Stein and Modern Painting: Beyond Literary Cubism." *Contemporary Literature* 22 (Winter 1981): 81–95.

Gilbert, Sandra M., and Susan Gubar, eds. *The Norton Anthology of Literature by Women*. New York: Norton, 1985.

Greenfeld, Howard. *Gertrude Stein: A Biography*. New York: Crown, 1973.

Griffin, Susan. "The Way of All Ideology." In *Feminist Theory: A Critique of Ideology*, edited by Nannerl O. Keohane, Michelle Z. Rosaldo, and Barbara Gelpi, 273–92. Chicago: University of Chicago Press, 1981.

Hooks, Bell. *Ain't I a Woman: Black Women and Feminism*. Boston: South End Press, 1981.

Hull, Gloria T., Patricia Bell Scott, and Barbara Smith, eds. *All the Women Are White, All the Blacks Are Men, But Some of Us Are Brave*. Old Westbury, N.Y.: Feminist Press, 1982.

Lauter, Paul. "Race and Gender in the Shaping of the American Literary Canon: A Case Study from the Twenties." *Feminist Studies* 9 (Fall 1983): 435–63.

Lubiano, Wahneema. "Messing with the Machine: Four Afro-American Novels and the Nexus of Vernacular, Historical Constraint, and Narrative Strategy," 44–87. Ph.D. dissertation, Stanford University, 1987.

Marcus, Jane. "Daughters of Anger/Material Girls: Con/textualizing Feminist Criticism." In *Last Laughs: Perspectives on Women and Comedy*, edited by Regina Barreca, 281–308. London: Gordon and Breach, 1988.

Moraga, Cherríe, and Gloria Anzaldúa. *This Bridge Called My Back: Writings by Radical Women of Color*. New York: Kitchen Table: Women of Color Press, 1981.

Ruddick, Lisa. " 'Melanctha' and the Psychology of William James." *Modern Fiction Studies* 28 (Winter 1982–83): 543–56.

Russ, Joanna. *How to Suppress Women's Writing*. Austin: University of Texas Press, 1983.

Spillers, Hortense J. "Notes on an Alternative Model: Neither/Nor." In *The Year Left 2: Toward a Rainbow Socialism*, edited by Mike Davis, Manning Marable, Fred Pfeil, and Michael Sprinker, 176–94. London: Verso, 1987.

Spivak, Gayatri Chakravorty. "Foreword" to her translation of "Draupadi" by Mahasveta Devi. In *Writing and Sexual Difference*, edited by Elizabeth Abel, 262–82. Chicago: University of Chicago Press, 1982.

Stein, Gertrude. *Three Lives*. New York: Vintage Books, 1909.

Steiner, Wendy. *Exact Resemblance to Exact Resemblance: The Literary Portraiture of Gertrude Stein*. New Haven: Yale University Press, 1978.

Sternhell, Carol. "Do Women Have Pens?" Review of *How to Suppress Women's Writing*, by Joanna Russ. *Village Voice Literary Supplement* February 7, 1984, p. 13.

Stimpson, Catharine R. "The Mind, the Body, and Gertrude Stein." *Critical Inquiry* 3 (Spring 1977): 489–506.

———. " 'Thy Neighbor's Wife, Thy Neighbor's Servants': Women's Liberation and Black Civil Rights." In *Woman in Sexist Society: Studies in Power and Powerlessness*, edited by Vivian Gornick and Barbara K. Moran, 622–57. New York: Basic Books, 1971.

Tompkins, Jane. *Sensational Designs: The Cultural Work of American Fiction, 1790–1860*. Oxford: Oxford University Press, 1985.

Wright, Richard. "Between Laughter and Tears." Review of *Their Eyes Were Watching God*, by Zora Neale Hurston. *New Masses* 5 (October 1937): 25–26.

Chapter 8

. . . .

Exiled as Exiler

Sara Coleridge, Virginia Woolf, and the Politics of Literary Revision

Bradford K. Mudge

Re-vision—the act of looking back, of seeing with fresh eyes, of entering an old text from a new critical direction—is for women more than a chapter in cultural history: it is an act of survival. Until we can understand the assumptions in which we are drenched we cannot know ourselves.
—Adrienne Rich, "When We Dead Awaken"

Writing on Sara Coleridge in September 1940, Virginia Woolf recognized the tragedy of a life lived only to a fragment of its potential (*Moth*, 111–18). Like her father's "Christabel," Sara Coleridge became for Woolf an "unfinished masterpiece" (114), whose genius was much in evidence but whose circumstances conspired against completion, stifling talent and denying possibility. The intimidating shadow of a brilliant father, the early death of a beloved husband, and the unending demands of parenthood all served to thwart the intellectual energies of a woman who by the age of twenty-two had mastered six languages, published two books, and proven herself in many ways the most Coleridgean of Coleridge's offspring.[1] Yet according to Woolf, whatever accomplishments were achieved—several children's books, a few essays, even the impressive editorial projects—pale in comparison to what might have been.[2] Constantly interrupted by the demands of female duty, Sara was a "heaven-haunter" (*Moth*, 114) unable to translate her visions into the words of men: she was "diffuse," "indefatigable," "incomplete" (115–16). Although better educated and more articulate than the imaginary Judith in *A Room of One's Own*, Sara became for Woolf another of Shakespeare's sisters, a silent heroine whose muffled story haunts our understanding of the past as it challenges the myths of our present.

Woolf's backward glance at Sara Coleridge was not without its jolt of recognition, for the daughters of educated men understood one another, and the Modernist daughter of the Victorian scholar and the Victorian daughter of the Romantic poet were closer than it first appeared.[3] Both had had to struggle for an education while brothers enjoyed the universities; both had been encouraged to believe in traditional female selflessness; both suffered from anxiety, insomnia, and "madness."[4] Like Woolf, Sara fought an ingrained cultural prejudice against women intellectuals; she was exiled by reason of gender from the traditional arena of inquiry. She was not, however, a novelist but a critic, a philosopher, and above all a theologian. She was also very much the proper daughter, and she labored long and hard on behalf of her father's reputation. When she died in 1852, after a horrific battle with breast cancer, she left thousands of pages of manuscripts—essays, journals, poems, and long theological dialogues in the style of Walter Savage Landor's *Imaginary Conversations*. Most were fragments.

Woolf could understand fragments. Thus Sara's twenty-six-page autobiography, written as she lay suffering in September 1851, became a telling document. Looking closely at the series of dots that end the memoir in midsentence, Woolf found an apt symbol for a woman who, like her father, was fated to "complete incompletely" (*Moth*, 118) but who, unlike her father, would receive little recognition for her labors. Toiling in the service of Coleridge's reputation, Sara pieced together his fragments at the price of her own. But Woolf saw too that although fettered by duty, Sara nevertheless discovered a kind of freedom in her editing, for there she "found her father, in those blurred pages, as she had not found him in the flesh; and she found that he was herself" (115). Editorial work became "not self-sacrifice, but self-realization" (115), a pathway to completion, a process by which father and daughter, separated throughout their lives, found themselves and each other in a labyrinth of words.

Yet Woolf might have wondered to what degree that self-realization was accomplished at the expense of self-expression. After finishing her monumental edition of her father's *Biographia Literaria* in 1847, Sara confided to her diary a passage that Woolf would have known:

> No work is so inadequately rewarded either by money or credit as that of editing miscellaneous, fragmentary, immethodical literary remains like those of STC. Such labours cannot be rewarded for they cannot be seen—some of them cannot even be perceived in their effects by the intelligent reader. How many, many mornings, evenings, afternoons have I spent in hunting for some piece of information in order to rectify a statement—to decide whether to retain or withdraw a sentence, or how to turn it—the effect being negative, the silent avoidance of error. The ascertainment of dates, too, and fifty other troubles of that kind, causes much work with very little to shew for it. It is something to myself to feel that I am putting in order a literary house that otherwise would be open to censure here or there. But when there is not mere carelessness but a positive coldness in regard to what I have done, I do sometimes feel as if I had been wasting myself a good deal—at least as far as worldly advantage is concerned. (Diary, October 28, 1848)[5]

Having worked for over a decade to repair her father's reputation, Sara grew dissatisfied with her "reward" and began late in life to question the value of her efforts. The endless concern with the minute particulars of someone else's corpus granted satisfaction, but of a distinctly subservient sort. Her phrasing—"putting in order a literary house"—tropes nicely on

the domestic parallel; both sets of chores demand a prescribed selflessness that tends to "waste" original talent. "What," she laments, "*might* I
have been?"

Clearly, the "self-realization" achieved in and through editorial labor
was not the uncompromised union Woolf suggests but a far more complex
phenomenon—psychologically, socially, and historically—that stands at
the center of a web of familial events rarely cause for speculation.[6] But
more the issue here is Woolf's revisionary ambivalence. On one hand, she
was deeply sympathetic to Sara Coleridge and women like her, celebrating
the "lives of the obscure" as forgotten but essential counterparts to the
patriarchal history of warriors and statesmen. To exhume women's lives
from the refuse heaps of male historians was, she felt, to take the first step
toward collective self-discovery. Yet on the other hand, Woolf's own exca-
vations were marked by a cultured wariness of and palpable disdain for
"minor" literary achievements. She was suspicious of the immethodical
and fragmentary Sara Coleridge if only because her "story" was incomplete, a failed telling whose hidden circumstances could not redeem a
tragedy of unfulfilled potential. I would like to argue that Woolf was both
"exiled" and "exiler," that her revisionary ambivalence acts out a conflict
between her desire for historical revision and her need for literary evaluation, that this conflict was rooted in the tension between her political
grievances and her literary achievements, and that this tension character-
izes much of her work during the 1930s. More important, perhaps, I
would like to argue that Woolf's dilemma raises serious questions about
the evaluative paradigms that continue to structure our critical practice
and vitiate our own attempts at historical revision.

Woolf's essay was occasioned by the publication of Earl Leslie Griggs's
1940 biography of Sara Coleridge, *Coleridge Fille*, and although polite and
complimentary, her review was no doubt intended to offer at least a partial
corrective to his solid but unimaginative account. Adding to Edith Coleridge's *Memoir and Letters of Sara Coleridge* (1873) and Mrs. E. A. Towle's
A Poet's Children (1912), Griggs's biography painted a formal portrait over
their rough and often inaccurate sketches.[7] A scrupulous researcher, he
made extensive use of the unpublished material, preferring whenever
possible to let the remains speak for themselves. But however sympathetic,
Griggs was unable to realize anything more than a general and very distant
understanding of his subject. Sara Coleridge would always be a "distinctly
minor figure" (vii), and his biography as a result seems to envision itself as

one long, definitive footnote to a universally accepted and unchanging "history" of great men and great events. Griggs gives no indication that Sara Coleridge's life offers anything more than a "minor" glimpse back to a famous father and certainly no suggestion that her life might continue to speak to the present, interrogating the very "history" that has condemned her to obscurity.

Reconstructing the people and patterns of history from another set of assumptions, Woolf knew that to focus solely on the "major" was to use a limited set of criteria and let innumerable questions go begging. She had mocked the tunnel vision of male historians in *A Room of One's Own* (1929) and so recognized that such self-assured selectivity was dangerous, inappropriate, and silently obfuscating.[8] She knew too that the real story often begins rather than ends with its supposedly minor details:

> And, like so many of her father's works, Sara Coleridge remains unfinished. Mr. Griggs has written her life, exhaustively, sympathetically; but still . . . dots intervene. That extremely interesting fragment, her autobiography, ends with three rows of dots after twenty-six pages. She intended, she says, to end every section with a moral, or a reflection. And then "on reviewing my earlier childhood I find the predominant reflection. . . ." There she stops. But she said many things in those twenty-six pages, and Mr. Griggs has added others that tempt us to fill in the dots, though not with the facts that she might have given us. (*Moth*, 111)

In Sara Coleridge's life, Woolf saw a mystery which Griggs's biography helped more to intensify than alleviate. His assurance as to both the status and the details of his subject could not keep the questions at bay. On one level, then, the series of dots symbolized a failure to complete, an inability to make or do what might have been; they signified a radical lack and nothing more. Sara's own writings could not, Woolf realized, rival her father's: "Like her father she had a Surinam toad in her head, breeding other toads. But his were jewelled; hers were plain" (*Moth*, 116). Considered formally, Sara's productions were distinctly "minor." On another level, however, as Woolf realized, the dots punctuated a faded tale illegible to her eyes, a muted story very much a part of the heard melodies of great men and great events. In the latter case, the dots defeated critical self-assurance, represented something just beyond her grasp, and so constituted a focal point into which all perspectives collapsed. Those mysterious dots thus wisely subsumed Woolf's own possible interpretations: with so much left unrecorded, with a life reduced to dots on a page, it became pointless to argue whether Sara Coleridge was the unfortunate victim of an oppressive society or a grateful martyr to the spirit of her father— always the "dots intervene."

If Virginia Woolf erred in her assessment of Sara Coleridge, she did so by too quickly accepting a mystery for which she thought there was no explanation. Written only six months before her suicide, Woolf's essay is unusually resigned to its own limitations; it is reluctant to question Griggs's use of the unpublished material and pessimistic about the possibilities for historical reconsiderations of "minor" women writers. However "sympathetic" (*Moth*, 111) Woolf finds Griggs's portrait, his brand of historiography aids and abets the very cultural forces that worked to marginalize Sara Coleridge as a nineteenth-century woman of letters. And, however qualified by its palpable sadness, Woolf's own acceptance of Sara as a fragmentary "Christabel" performs an analogous function, condemning Sara (albeit benevolently) with hierarchical standards of "taste" capable of flexibility but incapable of rejecting "style" and "taste" altogether.

Put another way, both Griggs and Woolf employ a system of valuation (generally historical for the former, more specifically literary for the latter) that presupposes the necessity of public performance, of "great works" produced by artistic or intellectual "genius." That system cannot accommodate the fragmentary remains of Sara Coleridge without immediately pronouncing them a failure. The result for Woolf was a double bind: she recognized a victim of cultural prejudice, of institutionalized prohibitions against women, only to have her aesthetic standards, which were necessarily canonical even when revisionist, tell her there were ample reasons for the "minor" status handed down by "History." In short, a desire for historical revision warred against the unchallengeable supremacy of "Art" and its accompanying (and unavoidable) dependence on hierarchy.

In another of Woolf's late essays, "The Art of Biography" (*Moth*, 187–97), for example, in a discussion of Lytton Strachey, she explores the question, "Is biography an art?" The answer is no. The reason is that "the novelist is free; the biographer tied" (188). The latter's work "is made with the help of friends, of facts"; the former's "is created without any restrictions save those that the artist, for reasons that seem good to him, chooses to obey." Although the categories do in practice overlap, a distinction is maintained: biography is a "craft" rather than an "art" (191). Whereas biography is necessarily limited by its extratextual referentiality, art is "a free world where facts are verified by one person only—the artist himself" (193).

As the masculine pronouns suggest, there is already a serpent lurking in Woolf's Eden, and, at the essay's close, when Woolf puts biography on a "lower level" just beneath the "intense world of the imagination," that serpent squirms more fully into view: "We are incapable of living wholly in the intense world of the imagination. The imagination is a faculty that soon tires and needs rest and refreshment. But for a tired imagination the proper food is not inferior poetry or minor fiction—indeed they blunt and debauch it—but the sober fact, that 'authentic information' from which, as Lytton Strachey has shown us, good biography is made" (196). The imperial "we" is a giveaway. To whom could it refer if not to a select few whose wide reading and good judgment guarantee their positions as purveyors of taste and tradition? Acclimated to sublime heights, they return intermittently to the world of "sober fact" to take a breather from their heady exertions and to recheck historical grounding.[9] The latter is an admittedly important process; "inferior poetry" and "minor fiction" were unquestionably for Woolf historical events worthy of scrutiny. But they were also corrupt (and corrupting) imaginative products: like the serpent in the garden, they promised knowledge but threatened purity. They were, as Woolf remarked elsewhere, "as great a menace to health of mind as influenza to the body" (*Diary*, 1:211).

The "intense world of the imagination," it would seem, was not entirely "free." However feminist its orientation, however much its dependence on and allegiance to the world of "sober fact," it remained structured by gradations of taste, standards of judgment which at a moment's notice could separate the "genuine" from the "inferior," the "major" from the "minor." Regardless of her political commitments, her hatred for patriarchy, and her disgust at the hegemony of the literary canon (not to mention of history in general), Woolf could not renounce her belief in the liberating world of art. She could not abandon the security of "Literature" as a category objectively verifiable and ideologically unfettered. To do so would be to relinquish "art" for "propaganda" and "disinterestedness" for "unreal loyalties" (*Three Guineas*, 85–144). It would be to turn her back on the one Victorian institution that had provided the means by which she could escape the incestuous house of her father and the stultifying role of Victorian woman: "The profession of literature," Woolf emphasized throughout *Three Guineas*, "is open to the daughters of educated men" (89). But however much these daughters were free to shout from its windows, the house of fiction had its own ways of exacting allegiance.

To question the degree to which Woolf's aesthetics worked to suppress her more radical politics is not to slight the power of what Jane Marcus has emphasized as the three dominant strands of Woolf's thought—"the mystical, the 'Marxist,' and the mythical";[10] for such a failure would have to ignore not only Marcus's persuasive arguments but also the work of a large group of feminist scholars who have convincingly revived Woolf's political vision.[11] My intention here is hardly to rediscover the flighty, weak, decidedly Edwardian Virginia of Quentin Bell's biography or simply to expose the conservative flank of an otherwise tough radical feminism. Rather, by focusing on Woolf's assessment of Sara Coleridge, I hope to see how the tension between Woolf's need for aesthetic standards and her desire for historical revision necessarily raises questions first about the use of major/minor distinctions in literary studies and then about possible alternative systems of critical valuation.

In other words, I agree with Carolyn Heilbrun that in her fifties Woolf wrote "'against her artistic grain'" (236–53), not in the pejorative sense that Leonard intended, for the quotation was originally his, but in the positive sense that Woolf struggled to overcome an inherited reverence for an "Art . . . rid of all preaching" (*Writer's Diary*, 183). In its place, she needed to establish an artistic vision intellectually honest and unrepentantly political. *Three Guineas* is the record of that need, and in it—as Heilbrun has argued—the suppressed anger of *A Room of One's Own* finds release. But if I am less willing than Heilbrun to acknowledge Woolf's success, it is because I believe that the conflict was never resolved satisfactorily, either by the artist herself or by the literary scholars who have revived Woolf's commitments only to overlook her prejudices.

Had Virginia Woolf examined the beginning of the 1851 fragment as closely as she did its ending, she might have ventured a more conclusive opinion, for in one revealing introductory paragraph crowd many of the issues centrally important to Sara Coleridge's life and work:

My Father has entered his marriage with my mother and the births of my three brothers with some particularity in a family Bible, given him, as he also notes, by Joseph Cottle on his marriage; the entry of my birth is in my dear Mother's hand-writing, and this seems like an omen of our life-long separation, for I was never with him for more than a few weeks at a time. He lived not much more, indeed, with his other children, but most of their infancy passed under his eye. Alas! more than any of them I inherited that uneasy health of his, which kept us apart. But I did not mean to begin with "alas!" so soon, or so early to advert to the great misfortune of both of our lives—want of bodily vigour adequate to the ordinary demands of life even under favorable circumstances.

In 1851, as in 1802, the "family Bible" represented both the Book of the Father and the father's book, conveniently superimposing one privileged institution over another. Absent from it was not Sara's name, which had been dutifully transcribed by her mother soon after her birth, but the legitimizing "hand" of her father, which alone could give that name its proper status. The names of her brothers were officially recorded with "some particularity" and thereby claimed by a sanctioned and sanctioning patriarchy, but her name is symbolically orphaned—exiled—inscribed by an authority not genuine but borrowed. The tone is resigned, sorrowful, with just an edge of bitterness: "Most of their infancy passed under his eye." Then, in the lamentations that close the paragraph, a reversal is engineered and a rationale put forth. The separation was caused not by difference, as the inscription suggests, but by similarity. "More than any of them," she "inherited" her father's "great misfortune"—a "want of bodily vigour." Appearances to the contrary, exile is circumvented, and unity is achieved through mutual infirmity.

The bonding that occurs between father and daughter in the closing sentences of the paragraph offers an interpretation that shields the ailing writer (then considering the mesmerism cures recommended by Elizabeth Barrett Browning) from potentially uncomfortable symbolism. The irregularity of the inscription suggests, as Sara notes, "an omen" of a "life-long separation," but obviously it also proclaims her marginal status as woman. Endorsed by a female hand, she inherits not the world of her father but that of her mother, and—conversely—her estrangement from him is also her exile from a world of freedom and opportunity. That this exile should be linguistically mandated, a consequence of her "dear Mother's handwriting," appropriately reveals the dilemma of the intellectual woman brought up to believe her writings were of no marketable value.

Whether intended or not, then, the opening paragraph from the 1851 memoir asks that the "life-long separation" between father and daughter be seen in terms of, among other things, sexual difference. The absent father is both the eccentric poet comfortably installed at Highgate and the patriarchal endorsement never a possibility; he is both the author and the authority, both the biological father and the law. Although the physical distance between them could easily have been overcome, the sexual difference was an unbreachable gulf enforced fervently by family, church, and state. So disfranchised from the beginning, Sara might have measured the inequities within her own narrative, stopping to reflect upon the difference between the maternal and paternal inscriptions and perhaps seeing there an apt emblem for her own marginal career as woman of letters. Still more reflective, she might have considered the obvious irony—that the greater part of her public labors had been spent verifying, legitimizing, and defending the words of her father, which, from the outset (and regardless of the charges of plagiarism), maintained a greater credibility than her own. Yet such reflection was at the time simply not a possibility, for Sara's identity had been forged by the very institutions that constrained her, and from her perspective those constraints were not her bondage but her liberation and her blessing. Thus it is not surprising that the "want of bodily vigour" which explains the "life-long separation" also becomes a valued legacy bonding father and daughter through shared adversity. Resignation is, after all, a Christian virtue, and Sara, like her father, depended heavily on a theology that accommodated and justified human frailty: she too suffered from constant ill health; she too battled a lifelong addiction to opium.

As the autobiography continues, the issue of health, both physical and psychological, emerges as a dominant theme and reveals substantially more than the author intended—more perhaps than Woolf would have cared to recognize. Sara depicts herself as the victim of warring parents and of the conflicting philosophies of the two households at Allan Bank and Greta Hall. Whereas the Wordsworths at Allan Bank (and their live-in guest Coleridge) encouraged rustic simplicity and a certain emotional honesty, the Southeys and Coleridges at Greta Hall were more refined in their behavior and less likely to be demonstrative. Caught in the middle, Sara faced a choice not only between parents but also between differing ideals of woman-as-young-girl, between alternate versions of "daughter." In the autobiography, then, arguments about her health are subsumed by the larger question of what it means to be a woman; and although the accounts of her father are marked by a palpable ambivalence, Sara had little trouble deciding in favor of his particular brand of female purity, of woman's spiritual essence. Such a move had the advantage of aligning father, monarch, and deity with a reassuring philosophic neatness, explaining in turn women's physical, social, and political infirmities as merely transient hardships to be rewarded in the life hereafter.

Thus, at the autobiography's close, Sara ponders her objectives and questions the relationship between her "childish experience" and her "maturer self": "Such are the chief *historical* events of my little life, up to nine years of age. But can I in any degree retrace what being I was then— what relation my then being held to my maturer self? Can I draw any useful reflection from my childish experience, or found any useful maxim upon it?" She then immediately returns—as if in answer—to her health, to Allan Bank, and to her father:

> I remember well that nervous sensitiveness and morbid imaginativeness had set in with me very early. During my Grasmere visit I used to feel frightened at night, on account of the darkness. I was then a stranger to the whole host of night-agitators. . . . And yet I was terrified in the dark, and used to think of lions. . . . My next bugbear was the Ghost in Hamlet. Then the picture of Death and Hellgate in an old edition of Par[adise] Lost . . . last & worst came my Uncle Southey's ballad horrors, above all the Old Woman of Berkeley. Oh the agonies I have endured between nine and twelve at night. . . . I dare not, even now, rehearse these particulars for fear of calling up some of the old feeling, which indeed I have never in my life been quite free from. What made it worse was that . . . it could not be understood by the inexperienced. . . . My Uncle Southey laughed. . . . Even mama scolded me. . . . But my Father understood the cause better. He insisted that a lighted candle should be left in my room. . . . From that time forth my sufferings ceased. I believe they would have destroyed my health had they continued.

Here, the bodily—"nervous sensitiveness"—and the psychological— "morbid imaginativeness"—are traced back to and conflated in the "old feeling," a primordial fear that appeared to the young Sara in various guises, as "the Ghost in Hamlet," "the picture of Death" from *Paradise Lost*, and most forcefully as Southey's "Old Woman of Berkeley." This (dis)ease, the ur-infirmity at the root of all others, was understood by no one except her father, and it is through this uncommon bond that we are to perceive and evaluate their relationship. And, more important, it is through their relationship that we are to perceive and evaluate Sara's life.

"The old feeling" is not a single experience or even a predisposition of character but a psychophilosophical given seen by Sara as a religious first principle, a sensitivity to be sure, but a sensitivity to the unchanging spiritual condition of man, whether it be called original sin, natural depravity, or congenital Coleridgean guilt.

And so the "Alas" with which the autobiography began echoes here to bring us around full circle, as the "lighted candle" that Coleridge leaves his daughter illuminates both child and adult. For the six-year-old girl, the taper dispels night fears and calms her immediate anxieties; for the forty-eight-year-old woman, it enlightens a lifetime of frustrations, explaining away parental neglect, male/female inequities, and, above all, the nagging feeling that natural talent had been wasted in the service of others. For one, the light is a physical comfort, for the other, a spiritual justification. To measure the distance between the little girl and the dying woman, between the experience and the interpretation, is to trace the process of an education and the events of a lifetime.

But the autobiography was never completed. It ends abruptly after only the first of what were intended to be eight separate sections. Each section, Sara confided to her daughter Edith, was to conclude with an appropriate "Moral of Reflection . . . some maxim which [that section] specifically illustrated, or truth which it exemplified, or warning which it suggested." Instead, as Woolf emphasized, the autobiography breaks off in midsentence: "On reviewing my earlier childhood I find the predominant reflection. . . ." Perhaps an unexpected visitor interrupted her writing, her own "person from Porlock" sent to dispel the creative vision. More likely, the interpretive assurance with which that sentence began was in fact lacking. Sara's "predominant reflection" was anything but predominant: the anxieties, fears, and confusions of childhood failed to respond to the soothing interpretive vision that the dying woman hoped would order her life as neatly as it had her father's works.

As Woolf could not have known, Sara's autobiography was written in the midst of a crisis of faith that had begun during the early summer of 1851 and was by that September reaching its zenith. Characterized by depression, insomnia, and raging hysterical fits, her illness is recorded in her diary; entries indicate that it was part of a larger pattern of doubts concerning those institutions that had molded her life. Earlier suspicions about the value of "putting in order" someone else's "literary house" bred further suspicions, which, when encouraged by the agonies of cancer, led her to question God's omnipotence and her own chance of salvation. Thus Woolf was right to suspect a mystery lurking behind those concluding dots. But she was wrong to assume that they automatically inscribed an inadequacy which necessarily prohibited further scrutiny, for with those dots Sara Coleridge denied the neatness of the roles into which she had been placed—the dutiful daughter, faithful wife, devoted mother—and questioned, with silent protest, the institutions to which she had given her lifelong support.[12]

Woolf's protests were not silent. Many were subtle, many tentative: she knew, as Sara Coleridge had learned, that there was always a price to pay. Nevertheless, in one form or another, Woolf wrote down her protests. By the mid-1930s, with Europe careening toward disaster and Woolf an established author in her fifties, subtlety was no longer a necessity so she allowed herself a "good gallop" (*Writer's Diary*, 267) over terrain that had long troubled her. The resulting book was, of course, *Three Guineas*. In it, "she was free," as Heilbrun puts it, "to assume a tone that is far from ladylike, wholly unconciliatory, beyond the charm of *A Room of One's Own*: she was able to indulge the glorious release of letting her anger rip" (241). Predictably, *Three Guineas* met with a cool reception, and even among Woolf's friends the reactions were mixed.[13] E. M. Forster would later direct a well-bred sneer at its "old-fashioned . . . Feminism" (33), although he left it to Quentin Bell to dismiss entirely. For Bell, the book is the "product of a very odd mind . . . [in] a very odd state." Like Forster, Bell believed his aunt was incapable of understanding the contemporary political climate: "She belonged, inescapably, to the Victorian world of Empire, Class and Privilege" (421).

Recent readers have been less content to leave Woolf fettered by the stays of "the Victorian world of Empire, Class and Privilege." In her essay " 'No more horses': Virginia Woolf on Art and Propaganda," Jane Marcus stoutly declares: "Snobbery, elitism, hatred or distrust of the working class—not true" (279); "*Three Guineas* is a socialist, pacifist, and feminist polemic" (267).[14] Arguing that Woolf's political vision was allied to and dependent upon the lower classes, or "lowbrows" as Woolf called them, Marcus demonstrates that the "Outsiders' Society" was not a naive rhetorical position but a vital first step toward the rejection of patriarchal nationalism and the subsequent establishment of an international socialism (277–79). In the course of her argument, Marcus effectively demolishes the effete "Virginia" of Leavis, Forster, and Bell, restoring to Woolf the courage of her convictions and suggesting to scholarship that it examine more self-critically the marketing of celebrated literary figures.

Yet " 'No more horses' " is itself unabashedly celebratory. Only once does Marcus question Woolf's ideological assumptions. "Pacifism is to me," Marcus writes, "an ethical luxury, a self-indulgence at some historical moments, but in Woolf it is understandable" (283). This passage occurs several pages after Marcus had encouraged her fellow "professional women, writers and teachers," to consider adopting Woolf's suggestions: "We are the guardians of culture and its future promise, *if* we do not join the profession on the same terms as men, but remain in poverty, intellectual chastity, and 'freedom from unreal loyalties.' The terms are hard. . . . What would happen if women followed [Woolf's] advice?" To answer the question and end her paragraph, Marcus quotes the following passage from *Three Guineas*:

> The slaves who are now kept hard at work piling words into books, piling words into articles, as the old slaves piled stones into pyramids, would shake the manacles from their wrists and give up their loathsome labour. And "culture," that amorphous bundle, swaddled up as she now is in insincerity, emitting half truths from her timid lips, sweetening and diluting her message with whatever sugar or water serves to swell the writer's fame or his master's purse, would regain her shape and become . . . muscular, adventurous, free.

Like all of *Three Guineas*, this passage deserves to be taken seriously by today's "professional women, writers and teachers"—but not reverentially. If Woolf's ideal culture—"muscular, adventurous, free"—achieves political efficacy via a "mystical" and "mythical" power traceable to Caroline Stephen, F. D. Maurice, and others, as Marcus has argued ("Niece," 7–36), it is no less nostalgic and uncritical for it. However admirable her convictions, the "culture" Woolf offers us is neither free from ideological constraints nor unhampered by the tensions of difference. Rather, like its patriarchal twin, it obscures the complexities of institutionally mediated production and reception as it rushes to escape "insincerity" and "half truth." To what degree, then, does Woolf's "culture," pacifist and separatist though it is, simply invert its nemesis, say, T. S. Eliot's decidedly fascistic and phallocentric "orthodoxy"?[15] Both share, it could be argued, the same assumptions about the role of art in society—in particular that art is a category of works imbued with lasting value of unquestionable authority, created by genius and recognized by taste. More important, both "exile"—with equal self-confidence—those "minor" works of insufficient merit.

As a child Woolf was steeped in Carlyle, Coleridge, and Macaulay (Bell, 53).[16] Although she labored to revise her father's lionizing assessments of the Victorian greats, it was no accident that Arnold's favorite word, "disinterestedness," was also Woolf's or that Coleridge's "clerisy" would reappear in different guise in *Three Guineas* (176). The notion of "culture" so dear to the mid-Victorians stabilized Woolf's "highbrows" and elevated her "lowbrows": it provided a fixed center free from the "infantile fixations" of male professions (127–41). Although Woolf recognized and lamented the extent to which literature was a profession inescapably dominated by financial interests and compromised by corrupt reviewers and critics, she nevertheless celebrated its relative freedom, compared, say, to the ingrained and claustrophobic sexism of religion: "Thus the profession of religion seems to have been originally much what the profession of literature is now. It was originally open to anyone who had received the gift of prophecy. No training was needed; the professional requirements were simple in the extreme—a voice and a market-place, a pen and paper" (123). The "gift of prophecy," the "voice," is synonymous with "talent" or "genius," an imaginative vision capable of translating itself into words. Regardless of the mercantile "middlebrows," literature still is, and presumably always will be, "open" to those who meet the qualifications. Like "culture" in the earlier passage, Woolf's "gift of prophecy" is presented uncritically: no allowances are made for its ties to and dependence upon "tradition"; no indication is given that "culture" has a habit of fashioning "talent" in its own image, of recognizing and encouraging only the "voices" to its "taste." Woolf offered her solution to the problem of biased reviewers in a footnote: "The suggestion in the text is not to abolish public criticism; but to supplement it by a new service based on the example of the medical profession. A panel of critics recruited from reviewers (many of whom are potential critics of genuine taste and learning) would practice like doctors in strictest privacy. Publicity removed, it follows that most of the distractions and corruptions which inevitably make contemporary criticism worthless to the writer would be abolished" (176). "Genuine taste" is the critical counterpart to "talent," and when both function smoothly, "culture" is at one with itself and its society. The price of such harmony, however, is suppression: those writers whose talents are abnormal, whose texts fail to meet certain standards of judgment, can either be marginalized as "minor figures" or dismissed entirely.[17]

Like Sara Coleridge, who struggled in her autobiography to order a life threatened suddenly by a late shift in perspective, by the unasked-for traumas of self-revision, Virginia Woolf struggled in *Three Guineas* to accommodate cherished beliefs within a newer and more radical feminism. As she had not done before, Woolf "let her anger rip" against the "unreal loyalties" that seemed to be at once society's unifying force and its irrational urge to self-destruction. If she allowed herself the luxury of one stable vantage point from which to get her bearings as she systematically exposed the rampant ills of patriarchy, the error is hardly grievous. In fact, it is no error at all. It is an ideological position historically specific and contextually understandable; it is, in other words, a position that arises not only out of Woolf's private experience but also in the context of larger challenges then affecting the status of art in society—in particular the challenges proffered by the European avant-garde.

I am not suggesting that the author of *Three Guineas* desired either a police state or a literary canon exclusively "highbrow." I am suggesting that Woolf's need to rethink patriarchal institutions encountered understandable difficulties concerning the institution of art. By "institution" I mean in particular the structure of assumptions and beliefs which mediate both the production and reception of art in society. Such mediation has always existed, but according to Peter Burger (who conveniently summarizes a whole line of thought on the subject), it was only during the first decades of the twentieth century that this mediation was exposed and questioned.[18] The challenge, significantly, came not from critics, who by definition supported the status quo, but from avant-garde artists who were displeased with the commodification of art in bourgeois society. By attempting to destroy the cherished notions of artistic autonomy so much a part of late nineteenth-century aestheticism, they hoped to reintegrate art into social praxis. Their failure to do so (Duchamp's "Ready-Mades" have now become the very "works of art" they were originally intended to challenge) in no way lessens the significance of their institutionally directed criticism. In fact, according to Burger, it should force the critic to acknowledge that the relationship between art and society is always institutionally mediated (Burger, 21–23).

The strength of Burger's work, and its significance both for Woolf's revisionary stance and for our own, derives from its recognition that one cannot adequately criticize formalism without first establishing a "categorical frame" that permits the relationship between the critic and the art work to be "thematized," that is, acknowledged and evaluated as part of a changing social context (Burger, 4). This frame, "the institution of art/literature," exposes and explains the essentially contradictory role of art in modern society: art is utopian and so protests against a less than ideal reality; but its truths are always already aestheticized and so remove themselves from the realm of praxis.[19] In other words, the utopian impulses are effectively short-circuited by a prefabricated set of assumptions which insists on the autonomy of art, on an otherworldliness that neutralizes political change and discriminates against all nonstandard works (Burger, 26–27, 90–95).

Because Woolf subscribed to an inherited autonomy aesthetic, literature was to her not an institutional construct but a categorical given: regardless of corrupt "middlebrows," it remained distant and holy, a house built by genius and appreciated by taste.[20] But because Woolf's motivations were largely political, because she sought to effect change through her art, her mystical and mythical idealism, that stuffy mansion quickly proved claustrophobic: its rooms were grand but confining, its halls spacious but cold. As a critic, she soon learned the value of exploring back corridors and forbidden cellars, where she met women such as Sara Coleridge who taught her the other side of history. As an artist, she used this knowledge to design her own house with fewer walls and more accessible views. Finally, toward the end of her life, she became a little distrustful of all literary architecture. Had she persisted with "The Pargiters," an experimental draft of alternating chapters of fact and fiction,[21] Woolf might have lost whatever residual elitism remained from her Victorian education and given us another avant-garde success. Such an experiment, had Leonard not stopped it, would have challenged the otherworldliness of the imagination and the claims of aesthetic norms to universal validity. It would not, of course, have destroyed the "institution of art/literature," but it would have been a gesture against the autonomy aesthetic that structured and continues to structure literary criticism as it is most often practiced.

Woolf's struggles, then, are of some significance for a discipline that acquired its legitimacy only during her lifetime and which still is—by definition—resistant to the study of "minor" figures. For as long as the distinction between literary and nonliterary remains operative, corresponding distinctions between major and minor follow logically. To rethink major and minor, one must rethink the ingrained systems of critical valuation which thus far have kept the concept of the "literary" securely in place. Through hard work and harder polemics the term can be redefined to include "minor" writers—the politically, sexually, and ethnically disfranchised. But the revisionist critic usually argues that the heretofore marginalized work has been marginalized only because of a previous failure to perceive exactly how the work embodies the scene of its struggles. In other words, the "minor" writer is shown to be as complex, subtle, engaging, or powerful as the "major" writer but on significantly different terms, the relevance of which becomes apparent only after contextual redefinition. Such a move challenges the values of the literary without questioning the framework. In Burger's terms, criticism has yet to overcome its dependence on the autonomous literary form, the well-wrought urn packed with whatever "stylistic" qualities are valued at the critical moment. Under the rubric "literary," all forms have the potential for justifying serious scrutiny, but once the autonomy of art has been exposed as a more or less contrived institutional frame, then, as Burger argues, "normative examination" gives way to "functional analysis" (87) and the scope of inquiry necessarily expands.

But what exactly is "functional analysis"? Although Burger does not elaborate, it would be as I envision it, a critical practice whose system of valuation would be structured so as to accommodate diverse cultural artifacts—an obscure autobiographical fragment as well as the acclaimed *Three Guineas*, or, for the sake of argument, a Disney comic book as well as Pound's *Cantos*. The claim is not as extravagant as it sounds, nor is it a gross and irresponsible conflation of literary criticism and sociology. Walt Disney's industrial fiction warrants serious consideration rather than knee-jerk dismissal, as Ariel Dorfman's two books *How to Read Donald Duck* and *The Empire's Old Clothes* make clear.[22] No one would argue that a comic book is the "literary" equivalent of a great Modernist long poem, but one might contend that the comic represents a mass-produced, pervasively influential form whose posturing innocence and self-effacing claims to be mere entertainment cloak a very powerful ideological force. It might also be argued that the Disney comic represents precisely the mass education Pound's *Cantos* were intended to counter and that High Modernism (Woolf's as well as Pound's) is the last hurrah of an elite culture deeply threatened by the rise in the eighteenth century of a literate populace and by its new "folk art," which for the first time challenged the supremacy of "high" art as it competed for limited financial rewards. My point here is that the two artifacts are deceptively separated in their critical "worth" by institutional predilections that favor stable, iconic, autonomous "works" that insist on lasting value by the very fact of their being literary. The comic book, on the other hand, makes no such claim. In fact, the comic book is quite content with its disposable form, knowing full well that it is easily disseminated and more easily replaced, if not with itself then with a suitable copy. Like the advertisement, the comic book is content to exist only for the moment of its consumption: it fully understands the power of ubiquity.

Although it might be pointless to argue whether the cultural influence exerted by the *Cantos* was greater or lesser than that exerted by Donald Duck, the very posing of the question situates the literary work within the cultural matrix where it belongs and forces the acknowledgment of alternative modes of valuation, of other ways of mapping the "literary" terrain so as to include the fragmentary remains of "minor" women as well as the more polished "works" of the "highbrow" sisters.

Sara Coleridge spent the greater part of her life "putting in order a literary house" only to realize on her deathbed that she could have built her own. Her autobiography is an attempt at revision, at looking back, at seeing with fresh eyes how she might have laid new foundations instead of refortifying the old ones put down by her father. Virginia Woolf built her literary house on sites cleared by Sara Coleridge and similar women; Woolf looked back to the "lives of the obscure" to find her own tradition, her own line of women writers working in the shadows of great men and great events. Even though she was convinced of their "invincible mediocrity," she persisted; she read their memoirs, their diaries, their "inferior fiction," and their "minor poetry"; she learned from them. They revised her understanding of history; she revised the way they were understood. It was, in Adrienne Rich's words, a mutually beneficial "act of survival."

The process of revision continues. To revise Virginia Woolf revising Sara Coleridge is to extend the act of survival; it is to question Woolf's unquestioned tenets as well as to champion her political and artistic integrity. It is also to question the paradigms that structure our own critical activity and to wonder about the possibilities for cultural studies less dependent on exclusionary standards and more receptive to the varied and often fragmentary voices of history.

Notes

A different version of this essay appeared in the Fall 1986 issue of *Tulsa Studies in Women's Literature*. I am indebted to Jane Marcus, Jerome McGann, and Clare Colquitt for their encouragement and assistance. Particular thanks go to Jane for her numerous suggestions and unflagging willingness to share her knowledge of Woolf and Woolf scholarship.

1. In 1822, at the age of nineteen, Sara published *An Account of the Abipones*, a three-volume translation of a work in Latin by Martin Dobrizhoffer. Three years later, she published *The Right Joyous and Pleasant History of the Facts, Tests, and Prowesses of the Chevalier Bayard*, a two-volume translation from medieval French. Originally intended to assist her brother Derwent with college expenses, neither translation was to be anything more than an amusement for Sara, chores to keep her busy during her long and often strained engagement to her first cousin Henry Nelson Coleridge. Like Mary Kingsley, the marginalized "heroine" of Woolf's 1938 polemic *Three Guineas*, Sara contributed much to "Arthur's Education Fund" (*Three Guineas*, 3).

2. *Pretty Lessons in Verse for Good Children* (1834), a collection of poems originally written for Sara Coleridge's daughter Edith and son Herbert, went through five editions. In 1837, Sara published another children's book, *Phantasmion*, a long and rambling prose fairy tale.

After Coleridge's death in 1834, Sara and her husband began what proved to be a protracted defense of the poet's reputation. Using the most effective strategy possible, they brought out Coleridge's unpublished material and republished works that were out of print, maintaining high editorial standards and frequently including critical essays as either introductions or appendixes. Between 1834 and 1843, they were responsible for publishing two volumes of *Table Talk*, four volumes of *Literary Remains*, the third edition of *The Friend*, and the fourth and fifth editions of *Aids to Reflection*, a single volume including the *Constitution of Church and State*, the two *Lay Sermons*, and the *Confessions of an Inquiring Spirit*. After Henry's death in 1843, Sara continued their project by publishing the *Biographia Literaria* in 1847, *Notes and Lectures upon Shakespeare* in 1849, *Essays on His Own Times* in 1850, and *The Poems of Samuel Taylor Coleridge* in 1852.

In addition to her editorial work, Sara published two reviews for the *Quarterly Review*, one on Tennyson's *The Princess* in March 1848 and another on Dyce's edition of Beaumont and Fletcher in September 1848.

3. According to Noel Annan, Leslie Stephen thought S. T. Coleridge "the seminal mind of the century" (314) and insisted that his daughter read Coleridge, like Carlyle, in great quantity. Stephen, however, had trouble coming to grips with Coleridge's moral weaknesses and could not balance the poet's private faults against his public virtues (313–15).

4. The quotation marks signify an informed wariness about the ideological

baggage that has accompanied and continues to accompany discussions of female illness. The term is meant not in the inherited and uncritical sense of Woolf's biographer Quentin Bell, for whom it seems to represent the logical culmination of a series of "natural" female traits—emotionalism, irrationality, disorganization— but rather in the sense of its ties to nineteenth-century hysteria and of its decidedly ambivalent stance in relation to the "cult of female invalidism" that fostered it. As Barbara Ehrenreich and Deirdre English have argued in *Complaints and Disorders: The Sexual Politics of Sickness*, hysteria involved both the acceptance of society's definition of woman as inherently "sick" and a powerful protest against "an intolerable social role" (42–43). For enlightening discussions of Woolf's "madness," see Kenny; and Marcus, "Virginia Woolf and her Violin." See also Vicinus.

5. I am grateful to Mrs. A. H. B. Coleridge and the Coleridge estate for permission to quote from the unpublished material.

6. Much attention has been paid to Coleridge's strained marriage, his off-and-on friendship with the Wordsworths, and his extended stay with the Gillmans, but scholars have failed to explore the process by which Coleridge was packaged and marketed by devoted family members after his death in 1834 and the ways those efforts have affected both the "Coleridge" read by the high Victorians and the "Coleridge" we read today. Scholarship has neglected to recognize the extent to which Sara Coleridge remade her father in her own image and for her own purposes.

7. Edith Coleridge, Sara's daughter, includes her mother's autobiography in her edition, and Woolf would have read it there. All references to the autobiography in this essay are from the original manuscripts at the Harry Ransom Humanities Research Center.

8. *A Room of One's Own* contains Woolf's most celebrated discussion of "minor" women writers. She argues that "masterpieces are not solitary births" (68) but are dependent upon and indebted to a long tradition of lesser-known predecessors (61–81). Nevertheless, as I shall argue, the standards by which works are judged to be either "major" or "minor" are left unquestioned; the cultured reader, Woolf implies, is automatically capable of recognizing "a work of genius" (53). Similarly, in another early piece, "The Lives of the Obscure," Woolf defends and applauds the "invincible mediocrity" (381) of second-string autobiographers as essential to the appreciation of "good books." To understand a literary period, she argues, one must be intimately familiar with its "gradations of merit" (381). But how those gradations come into being and by what process they order the literary universe remains a nonproblem.

9. Although my criticism here immediately recalls similar censures by Queenie Leavis, E. M. Forster, and Quentin Bell, my position could not be more different. I have no intention of denying Woolf's political vision, the political content of her novels, or her dependence on the world of "sober fact." On the contrary, I insist on all three: Woolf's "highbrow" responsibility for and dependence upon "lowbrow

... vitality" has been copiously and convincingly documented—first in "Lives of the Obscure" and *A Room of One's Own* and later in *Three Guineas*, "Sara Coleridge," and "Middlebrow." See also Marcus's " 'No more horses.' " Marcus refutes the criticisms of Leavis, Forster, and Bell but fails, I think, to recognize how Woolf's rage against "middlebrows" is in danger of turning an otherwise useful polemic into a prejudicial and exclusionary critical practice.

10. Marcus, *Virginia Woolf*, 2; see also Marcus, "The Niece of a Nun."

11. See, for example, Black; Carroll; DeSalvo; Moore; Silver; and Squier.

12. The ellipsis, appropriately, is an important but frequently unnoticed symbol in both *A Room of One's Own* and *Three Guineas*. Jane Marcus, in *Virginia Woolf*, explains the use of ellipses in a way that dovetails nicely with my own understanding of Woolf's late anxiety and alienation. Marcus writes: "The gender gap between Woolf and her enemies and the class gap between Woolf and her allies is most often expressed not in words, but in their absences, in ellipses, so that the dot dot dot of unfinished sentences and uncompleted thoughts, which increases dramatically throughout her writing career, is an exact representation ... of her own position in relation to her culture" (12).

13. Vita Sackville-West thought the arguments "misleading" (*Letters of Virginia Woolf*, 6:243, 257). Maynard Keynes, in Bell's words, "was both angry and contemptuous; it was, he declared, a silly argument and not very well written" (Bell, 441). Bell himself was disturbed by linkage between patriarchy and fascism: "The connection between the two questions seemed tenuous and the positive suggestions wholly inadequate" (441).

14. Although Marcus's essay appeared in 1977 and was immediately and repeatedly seconded, the debate is still very much alive. For a revealing glimpse of the two major combatants and a helpful summary of their disagreements, see Bell, "A 'Radiant' Friendship," and Marcus, "Quentin's Bogey."

15. I am thinking here of Eliot's remarkable 1934 essay "After Strange Gods," in which he preaches the value of a homogeneous "Christian orthodoxy" before railing against Yeats, Hardy, and Lawrence. Obviously an attempt to redefine earlier notions of "tradition" in light of his more strident religious beliefs, Eliot's "orthodoxy" uses "culture" to centralize and stabilize his ideal society. See also his "Religion and Literature" (1935).

16. See also DeSalvo's "1897."

17. Ethel Smyth, ever the iconoclast, challenged Woolf about the ease with which the latter made her aesthetic judgments. Woolf's response (*Letters*, 4:230–32) is revealing both for its evasive tactics and for its palpable tension between a need to "discriminate" and a fear that too often such discriminations are dictated "by habit" and so are "woolly headed" and exclusionary. To end an obviously uncomfortable discussion, Woolf writes: "I grant that having been born within the Polar region of Cambridge I tend by *education* not instinct to frigidify" (emphasis added).

18. I am thinking here too of the work by many recent leftist historians and theorists, among them Raymond Williams, Terry Eagleton, Fredric Jameson, and Edward Said. All depend in one way or another upon an understanding of the history of literary culture argued originally by Williams. Anticipated in his classic *Culture and Society* (1959) and elaborated in both *Keywords: A Vocabulary of Culture and Society* (1976) and *Marxism and Literature* (1977), this history traces the word *literature* from the fifteenth century to the present to illuminate a process of increasing separation from social praxis. During the fourteenth and fifteenth centuries, the word referred to a level of experience, a state of being widely read in all kinds of writings: one "had literature" in the general sense of having a broad education. By the late Renaissance, it had come to mean specifically the objects of that education, all types of books. Later still, during the eighteenth and nineteenth centuries, the term took its present meaning—the objects exclusively of imaginative production. This same process Burger discusses as the formation of "autonomous art," the gradual "detachment of art from [its] practical contexts" (46). He identifies three phases—Sacral Art, Courtly Art, and Bourgeois Art—and examines the changing modes of production and reception according to intended social function (35–54). See also Eagleton, 1–53.

19. Herbert Marcuse provides the *locus classicus* for any discussion of the paradoxes of elite culture (88–133).

20. For a useful discussion of Leslie Stephen's understanding of "literature" and his ties to Desmond MacCarthy and Queenie Leavis's notions of culture and criticism, see Annan, pp. 317–38.

21. See Leaska, ed.

22. Dorfman's work on industrial fiction and John Berger's analysis of advertisements are two persuasive examples of the value of critical attention paid to popular art forms. Whereas Dorfman illuminates the silent ideologies of Disney's fantasy world, Berger examines the interrelations between the development of painting and its representations and analogs in contemporary advertisements.

Works Cited

Annan, Noel. *Leslie Stephen: The Godless Victorian.* New York: Random House, 1984.

Bell, Quentin. "A 'Radiant' Friendship." *Critical Inquiry* 10 (June 1984): 557–66.

———. *Virginia Woolf: A Biography.* New York: Harcourt Brace Jovanovich, 1972.

Berger, John. *Ways of Seeing.* New York: Penguin, 1973.

Black, Naomi. "Virginia Woolf and the Women's Movement." In *Virginia Woolf: A Feminist Slant*, edited by Jane Marcus, 180–97. Lincoln: University of Nebraska Press, 1983.

Burger, Peter. *The Theory of the Avant Garde*. Minneapolis: University of Minnesota Press, 1984.

Carroll, Berenice A. " 'To Crush Him in Our Own Country': The Political Thought of Virginia Woolf." *Feminist Studies* 4 (1978): 99–131.

Coleridge, Sara. Autobiography. MSS housed at the Harry Ransom Humanities Research Center, University of Texas at Austin, where they form part of the extensive Coleridge Family Papers.

———. Diary. MSS housed at the Harry Ransom Humanities Research Center.

DeSalvo, Louise A. "1897: Virginia Woolf at Fifteen." In *Virginia Woolf: A Feminist Slant*, edited by Jane Marcus, 78–108. Lincoln: University of Nebraska Press, 1983.

———. "Shakespeare's Other Sister." In *New Feminist Essays on Virginia Woolf*, edited by Jane Marcus, 61–81. Lincoln: University of Nebraska Press, 1981.

Dorfman, Ariel. *The Empire's Old Clothes*. New York: Pantheon, 1983.

Eagleton, Terry. *Literary Theory: An Introduction*. Minneapolis: University of Minnesota Press, 1983.

Ehrenreich, Barbara, and Deirdre English. *Complaints and Disorders: The Sexual Politics of Sickness*. Westbury, N.Y.: Feminist Press, 1973.

Forster, E. M. *Virginia Woolf*. New York: Harcourt Brace Jovanovich, 1942.

Griggs, Earl Leslie. *Coleridge Fille*. London: Oxford University Press, 1940.

Heilbrun, Carolyn. "Virginia Woolf in Her Fifties." In *Virginia Woolf: A Feminist Slant*, edited by Jane Marcus, 236–53. Lincoln: University of Nebraska Press, 1983.

Kenny, Susan M. "Two Endings: Virginia Woolf's Suicide and *Between the Acts*." *University of Toronto Quarterly* 44 (Summer 1975): 265–89.

Leaska, Mitchell, ed. *The Pargiters: The Novel-Essay Portion of "The Years."* New York: New York Public Library, 1977.

Marcus, Jane. "The Niece of a Nun: Virginia Woolf, Caroline Stephen, and the Cloistered Imagination." In *Virginia Woolf: A Feminist Slant*, edited by Jane Marcus, 7–36. Lincoln: University of Nebraska Press, 1983.

———. " 'No More Horses': Virginia Woolf on Art and Propaganda." *Women's Studies* 4 (1977): 265–90.

———. "Quentin's Bogey: A Reply to Quentin Bell." *Critical Inquiry* 11 (March 1985): 486–501.

———. "Virginia Woolf and Her Violin." In *Mothering the Mind: Twelve Studies of Writers and Their Silent Partners*, edited by Ruth Perry and Martine Watson Brownley, 181–201. New York: Holmes and Meier, 1984.

———. *Virginia Woolf and the Languages of Patriarchy*. Bloomington: Indiana University Press, 1987.

———. ed. *New Feminist Essays on Virginia Woolf*. Lincoln: University of Nebraska Press, 1981.

_____, ed. *Virginia Woolf: A Feminist Slant*. Lincoln: University of Nebraska Press, 1983.

Marcuse, Herbert. *Negations*. Boston: Beacon Press, 1968.

Moore, Madeline. *The Short Season between Two Silences: The Mystical and the Political in the Novels of Virginia Woolf*. Boston: Allen and Unwin, 1984.

Silver, Brenda R. "*Three Guineas* Before and After." In *Virginia Woolf: A Feminist Slant*, edited by Jane Marcus, 254–76. Lincoln: University of Nebraska Press, 1983.

Squier, Susan M. *Virginia Woolf and London*. Chapel Hill: University of North Carolina Press, 1983.

Vicinus, Martha, ed. *Suffer and Be Still: Women in the Victorian Age*. Bloomington: Indiana University Press, 1973.

Woolf, Virginia. "The Art of Biography." In *The Death of the Moth and Other Essays*, 187–97. San Diego: Harcourt Brace Jovanovich, 1970. The essay appeared originally in the *Atlantic Monthly*, April 1939, pp. 506–10.

_____. *The Diary of Virginia Woolf*. Edited by Anne Olivier Bell assisted by Andrew McNeillie. Vol. 1. New York: Harcourt Brace Jovanovich, 1977.

_____. *The Letters of Virginia Woolf*. Edited by Nigel Nicolson and Joanne Trautmann. Vol. 6. New York: Harcourt Brace Jovanovich, 1980.

_____. "The Lives of the Obscure." *Dial*, May 1925, pp. 382–90.

_____. *A Room of One's Own*. 1929. Reprint. New York: Harcourt Brace Jovanovich, 1957.

_____. *Three Guineas*. 1938. Reprint. New York: Harcourt Brace Jovanovich, 1966.

_____. *A Writer's Diary*. New York: Harcourt Brace Jovanovich, 1973.

Chapter 9

. . . .

Exiled by Genre

Modernism, Canonicity, and the Politics of Exclusion

Celeste M. Schenck

They could not wait in exile forever.
—Louise Glück, "Hyacinth"

When I first mapped out an essay on what I'd like to call modernist women's exiles, I envisioned an article on the exchanges between gender and genre, raised exponentially to include geography in the case of those triply exiled expatriate women poets. The task has been more difficult than I imagined for two reasons: first, my perfectly sonorous third—gender, genre, geography—collapsed under pressure of a less concordant trio—race, class, and sexual preference; second, because Gilbert and Gubar's observation that "verse genres have been even more thoroughly male than fictional ones" (*Madwoman*, 68), with its corollary that women writers able to make themselves at home in the house of prose were exiles when it came to poetic genres, simply did not hold up as a theory in a period that willingly consigned poetic forms into the hands of genteel poetesses, keeping the "new poetry" safe for the experimenters, the form-breakers, and the vers-librists—that is, the men.

It may seem odd that I take up the banner of genre at a moment when Modernists were doing all they could to dislodge it as an evaluatory criterion of poetry, but in fact the debate raged in periodicals of the day in a manner I find chillingly gendered. In a 1914 polemic against that "decorative straight-jacket, rhymed verse," a *Little Review* essayist asks us: "Suppose I were a Bluebeard who had enticed a young girl into my dim chamber of poetic-thought. Suppose I took the little knife of rhyme and coolly sliced off one of her ears, two or three of her fingers, and finished by clawing out a generous handful of her shimmering, myriad-tinted hair, with the hands of meter" (Bodenheim, 22). Although the butchered victim in this fantasy is poetry, the hostility generated by rhymed verse extends metonymically to her largely female practitioners. For example, John Crowe Ransom, in "The Poet as Woman," an essay in condescending praise of Edna St. Vincent Millay, quibbles with her choice of the indeterminate word *comfort*, shortened to keep meter. Accusing Millay of obedience to "the mechanical determinism of metrical necessity," he turns the Procrustean metaphor back on her by ending his essay with an image of female dismemberment, once again, ostensibly, of poetry: "Procrustes, let us say with absurd simplicity, finds the good word *comforter* too long for the bed. So he lops off her feet" (110).[1]

But in the foregoing examples I have only described the woman poet's Charybdis. She is equally censured, often out of the other corner of the male critic's mouth, for being inadequately formal, that is, ill-suited to mastery of poetic genres by temperament and education. In the same essay quoted above, Ransom calls Millay "not a good conventional or formalist poet . . . because she allows the forms to bother her and to push her into absurdities. I imagine there are few women poets of whom this is not so, and it would be because they are not strict enough and expert enough to manage forms,—in their default of the disciplines under which men are trained" (103). William Archer says, apparently in praise of Alice Meynell:

> Few poetesses of the past have shown a very highly developed faculty for strict poetical form. I am not aware that the works of any woman in any modern language are reckoned among the consummate models of metrical style . . . ladies as a rule seem to have aimed at a certain careless grace rather than a strenuous complexity or accuracy of metrical structure . . . Mrs. Meynell is one of the rare exceptions to this rule. Within a carefully limited range, her form is unimpeachable. (Quoted in Schlack, 112)

It is little wonder, given the prescriptive nature of Archer's praise, that Meynell wrote a poem called "The Laws of Verse" in which she invites the erotic embrace of a controlling prosody and rhyme.

> Dear laws, come to my breast!
> Take all my frame, and make your close arms meet
> Around me; and so ruled, so warmed, so pressed,
> I breathe, aware; I feel my wild heart beat. (*Poems*, 173)

The double bind of the woman poet, as I redefine it for the female Modernist, her simultaneous exile *from* and *to* poetic form, almost makes comprehensible Edith Sitwell's defensive *ars poetica* in this peevish letter to Maurice Bowra:

> Women's poetry, with the exception of Sappho . . . and . . . "Goblin Market" and a few deep and concentrated, but fearfully incompetent poems of Emily Dickinson, is *simply awful*—incompetent, floppy, whining, arch, trivial, self-pitying,—and any woman learning to write, if she is going to be any good at all, would, until she had made a technique for herself (and one has to forge it for oneself, there is no help to be got) write in as hard and glittering a manner as possible, and with as strange images as possible—strange, but believed in. Anything to avoid that ghastly wallowing. (*Letters*, 116)

The ample quotation from Sitwell is intended to illustrate that this debate over genre not only installed itself along gender lines, inscribing itself in a familiar binary opposition between male Modernists and female poetesses, but cut across gender lines to enforce differences among women poets. In an essay titled "Some Observations on Women's Poetry," for example, Sitwell praises Rossetti's *Goblin Market*—"the perfect poem written by a woman" (59)—and censures Barrett Browning's *Aurora Leigh* —"Mrs. Browning used a technique and a manner which is only suitable to a man," that is, she avoids versification and the control it implies. The result, according to Sitwell, is a kind of ill health in Barrett Browning's poetry that is emblemized by the vision of her "horsehair sofa": "She is always prostrated and never in fine fighting trim—the pink of condition for a poet" (59). The issue for Sitwell, who, like Meynell, feels "we cannot dispense with our rules," is to achieve a glittering hardness that will compensate for the sickliness/softness of what Sitwell would call, excepting Sappho, Rossetti, and herself, "women's poetry." In drawing out the implications and undertext of Sitwell's judgment on Barrett Browning, I mean to expose the bind she is caught in. She is committed *both* to a separate tradition of women's poetry—"it is of a different kind altogether, needing different subjects and a different technique" (59)—*and* to outdoing male poets in fashioning a poetics that is anything but wallowing and soft. Her recourse to form, then, was both prescribed and understandably defensive.

Why might women poets be especially susceptible to the (contradictory) criticisms of being too strong/too weak, too rigid/too flabby, too hard/too soft?[2] Theodore Roszak, in an early discussion of the sexual politics of Modernism, "The Hard and the Soft," points to the sexual imagery in the discourse of the period more generally, to its obsession with male impotence, sterility, and fears of castration in the face of female strength; that is, he views the contrast of a male and female Modernism in terms of the familiar opposition of his title. Gilbert and Gubar destabilize this binary scheme at the end of their "Tradition and the Female Talent" by suggesting that the "female half of the dialogue is considerably more complicated than the male" because women writers respond to male anxiety with guilt of their own rather than with the heightened competency men fear (204). I would suggest, framing the problem in Sherry Ortner's now famous anthropological terms, that women are always subjected to competing stereotypes: they are both "beneath" culture—too mired in nature to master the codes or poetic forms—and (notably in and after the Victorian period) "upholders of" culture—hence, rigid, conservative, form-bound, repressive of spontaneity and experimentation. The whole idea of the "genteel" against which Modernism defined itself seems to be inextricably bound to these contradictory, even schizophrenic, notions of femininity. One wonders, for example, which of the two Max Beerbohm is censuring in his faint praise of Virginia Woolf's writing for its likeness to her father's: "If he had been a 'Georgian' and a woman, just so would he have written" (quoted in Gilbert and Gubar, "Tradition," 183). If gentility in poetry carries the disparaging connotation of soft and female, or worse, not male enough, it can also bear the opposite meaning of conservative and rigid, rhymed, and therefore masculine and hard. Given the impossibility of separating the two valences of the term, it is no wonder that women poets found themselves divided in the debate over genre.

Not only, then, must we contextualize the notion of poetic form during the period known as Modernism—conventional form, although alive and well in genteel Georgian verse, was the *bête noire* of the Modernist movement in poetry, and therefore, although devalued, comparatively open to women poets. I will also ask that we attend to the differences between the female voices of rear-guard and avant-garde modernism. If we listen to the more traditional meters of Anna Wickham, Charlotte Mew, Sylvia Townsend Warner, Alice Meynell, and even Edith Sitwell (not to mention the some five hundred British women who wrote strong war poetry during the years around 1914) as attentively as we now hear the daring verbal experiments of H.D., Stein, and increasingly Mina Loy, we must renounce, I believe salutarily, any hope for a unitary, global theory of female poetic modernism.[3]

My polemic must be taken in the context of the ongoing project of Modernism's revisionary history, that is, the critique of the ideology of Modernism from the vantage point of all the new politics—Marxist, feminist, neohistoricist. I could not argue for a reconsideration of Modernism's foreclosed archives, except after and in light of Georg Lukács's essay on Modernist ideology in *The Meaning of Contemporary Realism*, Lillian Robinson's and Lise Vogel's 1971 polemic *against* the detachment of culture from history in Modernist art and *for* the study of race, class, and sex as factors of exclusion, and, finally, feminist critical salvaging of H.D., Stein, and Loy from the overwhelmingly masculine domination of the period. Without the work of Susan Stanford Friedman, Rachel DuPlessis, and Cyrena Pondrom on H.D., Catharine Stimpson, Marianne DeKoven, and Shari Benstock on Stein, and Carolyn Burke, Virginia Kouidis, and Roger Conover on Mina Loy, it would not be possible for me to argue for further opening of the canon to women poets. After all, H.D. had to be carried out of the burning city on the shoulders of her literary daughters if Robert

Graves's dismissive censure of her is to be considered typical: "The only excuse to be made for those who once found H.D. 'incomprehensible' is that her work was so thin, so poor, that its emptiness seemed 'perfection,' its insipidity to be concealing a 'secret,' its superficiality so 'glacial' that it created a false 'classical atmosphere.' She was never able, in her temporary immortality, to reach a real climax in any of her poems. . . . All that they told was a story of feeble personal indecision; and her immortality came to an end so soon that her bluff was never called" (Riding and Graves, 122–23).[4]

But my business is not with the now safely restored H.D., or with Stein, or with Hugh Kenner's canonized Six, on which Modernist board only the sanitized Miss Moore sits as representative female (49–61),[5] nor even with what Virginia Kouidis calls, making a place for Mina Loy, the "Stein—Pound—Williams—Moore current of modernism" (24). In fact, the hard question I would like to pose is whether we feminist critics, in privileging those female poets who broke form with the boys (even if, as it turned out, they broke form *for* the boys), have reproduced the preferences of dominant critical discourse and extended the hegemony of an exclusive, in this case antigeneric, prejudice which consigned most women poets to debased use of tired forms. Shouldn't the canonizing of Stein and H.D., like that of Dickinson at the behest of the elegant deconstructors, give us pause, if it is accomplished at the expense of striking poets like Wickham and Mew, Wylie and Meynell, from the Modernist register? Furthermore, linking poetic practice to politics, might our collusion with the aesthetic Aryanism of the Modernist canon and its inevitable tendency to produce elite readers, even when we open that canon to women, amount to an enforcement of its exclusionary politics? Sonia Saldívar-Hull's reading of Stein in another essay in this volume poignantly forces us to confront a Chicana reader's alienation before Stein's racism and classism. How shall we choose to address those moments when Stein—formally and politically—has more in common with William or Henry James, Picasso, or for that matter Jacques Derrida, than with Ma Rainey[6] or Melanctha? Will the motley multiple determinants of literary modernism—gender, genre, geography, class, race, and sexual preference—finally force us to abandon a specious and essential, although for a time useful, difference between male and female Modernism?

My project here will be to isolate a few instances that roughen up the history of literary Modernism and present a paradox: if, as both Lukács and feminist critics have demonstrated, the radical poetics of Modernism often masks a deeply conservative politics, might it also possibly be true that the seemingly genteel, conservative poetics of women poets whose obscurity even feminists have overlooked might pitch a more radical politics than we had considered possible? I wish, in short, to question the equation both conservative Modernists and radical theorists have made between radical form and radical politics—even a critical theorist like Julia Kristeva might co-conspire in a Modernist hegemony that fetishizes formal experiment. The situation of marginalized modernists such as Wickham, Mew, Townsend Warner, Meynell, and Sitwell has much to tell us not only about the dispersive underside of the Modernist monolith but also about the politics of canonicity and even about inadvertent feminist adherence to a politically suspect hierarchy of genre.

"Exile Begins as an Apprehension Visited in Secret"

The female affinity for fixed forms has been explained variously—in terms of the woman poet's reproduction of the struggle against cultural containment, of her need to "rein in her strong, unruly feelings" by recourse to formal strictures like the straitjacket of rhyme mentioned above (Fried, 2), finally of formal counter to very real social and sexual marginality. Marianne DeKoven explains female reticence to engage in experimental writing by arguing that "women writers, until, literally, now [with Stein], have been struggling to gain the position which male writers have been free to see as false" (*Different Language*, xx). Elaine Marks, Susan Gubar, and Elyse Blankley all note the coincidence of Renée Vivien's exotic sexuality with her self-exile into rhymed Alexandrines in an expatriate tongue of a century before, and others suggest that her incarceration in sentimental, imitative verse parallels her bodily anorexia or her imprisonment within the "doomed lesbian" image of the nineteenth century (Faderman, 268). Similarly, Louis Kannenstine, in a massive dismissal of all of Djuna Barnes's early verse, considers that her "conventional use of metre and rhymes was perhaps intended to provide a neutral ground to counter the strain" of her sexual preference (23). I would argue that recourse to convention does not always constitute a desire for constriction—Debra Fried's stunning reading of Millay's sonnets, for example, demonstrates that the freeing-by-binding trope might very well prove more explanatory of male than female formal experiment. Although certain of the vague pastorals sandwiched between stories in Barnes's *A Book* might have merited Kannenstine's disdain, the rhymed, "matched accentual lines" (Field, 70) of *A Book of Repulsive Women* do not in my view function as a safety valve or counter to the transgressiveness of the subject matter, nor are they the result of pure "stylistic excess" (Kannenstine, 32). Mina Loy's formal experiments with "Pig Cupid," "rooting erotic garbage"—sans commas, sans rhyme—seem tame next to the sexual radicalism of Barnes's unnervingly regular, rhymed syllabic verse:

Someday beneath some hard
Capricious star,
Spreading its light a little
Over far,
We'll know you for the woman
That you are,

See you sagging down with bulging
Hair to sip,
The dappled damp from some vague
Under lip,
Your soft saliva, loosed
With orgy, drip. ("From Fifth Avenue Up," 1–2)

In short, an alternate sexual politics is surprisingly announced in the *Repulsive Women* "rhythms"—a politics that would both impose exile and profit by it, a politics that would defiantly set itself up in the conformity of rhyme and meter, a politics that would challenge the heterosexism and homophobia of the dominant Modernist discourse in perfectly rhymed verse. Still, Barnes would shortly, largely as a result of her prose, achieve canonicity among the avant-garde, and her place in the feminist canon will be assured by the publication of Mary Lynn Broe's forthcoming revaluation of Barnes, *Silence and Power*.

Whereas Barnes's lesbian eroticism may no longer provoke surprise, it does startle to find the following lines in Charlotte Mew's "On the Road to the Sea": "We passed each other, turned and stopped for half an hour, then went our way, / I who make other women smile did not make you" (29). The achieved smile by the end of the poem is associated with dying climactically: "Reeling,—with all the cannons at your ear." In "The Fête" female sexuality receives equally delicate but nonetheless explicit treatment:

At first you scarcely saw her face,
You knew the maddening feet were there,
What called was that half-hidden, white unrest
To which now and then she pressed
    Her finger-tips; but as she slackened pace
And turned and looked at you it grew quite bare:
    There was not anything you did not dare:— (Warner, 6–7)

"Absence," perhaps more than any other Mew poem, evokes both delight in female sexuality and conflict over its homoerotic expression. As anatomically suggestive of female anatomy as Sappho's imagery, Mew's adumbration of hooded female pleasures safe from the destructive beat of masculine hooves eases the traditional sapphic concern for a lost maidenhead, trampled by shepherds until only a purple stain remains upon the ground.

In sheltered beds, the heart of every rose
    Serenely sleeps to-night. As shut as those
Your guarded heart; as safe as they from the beat, beat
Of hooves that tread dropped roses in the street. (Warner, 47)

But the cost to the poet-speaker of answering the call of her female lover's eyes is conveyed in an arresting image of silencing at the hands of Christ:

But call, call, and though Christ stands
    Still with scarred hands
Over my mouth, I must answer. So,
I will come—He shall let me go!

Even more unsettling is the morbid but fascinating exploration of enveloping female eroticism in "The Forest Road" (Warner, 20–22), a poem pronounced pathological by a contemporary physician. It is, no less than Shelley's *Alastor*, a quest for what the speaker thinks is other and learns is in fact same. By the close of each, a binding love tryst gives over to death, as the poet-speaker confronts his/her own soul in the figure of the other. But whereas Shelley's poet's pursuit of an elusive maiden brings him to the grave, "The Forest Road" explores the contours of a female symbiosis that reads simultaneously as ecstasy and death. The poet knows she "could go free" if only she could separate from the other's enlacing hair: "I must unloose this hair that sleeps and dreams / About my face, and clings like the brown weed / To drowned, delivered things." Trying to quiet her female other, to "hush these hands that are half-awake / Groping for me in sleep," at the last she cannot separate from her. The image of double suicide that closes the poem marks a mutual female climax as well: as the "dear and wild heart" of the one has been broken in its breast of "quivering snow / With two red stains on it," the other determines to "strike and tear / Mine out, and scatter it to yours." In spite of its exploration of the dangers of giving in to the "poor, desolate, desperate hands" of the other, the poem ends ecstatically: "I hear my soul, singing among the trees!" Although Mew's biographers agree that her love for women remained to the end of her days a locus of conflict and psychic pain, her appreciation of female sexuality, in both benign and threatening manifestations, is at the heart of her best poetry.

The violence of "The Forest Road" is balanced by the delicate evocation of autoerotic pleasure in Mew's magnificent "Madeleine in Church." These lines fairly exult in the capacity for female self-enjoyment apart from the determining sexual presence of an other.

> I could hardly bear
> The dreams upon the eyes of white geraniums in the dusk,
> The thick, close voice of musk,
> The jessamine music on the thin night air,
> Or, sometimes, my own hands about me anywhere—
> The sight of my own face (for it was lovely then) even the
> scent of my own hair,
> Oh, there was nothing, nothing that did not sweep to the high seat
> Of laughing gods, and then blow down and beat
> My soul into the highway dust, as hoofs do the dropped roses
> of the street.
> I think my body was my soul,
> And when we are made thus
> Who shall control
> Our hands, our eyes, the wandering passion of our feet (Warner, 23).

This long poem of over two hundred lines, Mew's best poem, is composed of both varying rhyme schemes and stanza structures; each movement of this dramatic monologue is accompanied and marked by elaborate formal variation. In this section in particular, the incantatory rhythms and the sexual content of the lines invite enormous variation in length and emphasis, whereas other, less dreamlike and more conversational sections call for greater regularity in meter and line length. As a whole, "Madeleine in

Church" should be seen as the culmination of a genre, a revision of the Victorian Fallen Woman poem, which Mew appropriates to champion rather than punish female sexuality, a revision informed as much by her own sexual conflicts as by her impatience with traditional mythologies of the "pécheresse" (Mizejewski, 283, 301): Mew gives her modern magdalen both a voice—of which the canon, preferring to describe her, had deprived her—and entitlement to full sexual enjoyment, autoerotic, heterosexual, or lesbian.

Although Virginia Woolf once wrote to Vita Sackville-West that she had just met "Charlotte Mew, (the greatest living poetess),"[7] critics have only begun to revalue the corpus that Mew's contemporaries, Woolf and Thomas Hardy among them, and even some followers, most notably Marianne Moore, so admired. Val Warner's 1981 reissue of Mew's *Collected Poems*, accompanied by her complete prose, and Penelope Fitzgerald's tasteful but forcibly limited biography, *Charlotte Mew and Her Friends*, praised by Brad Leithauser in a kind but still somewhat patronizing review essay on Mew in the *New York Review of Books* (called "Small Wonder"), have brought her work back to light. Although a number of critics, most notably Leithauser, have singled Mew out for her "indigenous originality" (25), her distinctive voice, they tend to censure her at the same time for her small, unoracular formalism—"her pitch is refined and her scale is modest" (31). When they do attribute to her some "nervy bravado," they do so for the Hardyesque roughed-up rhythms, the ventriloquistic experiments with dialect, the perseverance of repeated rhyme which Marianne Moore would later make famous and acceptable (Leithauser, 26). In fact, "Madeleine in Church" is anything but regular in rhythm, anything but conventional in line length and stanza form—its enormous formal variety marks its dramatic and sophisticated shifts in tone. Additionally, in their haste to excuse her "measured and unspectacular" production aside the form-shattering norms set by a masculinist Modernism, these critics fail to read beyond what they see as rhythmical familiarity and rhyme to a strikingly unconventional content (Leithauser, 25). But the sexual radicalism of this untypically formal corpus has been overlooked even by feminist critics attuned to Mew's revisionary impulses. Even Linda Mizejewski's sensitive reading of the Fallen Woman poems stops at Mew's poetic protest against heterosexual inscription into femininity. Beyond Mew's personal and idiosyncratic voice, beyond even her occasional generic daring, is an elected erotic politics belied by the shape of the poems.

Not just the experimental female modernists, then, but a good number of those faithful to meter and rhyme as well wrote a poetry of marked sexual preference: Anna Wickham, married mother of four, who developed a passionate attachment to Natalie Barney late in her life, freely admitting to her "biting lust" (*Writings*, 46); Charlotte Mew, pictured in her *Collected Poems* in full cross-dress, a would-be lover of novelist May Sinclair; Sylvia Townsend Warner, who copublished *Whether a Dove or a Seagull* with her lover, effacing the distinction of authorship from the face of the poems in a perfect emblem of their symbiosis (Marcus, 59); and even Edith Sitwell, probably asexual but certainly galvanized by her intense relationship with her governess, Helen Rootham. Each shares a politics with the more critically fashionable Barnes, coding in what we have learned to call conventional poetry the secret exile of sexual preference.

"One steps aboard; / the boat slowly / abandons the port / and nothing has changed"

Anna Wickham, like her contemporary Charlotte Mew, has lapsed into obscurity for reasons that have everything to do with the form of her verse and the manner of her dress—Harold Acton, for example, found her poetry as unfashionable as her person (Smith, 2). Unlike Mina Loy, whose elegance after four babies was continually remarked, Wickham was large and haphazard in appearance (gypsylike if the critics were feeling kind). She once deliberately wore a wool jumper to an affair at which Edith Sitwell was sure to show up in gold brocade. Charlotte Mew always wore a tweed topcoat over her often frankly masculine dress and sported a "felt pork-pie hat put on very straight" (Monro, viii). Wickham was prolific (nearly fourteen hundred poems in twenty years) where Mew was spare (her first book came out in 1916, when she was nearly fifty), yet both wrote overtly feminist poetry that was highly recognized in its day. Thomas Hardy called Charlotte Mew "far and away the best living woman poet—who will be read when others are forgotten" (quoted in Fitzgerald, 174), and Anna Wickham had by 1932 an international reputation—anthologies of the day printed more of her poems than those of Walter de la Mare, Robert Graves, and in some volumes, even William Butler Yeats (Smith, 23). Neither Wickham nor Mew had anything like a formal education and no formal study of poetry, although Wickham's father apparently made her promise to become a poet. Mew destroyed everything that might constitute a record of her life except for the few pieces that make up her *Collected Poems* and some stories, and most of Wickham's papers and letters were lost during the 1943 bombing of her Hampstead home. Both Wickham and Mew questioned the church, but whereas Wickham's revisionary supplication of the feminized deity poignantly redresses banishment—"In nameless, shapeless God found I my rest, / Though for my solace I build God a breast"—Mew's resignation, in "Madeleine in Church," is complete—"I do not envy Him His victories, His arms are full of broken things" (Warner, 26). Finally, both Wickham and Mew committed suicide. The indignity of Mew's death by the ingestion of disinfectant was matched only by the carelessness of her obituary: "Charlotte New, said to be a writer" (Monro, xii). Wickham's fate is as banal: The London *Picture Post* did a feature on her in 1946 called "The Poet Landlady" (Smith, 28).

A closer look at the life's work of the colorful Wickham, a free-spirited, half-working-class Australian émigrée, who began her career as an opera singer and then divided her life between London and Paris, might cause us to agree with Stanley Kunitz that the neglect of Anna Wickham is "one of the great mysteries of contemporary literature" (quoted in Wickham, *Writings*, front blurb, n.p.). A pacifist who nonetheless supported the Great War effort, a deprived and unhappy wife who remained faithful to her husband during the entire course of their tumultuous relationship until his death, an acquaintance of Pound, Barnes, D. H. Lawrence, and Dylan Thomas who was as comfortable in a London pub as she was on the fashionable Left Bank, a staunch feminist and supporter of women's rights who harbored a masochistic sexuality founded in mother-lack and Catholic education, Wickham was an exciting mass of contradictions of which her poetry is the record. Her Australian childhood offered freedoms unknown to Englishwomen and seems to have stamped Wickham with a robust sense of sexual entitlement, a view of social inequity, and an authentic personal voice, all of which set her apart from other women poets of that period. For all the exhilaration of her Australian exile, however, the return to England and her sensitivity to inequities of class heightened her sense of herself as an outsider. The social rivalry between her mother's and father's families finds its way into poems like "Descent of Dorelia" and "The Little Old House." And her own marriage into a family of aristocratic birth initiated her into the oppression of the female spirit in

Victorian bourgeois culture. The rhyme scheme and alternating meter of the following poem sets off rather than contains the rage of "Nervous Prostration":

> I married a man of the Croydon class
> When I was twenty-two.
> And I vex him, and he bores me
> Till we don't know what to do!
> It isn't good form in the Croydon class
> To say you love your wife,
> So I spend my days with the tradesmen's books
> And pray for the end of life.
>
> . . . .
>
> I married a man of the Croydon class
> When I was twenty-two.
> And I vex him, and he bores me
> Till we don't know what to do!
> And as I sit in his ordered house,
> I feel I must sob or shriek,
> To force a man of the Croydon class
> To live, or to love, or to speak! (210)

There is defiance in the emphasis of the rhyme scheme and not a little irony in its metrical regularity. The poem is closer to folk balladry than to the genteel metrics of the Croydon class; we might even term it deliberately low-bred, even doggerel, a formal as well as political spoof on bourgeois values. This poem, "Dedication of the Cook," "The Angry Woman," "Definition," "The Wife," "All Men to Women," "Divorce," and "The Song of the Low-Caste Wife" criticize prevailing domestic politics, especially in their analysis of sexual difference within the culture that Wickham, marginalized by caste and country as well as gender, could see clearly as triple outsider. Wickham's formal conventionality is often the very vehicle of her poetic politics: her forced rhymes are meant to be funny and irreverent and to set off the political conflicts of which her poetry is made; they should not merely be read as unsophisticated concessions to the popular conventions of the day. "Meditation at Kew," outlining a poignant but humorous utopian program for marital reform, is the poetic version of her 1938 feminist manifesto, *The League for the Protection of the*

Imagination of Women. Slogan: World's Management by Entertainment (Smith, 27).

Alas! for all the pretty women who marry dull men,
Go into the suburbs and never come out again,
Who lose their pretty faces and dim their pretty eyes,
Because no one has skill or courage to organize.

What do pretty women suffer when they marry?
They bear a boy who is like Uncle Harry,
A girl who is like Aunt Eliza, and not new,
These old dull races must breed true.

I would enclose a common in the sun,
And let the young wives out to laugh and run;
I would steal their dull clothes and go away,
And leave the pretty naked things to play. (45)

Wickham's poems range from feminist pieces on marital relations and on the conflict between mothering and writing, to analyses of the domination of one class by another as in "Laura Grey," "Comments of Kate the Cook," "The Butler and the Gentleman," "Daughter of the Horse-Leech," and "Woman to a Philosopher." "Song of the Low-Caste Wife," unlike "Meditation at Kew," is rhythmically uneven and unrhymed, but it is no less than revolutionary in its analysis of the healthful dilution of the bloodline, its dramatization of the rift between herself and the women of her husband's family and class, its claim for "new myths" on the brains of "new men" mothered by underclass women, its valorization of lust and energy, change and growth, over "old glories" and "dead beauty."

What have you given me for my strong sons?
O scion of kings!
In new veins the blood of old kings runs cold.
Your people thinking of old victories, lose the lust of conquest,
Your men guard what they have,
Your women nurse their silver pots,
Dead beauty mocks hot blood!
What shall these women conceive of their chill loves
But still more pots?

But I have conceived of you new men;
Boys brave from the breast,

Running and striving like no children of your house
And with their brave new brains
Making new myths.

My people were without while yours were kings,
They sang the song of exile in low places
And in the stress of growth knew pain.
The unprepared world pressed hard upon them,
Women bent beneath burdens, while cold struck babes,
But they arose strong from the fight,
Hungry from their oppression.

And I am full of lust,
Which is not stayed with your old glories.
Give me for all old things that greatest glory.
A little growth. (165)

"The Angry Wife" is similarly unremarkable in its formal aspects but trenchant in its analysis of motherhood as both experience and institution. The poem first describes marriage in political terms—"If sex is a criterion for power, and never strength / What do we gain by union?" (202)—and then protests the institutional version of parenting which issues from that sexual politics, necessitating the (male) child's revolt against the mother.

I am not mother to abstract Childhood, but to my son,
And how can I serve my son, but to be much myself.

My motherhood must boast some qualities,
For as motherhood is diverse
So shall men be many charactered
And show variety, as this world needs.

. . . .

Why should dull custom make my son my enemy
So that the privilege of his manhood is to leave my house? (203)

"The Fired Pot" is a representative Wickham poem, combining personally registered awareness of the suffering of others with her characteristic directness about her own experience. In this poem, as in "The Song of the Low-Caste Wife," she claims a right to her own sexual desire; here, as in that poem as well, lust is a motivating energy that propels action and promotes change. In the monotonous life of the town she describes, it is, even when unconsummated, a mode of survival.

In our town, people live in rows.
The only irregular thing in a street is the steeple;
And where that points to, God only knows,
And not the poor disciplined people!

And I have watched the women growing old,
Passionate about pins, and pence, and soap,
Till the heart within my wedded breast grew cold,
And I lost hope.

But a young soldier came to our town,
He spoke his mind most candidly.
He asked me quickly to lie down,
And that was very good for me.
For though I gave him no embrace—
Remembering my duty—
He altered the expression of my face,
And gave me back my beauty. (47)

The reference to duty here is probably to the bounden husband to whom Wickham professed lifelong fidelity, but a humorous interpretation of those lines would not be uncharacteristic of her. She may in fact be referring to the wartime decree, under the Defense of the Realm Act, that it was a penal offense to communicate a venereal disease to a soldier.[8]

Finally, in "The Mill," the concord of heart at one with specific, palpably felt environment is expressed by means of a regularized rhyme scheme, the purposive flowing of alternating rhyme into matched concluding couplets.

I hid beneath the covers of the bed,
And dreamed my eyes were lovers
On a hill that was my head.
They looked down over the loveliest country I have seen,
Great fields of red-brown earth hedged round with green.
In these enclosures I could see
The high perfection of fertility,
I knew there were sweet waters near to feed the land,
I heard the churning of a mill on my right hand,
I woke to breathlessness with a quick start,
And found my mill the beating of your heart. (48)

I do not mean to suggest that the enormously uneven Wickham corpus remains undiscovered as a pretext of literary Modernism. Mew must be admitted to the canon as an overlooked treasure of the period, while Wickham remains important for reasons other than either experimentalism or formalism in verse. I would, however, like to see the personal and material specificity of "The Mill" have its history among our modernisms, reflecting—alongside Eliot's phlegmatic portrayals of deceptive lovers, Joyce's spoofs on the magazine romanticism of the day, Loy's send-ups of the masculine sexual principle, and Barnes's decadent New Woman poems—its own particular vision, neither ironized nor sentimental, of the way we loved then.

"No one comes after you / in this rain."

When Wickham writes at the head of her extraordinary autobiography: "I am a woman artist and the story of my failure should be known" (52), she compels the rereading I urge upon us here, not only to account for her disappearance from the annals of Modernism but also to understand the politics of our collusion as feminist critics in that exile. Wickham's poems of class consciousness are a salutary addition to a Modernist canon insufficiently concerned with the differentials of class and ethnicity. And next to Mina Loy's explorations of the decadent "Café du Néant" we will want to place Charlotte Mew's poems of France, among them "Pécheresse" and "Le Sacré-Coeur," "Monsieur qui Passe," and the Madeleine poem mentioned above, all of which analyze the uses to which female sexuality is put: "*Une jolie fille à vendre, très cher,* / A thing of gaiety, a thing of sorrow, / Bought to-night, possessed, and tossed / Back to the mart again tomorrow" (Warner, 31). Mew also wrote a handful of war poems during the years 1915–19, which are among the most iconoclastic and feminist of that period: rhymed, metered, and divided conventionally into stanzas, "The Cenotaph" and "May 1915" are pacifist hymns that re-member the "young, piteous, murdered face[s]" of the war dead by giving voice to grieving women, those "watchers by lonely hearths" who "from the thrust of an inward sword have more slowly bled" (Warner, 35).

Similarly, our analysis of Stein's linguistic iconoclasm should not eclipse Sitwell's accentual and rhythmic experiments. She set herself against the Georgian tradition of the day and counted herself among those Modernist poets who sought a reflection of the disintegration of Europe in their disruption of conventional form, although literary history has not pre-served her inclusion. For all the ornamentation of her verse and person, the idiosyncratic nursery vocabulary of the early poems, and the lapidary persistence of her imagery, Sitwell also wrote some of the best poems we have about World War II. "Gold Coast Customs," "Still Falls the Rain," and "A Mother to Her Dead Child" (*Collected Poems*, 237–52, 272, 286), representatively, reach beyond the Chinoiserie for which she has been limitingly known, beyond the occasion of the poems themselves—the devastating air raids of 1940—to broad cultural criticism for which she has been inadequately recognized.

Our work must also include greater attention to comparison among women writers, especially across the Modernist barrier of form. We must, for example, continue to read H.D. in context of other women poets, not merely as that Pound-fashioned founder of Imagism resultingly isolated from less "fashionable" women poets. Alice Meynell's revisionary mater-nal theology, for example, admittedly conventional in its formal expres-sion, bears comparison with H.D.'s feminized mythologies: Meynell's "Aenigma Christi" revises the mother-and-male-child configuration by centering upon the mother—"Yet I saw the whole / Eternal, infinite Christ within the one / Small mirror of her soul" (*Poems*, 195)—in much the way that H.D. encircles Mary at the end of *Trilogy*. Similarly, Meynell engaged head-on with the experience of World War I in her "Parentage" and "A Father of Women: Ad Sororem E.B." by aligning destruction with the patriarchal fathers and refiguring the place of the feminine in a recon-structed cultural ideology in much the way that H.D. maternally salvages the postwar wasteland in *Trilogy*. Although Meynell was of aristocratic birth, a devout, converted Catholic, and a happily married mother of eight, and H.D., by contrast, lived an expatriate life on the margins of conven-tional sexual and professional choices, both were ardent feminists with uncannily similar strategies for revising inherited mythologies. Our failure to read H.D. and Meynell together for the possibilities comparison offers enforces a masculinist Modernist prejudice against the practice of all but experimental form.

The differences among women modernists, particularly as established across the divide of poetic form, encourage us to think of genre, not as a pure, hypostasized, aesthetic category, but instead as a highly textured, overdetermined site of political contention, a literary space constructed often ex post facto from the conflicting materials of critical, political, racial, and sexual bias. A function of gender and geography, of class as well as critical consciousness, of exile at times imposed and at others elected, poetic genre not only divides male from female authors in the period we have come to call Modernism. I will argue in closing that, as a conflictual site, genre itself might serve as that Archimedean point of contradiction and comparison Myra Jehlen imagined in her "Paradox of Feminist Criticism," that necessary ground we stand so as to question our own assumptions. But Jehlen's scheme now requires revision: it is no longer the contrast between men's and women's writing that will save us from critical solipsism but the "radical comparativism" among women writers which we have just begun to practice, a comparativism alert to the politics of exile and exclusion that still underwrites canonicity.

Notes

I use the expression *politics of exclusion* to stand for a complex process by which women poets are exiled from canonical representation by both traditional critics and feminists. The term was first used, but differently, by Gayatri Spivak (276), to describe "moments on the edges or borders" of critical theories at which the "ideological trace" remains of their need to exclude the other to preserve identity or sameness. This essay was first presented at a 1986 MLA Division Meeting on Twentieth-Century English Literature, "Women Writers in Exile III: The Female Diaspora—(Dis)Placement and Difference." I thank Jane Marcus for inviting me to write on this topic and for her scrupulous attention to an early draft, and Susan Stanford Friedman, Lisa Ruddick, Rachel Blau DuPlessis, and the editors of this collection for valuable suggestions on subsequent versions. Shari Benstock and Susan Hastings generously shared personal copies of primary materials from European collections.

The three section heads are taken from a Michèle Murray poem, "Internal Emigrations," a meditation on the various forms the experience of expatriation takes—racial, sexual, cultural, and geographical.

1. See Gilbert and Gubar, "Tradition and the Female Talent," for similar examples of sadistic imagery in short stories by male Modernist writers.

2. I am grateful to Lisa Ruddick for encouraging me to deepen my analysis of this point and for suggesting the anthropological reading of the woman (modernist) poet's bind.

3. My polemic throughout this essay is the dismantling of a monolithic Modernism defined by its iconoclastic irreverence for convention and form, a difference that has contributed to the marginalization of women poets during the period and even division among them, a difference I have taken care to signal by substituting the plural and uncapitalized "modernisms" for "Modernism" as a marker of such

omissions and exclusions. It is my contention, shared by Susan Stanford Friedman in her unpublished essay, "Forbidden Fruits of Lesbian Experimentation," that the "presumed chasm between experimental and realist writing is misleading for the study of women's writing" (2). I also suggest that although a certain stylistic designation is lost if we open up Modernism to anything written between 1910 and 1940, we lose in at least equal measure if we restrict that literary critical marker of periodization to experimental writing alone. We lose, in short, all the other modernisms against which a single strain of white, male, international Modernism has achieved such relief.

4. Riding has since repudiated collaborative solidarity with Graves's position on "woman." See her response to John Wain's review of volume 1 of Richard Perceval Graves's (Robert Graves's nephew) study of the poet ("Taking His Measure," 59–60).

5. Marianne Moore and Elizabeth Bishop are the only women poets to be embraced unreservedly by the male Modernist establishment in a token stroke of inclusion that isolates them from other women poets. As a counter to Kenner's canonization of Miss Moore for her muscularity of style, her minimalism, her daring verbal experimentalism, in short, her "hardness" as a poet, I would direct the reader to Bonnie Costello's repositioning of Moore as a modernist. Rescuing her from Eliot's, Jarrell's, Blackmur's, and Ransom's approval of her "ladylikeness," Costello regenders Moore as a *woman* poet. Adrienne Rich, too, notes that "the woman poet most admired at the time (by men) was Marianne Moore, who was maidenly, elegant, intellectual, discreet" ("Re-Vision," in *Lies*, 39). Equally dangerous to women writers of this period is their reverse idealization—for their "ladyhood," or ethereal softness—in such articles as Earl Rovit's patronizing "Our Lady-Poets of the Twenties," published in 1980 and seemingly in ignorance of feminist criticism on Teasdale, Millay, Moore, and others. It is precisely this marginalization which Sitwell resists in the passages I quote above.

6. My allusion here is to the compelling peroration of Catharine Stimpson in a paper read at MLA (New York, 1986) on Stein and Moore. After establishing the links between them in a comparative move which I worry was meant to lend Stein credibility and status by comparison with the already credentialed Modernist Moore, Stimpson pays final, exhortative lip service to Stein's contemporary Ma Rainey, whose "laughter" and "songs" on another continent "also engendered Modernism." In fact, Stimpson's has been admittedly a "Tale of Three"—Stein, Moore, and the father whose gaze they both returned, Henry James. I worry similarly that the three panels organized by the 1986 Division of Late Nineteenth and Early Twentieth Century American Literature—"(En)Gendering Modernism: Gertrude Stein, H.D., Marianne Moore"; "Intertextual Modernism: H.D., Marianne Moore, and Gertrude Stein"; and "Disrupting Difference(s): Gertrude Stein and Marianne Moore"—may inadvertently erect a complementary Modernist canon to the one already in place: retroactively gendered but inadequately

flexible generically as to include Ma Rainey's exuberantly uncanonical blues rhythms and Mew's and Wickham's unexpectedly unconventional politics. My concern for the way an alternative canon might be positioned and co-opted does not displace my recognition of the difficulty feminist critics faced in getting Stein and H.D. into the canon in the first place.

I do not mean here to establish a simple equation between left wing politics and less experimental formal stances. Although not all Modernist experiments in form are uniformly tied to right wing sentiments, most that *are* happen to be male. For Woolf and H.D., however, most notably, the notion of breaking sentence and sequence was a way of rupturing political assumptions of great pertinacity and of making a radical criticism of power and status. I do not mean to imply, by asking that we review the work of less experimental poets of the period, that such leftward critiques remain the exclusive province of non-experimenters, but rather to include within our feminist rewriting of periodization poets who were not compelled, stylistically speaking, to "make it new." It is not that the sentence-breaking, female-authored works of that period necessarily collude with a reactionary politics, but that restriction of feminist critical interest to experimentalists may inadvertently work to reify Modernism as a term.

7. Woolf presumably met Mew at the bedside of Hardy's wife, Florence (*Diary*, 2:319 and n. 9; *Letters*, 2:140), and therefore we might conclude that the opinion of Mew's reputation, added parenthetically, might be that of Hardy, approved by Woolf herself. Earlier in the *Letters*, however, Woolf writes to R. C. Trevelyan that she has "got Charlotte Mews book" [*The Farmer's Bride*]. "I think her very good and interesting and unlike anyone else" (2:419).

8. I am grateful to Angela Ingram for sharing this insight.

Works Cited

Barnes, Djuna. "From Fifth Avenue Up." In *A Book of Repulsive Women*. Guido Bruno Chapbooks 2, 6, November 1915, pp. 1–2.

———. *Ladies Almanack*. 1928. Facs. ed. New York: Harper & Row, 1972.

Benstock, Shari. "Beyond the Reaches of Feminist Criticism: A Letter from Paris." *Tulsa Studies in Women's Literature* 3 (Spring–Fall 1984): 5–27.

———. *Women of the Left Bank: Paris, 1900–1940*. Austin: University of Texas Press, 1986.

Blankley, Elyse. "Return to Mytilène: Renée Vivien and the City of Women." In *Women Writers and the City*, edited by Susan Merrill Squier, 45–67. Knoxville: University of Tennessee Press, 1984.

Bodenheim, Maxwell. "The Decorative Straight-Jacket: Rhymed Verse." *Little Review* 1 (December 1914): 22–23.

Burke, Carolyn. " 'Accidental Aloofness': Barnes, Loy and Modernism." In *Silence and Power: A Reevaluation of Djuna Barnes*, edited by Mary Lynn Broe. Carbondale: Southern Illinois University Press, forthcoming.

———. "Becoming Mina Loy." *Women's Studies* 7 (1980): 137–50.

———. "Gertrude Stein, the Cone Sisters, and the Puzzle of Female Friendship." In *Writing and Sexual Difference*, edited by Elizabeth Abel, 221–42. Chicago: University of Chicago Press, 1982.

———. "The New Poetry and the New Woman: Mina Loy." In *Coming To Light: American Women Poets in the Twentieth Century*, edited by Diane Middlebrook and Marilyn Yalom, 37–57. Ann Arbor: University of Michigan Press, 1985.

———. "Without Commas: Gertrude Stein and Mina Loy." *Poetics Journal* 4 (1984): 43–52.

Conover, Roger, ed. and Intro. *The Last Lunar Baedeker*. Highlands, N.C.: Jargon, 1982.

Costello, Bonnie. "The 'Feminine' Language of Marianne Moore." In *Women and Language in Literature and Society*, edited by Sally McConnell-Ginet, Ruth Borker, and Nelly Furman, 222–38. New York: Praeger, 1980.

DeKoven, Marianne. *A Different Language: Gertrude Stein's Experimental Language*. Madison: University of Wisconsin Press, 1983.

———. "Gertrude Stein and Modern Painting: Beyond Literary Cubism." *Contemporary Literature* 22 (1981): 81–95.

DuPlessis, Rachel. "Romantic Thralldom and 'Subtle Genealogies' in H.D." In *Writing Beyond the Ending: Narrative Strategies of Twentieth-Century Women Writers*. Bloomington: Indiana University Press, 1985.

Faderman, Lillian. *Surpassing the Love of Men: Romantic Friendship and Love between Women from the Renaissance to the Present*. New York: William Morris, 1981.

Field, Andrew. *Djuna: The Life and Times of Djuna Barnes*. New York: Putnam's, 1983.

Fifer, Elizabeth. "Is Flesh Advisable? The Interior Theater of Gertrude Stein." *Signs* 4 (Spring 1979): 472–83.

Fitzgerald, Penelope. *Charlotte Mew and Her Friends*. London: Collins, 1984.

Fried, Debra. "Andromeda Unbound: Gender and Genre in Millay's Sonnets." *Twentieth Century Literature* 32 (Spring 1986): 1–22.

Friedman, Susan Stanford. "Forbidden Fruits of Lesbian Experimentation." Paper presented at the Modern Language Association, Chicago, Illinois, December 1985.

———. *Psyche Reborn: The Emergence of H.D.* Bloomington: Indiana University Press, 1981.

Gilbert, Sandra. "Soldier's Heart: Literary Men, Literary Women, and the Great War." *Signs* 8 (Winter 1982): 422–50.

Gilbert, Sandra, and Susan Gubar. *The Madwoman in the Attic: The Woman Writer and the Nineteenth-Century Literary Imagination*. New Haven: Yale University Press, 1979.

————. "Tradition and the Female Talent." In *The Poetics of Gender*, edited by Nancy K. Miller, 183–207. New York: Columbia University Press, 1986.

Glück, Louise. "Hyacinth." In *The Triumph of Achilles*, 14–15. New York: Ecco, 1985.

Gubar, Susan. "Sapphistries." *Signs* 10 (Autumn 1984): 43–62.

Hastings, Susan. "Two of the Weird Sisters: The Eccentricities of Gertrude Stein and Edith Sitwell." *Tulsa Studies in Women's Literature* 4 (Spring 1985): 101–22.

Jehlen, Myra. "Archimedes and the Paradox of Feminist Criticism." In *Feminist Theory: A Critique of Ideology*, edited by Nannerl O. Keohane, Michelle Rosaldo, and Barbara Gelpi, 189–216. Chicago: University of Chicago Press, 1981.

Kammer, Jeanne. "The Art of Silence and the Forms of Women's Poetry." In *Shakespeare's Sisters: Feminist Essays on Women Poets*, edited by Sandra Gilbert and Susan Gubar, 153–64. Bloomington: Indiana University Press, 1979.

Kannenstine, Louis. *The Art of Djuna Barnes: Duality and Damnation*. New York: New York University Press, 1977.

Kenner, Hugh. "The Making of the Modernist Canon." *Chicago Review* 34 (1984): 49–61.

Kouidis, Virginia. *Mina Loy: American Modernist Poet*. Baton Rouge: Louisiana State University Press, 1980.

Leithauser, Brad. "Small Wonder." Review of Fitzgerald's *Charlotte Mew and Her Friends*. *New York Review of Books*, January 15, 1987, pp. 25–31.

Lukács, Georg. "The Ideology of Modernism." *The Meaning of Contemporary Realism*. Translated by John Mander and Necke Mander. London: Merlin, 1963.

Marcus, Jane. "The Asylums of Antaeus: Women, War and Madness: Is There a Feminist Fetishism?" In *The Differences Within: Feminism and Critical Theory*, edited by Elizabeth Meese and Alice Parker, 49–81. Amsterdam: John Benjamins, 1989.

Marks, Elaine. "Lesbian Intertextuality." In *Homosexualities and French Literature: Cultural Contexts/Critical Texts*, edited by George Stambolian and Elaine Marks, 353–77. Ithaca: Cornell University Press, 1979.

Meynell, Alice. *The Poems of Alice Meynell*. London: Oxford University Press, 1940.

Mizejewski, Linda. "Charlotte Mew and the Unrepentant Magdalene: A Myth in Transition." *Tulsa Studies in Literature and Language* 26 (Fall 1984): 282–302.

Monro, Alida. "Charlotte Mew—A Memoir." In *Collected Poems of Charlotte Mew*. London: Duckworth, 1953.

Morse, Samuel French. "The Rediscovery of Mina Loy and the Avant-Garde." *Wisconsin Studies in Contemporary Literature* 2 (Spring–Summer 1961): 12–19.

Murray, Michèle. "Internal Emigrations." *Women's Studies* 7 (1980): 210–11.

Perloff, Marjorie. "Poetry as Word-System: The Art of Gertrude Stein." *American Poetry Review* 8 (1979): 33–43.

Pondrom, Cyrena. "H.D. and the Origins of Modernism." *Sagetrieb* 4 (Spring 1985): 75–100.

Ransom, John Crowe. "The Poet as Woman." In *The World's Body*. Baton Rouge: Louisiana State University Press, 1938.

Reilly, Catherine, ed. *Scars upon My Heart: Women's Poetry and Verse of the First World War*. London: Virago, 1981.

Rich, Adrienne. *On Lies, Secrets and Silence: Selected Prose, 1966–1978*. New York: Norton, 1979.

Riding, Laura. "Taking His Measure." *New York Review of Books*, September 24, 1987, pp. 59–60.

———, and Robert Graves. *A Survey of Modernist Poetry*. Garden City, N.Y.: Doubleday, Doran, 1928.

Robinson, Lillian, and Lise Vogel. "Modernism and History." *New Literary History* 3 (Autumn 1971): 177–99.

Roszak, Theodore. "The Hard and the Soft." In *Masculine/Feminine: Readings in Sexual Mythology and the Liberation of Women*, edited by Betty Roszak and Theodore Roszak, 87–104. New York: Harper, 1969.

Rovit, Earl. "Our Lady-Poets of the Twenties." *Southern Review* 16 (January 1980): 65–85.

Saldívar-Hull, Sonia. "Wrestling Your Ally: Stein, Racism, and Feminist Critical Practice," in this volume.

Salter, Elizabeth, and Allanah Harper. *Edith Sitwell: Fire of the Mind*. New York: Vanguard, 1976.

Schlack, Beverly Ann. "The 'Poetess of Poets': Alice Meynell Rediscovered." *Women's Studies* 7 (1980): 111–26.

Sitwell, Edith. *Collected Poems*. London: Macmillan, 1957.

———. "Modernist Poets." *Echanges* 2 (June 1930): 78.

———. "Some Observations on Women's Poetry: A Defense of the Theory That Male Technique Is Entirely Unsuitable to the Poetry of Women." *Vogue* (London) 65 (March 1925): 59.

———. "To Maurice Bowra, January 24, 1944." In *Selected Letters*, edited by John Lehmann and Derek Parker, 116–17. London: Macmillan, 1970.

Smith, R. D. Introduction. *The Writings of Anna Wickham*. London: Virago, 1984.

Spivak, Gayatri Chakravorty. "The Politics of Interpretations." *Critical Inquiry* 9 (September 1982): 259–78.

Stimpson, Catharine. "Gertrice/Altrude: Stein, Toklas, and the Paradox of the

250 . Celeste M. Schenck

Happy Marriage." In *Mothering the Mind: Twelve Studies of Writers and Their Silent Partners*, edited by Ruth Perry and Martine Brownley, 123–39. New York: Holmes and Meier, 1984.

————. "The Mind, the Body, and Gertrude Stein." *Critical Inquiry* 3 (1977): 491–506.

————. "The Somagrams of Gertrude Stein." *Poetics Today* 6 (1985): 67–80.

————. "Women Writers and the Avant-Garde." Paper presented at the Modern Language Assocation, New York, New York, December 1986.

Warner, Val. Introduction. *Charlotte Mew: Collected Poems and Prose*. Manchester: Carcanet (Virago), 1981.

Wickham, Anna. *The Writings of Anna Wickham*. Edited and Introduction by R. D. Smith. London: Virago, 1984.

Woolf, Virginia. *The Diary of Virginia Woolf*. Edited by Anne Olivier Bell assisted by Andrew McNeillie. Vol. 2. New York: Harcourt Brace Jovanovich, 1978.

————. *The Letters of Virginia Woolf*. Edited by Nigel Nicolson and Joanne Trautmann. Vols. 1 and 2. London: Hogarth, 1976, 1977.

Chapter 10

. . . .

Extra-Curricular Activities

Women Writers and the Readerly Text

Hilary Radner

She turned, as always, to analysis being a twentieth century woman and so
subject to the superstition that what the mind could understand couldn't any
longer hurt the heart.
—Marilyn French, *The Bleeding Heart*

Exiled from Within: The Woman's Novel

Many women writers have lived out their lives in exile, an exile that as a metaphor describes the status of femininity in the dominant intellectual discourse of Western European culture. In the conversations of Western European culture, the feminine voice is exiled from the public place—the political assembly, the court of law, the corporate boardroom—and seeks refuge in the private spaces of the home. Caught between these two conversations, women intellectuals occupy a paradoxical position in our culture. They participate in the public conversation to the extent that they define themselves by their professional role and their educational status; they stand excluded because their identity is circumscribed by their role in the home, in relation to children, lovers, friends, and family. Nevertheless, from Eleanor of Aquitaine to Eleanor Roosevelt, women have acted with force and intelligence. Their presence has permeated the social fabric with another discourse that is all the more pervasive because it remains unrecognized as a fundamental thread in the defining discursive patterns of Western culture.

The novel occupies a similarly contradictory position. A generative formation that provides a template for narrative production from the purple passion romance to the nouveau roman, the novel is both a "good read" and "literature," the object of private experience in the home and public discussion among intellectuals. As a symptom of social structure, the novel has a popular appeal that makes it the topic of mass communication research. As art, the novel is evaluated according to its relationship to a privileged canon of literary masterpieces.

Women's studies as an academic field reproduces this conceptual split by encouraging two basic approaches to feminine discourse. One approach reads popular culture texts as symptomatic of the feminine condition. The other attempts to legitimate certain women writers as artists by establishing them within the literary canon. Both approaches are necessary and useful, and both produce a similar result: the objectification of the text. For the mass communication researcher, the text is an object consumed by the other of mass society. Within the canon, the text is an artifact to be dissected and analyzed according to the rules of formal literary studies. From each perspective, the act of reading is documented as a process removed from the experience of the reader as scholar, in which reading becomes an objective rather than a subjective experience. Like the feminine voice, the private subjective experience of the novel is excluded from public scholarly discussion. The specificity of the novel, its articulation of conversation that is both private and public, is lost. Perhaps a discussion of this loss and its implications might illuminate the cultural role of feminine discourse, which is also excluded from the public conversation.

In losing sight of the novel as a subjective experience, we have overlooked the issue of novelistic pleasure—the pleasure of the text. The division of narratives into popular culture and literature corresponds to two distinct, rhetorically inscribed regimes of pleasure, two different ways of producing pleasure for the reader. Recalling Freud's general concept that neurotic psychic structures parallel quotidian or normal structures, we might see these two different modes of reading as two different symptom formations, hysterical and obsessional.

It would be a mistake to see these two symptom formations as producing a predetermined meaning. This distinction between two types of textual pleasure should suggest very little about interpretation of the text. The meaning of a text is largely the result of a personal and private negotiation effected by the reader. Formations of pleasure as generative mechanisms or "libidinal economies" (Turim, 97–98), in the sense that I am describing here, are the empty matrices that permit the generation of signifying practice, itself the domain of the reader. Formations of pleasure, I suggest, define the parameters of reading as experience rather than as interpretation. (This analogy might appear more apt if we recall that the interpretation of the symptom, as opposed to the diagnosis, must be left to the analysand or the patient.) These two symptom formations, though closely related, define two different libidinal economies: a pleasure in the symptom, generally associated with hysteria, and a pleasure in repression or deferral, generally associated with obsessional neurosis (Freud, *Introductory Lectures*, 301).

The popular culture text corresponds to the formation of symptoms characteristic of the hysteric—a pleasure in the symptom itself. The process has no ostensible goal except its own replication. The format romance is one of the more obvious structures that relies on this libidinal economy. Because the Harlequin reader knows the formulaic plot, she does not read for the plot but to enjoy the process of reading. Though following a completely different narrative structure than the format romance, soap operas recreate a similar libidinal economy. Rather than providing an ending that is too obvious, the soap opera lacks closure to emphasize a pleasure in the process of viewing. The soap opera viewer does not watch for the ending but for the continuity—the events going on rather than resolving themselves (Newcomb, 179). Like the formula romance, the soap opera relies on its ability to replicate its own highly predictable complications and to perpetuate itself as a source of textual pleasure.

A narrative structure that emphasizes process is often associated with feminine discourse (as is hysteria); in varying degrees, this emphasis on the textual experience is characteristic of popular culture as a whole. The slash-and-gash horror film that developed in the 1970s, for instance, is structured for a male viewer. These films build toward moments of intense narrative climax, but their climactic moments are sensationalist rather than intellectual. The mode of pleasure that this genre encourages recalls the hysterical symptomology associated with the feminine text, the formula romance and the soap opera, a pleasure of the text generated by the experience of textuality rather than by the pursuit of closure and the resolution of the enigma.

Literary criticism is governed by a libidinal economy that functions quite differently from that which prevails in the popular context. Literature offers pleasure as a goal rather than as a process—a pleasure in deferral and displacement, rather than a pleasure in the symptom itself. As such, it is an extension of a regime of reading that privileges the hermeneutic code—"reading for the plot," or narrative desire as "desire for the end" (Brooks, 52). From this perspective, reading to find out what it all means (solving the critical enigma in the larger sense) is analogous to reading to find out who did it (solving the immediate enigma of plot). Endings, unfortunately, in their finality are dangerous: culture depends on our ability to reproduce desire. Criticism offers its reader the opportunity to replicate the hermeneutic process through displacement rather than through repetition of symptoms (as is often the case with popular formula narratives). By analyzing the text, the reader dissects, reworks, and rewrites the narrative, each time recreating anew another narrative in his own image—reinscribing the enigma in his own terms as a sign of his position of mastery, repressing his experience of the text as pleasure in and of itself. This structure of displacement and deferral corresponds to the symptomology of the obsessional neurotic, who tends to take pleasure in repression.

A libidinal economy governed by displacement and deferral is characteristic of textual studies in academia as a whole. When the popular culture text becomes an object of scholarly research, it is transformed by the process of analysis. Within the academic arena, reading the popular culture text is governed by an economy of pleasure closer to that of literature than that engendered by the original context of popular consumption. This mutability may seem confusing at first, but, in fact, it underlines the similarity of position accorded by the academic institution to both scholars of literature and scholars of popular culture. Within the academic institution the text is always used as an instrument that empowers the scholar with a position of mastery over his own discourse. The choice between Marcel Proust and a format romance is not merely a matter of taste and status ascription but of symbolic positioning vis-à-vis the text. Excluded from this *dispositif* of academic reading is the position of the hysteric, in which the text is empowered as an other. It would be a mistake to see this relationship to the text as a mark of passive consumership. The hysteric produces the symptom; yet she gives herself over to its manifestation as though it were independent. Similarly, the formula romance reader has the illusion of being consumed by a story that she in fact produces as text.

Textual consumership is characteristic of the type of novel that Roland Barthes has called the readerly text (*S/Z*, 4–5), of which formula romance represents an extreme form. The reader seems to consume a product purchased by brand name often at a local supermarket or drugstore. At the opposite end of the spectrum, Barthes places the writerly text, which offers the reader the impression of writing his own narrative (*S/Z*, 4–5). The deliberate hermeticism of the French poet Stéphane Mallarmé, which demands an initiated, overtly active reader, illustrates this paradigm. The Mallarmé text requires an educated reader familiar with the codes that enable him to reproduce the writerly text for himself. Like the hysteric who refuses to recognize her control over her symptomology, the writerly reader refuses to recognize his lack of control, ignoring the cultural codes that overdetermine this text of mastery.

In summary, I suggest that hysteric and neurotic symptomologies, as libidinal formations generating two types of textual pleasure, correspond to two culturally constituted practices of reading. Texts do not belong to one category or another but are determined by the methodology of reading that produces them. For example, to be obsessed with the work of James Joyce within the institution of academia is legitimate, as long as this obsession engenders a process of rewriting and reproduction in the form of critical works. To be obsessed with Joyce outside academia—to read Joyce compulsively in the way that romance readers consume romances—

is to situate oneself outside the institution of legitimate cultural production. The genius of a neurotic symptomology is that it empowers the scholar to maintain a discourse of mastery in the face of all other discourses.

Like the woman intellectual, there is a genre that defies the master discourse of the neurotic: the woman's novel, which is perhaps the most novelistic of novels. If the essence of the novel is to produce a discourse that is both public and private, the woman's novel represents this intersection in exemplary form. This novel stubbornly rejects the status of high art. It is adamantly not against interpretation and demands to be understood in terms of its content. The woman's novel says, by and large, what it means to say, refusing to reveal its secrets under the scrutiny of the analyst by displaying these last for all to see, literati and nonliterati alike. Yet the richness of its language, the subtlety of its arguments, and its undeniable intelligence and self-consciousness defy the classification of popular culture. The woman's novel may be read either as popular culture or as literature, challenging the categories of High Modernism, reflecting the ambiguous social position of its preferred reader—the educated woman.

Methodologically, the woman's novel forces the reader to confront the limitations of a perspective that privileges either the formal characteristics of a text (reading as a literary activity) or its status as a symptom of larger social issues (reading as a popular activity). Thus the woman's novel has been ignored, or exiled, from the academic forum because academia has failed to generate an adequate methodology to represent this genre in its fullest sense. Similarly, one might say that this is an exile from academia of a subject that announces itself as feminine yet refuses both mastery and submission as defining instances. Thus the woman's novel represents, in the words of Angela Ingram, "an intersection point" that marks a specifically feminine subject who wanders "between two worlds, exiled from both."[1] For indeed this position has been carefully documented by such writers as Margaret Atwood, Margaret Drabble, Marilyn French, Joyce Carol Oates, and Susan Fromberg Schaeffer, among others—a position of estrangement accorded the woman who chooses to define herself by her intellect while maintaining her position as feminine.

As a genre, the woman's novel, then, represents the characteristic discourse of a certain class of women who have acquired a position of mitigated respect within the larger institution of masculinity. To hold this privileged position, these women must be able to assume a discourse of mastery, to operate within a regime of pleasure (or reward) modeled on obsessional rather than hysteric structures. The intelligence and acuity of social and psychological perception, the grounding of the novel in political and historical reality, and the elaborate systems of citation are all aspects of these novels that reflect a discourse of mastery. The efficacy of the form as an identificatory mode in which the reader gives herself over to the novel as a process controlled by the other of the text, the experiential properties of the genre, reflect hysteric structures of pleasure.

The dual function of the woman's novel is perhaps most clearly illustrated by a subgenre that I have termed the dissertation novel. *Falling* by Susan Fromberg Schaeffer, *The Odd Woman* by Gail Godwin, and *The Mind-Body Problem* by Rebecca Goldstein are examples of this subgenre— novels about women writing dissertations written by women who have written dissertations. As is often the case for many writers, the novel represents only one aspect of the author's professional life. The writers of the dissertation novel supplemented their more culturally legitimate project, the dissertation, with another form of discourse, the novel, that, though rewarding economically, is considered secondary within the institution of academia. The cultural value of the dissertation within the paradigm of legitimate discourse was inadequate in terms of the occulted discourse of private experience, in our society closely associated with a feminine identity. For one reason or another it was not enough that these women acquire professional status. They turned to novelistic discourse even though such production was either ignored or actively discouraged by the academic institution. Both a product of the education that formed the professional lives of these women and a form of resistance against the values promulgated by that education, the dissertation novel publicly negotiates the public and private discourse of the intellectual woman. The novels constitute a response to the inadequacy of a purely professional and academic discourse.

The genre as such marks the creation of a community in exile within the community of academia. The dissertation novel offers the academic woman a sense of community—at a price; it signals her estrangement from the community of the feminine as a homogeneous ideological category. Thus the academic woman as subject is created through a double movement of exile, exile from the community of male intellectuals and exile from the community of the feminine. Her position as "alien and critical" defines her status as intellectual and as woman, as a member of a community that is exiled within the very institution that has articulated her as an instance of estrangement.

To define this position it is necessary to rethink critical methodology, to find a position as a scholarly reader that is neither outside the text nor within it. Rather than asking how a text is structured, we might ask how a text creates a reader for itself. Or perhaps, more to the point, how does a text ask us to create ourselves as readers, to situate ourselves within the specific cultural context of a given reading formation? To do so, we must look at the cultural context in which a text is produced—the process by which a reading position is overdetermined by class, culture, education, and gender for a given subject. The approach known as cultural studies developed by the Birmingham Centre for Cultural Studies in Great Brit- ain has pioneered research in this area. (For a succinct account of the development of cultural studies see Streeter.) Television scholar Thomas Streeter summarizes the distinctive features of the cultural studies ap- proach: "Rather than conceiving of itself as founded on the search for objective knowledge, cultural studies sees itself as engaged with and part of a series of cultural and historical developments and processes. Cultural studies views itself as embedded in society, not outside society looking in" (75). In a certain sense we might say that the dissertation novel, because of its historical specificity (written in response to certain issues characteristic of a specific period), constitutes a cultural studies *sauvage*, a spontaneous body of work that self-consciously criticizes its own premises. The genre contests the hegemony of a Modernist perspective that privileges the minimalist text uncontaminated by the concerns of history and everyday experience. The dissertation novel is a dirty genre, an imperfect discourse that engages actively in the imperfection of the quotidian experiences of its readers.

The following analysis of *The Mind-Body Problem* illustrates these two crucial issues: (1) the way in which the genre functions as a point of intersection between two discourses, documenting the position of the academic woman as an instance of exile that is contained, normalized, and to an extent legitimated by the genre; (2) the way in which a given text within a cultural context creates a position for its reader, here a specifically feminine reader.

The Mind-Body Problem

Rebecca Goldstein, now a professor of philosophy at Barnard College, wrote *The Mind-Body Problem: A Novel* as a narrative reply to the impossibility of a philosophical epistemology that would resolve the ontological paradox of the mind-body problem—the topic of both Goldstein's own dissertation and that of the novel's heroine. The urgency of the mind-body problem, for Goldstein's heroine, derives in large part from her position as a woman attempting to establish herself in a field regulated by a system of "meaningfulness" produced by a male-dominated discourse. Through the concept of the "mattering map," the heroine tries to analyze the various and conflicting relationships of value that regiment both her mind and her body. *The Mind-Body Problem* attempts to reconstitute experience within an analytic framework, the experience of the dissertation, but also experience in more general terms that cannot be understood as meaningful within academic discourse.

As a genre, the dissertation novel renders meaningful precisely that aspect of experience that has been designated meaningless by the dominant discourse of academia. The genre thus represents a point of intersection between dominant or masculine discursive practice and occulted or feminine discursive practice, between legitimate textuality and institutionally illegitimate textuality, between the dissertation and the classical novel, between the production of writerly texts and the production of readerly texts. This novel actively represents femininity as a site of struggle and collusion. In *The Mind-Body Problem*, neither the heroine nor the author seems able to unravel the Gordian knot posed by the heroine's ontological dilemma; yet neither is willing to give up the position of privilege her education accords her. As a textual experience, the novel calls into play the complex social context overdetermined by class, gender, and education, the "mattering map," that circumscribes the intellectual woman.

The process through which I came to include Goldstein's novel in my bibliography provides an apt example of the social context in which the dissertation genre becomes meaningful. A fellow graduate student first brought *The Mind-Body Problem* to my attention. An advanced graduate student in her program had lent her the novel, telling her that it should be required reading for all women in graduate school. Several years later I chanced upon a paperback edition while browsing in a bookstore. I was struck by the novel, not because it seemed marked by transcendent reflections on the human condition but because it seemed so limited, so topical. If it lacked the valued qualities of the great novels of the nineteenth century, it was filled with insight into the particularities of my own situation. The novel's somewhat melodramatic account of the career and marriage of a young graduate student to a brilliant, older professor had little to do with my own life; however, the author-narrator's reflections on her work and fellow graduate students seemed extremely pertinent. The novel's strength lay not in its sense of the grand schema of life but in its transcription of quotidian detail.

I have described the process by which I discovered and read the novel because it seems typical of the way we as a culture decide to read fiction. We encounter novels by chance through the odd review in a magazine, or, more often, the recommendation of a friend or the gossip of academic circles—a circuit of information both personal and public. The relationship that my two friends and I had to this novel also seems typical. It was personal, inspired not by a desire to acquire a greater knowledge of the world at large but by a need to reflect on the particularities of our own situation, on those details of that situation that from a professional viewpoint would seem meaningless. Those details, reproduced as narrative, became meaningful within novelistic discourse.

This elaborate and idiosyncratic trajectory that brought us to read the same novel evokes the complicated mechanism through which, in Louis Althusser's terms, a subject is hailed, called forth, or "*interpellé*," by ideology (173–74). In practice, the act of interpellation is best understood not as a monolithic process in which a subject is defined and permanently subjected to a given ideology but as a series of complicated negotiations in which "subjection" is produced through numerous shifts and realignments at any given time. Negotiation takes place both in a vertical hierarchy of status ascription and in lateral configurations or social groupings of the same status. The choice to subject oneself, to see oneself as the inscribed subject of a given text, is generated through a number of lateral as well as vertical moves. To subject oneself to the canon involves a choice determined by a vertical hierarchy from professor to student. To choose a given text as the object of leisure, as an extracurricular activity, so to speak, involves a different type of subjection that is only marginally regulated by the institutional hierarchy.

In this particular instance, my position as a graduate student within a hierarchical structure played a crucial role in defining lateral rather than vertical influences. Relationships among individuals of the same status determined the value of *The Mind-Body Problem*. Significantly, the novel in and of itself was less important than the fact that it was a novel of a certain type. Admitting ignorance of *The Scarlet Letter* could be professionally damaging and might well undermine the status of a given individual within the peer group of fellow graduate students to which my friends and I belonged, especially his or her status within an institutional hierarchy. Although the decision to read or not to read *The Mind-Body Problem* does not involve the same cultural investment, it is nevertheless a culturally significant choice. Total unfamiliarity with contemporary writers similar to Rebecca Goldstein would affect the lateral positioning of the individual within the group. A member of this group of women needed a degree of competency in contemporary novels or conversation as the primary system of exchange within the group would stop. It would be a mistake, however, to see this group as either cohesive or completely unregulated by the dominant ideology of hierarchy. The configurations of the group could change from week to week or day to day, depending on who happened to be at the local coffee shop at a specific time. The characteristics of a member of the group were more consistent. These women had attended better than average schools, came from well-educated families, and were intellectually and professionally ambitious.

I cannot say that it is merely by chance that on a certain day I found myself in front of the book rack of the "intellectual" bookstore, as opposed to the local Dalton's or a record store, following a completely different itinerary. Education, culture, class, and gender had all conspired to encourage in me the impulse to read "serious novels" for fun. Similarly, when I pulled *The Mind-Body Problem* off the shelf, it was again not by chance. Education, culture, class, and gender were reinscribed in the very cover of the book itself—saying, hey you, this is written for you and about you. Because my position as a reader is overdetermined, I might have chosen the book by its title even if it had had an unappealing cover.

The process of selection was facilitated by a cover that reproduced the initial discourse that had impelled me to reach for a book in the first place. The cover was lavender, the design minimalist and subdued—tasteful according to the standards of the professional and intellectual middle class. The quotation that garnished the cover was from *Harper's*, a magazine that evokes a tradition of literary respectability. By stating that the novel "anatomizes the dilemma of the intellectual woman in an anti-intellectual society," the quotation reconfirms the novel's "seriousness" while evoking a feminine subjectivity. Consider how differently the quotation would have operated with the omission of the single word *woman*: "Anatomizes the dilemma of the intellectual . . . in an anti-intellectual society."

This femininity is reiterated through the reproduction of a painting. *Figure in Front of a Mantel*, by Balthus, Balthazar Klossowski de Rola, in which a naked young girl in the first stages of womanhood contemplates herself in what appears to be a mirror. Her breasts are small, her hips and legs heavy. She neither hides nor displays herself but is positioned in sharp profile, turned toward the mirror, rearranging her hair. Oblivious to the spectator, she is fascinated by her own image; she seems to be considering her condition, her nascent maturity. Consider again how different the effect would be if the rubric placed carefully below had read "Anatomizes the dilemma of the intellectual . . . in an anti-intellectual society." Without the single word *woman*, reflection and contemplation are transformed into a discourse of voyeurism and obsession originating in a male rather than a female subject. The omission of the word *woman* and of the first name of the author, "Rebecca," would return the depiction of a nude girl to its original context as a Balthus image—to its original trajectory of male possession, desire, and perversion, signaled by the signature of the male artist.

The use of the Balthus reproduction illustrates two crucial axes of textual practice characteristic of the woman's novel. The first is generated by the evocation of a culturally legitimate discourse. The cover exudes culture, taste, and education. Though the image of a nude woman looking in a mirror evokes the lurid sensationalism of romance or pornography, the colors, the unconventional pear-shaped body of the woman featured in the painting, the reproduction of a work by a very recognizable "blue chip" artist, and the quotation from a literary magazine all ground the invitation to read within a discourse of education and high culture.

The second axis of textual practice is more complex. It involves the systematic reinscription of masculine discourse within a specifically feminine topology. The use of the Balthus painting is a clear example. The author's name, a woman's name, emphatically inscribed in black as opposed to the blue used for the title, and the quotation from *Harper's*, also in black, frame the Balthus image from above and below. Thus the initial masculine obsession of the painting, its perversity, is rewritten in such a way that it says something—not about a male subject but about a feminine subject, who, if constituted for and by the male gaze, is nonetheless looking at herself for herself. The reappropriation of the body of the woman evokes a process of reterritorialization generated by the novel as a specific topos discovered by men (or rather produced through a conjunction of a patriarchal order and private capital) and yet colonized by women.

The novel is a woman's genre—charting a lost continent of experience that is not legitimated by the dominant masculine discursive class that nonetheless permeates the fabric—the text—of cultural practice. The dissertation novel in a way typical of the woman's novel as a whole shifts our attention from one process of structuration to an other—which is not hidden but, like a picture, a gestalt experiment, that can be "read" two ways, simply not perceived. It would be a mistake to consider that all novels function in this manner—even all middlebrow novels.

The male academic novel, for example, is almost always parodic, reproducing the dominant structure of meaningfulness in the unflattering mirror of social satire. Unlike the woman's novel, the academic parody does not speak in an other voice of other things. It speaks of the same things in a louder voice, exaggerating the features of the dominant structure. This is not to say that parody cannot have a subversive function, but rather that it is a product of the very discourse against which it situates itself. In *Small World: An Academic Romance* by David Lodge, our attention as reader is focused on the same figures, topics, theories, and issues that loom large in academic bibliographies. The dissertation novel returns our attention to another stratum of academic experience, to meaningless details, to the housework of academic life.

In *Marya: A Life*, another dissertation novel, Joyce Carol Oates devotes a chapter to the conflict between the first-person narrator and, in her words, a "black custodian" (233–50). The conflict is minor to the young woman's career; however, it provides the author and the protagonist the opportunity to dwell on precisely that aspect of academic hierarchy that does not appear on a vita or in a professional dossier—the occulted hierarchy of race, gender, and class. This hierarchy provides the core of a discursive practice, a crucial mechanism of academic life that regulates the quotidian functions of the institution but is never named as such by the dominant discourse of academia.

A novel such as *The Mind-Body Problem* is permeated by these two discourses—the dominant masculine discourse of meaningfulness and the occulted feminine discourse of meaninglessness. Through the narrativization of meaninglessness, the hierarchy of dominant discourse and occulted discourse is, if not reversed, at least called into question. *The Mind-Body Problem* underlines the antinomy of dominance and occlusion through a system of punctuation and quotation that structures the text into a series of chapters. The quotations, usually one, though chapter 8 offers two, are taken from the work of various philosophers (Wittgenstein, Jean-

Paul Sartre, Stuart Hampshire, Plato, and Nietzsche), with two exceptions, chapter 2 (a letter from Albert Einstein) and chapter 6 (a poem by
Anne Sexton).

This system of quotations is highly conventional, though as a rule
quotations are neither as long nor as frequent as those found in *The Mind-
Body Problem*. As a convention, it situates the discourse of the novel (as
fiction) within an intertextual network of cultural legitimacy. If the novel
itself is a melodramatic tissue of quotidian events, the quotations provide a
paradigm of practice that is not fictional, not quotidian, and eminently
meaningful within dominant discourse, in which philosophy functions as
the keystone in the monument of Western European intellectual life. The
quotations are markers, guarantors of cultural legitimacy available to the
reader should she care to invoke them. Skipping the quotations does not
negate their importance; their very existence acts as the guarantor of
cultural value. The significance of the generative cultural formation of
literacy and education (of which the quotation convention is symptomatic)
is underlined in all dissertation novels. The dissertation novel is explicitly,
rather than implicitly, produced by academic discourse. The novel's autobiographical subject (she who speaks) is defined through a specific historical and cultural institution, academia, which is, in turn, the object of her
discourse.

This privileged relationship to the ideological apparatus of education
and culture makes more obvious the nature of the novel as a site of
struggle between a dominant discursive class (culturally legitimate discursive practice evoked by the quotation system) and an occulted discursive
class (the meaningless discursive practice of the quotidian). It would be a
mistake to see this characteristic as unique to the dissertation novel; on the
contrary, it is a general characteristic of the middlebrow novel and of the
woman's novel in particular, which, in opposition to a genre such as the
formula romance, demands that its reader be familiar with the academic
codes of cultural literacy but take pleasure in a mode of reading that is not
academic. This split is intensified in the woman's novel because of the
ambiguous position accorded educated women in our society.

If we return to our earlier discussion of textual pleasure, the woman's
novel again represents a point of intersection between the two categories
of literature and popular culture. The structure of these texts seems to
lend itself neither to a writerly nor to a readerly regime of pleasure. If the
writerly text corresponds to obsessional symptomology and the readerly
text to hysteric symptomology, as this essay suggests, then the woman's

novel constitutes a hybrid form, a discursive system that perhaps best corresponds to analysis in the psychoanalytic sense. Analysis, the "talking cure," was the invention of a woman suffering from conversion hysteria. (For a detailed account of the case see Rosenbaum.) Her doctor discovered that if she talked through the circumstances that brought on her symptoms the symptoms would disappear. This process of talking through evolved spontaneously from the patient's apparent need to create a narrative of her experience, either in the form of fairy tales (which temporarily alleviated her symptoms) or of an autobiographical expression of her experience (which tended to have more permanently beneficial effects on her condition). The analysis of Anna O., as Freud calls her in his description of her case, was never successfully completed. Nonetheless, as Bertha Pappenheim she went on to become an important pioneer in social work, one of those strong-minded women whose energy and devotion bridged the gap between institutional responsibility and human charity. It was from her experiences with her doctor, Josef Breuer, that Freud evolved the technique of analysis.

The story of Anna O. is instructive because it may provide a parable on the power and frailties of feminine discourse. Her narratives and the technique of analysis grew out of the failures of a scientific discourse of mastery to control feminine experience. Thus psychoanalysis is founded on an experiential epistemology, a truth that cannot be replicated, generalized, or verified. The patient cannot be reduced to a systematic epistemological function. She can never be fully mastered by the analyst. It is always the patient, the analysand, who must solve the enigma of her illness, provide the truth of her experience as a narrative process. Unfortunately, the potential of analysis as an avenue of access toward the constitution of a feminine discourse of empowerment that is not a discourse of mastery has not yet been fulfilled. Recolonized by the therapist as an instrument of dominance, analysis quickly lost its latent function as a site of negotiation between dominant and occulted discourse. In a parallel move, the educated woman all too easily adopts the values and practices of her male counterpart. She comes to associate femininity with the disease, not the cure.

The novel effects a similar compromise. It offers an avenue of access to a history and a knowledge largely constructed outside a dominant discourse of meaningfulness. Yet if reading novels remains simply a leisure activity or an object of academic scrutiny, as a pursuit it can only reproduce distinctions of race, class, and gender. Neither analysis nor the woman's novel offers a solution to the dilemma of the intellectual woman. Indeed, it seems that if analysis or the novel as analysis becomes a goal in and of itself these practices are quickly circumscribed and contained within dominant discourse. There are no easy solutions, but it is clear that an academic feminism that does not interrogate issues of race and class and its own position of privilege becomes immediately suspect.

Anna O. enjoyed the privileges of the educated woman. Her education, her ability to converse in several languages, her intelligence, and her diligence all enabled her to make a valuable contribution to the development of psychoanalysis. As a woman, her name occulted, exiled from the scholarly discourse that surrounds her discovery of the "talking cure," she also represents the condition of estrangement that educated woman must take up to constitute herself as a subject within patriarchy. Until the condition of "talking" is rearticulated as cure and not as disease for women as a class, the intellectual woman will remain both the subject and the object of her own exile.

Note

1. I am deeply indebted to Angela Ingram for her thoughtful discussion of these issues.

Works Cited

Althusser, Louis. "Ideology and Ideological State Apparatuses." In *Lenin and Philosophy*. Translated by Ben Brewster, 127–86. New York: Monthly Review Press, 1971.

Barthes, Roland. *The Pleasure of the Text*. Translated by Richard Miller. New York: Hill and Wang, 1973.

_____. *S/Z*. Translated by Richard Miller. New York: Hill and Wang, 1974.

Breuer, Joseph, and Sigmund Freud. *Studies on Hysteria*. In *Standard Edition of the Complete Psychological Works of Sigmund Freud*, vol. 2. Edited by James Strachey. London: Hogarth Press, 1955.

Brooks, Peter. *Reading for the Plot: Design and Intention in Narrative*. New York: Knopf, 1976.

French, Marilyn. *The Bleeding Heart*. New York: Summit Books, 1980.

Freud, Sigmund. *Five Lectures on Psychoanalysis*. In *Standard Edition of the Com-*

plete Psychological Works of Sigmund Freud, vol. 11. Edited by James Strachey. London: Hogarth Press, 1955.

———. *Introductory Lectures on Psychoanalysis: Part II: General Theory of the Neuroses.* In *Standard Edition of the Complete Psychological Works of Sigmund Freud*, vol. 16. Edited by James Strachey. London: Hogarth Press, 1955.

Godwin, Gail. *The Odd Woman.* London: Penguin Books, 1974.

Goldstein, Rebecca. *The Mind-Body Problem: A Novel.* New York: Laurel, 1983.

Lodge, David. *Small World: An Academic Romance.* New York: Warner, 1984.

Lyotard, Jean-François. *Economie Libidinale.* Paris: Minuit, 1974.

Newcomb, Horace. *TV: The Most Popular Art.* New York: Anchor Press, 1974.

Oates, Joyce Carol. *Marya: A Life.* New York: Dutton, 1986.

Rosenbaum, Max. "Anna O. (Bertha Pappenheim): Her History." In *Anna O.: Fourteen Contemporary Reinterpretations*, edited by Max Rosenbaum and Melvin Muroff, 1–25. New York: Free Press, 1984.

Schaeffer, Susan Fromberg. *Falling.* New York: Macmillan, 1973.

Streeter, Thomas. "An Alternative Approach to Television Research: Developments in British Cultural Studies at Birmingham." In *Interpreting Television: Current Research Perspectives*, edited by Willard D. Rowland, Jr., and Bruce Watkins, 74–97. Beverly Hills: Sage, 1984.

Turim, Maureen. "Desire in Art and Politics: The Theory of Jean-François Lyotard." *Camera Obscura* 12 (Summer 1984): 91–106.

Chapter 11

. . . .

Alibis and Legends

The Ethics of Elsewhereness, Gender and Estrangement

Jane Marcus

Exile and orphanhood and bitterness and love,—
they weighed all four and found that exile was the heaviest.
The exile in a foreign land should wear all black
to match the lava-blackness of his heart.
—From "The Mourning Songs of Greek Women,"
    translated by Konstantinos Lardas

Afraid is a country with no exit visas
a wire of ants walking the horizon
embroiders our passports at birth
Johannesburg Alabama
a dark girl flees the cattle prods
skin hanging from her shredded nails
escapes into my nightmare
half an hour before the Shatila dawn
wakes in the well of a borrowed Volkswagen
or a rickety midnight sleeper out of White River Junction
Washington bound   again
gulps carbon monoxide in a false-bottomed truck
fording the Braceras Grande
or an up-country river
grenades held dry in a calabash
leaving.
—Audre Lorde, "Diaspora"

Alibis

To play with mimesis is . . . for a woman to recover the place of her exploitation by language without allowing herself to be simply reduced to it. It is to resubmit herself . . . to ideas—notably about her—elaborated in and through a masculine logic, but to "bring out" by an effect of playful repetition what was to remain hidden: the recovery of a possible operation of the feminine in language. It is also to unveil the fact that if women mime so well they are not simply reabsorbed in this function. They also remain elsewhere.
—Luce Irigaray (1977)

Feminist theory, as articulated in the voices of such poets as Audre Lorde and the anonymous Greek mourners of my epigraph, critic Nancy K. Miller, and psychoanalyst Luce Irigaray, situates the woman writer as the quintessential stranger in the paradise of male letters. Mikhail Bakhtin has established that the word in language is always half someone else's, a quotational polyphony of "double-voiced discourse." If this is so, then we may argue, as I have for Virginia Woolf, that the woman writer's voice is not only dialogic but triologic, and we may call women's writing a *triologue* or a triple-tongued discourse with her culture. She is already in exile by speaking *his* tongue, so further conditions of exile simply multiply the number of her "veils" and complicate the problem of exegesis.

My task in this essay is to attempt to understand the ethics of the woman writer's elsewhereness. For elsewhere is not nowhere. It is a political place where the displaced are always seen and see themselves in relation to the "placed." Dis/placement and difference as categories of political and gender exile from writing, speaking, and acting circulate around notions of fixed positions in a substantial Somewhere. As a critic trying to map these moves, one is like a blind cartographer sticking pins into a territory called Lost Bearings, especially as the extraterritorial space around the edges of one's map, where the marginal cluster together with the noncanonical, threatens to destabilize Placement and Place altogether. One is "put in one's place" by the process of "putting her in her place," in that the gesture of placement reveals itself as authoritarian and academic, the naming and judging game played by the alternate rules of "Who is most marginalized?" rather than "Who is central?"

Our feminist mappings of women's culture are a kind of ghostly treading on the dead bodies and songs of our ancestresses, the Judith Shakespeares of the past. Like Bruce Chatwin's vision of the "dreaming-tracks" of Australian aborigines in *Songlines*, we are tracing the "directions" plotted in women's songs across their own territory. Every rock and creek, desert and mountain bears the footprint and song print of women's iliads and odysseys. What we need is a new kind of compass for taking readings of the legends of women's maps and the maps themselves. A necessary awkwardness disables the critic at the start, as she balances one foot on the map and the other in the margins. Locating herself as she locates exiled writers, she becomes aware of the cartographer-critic's power to falsify the map, dissemble about the whereabouts of the extraterritorial creatures. (This was written before the startling Soviet announcement in the fall of 1988 that official maps of the Soviet Union had been deliberately falsified for over fifty years.) Some diasporas do not wish to be mapped and placed by what is perceived as the exiling agency itself. It may be dangerous for their survival. (Other exiled communities are confident that they take their culture with them into the promised land like Russian dissidents in the West, and are privileged by the press, while other exiled groups are ignored. When the drinking age was raised to twenty in New York, a club called Exile was opened for the privileged young people who can pay $10 cover charge to order "virgin" drinks. The *New York Times* reports [March 27, 1988, p. 16] that Afghan women exiled in a Pakistani refugee camp are being treated for depression at the loss of independence and return to purdah in exile.)

So the critic must engage with the ethical question of whether certain work is "outside her jurisdiction." But perhaps that is just my alibi or excuse for taking a position outside of "elsewhereness," when it is obviously not possible to do so, and for choosing such strange texts for exegesis: Stein's *Paris France*, Woolf's reputation as a critic, Elaine Showalter's essay on quilts, a piece of popular journalism called *The Silent Twins*, Sylvia Townsend Warner's stories "A Widow's Quilt" and "The Mother Tongue," and Warner's long out-of-print satire on the origins of story itself, *The Cat's Cradle-Book*. The critic's discourse is as necessarily "triologic" as the writer's, especially if she is negotiating between cultures and languages. Gayatri Spivak, for instance, asks white academics to consider the problem of collecting the writings of Third World women. Politically and ethically, critics and anthropologists may rob the writers of subjecthood by isolating them as objects to be studied. This also raises the vexed question of whether one may write across gender, class, race, or ethnic lines or just who may write safely about whom.

The Latin word for elsewhere is *alibi*. An alibi establishes one's innocence for not having been at the scene of the crime. But feminist criticism often romantically assumes that all women have equally plausible alibis for patriarchal crimes. This essentialist critical stance absolves the female from guilt, complicity, and responsibility. The exile from language, which Irigaray describes as universal for women, needs to be analyzed for each specific historical case. We can measure the extent to which each woman's art is alibi but cannot assert that all female art is alibi. Feminist criticism often acts as defense lawyer constructing alibis for women writers. And we have invented arguments for why our work is elsewhere in relation to the academy. How will future generations perceive these alibis?

The method of my alibi in this essay is etymological and metaphorical, contextual and historical, metymology. A medley on the map of exile, it tries to read the legends of exile on women's maps. A legend on a map proposes to teach us how to read (from *legere*). The map or chart (*fabula*) always needs a legend that explains its relation to the real world. We are just beginning to learn to read these legends. Let us not succumb to legend/trification (or patriarchal prettifying of these texts). In charting the politics of women's exile we are reading the legend on the map in that marginal space in the corner where legends traditionally appear or in the actual margins and rewriting the scale that measures distances. This reminds us of the difference between women's legends or stories and the legends about us (here we will reread the Bluebeard story). In invading this space we step on the territory of the canon-makers, whose control of the scale in which women's work is measured as small has created a powerful illusion of order and control of information through quantification in which so many inches equal so many miles. Reading the female *fabula* and her fables, we recalculate the distance of cartography's legend, its ideological geography as well as the feminine "scale."

For me the classic figure of the woman exile is Emma Goldman. Legend has it that J. Edgar Hoover stood on the dock to make sure the dangerous anarchist was really on the ship that was to return her by force to the Russia she had left, a Russia where she found herself as homeless an exile as she had been on entering the United States as a refugee. The contradictions of Emma Goldman's exile, forced and unforced, remind us that exile is a political condition of banishment from a threatened state. An exile is a stranger whether or not she has chosen her condition. A woman exile is, in addition, an uncanny figure, in Freud's formulation, for her very body means home and hearth, the womb/home of humankind. If she is homeless, lost, wandering, where are we, her daughters and sons? The uncanniness of the woman exile's position lies precisely in the contradiction it poses in raising her from object to subject in regard to the state, as a person in her own right, not, as she so often was, an addition to a male passport, losing her nationality with marriage. In much of our culture woman is nation, and nation is woman, both sign and signified. Stepping outside this system the self-conscious woman writer like Virginia Woolf claims that as a woman she has no country and wants no country, opting for the whole world as her country, equating exile by gender with the internationalism usually equated with Jews. In exile the woman rejects her role as representation of home/the mother's body to male desire and so is a threat to patriarchy as well as to the state.

Feminism is a natural medium and method for the examination of exile, for, in its explicit articulation of otherness, it places the critic in the position of exile, aware of her own estrangement from the center of her discipline, awkwardly measuring just how much marginalization she is willing to bear, negotiating dangerous identifications with her subjects, edgily balancing on boundaries and testing limits. But I worry that in the act of staging meetings on women writers in exile and collecting the essays into a book, we are privileging those who leave or are expelled over those who stay at home. The very act of studying exile sets limits and boundaries. Celeste Schenck's critique of the way feminist critics of Modernism have revived female Modernists, without questioning the value placed on experimental form and Joycean techniques, brilliantly and uncomfortably exposes internalized male values in such a practice, which leaves out the traditionalists, the rhymers, and some very good poets indeed. Since as critics we are bringing the artists we study home from exile, we may get carried away with our mission as liberators. Those writers who "keep the home fires burning" and the old forms dancing deserve our attention too. I anticipate the arrival of that old reprobate, Hierarchy, on the scene to rank states of exile as he previously ranked alienation. Is the political refugee in Siberia more of an exile than a lesbian poet in Iowa or a woman of color in a white culture? Can the loss of language be compared to the loss of nation? (Here I remember Geoffrey Hartman crying out at the end of a conference on feminist criticism, "Would you privilege the oppression of women over the oppression of Jews?")

Obviously, it is the ranking and privileging process which we must continually call into question, as well as our own roles as collaborators in mapping the boundaries of discourse. As soon as one thinks of exile as suffering, one is reminded of all the women artists who found their identity in exile. Ethel Smyth, the English composer and feminist, thrived on exile, and Georgia O'Keeffe chose a Spanish exile in her own country, where not speaking the language appears to have been an impetus to creativity. Gertrude Stein's double displacement articulated in *Paris France* allows her to work out from a third remove, as a painterly problem in figure and ground, why Paris stimulates her American writing identity. The pull of the words "peaceful and exciting" in the text underline the Parisian reality of war's banalities and express her respect for the French and the formal reserve against which she feels free to speak: "It is a secret but one does not tell it." Stein's voice here plays with disclosure, re-enacting the child's pleasure in secrets in a discourse interrupted by static (like a radio dispatch in wartime) that relates the child's discourse to diplomatic discourse during the war as a kind of "secret service" to the state. Unlike Woolf in *Three Guineas*, also first addressed to an America that had not entered the war, Stein does not advocate pacifism but grounds her plea for both England and the United States to enter the war in a connection between her nostalgic little girl self remembering Paris in America and the French girl, Helen Button, who is at the center of the text. The "Helen" recalls the woman over whom the Trojan War was supposedly fought, and the "button" the clitoral sexuality of "Tender Buttons" as well as Jacques Lacan's "mattress buttons," those words which pin language to the real world. "The world is all round and everybody knows all about it," she repeats, until the reader realizes just how few people know that the world is round in the sense of having a scientific education. If everybody really knew all about everybody else there would be no war, no point in Stein's geography lesson. She claims that "that other country that you need to be free in is the other country not the country where you really belong," and she pledges allegiance to that "other country": "After all everybody, that is, everybody who writes is interested in living inside themselves in order to tell what is inside themselves. That is why writers have to have two countries, the one where they belong and the one in which they live really. The second one is romantic, it is separate from themselves, it is not real but it is really there" (2).

Exile is obviously exhilarating for some artists, depressing for others. Natalia Ginzburg claims that writing redeemed her from exile; making a story was, in effect, building a home: "When I write stories I am like someone who is in her own country, walking along streets that she has known since she was a child, between walls and trees that are hers." On one's own map, one can be real; self and world are created in words.

Displacement and distance are obviously different for women who are already displaced by gender within their home cultures. But it is a mistake to think that all female experience of difference is the same or that all exiles are equally victimized or empowered. A female appropriation of a new distance, radically altering perspective by a close, enlarged, concentrated view of one object, a flower or a mountain, makes Georgia O'Keeffe's paintings suggest a specifically female way of seeing (up close and personal) in an exile's geography, which seems a graphic reflection of the spatiality of female Modernism. Like Rhoda's careful placement of the square upon the oblong in an architectural vision of music-making in Virginia Woolf's *The Waves*, for the exiled woman artist the making of a work of art is a reproduction of housekeeping. Like Rhoda, she "makes a perfect dwelling place." Words, paint, and musical notation are the brooms and brushes of exilic art as homemaking. Making something out of nothing makes somewhere out of nowhere, a mimetic of rebirth, childbirth, or self-making for the exiled artist, a process politically and intimately bound up with domestic labor.

As we debate these issues intellectually and privilege homelessness as impulse to art, let us remember that our cities are full of the nonwriting homeless. There is an ethic to the study of elsewhereness, which urges us to be aware that homelessness hurts. As we analyze the discourse of displacement, refugees from political and racial oppression all over the world and at our very doorsteps are negotiating their own status as legal and illegal aliens from South Africa to the Soviet Union, from New York City to the Texas border.

Border disputes between feminist critics and the establishment have largely been settled. Feminist criticism itself is no longer beleaguered on the boundaries of academia or wandering in the wilderness, making mountains out of its marginality. Those mountains made very good platforms for preaching a radical message to inflexible institutions. But the academy has bent a bit, and in some quarters feminist criticism has been domesticated and is happily settling down and learning the language. Yet some unregenerate Hilda Wangels still retain their mountain manners and stomp the halls in their hobnailed boots and knapsacks, determined to force the "master builders" into crowning their patriarchal spires with women's aspirations.

In this essay I question our notions of female diaspora and sketch a little map of gender in exile by raising some issues of critical practice, canonicity, language, and genre critiques, in the service of a social analysis of exile and art as they intersect with notions of individual genius, collective culture, and the relation of women's art to the social text of domestic labor.

Estrangement seems built into the female condition. May we say, then, that all women artists are strangers—though some women are stranger than others? This otherness is not universally experienced, nor is it universally acknowledged. A negative ranking process obtains as a subtext of the study of exile in which a Holocaust victim ranks higher in the hierarchy than Virginia Woolf, whose exile was internal, despite her mapping of the Outsiders' Society in *Three Guineas* as a united front of pacifism, feminism, socialism, and antifascism specifically linking working-class men to women of all classes in their marginality. I was taken to task by a feminist critic for comparing Virginia Woolf's "alien and critical" stance in British patriarchy with Walter Benjamin's position in Weimar Germany. "Thinking Back through Our Mothers" linked Woolf and Benjamin in their radical homelessness as woman and Jew, reading their suicides as both private and political acts. As critics Benjamin and Woolf were administering a culture for those who despised them and also needed them, for, as Terry Eagleton has often pointed out, the oppressed are natural readers of the culture that oppresses them. This insider/outsider position is itself a potent form of exile in which class, race, and gender clash and overlap in different ways than for the dominant.

Why is it so shocking to compare Virginia Woolf to Walter Benjamin? British patriarchs were less life-threatening to women than Nazis were to Jews, of course. Benjamin has been canonized as a thinker and Woolf as a writer, and hence it is audacious to consider Woolf's political essays and her literary criticism as theoretical because they do not name themselves theory. In fact, though Woolf called *A Room of One's Own* "talks to girls" rather than *A Discourse on the Theory of the Female Speaking Subject*, it is precisely our responsibility as critics to name theory where we find it, to place it on our contemporary maps. As Benjamin's experience of Jewish exile enabled him to create a portrait of "Paris, the Capital of the Nineteenth Century," Woolf's experience as an exiled woman enabled her to create "London, the Capital of the Patriarchy." Gertrude Stein, whose identity as Jew, woman, lesbian, and American was even more tortured and complex, takes up where Benjamin left off in naming Paris 1900–1939 as the *background* of all modern art.

The reputation of Virginia Woolf as a serious literary critic, a theorist of the relations of pacifism to feminism, socialism to antifascism, who argues that the origins of fascism are not in nationalism but in the patriarchal family, is itself in exile in her own country and, most surprisingly, among feminists in her own country. Her work is already, however, so canonized in the United States among feminists that a critic such as Bradford K. Mudge can make a serious critique of the flaws in her categories of "major and minor" and the blind spots in her proto-Modernist search for a way around philosophical questions of value in literature. It is instructive to look at the difference between the social texts in the United States and Britain, a difference which in America allows a radical critic like Mudge to fault Woolf for not being radical enough, while in Britain, her anti-Leavisite position is read (against all evidence in the texts) as conservative and elitist. There are times when I think that this outrageously funny mistake is entirely owing to the lack of earnest preaching in her style, that it is hard for many British readers to break Woolf's cover because she does not make dogmatic pronouncements. The French find no problem with this, as the wish of the critic to share pleasure with her readers is not culturally foreign to them, nor is it at odds with the most radical ideology. P. N. Furbank, the biographer of E. M. Forster, reminds his readers as he reviews the first volume of Woolf's essays that she was traditional in her outlook, sharing the "gentlemanly" values of other *Times Literary Supplement* (*TLS*) critics, their "good-mannerliness and imperviousness to ideas." "Even," he writes, "the unreceptiveness to ideas acquires a special value from her purposes; for a flight from 'ideas'—and one can hardly remember a single reference to *theory*, whether philosophical or political or psychoanalytical, in these essays of hers—was actually a facet of her aesthetic modernism and the most radical gesture she had to offer against Victorianism in the shape of Buckle or Leslie Stephen" (1393). We are to suppose that Mr. Furbank knows theory when he reads it: it wears a professor's gown and dictates in a professorial tone. That theory may be made collectively as an activity created by the writer in conversation with the common reader does not occur to him. Theory must mark itself as the discourse of theory or it is not theory. Woolf does not *refer* to theory because she is making theory in a new collaborative form which includes the reader as co-maker. What he calls "gentlemanly" is Woolf's creation of the female form of conversation as criticism. His legend/trification exiles her from the ranks of intellectuals and other women writers and domesticates her radical internationalism as English, male, effete, and elite. But

Furbank remains extremely puzzled by Woolf's earliest essays in musical theory, on Wagner and Bayreuth. I reprinted chunks of these unavailable essays in my early work on musical structure in Woolf's work so they have been generally available in the United States as contributions to her "exiled" status here as a *thinker*. Even Andrew McNeillie, introducing the first volume of Woolf's essays, fails to understand the importance of Woolf's apprentice essays in the *Guardian* (*Church Weekly*), an "unlikely outlet" for her writing. He notes that it was Violet Dickinson who got her the job as reviewer so she could make money and support herself. That is, her career was established with the help of women friends in an obscure and unlikely place. He considers her work for the *TLS* as the real apprenticeship. Since Furbank cannot "remember" the expression of any ideas in Woolf's writing, he counts her among the blissfully anti-ideological English. Since McNeillie cannot count as an inaugural act the introduction of one woman writer to an editor by another woman, we are bound to map her exile for ourselves in women's history and the history of ideas.

the ignorance that they are allowed to possess . . .
—Gayatri Spivak

> One cannot understand understanding as emotional empathy, the placement of the self in the other's position (loss of one's own position). This is required only for peripheral acts of understanding. One cannot understand understanding as a translation from the other's language into one's own language.
> —Mikhail Bakhtin (180–81)

As I write, I have been trying to imagine how Woolf would have responded to a book about exile from language called *The Silent Twins*, which has haunted me as a purely vicious example of murdering to dissect and a caution to literary critics and psychoanalysts about the distortions and victimizations that may accompany well-meaning attempts to study and analyze the "other." Marjorie Wallace, an articulate white liberal reporter, "rescues" the jailed, mistreated, and misunderstood black victims. This "rescue" is a specious alibi for her own "elsewhereness" from racial responsibility and an exploitation of their triologic cross-cultural discourse that keeps them elsewhere, at a distance, and off the scale of Wallace's map of British culture. Her objectifications are astonishing; their diary entries are printed and yet their very subjectivity is stolen from them by her brisk commentary and half-baked analyses. Mr. Furbank would have no trouble recognizing the theorist's voice here. It announces itself as master of these puzzling texts and equally puzzling lives, rousing the reader to join her in blaming the victims (or maybe their mother, or maybe their inattentive woman social worker. Oh, hurry, get them to the male professionals before they destroy each other.)

The West Indian twins June and Jennifer Gibbons, who stopped speaking in early childhood but wrote volumes of novels, letters, and diaries and produced an enormous body of fantasy plays incorporating dolls, drawings, and poems (this mass of writing is to me a black and white quilt that resists from behind the text Wallace's legend/trification of it, in the image of its storage in large black plastic garbage bags) are now in Broadmoor, England's prison-hospital for the criminally insane. The white reporter Marjorie Wallace has written this terrifying book out of a morbid fascination with what she sees as a new version of the Brontës' Angria, ransacking the writing for exotic thrills in vicarious victimization, a tale of "genius and destruction," the jacket says, shaped by the ignorant, well-meaning efforts of the reporter into a story of the evil domination of one twin by the other, a modern Gothic romance of gender and racial exile, in which the black female victims are blamed for their own oppression. Wallace ignores the power of the state, the schools, social workers, prisons, and parents over the twins and concentrates on how one coerces the other into silence.

The reader is appalled and instantly exiled by the blind racism of the text, which jauntily compares the girls hidden in their duffle coat hoods to members of the Ku Klux Klan, comments on their obsession with their silver bangle bracelets without the slightest idea of the meaning of those bracelets in West Indian culture, and evokes a savage, undifferentiated Africa, where twins are considered bad luck, while noting that the Gibbonses were often the only black family in the small English towns where they lived. Wallace never connects this fact to the development of writing, of the world and self-creation of June and Jennifer's silence, exile, and cunning, nor does she question why prison seemed to them a protecting "home" when they sought to be arrested. The twins had identical dreams (which they recorded) of being smothered by some huge object once they were safely (?) locked away from their family. Wallace attributes this dream to an origin in an attempt by one of their siblings to smother them as babies. Incest never occurs to her because the fine education of the father somehow exempts him from responsibility or blame, even though the twins first stopped speaking to him. Their silence extended to the rest of the family only, it appears, when that silence was not heard as a cry for help.

Now that they are drugged into nonwriting silence and "good" behavior in prison, Wallace pities June and Jennifer Gibbons only because, ceasing to write, they cease to be of interest. She does not explore the social question of racial oppression and cultural exile for the West Indian child of assimilating parents, who deprive their children of any cultural context in which to function, nor does she analyze the triologic nature of the inter-locking polyphony of the twins' voices intersecting with white English and American culture or see their immersion in and mastery of American TV and rock music culture, of Pepsi-Cola, drugs, sex, and violence and their awesome powers of writing that culture as an art of the exiled. Nor is the mother's abandonment treated as part of a pattern of defense against the admission of incest. Yet one cannot claim to "understand" in Bakhtin's sense the twins or their family as Wallace does. We read *The Silent Twins* as a cautionary tale about the dangers of projecting one's own plot on the recovery of the exiled and the silenced, of abuses almost inherent in the process of rescuing the abused, of distance increased rather than de-creased in enacting the exile's return. In a prize-winning poem called "Elective Mutes," Lucie Brock-Broido quotes the diaries with respect for June Gibbons as a writer and a speaking subject in exile. She writes, "No one can hear us talk, we mute we shy," and "We will talk patois, speeded / up 78 on the record player, so no one else can / understand. We do we know / the languages of hemlock, jimson weed" (38–39).

Magpie Criticism

While the voices of June and Jennifer Gibbons sing the plight of the colonial's return to the rejecting mother country, echoing the voices of the caretaker's children singing for their supper patronized and misunder-stood in Woolf's *The Years*, other forms of exile obtain closer to home. As the first essay in a planned history of American women writers, Elaine Showalter's "Piecing and Writing" limits the black woman to piecing and excludes her from writing by silent omission. Beginning in the already strongly established critical practice of the comparison of women's writing and cultural production to weaving and sewing, a practice worth cri-tiquing, Showalter asks, "Do we need to develop new forms of inquiry in order to account for a female tradition which is also multi-racial?" (233).

The trajectory of the essay closely follows the established pattern of a particular week of many Women's Studies classes across the country in which, using Elaine Hedges's classic, *In Her Own Image*, we read the history of quilt-making along with the texts in which quilt-making and American culture collide. Asking us to consider whether it is time to "deromanticize the art of the quilt," Showalter calls this practice into question while celebrating its achievements.

But something strange happens. Elaine Hedges and other experts dispute Showalter's reading of *Uncle Tom's Cabin* in relation to the log cabin quilt. In her readings of "A Jury of Her Peers," and other quilting texts up through a Bobbie Ann Mason story, Showalter's text, which has seemed inexorably to build up to a reading of Alice Walker's "Everyday Use," generally acknowledged as the quintessential quilt story, veers off in a misguided deconstructive turn. "Everyday Use" forces us to confront the answers to all the questions posed by the essay about gender, race, and American culture. Instead of reading it, or Alice Walker's novel *The Color Purple*, Showalter asks if there is not something "self-destructive" in feminist efforts to reclaim female art forms, which may in fact turn out to be burdens. She warns us not to "exaggerate the importance of women's culture."

I doubt if it is possible to exaggerate the importance of women's culture, despite the gains made over the last decade in recovering our past. The fear of "exaggeration" succumbs to legend/trification on the issue of the scale of canonical measurement of women's achievements. And it seems to me significant that Showalter's essay turns before the precise moment of what, in our Women's Studies classes, is the triumphant experience of reading "Everyday Use." Showalter cites Alice Walker as an essayist and critic on black women's quilts but alienates and exiles her as an artist by absence from her (rightful, surely?) and generally acknowledged position as the great artist she is in her full exploration of all the issues raised by Showalter in connecting the quilt to American culture. Specific in its recreation of 1960s experience of the Black Muslim and Black Is Beautiful movements, "Everyday Use" also wittily explores the very difference between pragmatic American critical practice and pure aesthetic theory, which seems to be the real problem with Showalter's stance. Walker works out the urban/rural problem and the drive to find one's "other" roots and one's family roots in American culture, and she enacts in splendid complexity the mother/daughter experience, invigorating the current debate about "fluid boundaries" and psychological differentiation with a full portrait of a strong and wise mother and *two* daughters, neither of whom is rejected in a powerful drama of exile and return within the mother country. What Showalter's exclusion of this story enacts most clearly is the question before feminist critics today of whether our critical practice, like Grandmother Dee's quilts, is to be framed at a distance from life as an aesthetic object or whether it is to be put to everyday use.

Does the deliberate exile of Walker from Showalter's text signify the exile of the critic from our common critical practice? She warns us against sentimentalizing women's culture. But I remain puzzled by the estrangement I feel as a reader deprived of a *denouement* by the omission of the most resonant quilt story from its place in her narrative. There is a big hole in Showalter's quilt, a hole where race is erased along with acknowledgment of her critical predecessors like Elaine Hedges. Race is a major part of the pattern, and it surely must be pieced into any American quilt, in this case as the centerpiece. Much of Walker's story is taken up with the notion of aesthetic value and the roots of folk art in necessity and poverty, in community and cultural heritage. The quilt is part of American communal women's work, produced as housekeeping skills were passed on in newly formed communities. The quilt is itself a map of women's history. The danger is not in sentimentalizing women's culture but in isolating the quilt from its context or the quilt story from the social text of gender and race. The danger lies in valorizing the individual artist, quiltmaker, or writer over the collective, divorcing the quilt as an aesthetic object from its roots in female experience of domestic labor. But the most serious danger is the elsewhering or erasure of the black woman artist from her place in American culture.

When Showalter asks, "Is it time to bury the burial quilt rather than to praise it?" (245) the answer, for me, comes from a British writer, Sylvia Townsend Warner, herself exiled from the canon perhaps because of her work in many genres combined with a left-wing and lesbian identity. Townsend Warner's late (1977) short story "A Widow's Quilt" (in *One Thing Leading to Another*) demonstrates the consequences of cultural displacement, the shocking result of the individual's attempt to make for herself what should be made for her by members of a community to which she has contributed. "A Widow's Quilt" is a feminist critique of the loss and devaluation of women's communal culture exiled from its origins in work. Charlotte visits the American Museum in Somerset and becomes obsessed with the sight of a widow's quilt from America, hanging in the museum. Already out of context as "folk art," the quilt inspires Charlotte with the desire to be a widow, to kill off her unloved husband by sewing a shroud/mourning robe. She rushes home to London and unearths her old blackout curtains left from the war. She adds the brocade from her wedding dress to "that lustreless soot-black, dead rook black" (128) of the curtains for her own widow's quilt. Stitching into it all her pent-up hatred for her husband and her wish for his death, she works in secret and alone at "her one assertion of a life of her own" (129). The American tradition of the communally created cover worked for the bereaved widow by her friends (as Kay Turner demonstrates in her lectures at the University of Texas) is here mocked by Charlotte's vicious single-mindedness. "Stitching away at Everard's demise" (132), she neglects to provide a stuffing or backing for the quilt and is instructed by her visiting sister in how to do it, at which point the quilt becomes too heavy, "a drudgery—another marital obligation, almost another Everard" (132). Charlotte has a heart attack rushing back with the last spool of thread to finish the quilt. Charlotte has been estranged from her roles as wife and homemaker, having refused childbirth, friendship, and sisterliness, and her body has rebelled at its exile from a life of shared work and pleasure. Her husband gives the quilt to her sister, telling her that Charlotte had called it a "Magpie Quilt." The lie is, of course, the truth of her own scavenger-bird relation to American women's quilt culture, a comment on the appropriation of form without context, art divorced from the common workroom and the common ceremonies of life and death. The magpie misnomer names very nicely the terrible price of decontextualization.

Much recent criticism bears the mark of Charlotte's Magpie Quilt as self-deluded obsessive piecing done in isolation from work and community. But this estrangement can be overcome. We cannot be silent at the displacement of race in the name of feminism or its banishment to the borders. If we are engaged in making a widow's quilt in memory of lost and exiled women artists, we need to piece our past together with the historical stuffing and backing appropriate for its "everyday use."

Magpie criticism, imitating the thievery and chattering of the bird in question, will obviously continue to flourish. But feminist, Marxist, and new historicist critiques of genre and canonicity are bound to have some effect on hegemonic culture. Printed next to Sylvia Townsend Warner's "A Widow's Quilt" in *One Thing Leading to Another* (the book has been exiled to the remainder pile, I learned from a recent catalog) is a 1948 story called "The Mother Tongue" originally published in *Housewife*. As Gayatri Spivak says, "there is safety in specificity." The story is a demonstration of Irigaray's claim, quoted at the beginning of this essay, that women are exiled from patriarchal language; they speak and write but maintain a problematic elsewhereness from their own discourse. In *Virginia Woolf and the Languages of Patriarchy* I have argued that Woolf deliberately valorizes the charwoman figure in all her novels as the origin and fount of language, invoking the rhythms of housework as the source of speaking and singing. The roots of culture, Warner suggests, are in domestic labor; ownership has been appropriated by the wrong class and gender. In "The Mother Tongue," Townsend Warner deconstructs the listening/speaking problem and anticipates contemporary debates about the relation of language to thinking. As the hegemonic listener from the dominant culture, Miss Oliphant from the Acclimatisation and Training Centre for Displaced Persons decides that "her" refugees should retain some of their native Polish for "the language in which one says one's prayers is one's native tongue" (135). The two "clever" girls are sent to work in an orphanage in the town, and Magda becomes a servant on a farm. Miss Oliphant wants everything to be "nice," for them to meet on Sundays and speak Polish—"the Poles are natural-born linguists—think of Joseph Conrad" (135). As a domestic laborer, Magda has no need for speech and soon loses both her English and her native Polish: "As a fish slides through the net and drops back into the water, Magda escaped from the mesh of words, vanished from conversations." She lives "unsignalized." "Behind not speaking lies the unspoken" (136):

> But a language is a thing which can only be possessed by those who possess it in common. Language is a dozen voices clinging to the rope of a litany. Language is a hundred voices clattering against each other in the market place. Language is the lamentation of thousands crying out in terror and anguish. Language is the uproar of millions, a rustle of questions sprouting thick as corn all over Europe, saying, *What now? When? Whither?* And presently language is a hundred voices clinging to the rope of a new speech, saying, *I-am-glad-to-see-you. Please-have-you-the-needle? Thank-you-very-much.* (136)

Magda finds speech again at the funeral of a farm laborer. As his coffin is lowered into the ground, she begins to lament her own "innumerable dead" "on the brink of a stranger's grave." She fills her mouth with earth—"Her outcry was of no language" (139), and she stands at the graveside listening for a reply.

Translations

but cats in peace-time or in war-time, they sit and watch and prey.
—Gertrude Stein, *Paris France*

"So you speak cat?"
"A little," I replied. "I understand it
better than I can speak it."
—Sylvia Townsend Warner, *The Cat's Cradle-Book*

There is a peculiar and fascinating transgression of taste and literary notions of "high" culture in Sylvia Townsend Warner's use of the devalued genres of the fairy tale and the fable. It is instructive to look at the ways in which lived forms of exile invigorate her use of exiled literary forms. Her particular version of the female triologic imagination engages itself naturally with the moral tradition of the teaching forms of children's literature. What effect did her lesbianism and communism have on her choice of genres? In rescuing archaic forms from their exile in genre limbo, she transforms the fantastic into a kind of superrealism. Ethics and ideology have a presence/absence in the stories like the wings of her tame elves—they are there, neatly folded on every elf's back, but it is impolite to use them at this moment in their culture. The particular form of elsewhereness pertaining to the Modernist left-wing woman writer, I would argue, is defined in the way she deconstructs a norm of socialist realism as a vehicle for the expression of both ethics and otherness. This is evident in the surrealist elements in Elsa Triolet's fiction, in the occult powers in Rebecca West's *Harriet Hume* and the poltergeists in *The Fountain Overflows*, the prophetic dreams associated with epilepsy in Elsa Morante's *History: A Novel*, the lyric phantasmagoria combined with Dickensian realism in Emily Coleman's *The Shutter of Snow*, the subversion of fable in Virginia Woolf's *Flush*, as well as the perversion of biography and history in *Orlando*. In this context Warner's fables and fairy tales join company in the countercanonical.

Banishment, exile, incest, and the problems of refugees and language/translation are themes that recur in her fiction. The experience of outsidership haunts her choice of form—within the structure she is decorously, even brilliantly, writing elegantly polished English prose. She does not rupture the sentence or the syntax; the challenges are to fundamental belief systems. The challenge is to "humanism" in its arrogant self-reflexivity. The allegorical urge to moralize is evident in the choice of genres like the fairy tale and fable, natural and obvious for a writer with a political message. But what is exciting about Warner's use of these forms is the witty and devastating way they refuse reassurance to the reader, and by destabilizing genre, she destabilizes gender, nation, community and order, language and history. Difference is disquieting; even in the Kingdoms of Elfin, there are changelings, and human and elf worlds collide and inter-mix; a baby is nursed by a cat. In *Lolly Willowes* (1926) Townsend Warner reinvented fantastic realism for the twentieth century. In *Kingdoms of Elfin* (1977) and *The Cat's Cradle-Book* (1940) she domesticates fantasy fiction, grounding it firmly in reality but morally interfering with readers who use fantasy as escape. There is no escape from Warner's ethics; she always has the reader cornered.

Both *The Cat's Cradle-Book* and *Kingdoms of Elfin* are remarkably post-Modern in their revolutionary unsettlement of the reader's notions of reality and upsetting of race, class, and gender issues (as in *Flush*) by moving the site of action to interspecies interaction and attraction. If either volume were signed Calvino or Borges, it would be instantly lion-ized as brilliant experimental fiction. In fact, I strongly suspect that Um-berto Eco's *The Name of the Rose* had its origin in a reading of Townsend Warner's novel about a fourteenth-century convent, *The Corner That Held Them*. An Englishwoman's books about cats and elves, however, are probably at the bottom of every active interest group's list for revision of the canon. Yet it is clear to me that *Kingdoms of Elfin* articulates the *angst* of Italo Calvino's *Invisible Cities* much more acutely because it dismantles patriarchal privilege along with so many other hierarchies. In the same sense, *The Cat's Cradle-Book* anticipates the critique by Gayatri Spivak, Edward Said, and others of anthropological methodologies that project patterns of behavior onto the objects of study, robbing them of subject-hood. The questions Warner raises about language and story, the modern search for an ur-language and an ur-story and the ethnography of speak-ing in *The Cat's Cradle-Book* are both serious inquiries and marvelous mockeries of the scholar's pursuits. The undecidability of the title evokes mystery; it is a primitive way of weaving with string on the fingers, forms of which were used to tell the position of the stars, a game for children; and, importantly, it evokes the superstition that the domestic animal might harm the human baby, guilt at exploitation of the animal, and fear at how much it knows about humans.

A Townsend Warner revival will probably have to await publication of her diaries, letters to Valentine Ackland, and a biography, though Wendy

Mulford's *This Narrow Place* is an excellent beginning. She eludes classification like one of her own changelings or slightly extraterrestrial creatures, always crossing genre boundaries. The power of Townsend Warner's realistic fantasies lies in their radical evocation of reality, not in escape from it. Like Kafka's *Metamorphosis*, they increase our concern for human suffering in the real world by crossing boundaries between the animal and the human. The estrangement called up by such dislocations is named "didactic romance" by Robert Scholes in his work on structural fabulation, and Christine Brooke-Rose brilliantly analyzes in *A Rhetoric of the Unreal* some variations in narrative structures of the fantastic. But neither critic looks at gender's relation to language and plot formation, that female sense of elsewhereness which Irigaray describes. Warner's triologic female "elsewhereness" is uncanny because of its domestic familiarity. This quality of "even stranger than strange" (which also occurs in Angela Carter's work) lies in its specifically female juxtaposition of the alien and the cozy. Warner is an expert in transgression of taste, as in the line "She was, after all, a British fairy." This sits right on the edge, jolting the reader's expectations. The roof literally falls in on an aged brother and sister in the stunning story "The Love Match" (1947), leaving the villagers and the reader to ponder a lifetime of incest. In "The Climate of Exile" in *Kingdoms of Elfin* Warner works out the difference between active and passive forms of exile, an allegory equally suitable for political dissidents or homosexuals on the question of life in or out of the closet. The triologic structure of this story pits a religious exile against a political poet against the citizens of Catmere, a state that supports itself as a "home" for wayward exiles. The artist, Snipe, cannot bond with Bodach, the mystic, because of his transgressions of narrative taste. In telling his story, Bodach "ruined the effect of the narrative" (161) by casually announcing that he had flown without wings and that his wings had "rejoined him." (They are, after all, British fairies.) Bodach breaks his vow of poverty, chastity and *gravity*, or grounding in exile and in narrative convention. Snipe wastes away because there is nothing to rebel against: "he knew the final intimidation of exile: he was afraid to go home" (168). The obvious lessons here, both political and rhetorical, are about "ruining the effect of the narrative," changing the plane of the plot in writing exile—wings. The project of feminist criticism is to change the scale of the legends on our maps of women's culture. Showalter thinks that we exaggerate, but it is important politically that we do not succumb to the plea from conservative feminism for legend/trification.

Bluebeard's Daughters

The Cat's Cradle-Book (1940, reprinted in England in 1960, dedicated to Ludwig Renn, the antifascist writer) also breaks fiction's vow of "gravity." Further out than Woolf's *Flush* on the border of interspecies relations, this brilliant fable robs humanity of its pride in the origins of narrative. Aesop's fables, and those of his successors, make a direct connection between the human and the animal, but Warner's are human-centered and do not question the assumption that storytelling, the art of narrative, is what separates humans from animals. Warner's text is unsettling (and long out of print) because it declares that *the origin of narration is in lactation.* Narrative is a function of nurturing. Storytelling is a mental form of nursing, and mothers are the first storytellers, not fathers. Homer, we may now assume, was a Greek cat; the origins of literacy are even more oral than we thought. Our first ink was milk. The look of narrative origins is very different if we imagine it as white on black, not black on white. If "man" is not differentiated from animals by his symbol-making capacity, then where is the difference? Culture, making sense of the universe, is a female activity, and, further, it comes to humans through that despised animal, the cat, which has been described in Western culture with all the characteristics of the female cultural other.

Reproducing the structure of the anthropologist's investigation of the "other," the narrator is asked at the opening of the book, "Have you ever thought about the culture of cats?" The triologic structure of the text involves the cats and their texts, their collector and explicator, and the reader-narrator. She joins the cat-culture expert, a mock-heroic fairy-tale prince, for a brief fling, listens to his adventures, reads the cat narratives, and returns when all the cats are dying of a plague. The book we are reading contains sixteen cat narratives from the original "cat" and the fables, because cats live with people, are about both animals and humans. In the introduction the young man who is collecting the cat stories tells her (shades of the critique of "experience-based feminist criticism") that his discovery that cats were the first storytellers arose when first he fell in love with Haru, a Siamese, in Ankara. "There she stood in the moonlight, poised, rocking lightly like a soap-bubble. Then with a cry of joy, raucous and passionate, she sprang onto my bed" (17). Haru dies when he won't let her out when she is in heat, and the narrative is charged with frustration at the impossibility of physical consummation of their love. He calls Haru "an exquisite story-teller, in the purest, most classical tradition of narrative," his "lost Scheherazade" (17). After her death he resolves to understand her civilization and discovers that even alley cats tell beautiful stories: "Yes, here, in a disused pig sty in Norfolk, a poor unlettered tabby was repeating to her kittens a story of Indian life which I had first heard from the lips of my Siamese cat in Ankara" (21). As Zora Neale Hurston deconstructs her own role as collector of tales in *Mules and Men*, the narrator asks him, rather cattily, whether his cats are raw material or collaborators in his study, the precise question contemporary critics ask. He avoids an answer by claiming that they are "sources" and that he must get his material from them without making them self-conscious. Mrs. O'Toady is his best source; she has the widest repertory and is "inexhaustible" (22). He has no interest whatever in Mrs. O'Toady's subjectivity. Totally absorbed by his personal explication of guilt at his exploitation of Haru in scientific classification of the cat narratives, he neglects the living cats or brings upon them an inexplicable "murrain." This recalls the plagues brought by liberal colonialists upon the "exotic" peoples they studied. And it constitutes a splendid and effective critique of our own practice of romanticizing those whom Victor Turner called the liminal, the marginal outsiders, the cultural aliens.

Narrative flows with mother's milk, and kittens are "trained up in a catly frame of mind" "at their mother's tails" (22). Mother cats are the guardians of memory, and their fables, unlike Aesop's, are not "propaganda." The two characters read the typescripts of the stories and argue about the "ur-text." Their richest sources are nursing mothers—"The text comes from Meep—another excellent mother and narrator" (23). Having chased down many an ur-text myself, I am chastened by Warner's fix on the fixation with first or best texts, with finding origins. Oceans of spilled milk/ink have flowed in such endeavors. We are also sent back to the legend/trification of the map of black female exile by Marjorie Wallace in *The Silent Twins* and the startling absence of Walker's "Everyday Use" from Showalter's narrative of American culture.

The effect of these statements is to upset the reader's human-centered notions, as well as ideas about nationality and language: "Why not suppose that our stories came to us from the cats?" (27–28) the young man asks the narrator. She is to clear her mind of humanism, now revealed as a form of chauvinism, and ethnography, to see that the best folk tales are objective and catlike, praising "sensibility and reserve" rather than chivalry and daring, and that "the proper study of catkind is man" (29). "For ages the languages of men have kept them apart. For ages the cat language has been catholic, explicit, unvarying. I understand it, you understand it, every child picks up an inkling of it" (28). By deconstructing cat culture, Warner silently claims objectivity for the female and relegates war stories to the now subliterate human narrative. When they discuss publishing the stories with variant texts and the difficulty of convincing people that this is a serious work of scholarship, Townsend Warner anticipates the problems all outsider groups have with the upholders of the canon: "Cat is not a recognized language. How are you to convince people that what is roughly a vocabulary of mew and guttural can convey such fine shades of meaning?" (31).

When all the cats but one die of the plague and the young man leaves, the narrator collects the fables in the book at hand. The best is called "Bluebeard's Daughter" (157–80), and it investigates many levels of difference. What is most haunting about the story is that it forces one to realize in its retelling of one of the most popular stories in Western culture that as women living in patriarchal history we are all Bluebeard's daughters. The fathers have murdered our mothers, locked up the history of their personal relations with women, and essentially the whole history of women, and killed the women who were curious enough to want to know it. For men have been the knowers and the tellers, and they have named the curiosity of women and cats a sin punishable by death. In this tale Warner reclaims "curiosity" as a suitable moral and intellectual activity for women, and she is also retelling the Zeus/Athena headbirth myth explicitly as a story in which the father's daughter does not carry on patriarchal values.

Historians have suppressed her because it is unreasonable that Bluebeard could have been a good father when he was such a bad husband. Djamileh is, of course, discriminated against because of her father, and she not only inherits his hair ("A deep butcher's blue") but she has purple lips, and "the inside of her mouth and tongue were dusky blue like a well-bred chow-dog's" (160). I cannot help but read the mark of the patriarchy on Djamileh's mouth and tongue as the ink of all the patriarchal texts on which women have been nurtured as their father's daughters. Her guardians persuade her to give up study to marry, and all goes well until her husband wants to unlock all the doors of her father's castle, including the one marked "curiosity killed the cat." She hides the key; he breaks down the door and breaks his leg falling into the room (which does not contain any mysteries). She advises him that since they cannot contain their curiosity the best thing to do would be to sublimate it in science, and they spend the rest of their lives as astronomers.

The Bluebeard myth is an important key to Western culture's naming of woman's intellectual curiosity as sinful and dangerous; man sets the test and woman always fails it and dies. The most powerful revision of the story is Béla Bartók's brilliant 1911 opera *Bluebeard's Castle*, which became a classic after World War II. Bartók reclaims Bluebeard as "everyman," done in in old age (he never murdered his earlier wives) by his last wife, Judith, who wants the "keys" to all his previous relationships. She is a villainess because she will not let him keep his memory private and intact. By naming her Judith the opera makes her a Jewish killer and remakes Bluebeard as a kindly Holofernes. George Steiner uses the opera (*In Bluebeard's Castle*, 1971) to critique the Bluebeard of establishment culture that will neither come to terms with the Holocaust nor take science seriously. He reads Judith's curiosity not in terms of gender but as the human urge to open all doors. Against these very powerful misreadings, legend/trifications, and rehabilitations, one may place the Warner story along with Angela Carter's more Gothic feminist version of the story in *The Bloody Chamber*, in which the heroine is rescued at the last minute by a blind piano-tuner and her mother riding on horseback against the tide. Carter's story was written as a tribute to Colette. In *Wayward Girls & Wicked Women* she reprints Suniti Namjoshi's "Three Feminist Fables," one of which, "A Room of His Own," rewrites the story so that Bluebeard kills his wife precisely because she has *not* opened the door out of respect for his privacy.

I propose that Sylvia Townsend Warner's "Bluebeard's Daughter" is a direct response to Virginia Woolf's fable "Shakespeare's Sister" in *A Room of One's Own*. The martyr is replaced by the survivor. The patriarchal predecessor is created in his roles as mother-murderer and father. Townsend Warner does not imagine that we can escape the mark of the patriarchy or bleach out the blue from our bodies. But she does express a hope that the father's daughter can reroute the energies of her husband into a joint scholarly pursuit. Perhaps it is utopian, but it is an alibi we can take seriously. Townsend Warner's feminist and socialist fables articulate the ethics of elsewhereness. She domesticates estrangement and asks us to examine our own complicity in "othering" even when we think we are working to expand the canon. Master text, master race, master language— all define themselves by the other. The language of cat with its gutturals

292 . Jane Marcus

and mews may be seen as a folk version of Kristeva's demoded demotic "semiotic," an eternal other mother tongue. Even as Warner teaches it to us she warns us against romanticizing our own liminality and that of our subjects.

Irigaray's "elsewhereness" can be an alibi for female lack of responsibility at not being responsible for the violence done historically by patriarchal language. As an ethic it lets us off the hook as criminals in racist and colonialist mappings of history. Its truth to women's experience of exile from language is real enough and cannot be written off. But as critics we surely should beware of a stance and a practice that gives us an alibi for so many cultural crimes. We can catch ourselves and each other in the practice of "magpie criticism," detecting the alibi in the alibi in our work and that most subtle and dangerous alibi of all, the one that excuses us from political action because we are engaged in writing criticism.

Note

My thanks to Mary Lynn Broe and Angela Ingram for taking on the task of editing this volume, which began with the 1986 MLA Twentieth Century English Literature Division meetings, and for their helpful comments on this essay. I would also like to thank the participants in the three sessions and the audiences for stimulating dialogue and Louise Yelin and Ingeborg O'Sickey in particular for their response to this essay. (As we go to press, Angela Ingram points out that Michael Seidel also uses the idea of the alibi in *Exile and the Narrative Imagination* [New Haven: Yale University Press, 1986].)

Works Cited

Bakhtin, Mikhail. *The Dialogic Imagination*. Edited and translated by Michael Holquist and Caryl Emerson. Austin: University of Texas Press, 1981.

———. "Notes." In *Bakhtin: Essays and Dialogues on His Work*, edited by Gary Saul Morson, 179–82. Chicago: University of Chicago Press, 1986.

Bartók, Béla. *Bluebeard's Castle*. Opera composed in 1911 to a libretto by Bela Balasz. Set in English by Chester Kallman for 1966 London recording and notes of a performance conducted by Istvan Kertesz with Christa Ludwig and Walter Berry, produced by Erik Smith. See notes of a dialogue between the conductor and Christa Ludwig on Judith's role.

Brock-Broido, Lucie. "Elective Mutes." *Harper's Magazine*, May 1988, pp. 38–39.

Brooke-Rose, Christine. *A Rhetoric of the Unreal*. New York: Cambridge University Press, 1981.

Carter, Angela. *The Bloody Chamber*. New York: Harper & Row, 1981.

———, ed. *Wayward Girls & Wicked Women*. London: Virago, 1986.

Castro, Jan Garden. *The Art and Life of Georgia O'Keeffe*. New York: Crown, 1985.

Chatwin, Bruce. *Songlines*. New York: Elizabeth Sifton/Viking, 1987.

Furbank, P. N. Review of *The Essays of Virginia Woolf. Volume 1*, edited by Andrew McNeillie. *Times Literary Supplement*, December 12, 1986, p. 1393.

Ginzburg, Natalia. *The Little Virtues*. New York: Seaver Books, 1986.

Gunew, Sneja, and Gayatri Chakravorty Spivak. "Questions of Multiculturalism," in this volume.

Hedges, Elaine R. "The Needle or the Pen: The Literary Rediscovery of Women's Textile Work." In *Tradition and the Talents of Women*, edited by Florence Howe. Urbana: University of Illinois Press, forthcoming.

Ibsen, Henrik. *The Master Builder*. London: Heinemann, 1983.

Lardas, Konstantinos, trans. "The Mourning Songs of Greek Women." *College English* 49 (January 1987): 37–41.

Lorde, Audre. "Diaspora." In *Catalyst* 1 (1987).

Marcus, Jane. "Thinking Back through Our Mothers." In *New Feminist Essays on Virginia Woolf*, edited by Jane Marcus, 1–30. Lincoln: University of Nebraska Press, 1981.

———. *Virginia Woolf and the Languages of Patriarchy*. Bloomington: Indiana University Press, 1987.

Miller, Nancy K. "Emphasis Added: Plots and Plausibilities in Women's Fiction." In *The New Feminist Criticism*, edited by Elaine Showalter, 339–60. New York: Pantheon, 1985.

Mudge, Bradford K. "Exiled as Exiler: Sara Coleridge, Virginia Woolf, and the Politics of Literary Revision," in this volume.

Mulford, Wendy. *This Narrow Place: Sylvia Townsend Warner and Valentine Ackland: Life, Letters and Politics, 1930–1951*. London: Pandora, 1988.

Namjoshi, Suniti. "Three Feminist Fables." In *Wayward Girls & Wicked Women*, edited by Angela Carter, 85–86. London: Virago, 1986.

Schenck, Celeste M. "Exiled by Genre: Modernism, Canonicity, and the Politics of Exclusion," in this volume.

Showalter, Elaine. "Piecing and Writing." In *The Poetics of Gender*, edited by Nancy K. Miller, 222–47. New York: Columbia University Press, 1986.

Smyth, Ethel. *Impressions That Remained*. New York: Knopf, 1946.

Stein, Gertrude. *Paris France*. 1940. Reprint. New York: Liveright, 1970.

Steiner, George. *In Bluebeard's Castle*. New Haven: Yale University Press, 1971.

Walker, Alice. "Everyday Use." In *In Love and Trouble*. New York: Harcourt Brace Jovanovich, 1973.

Wallace, Marjorie. *The Silent Twins*. Englewood Cliffs, N.J.: Prentice-Hall, 1986.

Warner, Sylvia Townsend. *The Cat's Cradle-Book*. New York: Viking, 1940.

———. *Kingdoms of Elfin*. New York: Viking, 1977.

———. *One Thing Leading to Another*. London: Women's Press, 1984.

Wexler, Alice. *Emma Goldman: An Intimate Life*. New York: Pantheon, 1984.

Woolf, Virginia. *The Essays of Virginia Woolf*. Edited by Andrew McNeillie. Vol. 1. New York: Harcourt Brace Jovanovich, 1986.

———. *Three Guineas*. New York: Harcourt, Brace and World, 1938.

———. *The Waves*. New York: Harcourt Brace Jovanovich, 1931.

· · · · · · · · · · · · · · · · · · · ·

Exile, Jews, Women, Yordim, I—An Interim Report

Esther Fuchs

Woman in exile, it's me: a feminist in Hebrew literature, a Hebrew critic in the Department of Oriental Studies, an Israeli among Jews, Jew among Americans, a Sabra in Saguaro land, a *yoredet* in Israel, not yet at home in Arizona, no longer at home in Tel Aviv.

To be a feminist in any field is hard enough, but to be one in a relatively small area, dominated by male-centered scholars for whom feminism is at best an American fad, is not only hard but dangerous. I did not realize that I was putting my job on the line when I began, around 1981, to deliver papers about women in Hebrew literature at the Association for Jewish Studies (AJS). What I felt at the time was frustration rather than anxiety. For it was clear to everybody that I was discussing a relatively trivial form of exile. When the proper alienation was that of the (male) Arab/Palestinian or the (male) Jew in the contexts of Hebrew and European literature, I stooped to quibble about the status of female characters in Israeli fiction. I was clearly discussing the wrong kind of alienation. It was the wrong subject, in the wrong field, at the wrong time and place.

I felt frustrated at the smugness of the high priests of my field, and, especially, at the coy submission of many of the women critics, who were assiduously pursuing the really great (male) authors and the really great topics, approved and ratified by their clearly influential male advisers and mentors. I was frustrated with myself for playing the insider, knowing full well I did not belong in that context. But then, what were the alternatives? There wasn't and still isn't an organized section for Hebrew literature at the Modern Language Association, or, for that matter, at the Middle Eastern Studies Association or the National Women's Studies Association. How many in these learned associations care about women in Hebrew literature? More important, with whom could I have a productive debate about the issues that were concerning me? So I went on giving papers at the Association of Jewish Studies until, in 1985, I think it was, I had to stop in the middle of my presentation. My throat muscles tightened up, my lips went into contortions, and I could not for the life of me control my tongue. The stunned audience remained silent as I rushed out of the lecture hall. In Massachusetts General Hospital they explained to me that I had an allergic reaction to the Stelazine that was prescribed for my gastritic pains. As I lay in my Copley Plaza room, pumped full of valium, I vowed to the darkness around me to never return to the annual AJS meetings.

I said I did not know that doing feminism in Hebrew literature might have cost me my career. This is not quite true. I did know that when one comes up for tenure, one needs approval from the high priests of one's field, and as the notoriously rebellious daughter, I should not have counted on the fathers' support. I was naive enough to believe that academic integrity will win over politics. I was wrong, of course.

But my gastritic attacks began long before the promotion and tenure review. They began around the time I completed the manuscript of the book I was later to entitle *Israeli Mythogynies*. These attacks were diagnosed as psychosomatic, related to stress and anxiety. In my sessions with my therapist, guilt rather than fear of professional failure was the constant motif. I was guilty of treason. I had betrayed my literary heritage, my Jewish identity, my teachers, the fathers of my culture, of my nation. Mine is a small nation, lacerated and broken and much maligned. I had betrayed the Jew and the Israeli in me. No matter how much my shrink and I were working on my guilt, I still felt responsible for spitting into the well from which I drank, as the rabbinic idiom goes. The gastritic pains intensified when I began to work on *Sexual Politics in the Biblical Narrative*, a critical analysis of the characterization of women in the Hebrew Bible.

The strongest support for my work came from the Women's Studies Program at the University of Texas. It did not occur to me, however, that there was nothing my sisters and allies could do when the promotion and tenure committee (nicknamed by a friend the Pope's Testicles) proclaimed its final word. Suddenly, the scholars who were so enthused about my papers were helpless against the word of the alleged specialists in my field. After all, most of them were in English, French, psychology, linguistics, anthropology—what could they say? They know nothing at all about Hebrew literature. The very ones who praised me for daring to challenge the powers that be in my field were also the first to beat a quick retreat. A letter of protest was sent to the dean. But we all know how much such a letter weighs over against the judgment of those who know best. To be brief, we could all commiserate about the alienation of feminists in our respective disciplines, but in my case, alienation from my field meant the end of my career. There are no senior scholars in my field who are feminists or even female. I did not think that made a bit of difference when I first began to do research on women in Hebrew literature and the biblical narrative.

Would I have done it differently had I had to do it all over again? Would I have stuck to the safer route of doing S. Y. Agnon and playing the obedient daughter with the fathers who applauded my work on the Israeli Nobel Prize Laureate?

The pink blotches on my left cheek began to appear during my visit to Israel in 1982. They too were later diagnosed as psychosomatic. Were the symptoms different because this exile was so very different? After all, I was in my own country, speaking to my own people, in my own language. Instead of rage, I felt embarrassment. I remember, now, having given a paper on Amos Oz's representations of women in Nurith Gertz's seminar on contemporary Israeli fiction at Tel Aviv University. The students looked at me as if I were a rare astronomical exhibit. Then came the questions. Am I saying that Amos Oz is a misogynist? Am I saying that he does not understand women? How can I even talk about women in his fiction; they are, after all, artifacts made of words. Can't I see that Hannah Gonen in *My Michael* is really a symbol of the state of Israel? That was in 1982, I think. I spoke Hebrew and presented my ideas in Hebrew; the class was conducted in Hebrew, but it might as well have been conducted in Japanese.

I think I know now that I tend to feel either guilt or panic when I feel deeply estranged from people I care about. I cared about those students, and I knew I could not reach them. The same sense of disconnection overwhelmed me after I delivered a paper entitled "Gender and Characterization in the Palmah Generation" at the Ninth World Congress of Jewish Studies. That was in August 1985. The air was thick with hostility. Though coming from professionals, the gist of the questions was the same: what do women have to do with the important subject of this panel? The chairperson gave me a minute to answer eight aggressive comments/

questions. I don't remember my answer, but I remember the anger. And I think now that much of what was not said loudly and clearly was something like this: "You are a native Israeli, surely you could speak to us in our own language, the language of the books you criticized so eloquently here. Just who do you think you are preaching to us in Western terms about our own literature? Have you forgotten who you are and where you came from?"

I was very harsh on myself on the way from Jerusalem to my parents' home in Tel Aviv. I berated myself for having done a disservice to feminist theory and for having sabotaged my own attempt to legitimize a feminist discourse in my field. You should have spoken in Hebrew, after all this is Israel, this is your own language, this is the language in which the books were written. They are right. But on the other hand, I answered myself, on the El Al jet that took me back to Tucson, I did speak Hebrew to Hedvah Yisachar, who interviewed me two days later for the Israel Public Broadcasting Services (it's not as big as it sounds, a group of little huts on the outskirts of Tel Aviv), and that did not make me feel any better. Hedvah's questions were sympathetic, and both of us spoke Hebrew, but I could not rid myself of the sense of exile. When I read the published version of the interview in *Na'amat*, the journal of Israel's working women, I realized that her questions were not so much addressed to a feminist scholar as to an Israeli *yoredet*—a descender from the (high) holy land. Hedvah wanted to know how my decision to leave Israel is related to my feminist critique of Hebrew literature. Is it that there are not yet well-developed women's studies programs in Israeli universities? Why did I find Tucson to be more congenial for my work? I wanted to tell Hedvah that she was wrong—I do not feel that the United States is more congenial to Hebrew literature—but I didn't. If I had, I would have admitted that I feel guilty about my emigration from my homeland. And I didn't feel like admitting that.

For despite my contempt for ideologies that proclaim certain places as the "proper" homes for certain individuals or groups, there is always that other voice, my mother's voice. The voice says something like this: "She [the country] is an ugly mother, she is a poor mother, but she is our mother." I wonder now to what extent my mother was talking about herself, and about the fact that in leaving Israel, I really left *her*. I wonder to what extent she was trying to make me feel guilty for breaking away from the stifling love I will end up seeking always in the wrong places, in the wrong people. But this is, after all, a moot question. Whether she meant it or not, whether I consider the concept of *yerida* an ideologically manipulative metaphor (as opposed to *aliya*—immigration to Israel), the fact remains that I am still offended when identified as a *yoredet*. I know it is preposterous to think that I betrayed my country simply by having left her. Yet whenever I hear that word, I feel like someone who just got her face schpritzed up with tomato juice. Tomato juice is a benign substance, and it does not sting as much as "kike" does.

What would I then compare this schpritz with? How about a word that might or might not be out of circulation, but which I heard with my own ears back in 1975 as a graduate student at Brandeis University. The word I heard, attributed with varying degrees of contempt, was DIB, an abbreviation of Dumb Israeli Bastard. It was not said with venom, mind you; it was, rather, uttered with a patronizing shrug: "S/he's just a DIB, give her a break." I was new to the United States and had no idea how widespread the use of this word was, but for some reason, I could not forget it, though I never heard it again after I left Brandeis. Why am I making such a fuss about it now? Because of the strenuous denials. When I mentioned the DIB incident in passing to the Professional Women's Section of the local chapter of Jewish Federation who invited me to speak about my research work on women in Israeli literature, there was a stir in the audience. The people who came to shake my hand protested too much. They were much too much concerned. They kept repeating that it was just a fluke, that I must forget it. Nobody says DIB anymore, certainly not in Tucson, Arizona. When a local journalist did an interview with me, the editor of the local Jewish paper asked me if I would mind her dropping this word from the text. It was not going to change the substance of the interview, after all.

That is, I guess, one example of exile: when the pious shushing is under way, when people are denying that problems exist, and when both Israelis and Jews are pretending that there are no differences, no difficulties. At moments like these, I am beginning to miss "home" and the more direct approach even when it leaves a red stain across my mental face. There is something about the crudeness of family members that often beats the insistence of polite hosts that you are more than welcome to stay.

Suspended between two kinds of exile—is that where I am? At least two kinds. Serves you right: nobody forced you to do Hebrew literature; if you did anthropology, you wouldn't have to be tortured daily by so many questions about your identity and the meaning of your life. Serves you right: who forced you to exchange for Sabras the Saguaros of Arizona? In other words, I cannot avoid the thorns. They are wherever I go. They prick, they sting. I am beginning to think now that maybe it's not the place at all, maybe it's my skin. The skin of children of Holocaust survivors can never be too thick. I will probably feel estranged wherever I go. The logic is something like this: if my parents suffered so much, I have no right to be happy. The logic is something like this: children of Holocaust survivors have no home.

And even as I am thinking of women and exile, I am becoming suspicious of its appeal to so many feminists today. Why is the context now so congenial to pondering the state of women and exile? Why did I respond with so much enthusiasm to the concept? Exile presupposes that there is a thing called home. My parents told me that Polish anti-Semites used to taunt them with the slogan: "Jews to Palestine." When contexts become congenial to the examination of exile, it means among other things that one presupposes, or takes for granted, the concept of home. Beyond the exile/home dichotomy there must be another way of thinking about women in literature, feminism in the academy, I, Jews, Israelis, Yordim, the Holocaust, the universe, time, home, thinking, questions.

Part 3

. . . .

The Politics of Exile

Ideologies and Isolation

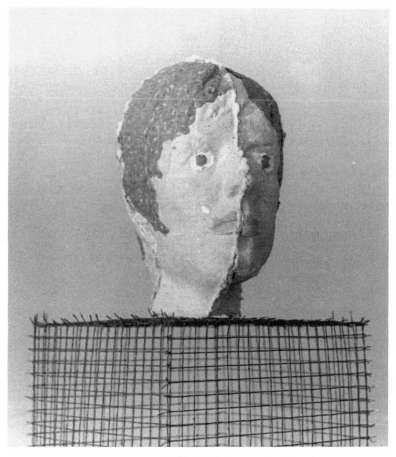

Dementia
Sculpture by Karin Connelly

Chapter 12

. . . .

Gender, Colonialism, and Exile

Flora Annie Steel and Sara Jeannette Duncan in India

Rebecca Saunders

In some deep sense, the British in India during British rule felt themselves to be in exile. The condition of exile resulted in people divided against themselves—exile created a split in the mind of the colonizer between the temptations of freedom from restraint on one hand and the need for self-imposed restrictions on the other. Much of the pressure of maintaining a balance between these needs so that imperialism could function properly was on the women. Not only did women have the problem of reconciling this conflict within themselves, they also had to take on the burden for men and for the culture at large.

To many Anglo-Indians, the world seemed somewhere else, and living with the pressures of exile was a daily concern. Novelist Flora Annie Steel describes the intense excitement felt by the British on the arrival of mail from home: "There is always a suspense about that moment of search among the bundles . . . for the thin packet of private letters which is the only tie between you and the world . . . when hope of home news is superadded, the breath is apt to come faster." She understands that such "a scene, trivial in itself, points an inexorable finger to the broad fact underlying all our Indian administration, that we are strangers and exiles" (*On the Face of the Waters*, 126).

Even more important than the letters themselves was their function as a reminder of all that home stood for. The sense of exile was reinforced through an elaborate cult of home, which included activities such as cultivating English pansies and daffodils that did not thrive in India and having a piano in the drawing room despite the humidity. Because of their isolation, members of the community drew close together; they were intolerant of the Indians they ruled and rigid toward each other. Forster's picture of the small-minded, pompous Anglo-Indian in *A Passage to India* remains our dominant image of them.

Fostering the cult of home was only one way in which wives and mothers eased the tensions and contradictions in Anglo-Indian life. Exile caused a rigidity in the behavior of the memsahibs, a snobbery that precluded knowing Indians except as servants; and the memsahib was a popular target for critics of empire. George Orwell concludes his 1934 novel *Burmese Days*:

> Elizabeth accepted him gladly. He was rather old, perhaps, but a Deputy Commissioner is not to be despised. . . . They are very happy. Mr. Macgregor was always a good-hearted man, but he has grown more human and likeable since his marriage. His voice booms less,

and he has given up his morning exercises. Elizabeth has grown mature surprisingly quickly, and a certain hardness of manner that always belonged to her has become accentuated. Her servants live in terror of her, though she speaks no Burmese. She has an exhaustive knowledge of the Civil List, gives charming little dinner parties and knows how to put the wives of subordinate officials in their place—in short, she fills with complete success the position for which nature had designed her from the first, that of a burra memsahib. (243–44)

Orwell's memsahib is a perfect example of the disliked wife of the administrator, perhaps the role nature intended for her but certainly the one imperialism designed for her. Women like Elizabeth stood for restraint that had to be imposed on themselves and their men in the form of rigid social behavior.

Anglo-Indians saw themselves as the standard-bearers of civilization. Their mission was to impose the order of their culture on the chaos of India. But often the reasons for their presence in India were less than altruistic. Some came to escape poverty, overcrowded families, and unemployment in England; others came for adventure and for the challenge of exciting work. Maud Diver, another Anglo-Indian novelist, writes:

That half-legendary country was then attracting, like a magnet, the most promising and adventurous young men in the three Kingdoms. From copious Georgian and early Victorian families—from country vicarages, where money was scarce and children plentiful—brother followed brother to India: some seeking a career, some a fortune; the racial spirit of adventure quickened, no doubt, by the narrow bounds and piously rigid discipline of the period. In effect, it may almost be said that the dullness of British homes has been the making of the British empire. (*Honoria Lawrence*, 25)

Escape from triviality or routine has, even in this century, been a motivation for people to leave their homes for the frontiers. Doris Lessing's father, for example, preferred his failure in Africa to the confines of office life in England. And one of Kipling's themes is the pettiness of life at home, the triviality that those who venture to the frontier have escaped.

Anglo-Indians drew toward their own culture so fiercely partly in reaction against the liberation life on the frontier afforded them, for the sense of freedom must have seemed dangerous. In the popular literature of the time, the feeling of escape from a stifling environment is usually enjoyed by men. If their wives successfully performed their roles, they became rigidly dutiful, rejecting as much of India as possible. Memsahibs were useful in perpetuating imperialism because they allowed the men to indulge in private satisfactions without their conscious knowledge. Elizabeth's making her man "more human and likeable since his marriage" is an example. She calcifies into a convenient representative of home values; he is then free to enjoy a challenging life of hard work among the Indians with no threat of "going native." Diver suggests the interdependency of restraint and chaos, Britain and empire, patriarchy and imperialism, when she quotes the Count von Konigsmark in her apology for the memsahib, *The Englishwoman in India*: "What would India be without England, and what would the British Empire be without Englishwomen?" (epigraph).

But women also went to the colonies to escape the confines of life in England. Popular novels of the time depict two types of such women: besides the dutiful memsahib (who, like Orwell's Elizabeth, mistreats Indians), there is the woman who succumbs to the temptation of a freer life. Diver writes that "frontier life in those earlier times still preserved its distinctive flavour of isolation and hazard, which had been the making of its men, and the making or marring of its women" (*Captain Desmond, V.C.*, 4). The challenge of empire brings out the best in men, but women can go either way.

The bad woman succumbs both to freedom and to a dangerous cultural influence; she must be strictly guarded against. The unconscious worry over unlimited freedom was focused on the memsahib and her reaction to India. This pressure resulted in the precarious position of the memsahib: she was expected to maintain strict standards but was resented for doing so; if she failed to maintain standards, she was harshly judged. Thus the freedom and sense of adventure of the frontier could lure Westerners because the memsahib's presence there assured that control would be maintained.

Popular novels illustrate how exile affects patterns of thought in those memsahibs who were also writers. Despite the importance of women in fostering the cult of home and in being the agents of restraint, these writers felt a strong need to justify women's existence on the frontier because the memsahib was so often criticized. This essay will examine the way two writers handled the tensions and pressures imposed by exile.

Flora Annie Steel, in trying to come to terms with the contradictions she found in her society, attempts a new kind of female character in her novel *On the Face of the Waters*, one of questionable character and who is not a paternalistic devotee of the cult of home. Alice Gissing is a fallen woman, but her moral lapse is not the point of her appearance in the novel. Most Anglo-Indian stories about fallen women are chronicles or, at times, explanations of their downfall (for example, Alice Perrin's *Woman in the Bazaar*, 1926). Steel, however, uses Alice Gissing's loose morality to make a larger point about the character of the British in India. At the same time, she allows herself to experiment with a new character type. Steel's struggle with Alice Gissing, as she tries to make her fit her perception of the real meaning of the British in India, reveals the split in her psyche as a writer living in a state of exile. Steel feels tensions between the potential freedom to satisfy personal desires stimulated by life in the colonies and the need to justify not only the British presence in India but, more particularly, the female presence there. Steel sensed that women were undervalued in the colonies, despite their market value as wives,[1] and sought to establish their real value in perpetuating imperialism. Her struggle with Alice parallels her own struggle to be an artist, to critique the society in which she lived; her failure with Alice reflects her failure to shake off the restraints imperialism imposes on its agents and its writers in order to perpetuate itself.

It took a writer doubly exiled to recognize that the relations between the dominant and the colonized cultures produced people divided against themselves. Sara Jeannette Duncan, a Canadian who lived in India and was not closely involved in ruling Indians, illustrates the psychic split in well-meaning British socialists in her novel about the beginnings of Indian nationalism, *The Burnt Offering*. But more unusually, she is the first to create an Indian woman who internalizes the ideals of her oppressors and as a result is torn between the two cultures. In her interest in the intersection of public life and private needs, Duncan admitted as few did that people were in the colonies largely to indulge in personal satisfactions—to be free from the constraints of home, to be rulers of a subject race, even, if they were women, to be like men—victimizers instead of victimized.

Life was varied and adventurous for Flora Annie Steel, who married a civil servant and lived in India from 1867 to 1889. She was actively involved in Indian life and politics—the kind of memsahib who never appears in the fiction of Anglo-India. Steel doctored Indian women, taught boys, and started schools for girls. Her life was an example of the range an Englishwoman could have in Indian affairs, but few chose to live this way.

Steel was a serious writer; of the 1857 rebellion, the subject of her novel

On the Face of the Waters, which she researched for years, she says, "The Indian Mutiny was then the Epic of the Race. It held all possible emotion, all possible triumph" (*The Garden of Fidelity*, 226). Clearly Steel felt herself called upon to write an important novel of Anglo-India.

Yet she could not escape the conventions of the colonialist adventure genre in which Indians (or any non-Europeans) are seen as the other and the Western self is tested against this other, who is essentially passive but capable of unbelievable violence when aroused. These conventions, fed by the condition of exile, have powerfully shaped the way we see people in colonized countries. Steel's intention, as she states in the preface, was to bring the two races closer to forgiving and forgetting what went on during the mutiny. But her attempt ends up a revenge novel that flatters the British ruling class.

Steel succeeds in the first chapters of *On the Face of the Waters*; she writes convincingly of the British inadequacy in handling events that led to the crisis and of the slackness of their moral life in general. Out of her critique comes a new type of female character, one who reveals unexpected possibilities in the unusual circumstances of life on the frontier and who becomes a model for Steel of appropriate female behavior. One of the freedoms available to this writer was a wide range of subject and expression.

Alice Gissing, who is decidedly not the heroine of the novel, is a frank woman and is described with frankness. *Clear* is the adjective that occurs most frequently in her portrait. She appears first as a flirt who eggs her lover on to absurd actions just for fun. But she becomes increasingly unusual, not least because of her difference from the typical memsahib. Steel uses Alice's bluntness to force her readers to put aside conventions; they are reminded that this is not England and that morals, characters, and motives are different here. Alice is an adventurer who marries first for the good looks of a man who had some "dark" blood in him (which in itself puts her beyond the pale for the times). After his death, "she had chosen wealth in the person of Mr. Gissing. Had he died, she would probably have married for position; since she had a catholic taste for the amenities of life" (48). With her husband in the background, Alice defies her society by traveling about openly with both a lover and an admiring young boy.[2] She lives with none of the cult of home (at the Gissings' house, "Everything was frankly, staunchly of the nabob-and-pagoda-tree style"), and in this she is contrasted with Kate Erlton, the heroine of the novel. Alice and her businessman husband, a class of people traditionally ignored by both

Anglo-Indian and adventure writers, prefer "India where they were received in society to England where they would have been out of it" (48). They are accepted only because of Mr. Gissing's money; even so, Alice is comfortable in her place slightly outside of both worlds.

Alice remains apart from the interests of her Anglo-Indian community. She knows the sources of her advantages—not only does her husband profit enormously against his Indian competitors, but also Alice, had she stayed in England, would have been the victim of a rigid class structure and a severe morality. She does not pretend to sentiments she does not feel, those expected of memsahibs. Early on Steel identifies Alice's "male" sensibility when she writes that Alice is "of that class of women who sin because the sin has no appreciable effect on them, but leaves them strangely, inconceivably unsoiled." Her "imperviousness," which is "as a rule, considered the man's privilege only" (51), is the source of her freedom.

Although Alice illustrates the freedom from restraint possible for women, her detachment pinpoints problems in the Anglo-Indian world as Steel sees it. For example, as Alice drives through an Indian festival crowd with her young admirer, he complains: "How the beggars stare. . . . let us get away from these grinning apes." Alice rebukes him: "They don't grin . . . they stare like bank-holiday people at the wild beasts in the zoo" (58). Alice's image reverses the young man's comment, which could be a quotation from any seasoned Anglo-Indian. The British become, in her eyes, the wild creatures, while the curiosity of the Indians, which repels her admirer, is reduced to the same curiosity expressed by any ordinary British crowd on holiday. But Alice does not deflate the boy's racist pretensions because she particularly likes Indians. Her comment derives from her detachment from the conventional passions of ordinary Anglo-Indians. She ignores the pressure to conform to the behavior expected of the memsahib, in this case the need to see Indians as less than human, as "not like us."

Alice's sense of curiosity and adventure free her to see the British as Steel must imagine an Indian might see them. A licentious feeling in the air makes the boy try to restrain her, but Alice moves deeper into the crowd to see what the Indians are laughing at. What she sees shocks her: "Two white-masked figures clasped waist to waist were waltzing about tipsily. One had a curled flaxen wig, a muslin dress distended by an all too visible crinoline giving full play to a pair of prancing brown legs. The other wore an old staff uniform, cocked hat and feather complete. The flaxen curls rested on the tarnished epaulet, the unembracing arms flourished brandy bottles" (60). The young man wants to fight someone over this insult to his lady and to the ruling race, but Alice knows instinctively how to handle the situation. She laughs and urges him to also: " 'Don't be a fool!' she whispered fiercely. 'Laugh! It's the only thing to do.' " Steel goes on to say, "Later she [Alice] declared she was glad to have seen what she had seen. Englishmen did drink and Englishwomen waltzed. Why then shouldn't the natives poke fun at both habits if they chose?" (60–61). And she claims her young man "abused" her for rushing to avenge her honor.

This is a rare moment in Anglo-Indian fiction. White women at that time did not go to Indian festivals; many refused even to shop in the bazaars. It is also unusual that the Indians in this scene get away with making fun of the morals of their rulers. Such ridicule was not allowed in Anglo-India. Steel herself in her autobiography insists that the illusion of dignity be maintained at all times, and the young man, of course, is the embodiment of conventional notions of honor. Finding himself in uncertain India, he grasps at conventions; Alice simply readjusts her vision.

Through this interesting renegade character, Steel looks at the British critically, even as figures of fun, as they must often have appeared to Indians. But Steel cannot be more openly critical than this; no one except a character outside the group would have been free to let the incident pass. The novel's hero, Jim Douglas, who was at the scene as a spy, felt obligated to kick the offending Indians—but not before complimenting Alice by shouting "Bravo!" when she laughed.[3]

Alice becomes even more closely identified with Jim, the male adventurer hero. Not only does she ignore the ordinary complex of feelings associated with Anglo-India, she refuses to act in the ways generally expected of Western women. Her charming entrance at a dinner that she and Jim both attend is abruptly interrupted when what looked like a branch turns out to be a snake. Jim seizes her from behind and holds her, and the moment is intensely significant for him: "He never forgot the passionate admiration which made his hands relax to an infinite tenderness, when she uttered no cry, no sound—when there was no need to hold her, so still did she stand, so absolutely in unison with the defiance of Fate which kept him steady as a rock" (129). This image of her haunts him for the rest of the novel. Alice's lack of conventional femininity becomes Jim's standard of measure. When he rages against women (which he frequently does—it is part of Steel's strategy for justifying women's presence on the frontier), he remembers Alice: "He wondered irritably if there was anything in the world into which this eternal question of sex did not intrude. And then, suddenly, he seemed to feel Alice Gissing's heart beat beneath his hand: there had been no womanhood in that touch" (133). And elsewhere: "Alice Gissing had not struggled in his hold because she had been in unison with his ideal of conduct" (184).

For Steel, this denial of womanliness is a fundamental value. The control of sex or passion is also held up as a test of manliness. Early in the novel a doctor exclaims: "Passion, Love, Lust, the attraction of sex for sex . . . nothing is easier knocked out of a man, if he is worth calling one—a bugle call, a tight corner—" (56). Steel extends this test to women on the frontier through Alice, who is womanly in that she charms and flirts. But in a crisis, she is cool. Adventure novels provide the tight corner, the crisis of the unexpected that becomes the test of personality. Thus part of Steel's elaborate justification of women on the frontier lies in this character. Alice proves that women can be manly, too, and for Steel manliness is essential in the running of an empire.

In making Alice similar to Jim, the hero, Steel emphasizes the real freedom that Alice experiences in India, which may be why Steel is so enthusiastic about her. Alice is, if anything, a victimizer, and her detachment, her refusal to play the female role of restraining the adventurous spirit, allows her to enjoy her life. When one of her admirers complains in the classic vein: "India is a beastly hole . . . things are so different—I wish I were out of it," Alice replies with a comment rarely found in Anglo-Indian literature: " 'You've got liver,' she said, confidentially. 'India is quite a nice place' " (51).

But Alice becomes the victim of Steel's division within herself. Steel cannot keep her outside of the group forever. Alice becomes a heroine halfway through the novel when she dies saving a white baby boy from an attack by an Indian religious fanatic at the outbreak of the rebellion. Her death reconciles Steel's criticism of Anglo-Indian life with the Anglo-Indian's idea of racial superiority. Alice may be a fallen woman, but under the stress of crisis her racial nature surfaces and causes her to perform a heroic act.

In contrast to Alice, Steel creates a conventional heroine, Kate Erlton, and she too illustrates the importance of women to empire. Kate is the memsahib typical of novels of the time. Her home is an exact replica of an English home. Here Steel puts her finger on the real role women played in empire. Although British leadership qualities are shown as enabling their soldiers to meet the Sepoys' challenge, their protective attitude toward women also spurs them on to victory. And Kate inspires this protective attitude.

In many adventure tales, the presence of women and children on the frontier provides the men with justification for any behavior. When Kate is feared lost after the fighting starts, Jim in a rage "would find and save Kate, or—*kill somebody*. That was the whole duty of man" (359). The need to protect women and children does more than justify the revenge taken by the British—it becomes proof of cultural superiority, qualifying Britain as a civilized nation and therefore the proper ruler of Indians. The protective attitude forms a large part of Steel's ideal of manly (and womanly) behavior. It also justifies the woman's place on the frontier, in the empire.

The proper valuation of women and the traits they are valued for become clear in a comparison of Tara, a servant of Jim's, with Kate. Tara is the popular stereotype of an Indian woman; she is passionate and over-sexed, devoted to but also in love with her master. Benita Parry has pointed out that for Steel, "Eastern love is a scorching and all-consuming experience which involves only the body and is a surrender to man's baser instincts, whereas Western love is that sentiment that engages the finer feelings" (129). Tara succeeds only in annoying Jim with her love: "The mystery of such womanhood . . . oppressed him. Their eternal cult of purely physical passion, their eternal struggle for perfect purity and constancy, not of the soul, but of the body, their worship, alike of sex and He who made it, seemed incomprehensible" (72).

In contrast to Tara's sexuality is Kate's trancendence of it. Women like Kate are important in preserving the image of paternalism. Jim orders Tara to protect Kate and the white baby Alice Gissing died saving because both are trapped in Delhi by the mutiny. They hide in a hovel in an obscure part of the city. Kate quickly establishes an English drawing-room atmosphere: "Kate took to amusing herself once more by making her corner of the East as much like the West as she dared. That was not much, but Jim Douglas's eye noted the indescribable difference which the position of a reed stool, the presence of a poor bunch of flowers, the little row of books in a niche, made in the familiar surroundings" (266). At first Jim resents this, "telling himself, once more, that women were trivial creatures," but soon he finds something that transcends their situation and gives meaning to it in the surroundings Kate has created: "Here he was looking at a woman who was not his wife, a child who was not his child, and feeling vaguely that they were as much a part of his life as if they were. . . . The mystery of fatherhood and motherhood . . . seemed to touch him here, where there was not even love. Yet it was a better thing. The passion of protection, of absolute self-forgetfulness, seeking no reward, which the sight of those two raised in him, was a better thing than that absorption in another self" (324–25).

Kate conjures up a vision of paternalism that is precisely what the mutiny threatened, for on a larger scale the protection of the weaker in exchange for their obedience is what imperialists like Steel believed was the true situation in India. The vision Kate inspires guides Jim to take revenge on the Indians; any thought of what the rebellion was about in the first place is successfully deflected.

Tara, in contrast, cannot understand what she sees in the roof house. Her nature, struggling to comprehend, is defined as she, "crouching in the corner, watched . . . with hungry, passionate eyes. Here, in this group of man, woman and child, without a personal claim on each other, was something new, half incomprehensible, wholly sweet" (364). She (and, by implication, other Indians) cannot see beyond her own needs.

The point is that the Englishwomen both represent and foster a different passion, the wider claims of paternalism. Indians, Steel implies over and over, can see women only as sexual objects; their institutions of purdah and polygamy, in turn, create heavily sexed attitudes in the women. Rather than seeing Indian women, as many earlier writers did, as the ideal of womanliness, Steel finds in them a passionate femininity that not only destroys relationships between women and men but harms the culture as a whole. The proper attitude toward women proves British cultural superiority; the Indian response to women causes the rebels to do foolish things. Incredibly, in Steel's version of the mutiny, it is the taunts of harlots that spur the sepoys to violence.

The virtue of Western civilization makes the British fight and fight well; its absence contributes to the Indian defeat by making Indians fight for the wrong reasons and lose heart quickly. Just as Jim Douglas, however reluctantly, recognizes the values represented by Kate's domesticity, so do the soldiers awaiting orders to storm Delhi. General Nicholson says to Jim in a statement that sums up the paradoxical position of women on the frontier: "As for the women and children—poor souls—they have been in our way terribly; but—we shall fight all the better for that, by-and-bye" (357).

A step away from Jim's gentle protectiveness of Kate, however, is a lust for revenge and an excuse for killing based on the thought of what Indians might be doing to British women and children: "Men were beginning to think with a sort of mad fury of women and children in a hundred places to which this unchecked conflagration of mutiny was spreading swiftly" (286). Women on the frontier may serve as reminders of deeply held cultural values, but they also conveniently help perpetuate some of imperialism's most murderous features.

Steel worked within the confines of a society in exile; she could not step outside of it as a serious critical artist. She attempted to reconcile the contradictions she found in Anglo-India (specifically, between the ideals of empire and the actual behavior of the English), and she used the figure of the memsahib as the focus of that reconciliation. Kate's conventionality makes Alice's adventurous, unconventional presence in the novel all the more striking. Kate and Alice represent the two ways of women on the frontier. Kate suggests the restraint that must be imposed on the sense of freedom that arises from living far from the restrictions of civilization— though, paradoxically, she grants a license for other, more horrible freedoms; Alice is a woman living out a life she could never have had at home.

That Steel kills off Alice and thereby incorporates her into the group indicates her own balancing act as a writer. As a committed administrator of Indians, Steel could not resist subordinating the interesting detail to the emotionally compelling idea: Alice Gissing must become a representative of the race and its mission in India. The possibility of developing a new character from a new range of subjects available to writers at this time of great turmoil is subordinated to the dictates and needs of imperialism.

Although any real sense of self-sacrifice on Alice's part is undermined because she has just discovered herself pregnant with Kate's husband's child, the others in her community perceive her as a heroine. She perfectly, and ironically, fulfills the function of the memsahib when her death drives her young admirer into a gristly killing rampage. A short quotation will suffice to show the lurid quality of Steel's writing here: "How could he think of leaving those devils unpunished, leaving them unchecked to touch her dead body, while he lived! He gave a little faint sob of sheer satisfaction as he felt the first soft resistance, which meant that his sword had cut sheer into flesh and blood; for all his vigorous young life made for death, nothing but death. Was not she dead yonder?" (233).

As powerful a character as Alice is, she cannot be sustained throughout the novel because she never gives up her freedom to become a proper memsahib. Steel has to force it on her. But Steel here is as much the tool of imperialism as any memsahib. Alice is sacrificed to women's larger role of helping Englishmen control Indians. The sacrifice of Alice shows an urge for women to deny their victim status and identify with men that is greater than the urge to celebrate any personal freedom a woman could have had away from the constraints of home. Put another way, collaborating in defining Indians as other, Englishwomen can be considered part of the British triumph against them. Thus Englishwomen are no longer other but us, intricately bound up with male triumph.

Sara Jeannette Duncan, an exile of a different kind, was a Canadian journalist who married a museum curator and went to live with him in Calcutta.[4] Although her husband was British, for most of their time in India they were journalists, not Anglo-Indian officials. She was not actually involved in ruling Indians, which may in part account for her ability to see through the stereotypes so essential to Anglo-Indians. In her novel about the beginnings of Indian nationalism,[5] *The Burnt Offering* (1909), she does not disguise the tensions of Anglo-Indian life as heroism or dedication to duty. She is even more unusual in showing some of the tensions in Indian life as well (that is, the lives of Indians who were not servants, peasants, or princes). She recognized more intelligently and generously than other writers that the Indian protests in the wake of the 1905 partitioning of Bengal were a sign of growing nationalism and not just the ravings of a few fanatics. And she concludes a novel in which an act of terrorism is the culminating event by extending generosity to both sides: "And so it passed into the history of a people whose virtues began, shortly afterwards, to be discovered by many persons hitherto, perhaps, a little blinded by their own" (316).

In novels and short stories featuring female adventurers, Duncan explores what people really were like once they left the conventions and securities of England for the frontier. Like Steel's Alice Gissing, Duncan's women are obviously in India for adventure, looking for wider horizons (Duncan herself traveled around the world in 1888 with a female friend). Judith Church in *His Honour, and a Lady* saw the key to a more exciting life in her choice of an Anglo-Indian administrator for a husband, despite her qualms: "With an inordinately hungry capacity for life she had the narrowest conditions to live in . . . he was her opportunity, and she had taken him, with private congratulation that she could respect him and private qualms as to whether her respect was her crucial test of him" (13).

Once in India, Judith openly revels in the possibilities her role as memsahib provides: "It is intoxicating . . . to be confronted with something to assume and carry out, a part to play, with all India looking on" (15–16). Such sentiments appear in Steel's autobiography but never emerge in her fiction. Duncan gives us one of the first sympathetic views of the memsahib that is not an apology.

In *The Burnt Offering*, Duncan recognizes the variety of personal motives that people have for being in India, which are often at odds with their professed motives. Anglo-Indian police attempt to capture the suspected mastermind of a terrorist conspiracy, Thakore Ganendra, but their efforts are hampered by a visiting radical member of parliament, Vulcan Mills, and his beautiful daughter Joan. The Millses come to India to "see for themselves," to stir up feeling against the Anglo-Indian government, and to report on its outrages to those at home.

In depicting Vulcan and Joan Mills, Duncan was in complete agreement with Anglo-India.[6] No one was more heartily disliked than the uninformed visitor from England who had already made up his or her mind about India. Despite their good intentions, the two Millses misread most of what they are exposed to, determined to see only the worst of the British and the best of the Indians.

Their conversation with Indian leaders reveals their bias, yet Duncan's characters are never one-dimensional; Mills is right about many of the administrative problems in India. Told by a moderate that the British government has always meant well, he replies: "With the people groaning under the most corrupt and oppressive police known to modern civilization! With the masses still sunk in—in their primitive ignorance, and the educated classes debarred from any voice in the affairs of their own country!" (26)

But he misses the importance of religion and of traditions to the Indian leaders with whom he is discussing the strategies of change, ideas that, particularly at this time, were changing the tone of Indian protests. Ganendra suggests:

"I don't know whether you will agree with me in thinking that the worst home rule is better for a people than the best foreign rule? . . . I will go no further, and say that the better a government by foreigners the more demoralizing it is to the subject race. . . . "

"It's arguable," he [Mills] said. " . . . but why should we suppose that after all these years of the Western model, the government of India by the Indians should be so bad?"

"I fear it is because of the Western model," Ganendra smiled again. "But . . . give us back our Mother, and we shall not trouble about the fashion of her dress." (29)

This conversation indicates one division in Indian thinking at this time: whether to stay within the system of empire and agitate for constitutional reforms or to reject Western models. But the question of Western models is not even seen as a question by Mills, who assumes their superiority.

Neither is his daughter Joan immune from patronage of the Indians she believes she has come to serve. In a conversation with Bepin, a disciple of Ganendra, Joan notices that Bepin gazes at Ganendra "with a look of devout and adoring attention that was new to her in the history of the human face." But she has no idea of the importance of the guru to Bepin and deeply offends him when she says of Ganendra, "He looks a dear" (30).

In his position as a member of the dominant culture, Mills is deaf to what his Indian friends tell him. But more than that, the freedom he has in India to indulge in cultural superiority motivates him. Mills is adored and respected by the Indians he meets except for one—a priest, Yadava. Mills expects Indians to agree with his radical ideas; therefore, he is caught off guard when he encounters this moderate. Angered by Yadava's insistence on the importance of religion, Mills adopts his usual stance:

"There's nothing diviner, sir, . . . than representative institutions.

"Oh, they are the bulwarks of Western liberty," responded the priest suavely, "but we in India have another kind of freedom."

"There is no other kind . . . and you in India must rouse yourselves to feel that. . . . It is what I preach to my friends here day and night." (179)

Mills's personal needs surface in his violent reaction to Yadava's opposition—needs that, at least until now, have been satisfied by the relations between colonizer and colonized:

Vulcan spoke with rapid anger. His face was pale, and he caught at his beard with a hand that trembled . . . he had this afternoon experienced the first sign of opposition from a people that had to him also become a subject race, subject to his theories, his prejudices, and his personal power. He did not take it well. I fear he would have made an autocratic Deputy Secretary, or a Collector who would have oppressed the people sadly for their good. (181)

In a literature full of self-justification, Duncan's novel stands out for its consciousness of one of empire's strongest lures, the chance to indulge in fantasies of one's moral progressiveness and superiority. Mills extends his reformer's role at home to the people of a whole continent.

But Duncan's most startling achievement in this novel is her awareness of the cost to an Indian woman of internalizing the ideals of the dominant culture. The Rani Janaki has a complex personal history (which in itself is rare in Anglo-Indian literature). Her life demonstrates the tensions created by the mix of the two cultures that created her, and with one slight exception, she and her father, Sir Kristodas Mukerji, are the only characters who change. Thomas Tausky writes that "Duncan has given to an Indian character the moral uncertainties and sensitive if not always successful responses to difficult situations that in previous works she had reserved for her most cherished English ladies" (255).

The Rani's father had been "one of the strictest and most ascetic leaders of the Brahmin community" (36). Janaki was married at six and widowed at seven and followed the rituals of Brahmin widowhood. As compensation for her austere life, Sir Kristodas educated her and, increasingly Westernized himself, sent her to England:

> She fell into a family of a Radical don of Oxford, where for five years she was treated with indignant pity and taught to think politically. . . . She was also led . . . to see some absurdity in her career as a Hindu widow, so that she stood intellectually quite outside herself in that capacity. Her widowhood shrank into the core of her being . . . and so clever and charming a person grew up round it that in the end she hardly knew it as there. (41)

The potential for tension lies in Janaki's pull toward radical nationalist politics and away from her father's loyalist approach and in her love for a liberal Anglo-Indian official, John Game. She begins to change early in the novel when she discovers that Game has fallen in love with Joan Mills. And her change will take her solidly back to the culture of her birth.

The blend of East and West gives Janaki insight and tolerance, putting her in sharp contrast with the other characters, who act out roles determined for them by their position in empire. She has a better grasp on the ways of both cultures than Joan Mills does. Early in the novel, Joan accompanies Janaki to a Ladies' League party. The motives of the ladies giving the party are complex, but Joan sees them as patronizing. Janaki tries to explain:

"I do not know why, but suddenly they decided they would know us
. . . the ladies of Calcutta, the burra-mems. They found they had a
duty not only to those who go about like me, but to all the little ladies
who keep purdah. It was very kind."

"It doesn't sound *real*," said Joan, who had no desire to find it real;
and Janaki, smiling, repeated—

"It was very kind." (109)

There are, predictably, awkwardnesses at this party, and Janaki spends
much time reassuring the mems that the Indian women are enjoying
themselves. Joan is out of her depth: "It seemed that for the Rani Janaki at
least the kind ladies . . . had accomplished something appreciable. But she
[Joan] did not pause to weigh it, having nothing, indeed, to weigh it
against" (112). Joan has never really looked at another culture and is not
aware of complexity. Janaki is patient with these tensions: she knows
enough not to force her interpretation on any situation.

One of the Bengali women is finally induced to sing, and she sings a
radical patriotic song that she has composed. Joan is surprised, even a little
shocked, having expected Indian women to conform to her idea of oppressed womanhood. And she is further surprised when Janaki explains:

"Every Bengali woman in this room is in her way a politician. But,
naturally, they will not speak of that."

"*Naturally?*" exclaimed Joan. "Is any one afraid to talk politics,
under the British flag?"

"We will say that they are shy," is the reply. (113)

Like her father, Joan cannot understand a different approach to politics
(or parties). She cannot escape the reformer's clichés, nor is she satisfied
with the Indian women who do want reform. She reveals the same mixture
of cliché and condescension in her comments on the women of an Indian
family who have befriended her. After a visit during which she discovers
that the ladies are boycotting English goods, "Joan . . . came home a little
disconcerted. 'Oh, to get at them!' she said to her father. 'They are
darlings, but they have no breadth of view—no breadth of view whatever' "
(104). Duncan makes it clear that Joan will not respond to what she
actually sees in the women she expects to influence. Secure in her convictions, Joan has an easier time of it than Janaki.

The price of insight for Janaki is that she is outside both worlds. The
strain of balancing the demands of two cultures paralyzes her. Janaki's

comment on the song of the women reveals her sense of her own alienation, that the polite violence of one culture imposing itself on another has
silenced her: "'Their husbands and fathers are moderates—but they
sing,' said Janaki significantly. 'I, too, am a moderate, and I do not even
sing. I think,' she added in a lower tone—and Joan could not see her face
for a fold of her sari—'that I have lost my voice'" (115).

As Janaki watches Game's love for Joan develop, she gradually reverts to
the old habits of her widowhood as she battles for an identity to help her
face her suffering: "Mrs. Foley . . . said to her husband that Janaki seemed
to grow more and more 'native' as John Game's courtship went ingenu-
ously on" (105). The problem is compounded by her secret support of the
nationalist movement, which is planning an attack on some Anglo-Indian
officials. Finally, Janaki begins again her penances as a widow and cries in
a passionate outburst to Mrs. Foley: "'The abolition of *suttee*,' said this
Hindu widow, entrapped in the snares of the flesh. 'It was a cruel thing to
abolish *suttee*'" (221). Dramatically, she grasps at one answer to her suffering from her own culture while demonstrating that all of her resources
for living have been abolished by the other. Her cry shows the depth of her
rejection of what have been presented to her as the ways of a more
enlightened civilization.

Instead of the scorching love we saw in Steel's Indian woman, Tara,
Janaki's love for Game is so quiet that he never even notices it, and the
supreme devastation for her comes when she betrays her political beliefs
to warn him of the terrorist plan. He brushes off her sacrifice; like many
Anglo-Indians he misses the seriousness of the nationalist movement.
Game dies as a result of the attack Janaki warned him of. Duncan condemns the terrorist attack, and Anglo-India is exonerated because the
attack occurred right at the moment of the 1909 Minto-Morley reforms,
which granted Indians more positions in government than ever before.
Game is a hero.

But Game is also dead, and Duncan gives this Indian family the last
word as they make a dignified, profound rejection of their Westernized
life. Sir Kristodas has also returned to his former self because of the
pressures of having to preside over a case of sedition brought against his
lifelong friend Ganendra. (Kristodas was appointed to this case to show
that Hindu judges were allowed to try important cases.) In the end, he and
Janaki retire from public life with their guru. They resign themselves to a
life of contemplation, but the resignation results from the pain and depri-
vations they have suffered in their involvement with the Westernizing of

their world, certainly not from any "natural" racial passivity. Their seeking is not passive:

> Henceforth from holy place to holy place, they will gather that wisdom of the heart . . . which is the gift and the glory of the Mother whose children they are. Henceforth . . . they will endeavour to forget that which *so imposed itself as life* [italics mine]. Life not having pleased them, they have exercised towards it the profound and delicate option which is their inheritance; they have left it in the world. . . . Let us dream that the Mother is well pleased with these her children, the Mother whose sanctions are won with no heathen oblation— (319–20)

They have come into their own by reclaiming their own; we feel that India as a nation will also. But no prescription is being made here. Duncan carefully refrains from saying that Indians should return to their traditions, even though that is what Gandhi and others were beginning to say then. She implies that Indians will do what they have to do, and as a Westerner in the rare position of being merely an observer, she applauds them.

In addition to both being memsahibs, Flora Annie Steel and Sara Jeannette Duncan are linked by their depiction of empire as a place to indulge in personal satisfactions. But Duncan was conscious of this feature of empire and Steel was not. Duncan's example illustrates the depth of exploitation in the colonial experience, whether emotional or material. Duncan was in a sense doubly exiled; for her the challenge of the frontier took place on a different continent. In India, she could be herself, and she succeeds in an area where so many others fail, not necessarily because of her brilliance or political insight but because she is content to be an observer, not a prescriber.

Exile can turn writers into ideologues. The urge to convince and to justify was strong among women writers on the frontiers who already felt undervalued. Steel wrote what may be thought of as a woman's adventure novel, inverting the elements of adventure so that her work remains that of a woman who could not glory outright in the emotions of adventure.

The life of exile these memsahibs lived, even when it did not restrict them to the confines of the group, as it did not restrict Steel, limited them by the conventions of the imperialist mentality. They had an interest in keeping empire going, in perpetuating the relationship between colonizer and colonized. When empire was the subject, or even the background of a novel, it was difficult for the British to enlarge their imaginations, to tolerate ambiguity, and not to lose sight of interesting details. Duncan's cosmopolitanism provides a fuller picture of life in the empire than Forster's famous visit to India.

Notes

1. Women who arrived by the boatload to find husbands in India were called the "fishing fleet." Those who went home the next year unmarried were the "returned empties."

2. Barbara Wingfield-Stratford writes about the phenomenon of the young admirer in the life of the memsahib in *India and the English*, 1923: "It is curious to see . . . Mrs. Smith . . . just because she happens to live in India, be in actual fact a dashing mondaine whose only thoughts are of amusement and who has a different 'boy' every month. For in India nearly every woman under fifty has a 'boy,' whom she rides and dances with, goes for walks with in the hills, and who is in constant attendance on her at the Club" (37). That Alice has a "boy" in addition to a lover adds a dimension of decadence to her portrait.

3. In Anglo-Indian literature, certain male characters do have insight into the minds of Indians. They are spies, always excellent at disguises, who move freely among the Indians and learn their secrets. Spies are far more insightful than administrators, in whose pay they often are, and Jim Douglas in this novel is such a one. Spies function often to criticize administrative blindness; they are the mouthpieces for writers such as Steel and Kipling to rail against the obtuseness of the government.

Doubtless, Steel was directly influenced by Kipling in her creation of Jim Douglas. Kipling's Kim, for example, was trained as a spy (disguised as a surveyor). A rationale for these character types is that to rule successfully, the government must have firsthand information about its subjects. But spying is also for the adventurous and even the playful. Kipling's character Strickland, from "Miss Yougal's Sais" (*Plain Tales from the Hills*) finds prying into native life "the most fascinating thing in the world" (25).

But spying is clearly a male activity; the woman Strickland falls in love with agrees to marry him "with the strict understanding that Strickland should drop his old ways, and stick to Departmental routine, which pays best and leads to Simla" (29). Alice cannot be a spy, but Steel gives her a spy's angle of vision instead of making her the restraining influence.

4. Duncan was born in 1861 in Brandford, Canada West. She was one of the first Canadian women to work in a newspaper office. At the age of twenty-seven, she set off for a trip around the world with a friend, Lily Lewis, and wrote about it

in her first best-seller, *A Social Departure*. In India, she met Everard Cotes, a museum curator and journalist, who proposed to her in front of the Taj Mahal. She accepted him but continued her trip, returning after a year and a half to marry a man she had known only a few weeks. They lived in Calcutta and Simla for the next thirty years. Duncan died in England in 1922.

5. Two other novels that dealt with Indian nationalism appeared in the same year. *The Bronze Bell* by L. J. Vance and *Cecilia Kirkham's Son* by Mrs. Kenneth Combe. But the honor of being first is usually given to Edmund Candler's *Siri Ram* (1912). Candler is harshly antagonistic toward Indian nationals, and his novel is an index of what intelligent Britons were thinking then. A comparison with him shows how far ahead of her times Duncan was.

6. Flora Annie Steel comments on such visitors from England in the following passage from a short story "For the Faith" (*The Flower of Forgiveness*, 1894). She begins by illustrating the devotion of an old servant for his young white master:

"You see them often, these old anxious-looking retainers, waiting . . . with wistful, expectant faces.

"And some beardless youth, fresh from Eton or Harrow, says with a laugh, 'By George! are you old Munnoo or Bunnoo? Here! look after my traps, will you?' And the traps are duly looked after, while the Philosophical Radical on the rampage is taking the opportunity afforded by baggage parade to record in his valuable diary the pained surprise at the want of touch between the rulers and the ruled, which is, alas! his first impression of India. In all probability it will be his last also, since it is conceivable that both rulers and ruled may be glad to get rid of him on the approach of hot weather. Mosquitoes are troublesome, and cholera is disconcerting, but they are bearable beside the man who invariably knows the answers to his own questions before he asks them" (54).

Works Cited

Diver, Maud. *Captain Desmond, V.C.* London: William Blackwood, 1907.

———. *The Englishwoman in India*. London: William Blackwood, 1909.

———. *Honoria Lawrence*. New York: Houghton Mifflin, 1936.

Duncan, Sara Jeannette. *The Burnt Offering*. 1909. New York: John Lane , 1910.

———. *His Honour, and a Lady*. New York: D. Appleton, 1896.

Fowler, Marian. *Redney: A Life of Sara Jeannette Duncan*. Toronto: Anansi, 1983.

Kipling, Rudyard. *Plain Tales from the Hills*. New York: Oxford University Press, 1987.

Orwell, George. *Burmese Days*. New York: Signet, 1963.

Parry, Benita. *Delusions and Discoveries*. New York: Penguin Press, 1976.

Perrin, Alice. *The Woman in the Bazaar*. London: Cassell, 1926.

Steel, Flora Annie. *The Flower of Forgiveness and Other Stories*. 2 vols. London: Macmillan, 1894.

———. *The Garden of Fidelity*. London: Macmillan, 1929.

———. *On the Face of the Waters*. London: William Heinemann, 1903.

Tausky, Thomas E. *Sara Jeannette Duncan: Novelist of Empire*. Port Credit, Ontario: P. D. Meany, Publishers, 1980.

Wingfield-Stratford, Barbara. *India and the English*. London: Jonathan Caper, 1923.

Chapter 13

. . . .

Un/Reproductions

Estates of Banishment in English Fiction after the Great War

Angela Ingram

The Home Front

L ooking for a fourth term to add to "poverty, chastity, derision," Virginia Woolf says, in *Three Guineas*, "we have no time to coin new words, greatly though the language is in need of them. Let 'freedom from unreal loyalties' then stand as the fourth great teacher of the daughters of educated men" (78). Later, she decides that "we can best help . . . prevent war *not* by repeating [educated men's] words and following [their] methods but by finding new words and creating new methods" (143; my emphasis). Just such redefinition and apparent contradiction have been crucial to our approaches to the word *exile*. Fatherland is redefined by mother tongue, interdiction by exhilaration, canonicity by cannon fodder. Intellectually and emotionally estranged from Triple Alliance and Triple Entente, from Axis and Allies, to make one in the triptych of this collection one had to re-revision exile and expatriation—terms which, as several writers in this collection suggest, we might do well to regard with suspicion.

Estates of banishment constitute a particularly gendered exile. *Estate* as a "special state or condition" is obsolete except in "man's, woman's estate" (*OED*). But I am more concerned with *banishment*. To ban is "to summon by proclamation (usually to arms)" and to "curse, anathematize, interdict"—a nice lexicographical leap from exile to what happens to opponents of God and his church. *Ban* also gives us "banal: of or belonging to compulsory feudal service." Such lexical permutations encourage one to juxtapose texts of two kinds which in some way responded to England's summons "to arms" in 1914 and afterward. Some texts subverted the "summons" and met with interdiction and exile; some are banal: like the banned books, they addressed dangerous topics, but they did so in ways that complied with the compulsion of feudal service.

That service entailed producing children for the "Great" and for the next war; it was dangerous to question a quasi-official motherhood-for-militarism program whose origins lay in imperialist expansionism.[1] Such a program was defined in autumn 1916, when seventy-five thousand copies of a pamphlet, originally a letter to the jingoistic *Morning Post*, sold in a week. A response to a soldier's appeal for peace, it demands that British mothers be heard,

> seeing that we play the most important part in the history of the
> world, for it is we who "mother the men" who have to uphold the

honour and traditions not only of our Empire but of the whole civilised world. . . .

We women . . . will tolerate no such cry as "Peace! Peace!" when there is no peace. . . . With those who disgrace their sacred trust of motherhood we have nothing in common . . . . We women pass on the human ammunition of "only sons" to fill up the gaps, so that when the "common soldier" looks back before going "over the top" he may see the women of the British race at his heels, reliable, dependent [*sic*], uncomplaining. [And baying?] . . .

A "common soldier", perhaps, did not count on the women, but they have their part to play, and *we* have risen to our responsibility. We are proud of our men, and they in turn have to be proud of us . . . . Women are created for the purpose of giving life, and men to take it. Now we are giving it in a double sense. (quoted in Graves, 228–30)

The letter/pamphlet was signed "A Little Mother." "The Queen was deeply touched"; one soldier claimed it had done more for soldiers than Florence Nightingale had; it made a "Bereaved Mother" feel she would "gladly give [her dead] sons twice over" (Graves, 228, 231). I quote the letter at length because its sentiments are so representative and so utterly repulsive.

That was in 1916, the year of compulsory conscription. Late in 1917 Mrs. Alec Tweedie's *Women and Soldiers* daringly suggested that women were not merely wombs for war,[2] emphasized (repeatedly) how well women had "done their bit," and chided "poor men" for failing to realize the versatility and intelligence of (upper- and middle-class) women. "Men have become fighters and women have become soldiers. . . . Today every man is a soldier and every woman is a man. Well, no—not quite; but, speaking roughly, war has turned the world upside down; and the upshot of the topsy-turvydom is that the world has discovered women and women have found themselves. And a new world has been created" (1–2). These words sound wonderful, but Mrs. Tweedie's demands for decent wages, child care, and cooperative housing clearly spring from her belief in the paramount importance of "new-world" women's reproductive functions: "The undertaking by women of too heavy physical work may so injure them that the would-be mothers of the future may fail to bear off-spring" (21). And her last chapter, "After the War?" begins: "One shudders to think of a future with a large part of the world populated by women. Women are made to mate with men and men with women. It may take a whole generation to *stamp out the surplus of women* and begin to readjust society again" (162; my emphasis).

"Women pass on the human ammunition"; "women are made to mate with men": during the war such ideas were upheld by DORA—the Defence of the Realm Acts, which sprang fully armed from the heads of the fathers on August 8, 1914, getting through the House of Commons in five minutes (Williams, 23). Giving His Majesty in Council powers "for securing the public safety and the defence of the realm," DORA was designed initially to protect docks, railways, and communications. She grew mightily, though, as such patriarchal matriarchs are wont to do: it became criminal to whistle for a cab in London after dark, stand a soldier a drink, feed bread to sea gulls, communicate venereal disease to a soldier, write, for oneself, criticism of the war. Under DORA, "Orders in Council could be issued forbidding almost any activity the Government considered harmful; new crimes could be created overnight" (Cole and Postgate, 536).[3] So defending, DORA came to promote, even compel, nationalism, militarism, and the endless production of ammunition—manufactured and human. Concomitantly, she punished individualism, pacifism, internationalism, and reluctance to produce cannon and cannon fodder. Anti-government publications, from both Right and Left, were prosecuted, and pacifist pamphlets were seized by the dozen. Two books banished by DORA are particularly interesting because they prophetically identify a number of attitudes later consistently anathematized by postwar Tory governments.

Little Mothers wrote letters prescribing women's proper roles; Ellen La Motte's *The Backwash of War* (1916) seems to describe the Little Mothers. La Motte explains her title thus: "The War's slow onward progress stirs up the slime in the shallows, and this is the Backwash of War. It is very ugly. . . . Little lives foam up . . . ugly, weak, hideous, repellent," which afterward "will consolidate again into the condition called Peace"—a peace unrealizable until there are "clean little lives" (vi). We get a sense of those "little lives" from her description of soldiers showing each other pictures of their wives:

> Pathetic little pictures . . . of common working-class women, some fat and work-worn, some thin and work-worn, some with stodgy little children grouped about them, some without, but all were practically the same. They were wives of these men . . . the working-class wives of working-class men. . . . Ah yes, France is democratic. . . . All the

men of the Nation, regardless of rank, are serving ... but the trenches are mostly reserved for men of the working class, which is reasonable, as there are more of them. ...

There was much talk of home, and much of it was longing, and much of it was pathetic, and much of it was resigned. And always the ugly little wives, the stupid ordinary wives, represented home. And the words home and wife were interchangeable and stood for the same thing. (98–100)

Wives are not allowed at the front; they might tell their husbands things the censors would habitually cut out of letters. It is not "the woman but the wife that is objected to. There is a difference. In war it is very great" (102). "Wives are forbidden, because lowering to the morale, but women are winked at, because they cheer and refresh the troops. After the war, it is hoped that all unmarried soldiers will marry, but doubtless they will not marry these women who have served and cheered them in the War Zone. That, again, would be depressing to the country's morale. It is rather paradoxical but there are those who can explain it perfectly" (103–4). Emphasizing the stalemate, castigating those officers who award medals to all *mutiles* (most shipped back to Paris to parade the streets and encourage the others), damning those who nurse an unsuccessful suicide so that he can stand up to be shot, locating "women" but not "wives" at the front, La Motte hardly would have helped the Little Mothers ("stupid, ordinary wives") cheerfully to pass on the human ammunition. She describes far too graphically and angrily the unimaginable mutilation of that "ammunition" and the uses to which it was so cynically put.

La Motte's book was "kept out" by an officialdom that demanded bellicosity, the production of ammunition, and unquestioning loyalty to "the Nation."[4] Two years later, DORA banned Rose Allatini's pseudonymous *Despised and Rejected*. Two days before the German commanders agreed to evacuate their troops preparatory to signing the armistice, Allatini's publisher was fined £460 for making statements "likely to prejudice the recruiting, training, and discipline of persons in his Majesty's forces."[5] The book was "a pacifist pamphlet in the disguise of a novel"; the presiding alderman contemplated imprisoning the publisher, for though the novel's "obscenity" was not on trial, he did not "hesitate to describe it as morally unhealthy and pernicious" ("Publisher").

Despised and Rejected certainly is propaganda but (albeit sometimes depressing) not a bad novel. It is set in the period from summer 1914 to late

1916. Its prewar section delineates a society that valorizes male public school sportsmanship and stiff-upper-lippedness, marrying off daughters and having the vicar to tea. One does one's bit, has neat lawns and neat moustaches (men only), travels to the City (men only), improves the efficiency of manufacturing and mining—as long as doing so does not necessitate improving working conditions. One distrusts artists and foreigners (especially Jews) because they obviously don't do *their* bit. Allatini then shows the easy transition of bourgeois patriarchal values from an "armed peace" to a war economy that rewards profiteering, insanely bellicose patriotism ("giving" sons to war replaces marrying off daughters and both are done in competition with the neighbors), and doing one's bit for Kitchener.

Those home front values are anathema to the novel's co-protagonists. Presented first as a lesbian, Antoinette ridicules her family's attempts to marry her off and eventually falls in love with Dennis, a homosexual composer, who declares himself a conscientious objector and ultimately follows his socialist-pacifist lover, Alan, to prison. Antoinette's other male acquaintances, with a "metaphorical clanking of spurs," go off to be "instructed in the art of 'showing Fritz the stuff old England [is] made of'" (149). Those who do not approve of the clanking are Allatini's heroes; to identify them all one needs, like Koko, is a little list. They are pacifists (from "absolutists" to those who eventually "rat"), "potential" lesbians, homosexual men, socialists, Jews, Irish nationalists, actors and artists, Christians who dangerously believe gospel to be gospel, and an eighteen-year-old so terrified to contemplate pain at the front or in prison that he kills himself. At Dennis's tribunal there are left-wing journalists and an elderly suffragette; at home, Dennis's mother bewilderedly apologizes for being a mother first and British only second.

We learned from George Dangerfield that Liberal England strangely died from a surfeit of workers, women, and the Irish.[6] Add the long-standing belief in a Jewish conspiracy, the monarch's conviction that homosexual men ("chaps like that") shot themselves, the decision *not* to reprieve Roger Casement from hanging when his "addiction to perversion" was discovered, and it is clear that, favoring such unpatriotic riffraff, Allatini's novel endangered "the public safety and the defence of the realm." (Out in the real world Sylvia Pankhurst organized a demonstration against conscription: "All the rebels of those days . . . were with us: Socialists, Anarchists, Individualists, Trade Unionists, Left Wing Industrialists,

Pacifists—those who hated capitalism and compulsion—those who opposed the war" [*Home Front*, 215].)

Despised and Rejected accurately and courageously identified that fascist "germ" in patriarchy which Virginia Woolf was so comprehensively to analyze in *Three Guineas*: it is nurtured in boys'-school team spirit and girls' marriage competitions; it logically matures to compelling boys to kill other boys for the fathers' defense and to compulsory motherhood. The solicitor for Allatini's publisher claimed that the "title 'Despised and Rejected' referred to the abnormal sequal [*sic*] tendencies of the hero, and not to his pacifist views." Like La Motte, who links brutal militarism, class exploitation, and the hypocrisies of the double standard, Allatini conflates, and champions, multiple "crimes" against the patriarchal state, which despises, rejects, and punishes those "Ishmaels" who refuse to pass on *any* ammunition.[7]

Unpopular in Whitehall

War taught the fathers that wage-earning women could usefully release men for the front, but making human ammunition was far more valuable. A 1917 newspaper article claimed that the war had brought home "the value of the mother as a national asset"; *Labour Woman* (shame!) published an essay that said, "Whatever a childless woman may do for the community is nothing to the service rendered by her who gives it healthy and good children" (quoted in Braybon, 118, 124). Postwar, such attitudes were ubiquitous: to render service women must have babies, and with two million unemployed (the same number as the "surplus" of women), the state's objective was to force women from the labor force and into labor. The *News of the World* gave prizes to "every 'proud mother of ten children'" (quoted in Hall, *Passionate Crusader*, 150).[8] Sexologists and "sex-reformers," Sheila Jeffreys suggests, had a field day urging women to have reproductive sex. Although theirs might not have been the only views promoted, there certainly was a quasi-official policy that not having heterosexual intercourse endangered women's health, and there were suggestions (less loud, perhaps, than in Germany) that polygamy might solve the "problem" for all those surplus, frustrated women (165–93).[9]

Fiction critical of attempts to replace the millions killed or maimed courted exile through censorship. The criteria changed, though, and in-

stead of DORA the Obscene Publications Act had to serve.[10] That act
defines as obscene "matter" that might tend "to deprave and corrupt those
whose minds are open to such immoral influences." To twentieth-century
officialdom, Morris Ernst suggests, that usually meant the "explicitly
sexual" (xiii). But not always. The fathers acted to ban anything that, even
indirectly, impugned their attempts to reconstruct a comfortable Edwardian world in which men were men and women were breeders. Their
version of "obscenity" harks back to the word's first recorded English
usage in Shakespeare's *Richard II*, where the Bishop of Carlisle tries to
prevent the pretender, Bolingbroke, from ascending the throne (despite
his claiming Richard's acquiescence):

> What subject can give sentence on his king?
> And who sits here that is not Richard's subject?
> . . . .
> And shall the figure of God's majesty,
> His captain, steward, deputy elect,
> Anointed, crowned, planted many years,
> Be judg'd by subject and inferior breath
> And he himself not present? O, forfend it God
> That in a Christian climate souls refin'd
> Should show so heinous, black, obscene a deed! (IV.1.121–31)

God's majesty in the 1920s was "figured" by a Tory government concerned to foster paternity in anyone capable of it. The divine identification
had immaculate justification. In 1909, for example, Oxford's first professor of military history had proclaimed, "The mark of the State is sovereignty, or the identification of force and right, and the measure of force
and right and the measure of the perfection of the state is furnished by the
completeness of this identification." Commenting on this statement in
1928, Caroline Playne wrote, "It is impossible to carry this amazing
doctrine further. The Sovereignty of the State is . . . absolute, . . . akin to
that which the Old Testament attributes to the Deity. . . . Upon competition between States rests the order of the world" (159). One way European states were competing was in population growth, and, *patria* and *pater*
being synonymous, it was "obscene" to suggest that prospective paters and
maters were not patriotically producing new soldiers.

   That Radclyffe Hall's *The Well of Loneliness* suggests just that is *one*
reason, I think, it was banned in 1928. Though it patriotically describes

women supporting the war effort, it shocked the magistrate by showing how "some women of standing and position engaged as ambulance drivers at the front were addicted to . . . horrible tendencies," "unnatural offences between women" presented as not "in the least degree blameworthy" (quoted in Brittain, 98–101). Not only were the antimummies blame*less*, but Hall suggests that the lesbians who "came out" to help defend the realm, "as though gaining courage from the terror that is war" formed "a battalion . . . that would never completely be disbanded. . . . They had found themselves," she says: "Thus the whirligig of war brings in its abrupt revenges" (275). This is tantamount to saying, in nicely turned neo-Shakespearean language, that the fathers who made the war (which they were luckily too old or too "necessary" to fight in) created what that noisy fascist publicist James Douglas called "the plague stalking shamelessly through great social assemblies" (quoted in Brittain, 54). And against that "battalion" the heterosexual hordes are not reproducing themselves very efficiently. Hall's hero, Stephen, is an only child, despite her parents' trying seventeen years for a son; the family retainers are childless; the neighbors' horrid son is killed in the war (patriotic but unreproductive); the horrid daughter produces children but (to compensate?) wants all the useless elderly killed off. The novel's good "mothers" are Stephen's unmarried, childless governesses.

The war's "revenges" constitute, ironically, a very dangerous kind of parenthood. Valérie Seymour (the Natalie Barney character) contends that "nature was trying to do her bit [one appreciates the wartime cliché]; inverts were being born in increasing numbers, and after a while their numbers would tell, even with the fools who still ignore Nature. They must just bide their time—recognition was coming" (Hall, *Well of Loneliness*, 413).[11] Mother Nature thus defined is obviously not the sort of producer the fathers wanted. To make matters worse, at the end of the novel Stephen becomes a mother—not of useful human ammunition but of the whole homosexual race: "Her barren womb became fruitful—it ached with its fearful and sterile burden . . . with the fierce yet helpless children who would clamour in vain for their right to salvation. They would turn first to God, and then to the world, and then to her" (446). Delivered of her "burden," Stephen is thus mother-god-intercessor, and the magistrate (understandably) considered "the way in which the Deity was introduced . . . singularly inappropriate and disgusting." Poor paters in their Christian climate! In 1918 Allatini's homosexual pacifist is Jesus;

in 1928 Hall's very butch dyke is the Virgin Mary. A wonderful in/version of the motherhood and war equation, this is not the way to beget soldiers.[12]

The Well of Loneliness does not attack patriarchy so much as sets it aside on precisely those grounds where it needed most defense—its ability to reproduce itself. One might read an attack on reproductiveness in the description of the "aggressively normal" Monsieur Pujol, father of six with another on the way, who keeps a bar for "inverts" and gloats paternally over the horror stories of their lives (388–89). But he is French, and sneering at French fecundity in 1928 might have been deemed rather patriotic. But as the chairman of the court that denied the publisher's appeal against banning observed, "This is a disgusting book when properly read." Reading it "properly," the fathers found it raised too many questions about postwar England and answered them in ways they considered unproductive—un/reproductive.

Associated hindrances to patriarchal (re)production are suggested by E. M. Forster and Virginia Woolf in a letter protesting censorship of *The Well*. Lesbianism exists, they say, scientifically and historically recognized; now novelists have been forbidden to mention it: "May they mention it incidentally? Although . . . forbidden as a main theme, may it be alluded to, or ascribed to subsidiary characters? . . . Is it the only taboo, or are there others? What of the other subjects known to be more or less unpopular in Whitehall, such as birth-control, suicide, . . . pacifism? May we mention these?" ("New Censorship"). It may be true, as Norman St. John-Stevas claims, that the Obscene Publications Act was not concerned to "control" public morals (93), but it seems clear that the fathers acted to ban anything approaching the anti-patri plan the letter indirectly outlines (while leaving unscathed what the letter calls "subjects . . . officially acceptable, such as murder and adultery").[13]

Several subjects "unpopular in Whitehall" are intrinsic to Norah James's *Sleeveless Errand*, banned early in 1929 and so exiled it has been designated "probably the most suppressed novel ever published in England" (Kunitz and Haycraft, eds., 716).[14] James called it a "kind of sermon against the stupidity and futility of the life a section of the post-war generation was leading" (*Democracy*, 231); the prosecutor said it was "told in the form of conversation by persons utterly devoid of decency and morality, who for the most part were under the influence of drink, and who not only tolerated but even advocated adultery and promiscuous fornication. Filthy language and indecent situations appeared to be the keynote. . . . The name of God or Christ was taken in vain more than 60 times in a way that shocked. [He] quoted . . . the saying of one character, 'For Christ's sake give me a drink' " ("Seized Novel"). Yes, someone does say, "For Christ's sake give me a drink," and someone else, "Christ, here's David, sozzled as usual." Told she uses "an awful lot of bad language," the heroine, Paula, says, "Do I really? . . . What's it matter?" (121). Indeed, what's it matter? Surely the novel was banned less for its "bad language" than for its attack on the soldier-producing state?

Sleeveless Errand begins with Paula's rejection by her male lover and determining on suicide. She encounters Bill, who, having just found his wife naked with a male friend, decides to join her. At various bars and clubs they meet drunken men, female prostitutes, and Paula's "Crowd," who interminably discuss money, sex, work, and how bloody life is. Next day Paula pays her bills, makes her will, hires a car, and drives them to the South Coast. A chance encounter with a seedy seaside troupe involves them in more drinking (and discussion of money, sex, work . . .). Then, having persuaded Bill to return to his wife and have children, Paula drives to the cliffs and runs the car over.

Its "profanity" notwithstanding, *Sleeveless Errand* seemed to reviewers such as Edward Garnett, Desmond MacCarthy, and Arnold Bennett a "moral tale" to dissuade people from the hard-drinking, careless London "crowd" life.[15] It *was* moral, and the moral of the subtext outraged the Tory government and its constituency. It was an indictment of the war they had made "for democracy" ("Democracy! Christ what a farce!" says Paula), as well as of the continuing hypocrisies and contradictions of the postwar society they sustained. In that society people were failing to have children or were practicing birth control; women were still going out to work, and a number were getting divorces (so many that the home secretary forbade "the publication of unnecessary details in divorce cases" [Brentford, 22]). Some men, like James's Bill, were not "letting" their wives have children; some, again like Bill, were realizing that shell-shock victims (sixty-five thousand in special hospitals in 1928) would be better off dead.[16] With perfect logic James damns the war, the men who made it, the church that loudly supported it, the fools who went to kill and die in it, and, most of all, the survivors—especially the unreproducing women:

"Look at the girls today. They resent not having what they call the 'good time' we had during the War, when sexual control . . . went by the board. . . . They want . . . the same thing . . . although if they get found out, the world makes them suffer . . . just as much as it made women suffer for the same thing before 1914. . . . They find . . . a large proportion of the men with whom my generation would have mated were wiped out . . . and the majority of those left have married. . . . The youngsters with whom they should be mating [are] taken up by the older women." (234–35)

Paula's generation is "damned," and "both our mothers and our sisters have been smeared with the same poison." Competing with younger women for younger men, "older women" find "even the very prostitutes hate [them] because the men need them so much less now."[17] Any solution, Paula suggests, is cataclysmic: "If only some wise Providence would wipe out with one sweep all the so-called women war-workers who are unmarried, or who, married and healthy, have purposely avoided having children, then there might be some chance of England pulling herself out of the moral mire she's staggering about in now" (237).

All this seems neatly to concur with Mrs. Tweedie's desire to "stamp out . . . surplus . . . women"; the fathers should have rejoiced. James's approval of suicide and birth control, however, and her claims that only professional female prostitutes were not "damned" and only "homos," not promiscuous, seem to rub the noses of the men in Whitehall firmly in their own "moral mire."

Banishing *Sleeveless Errand* was perhaps the last flag-wag of God's Tory deputies, especially of Sir William Joynson Hicks, the home secretary, who, out of office in 1929, wrote a pamphlet titled "Do We Need a Censor?"[18] He proved that we did. The specifically political nature of banishment is suggested by the publication in 1930–31, under the short-lived Labour government, of "Helen Zenna Smith's" war trilogy, which, far more crudely than La Motte, or Allatini, or James, condemns patriotism, the home front mentality, and the call to have babies, especially with war heroes (and the more mutilated, the more patriotic to marry them).[19] The ban, in other words—though this may be a gross oversimplification—seems to have changed with the change in ministries. And it is noteworthy that by 1932 even Anglican bishops supported international peace movements (J. Stevenson, 366).

Love, Service, and "Thousands of Old Maids"

By and large, of course, Tory patriarchal priorities were sustained in and by contemporary fiction, some of which does raise questions about "surplus" nonmothers and working women and lesbians but answers them in narratives that are banal in at least the sense that they are written under the equivalent of "compulsory feudal service." Thus they avoid banishment. Two very different novels are especially illustrative of what I mean.

Sylvia Stevenson's *Surplus* was published in 1924. The title most obviously applies to Sally Wraith, who is, consistently, "surplus." Sacked by a motor firm that treats her like a clerk, not a sales agent, she sets up house with another former wartime driver, establishing a motorcycle taxi service while Averil designs posters and paints. Averil is commercially unsuccessful until a friend gets her a big commission; eventually she leaves and marries him. Sally's motorcycle falls apart; Sally falls apart. After vegetating at home for a while, she gets a job in a third-rate London teashop, a dead-end existence that ends when she agrees to marry a colonial farmer (to whom she once sold a car) and accompany him to East Africa.[20] That *should* solve the "surplus" problem.

As reviewers recognized, however, the novel's real focus is Sally's all-consuming (physically "unconsummated") love for Averil. Averil is surplus only until she does as all girls must—marry and "start a family." The better to identify the problem, Stevenson has the cheerful, pudgy psychiatrist Averil eventually marries explain to Sally that, like "lots of women nowadays," she has repressed the great instinct for self-perpetuation (the *only* other allowable instinct being for self-preservation) and is therefore abnormal. Sally gamely rejects the "early Victorian" idea that "the only thing women exist for is to have families," claiming that "heaps of women don't want children." Replies the Freudian feudal father, "Only the abnormal ones. And even they do, right down underneath. Only their conscious minds take charge and persuade them that, as there aren't enough men to go round, they had better not waste their time wanting what they can't get." The argument for male "self-preservation" (that which prompts men to "defend" themselves by going to war) and female "self-perpetuation" (that which men tell women to endorse by reproducing) runs to ten pages (129–39). Much later, Sally does tell herself she will have a child—for her "an occupation" and the colonial farmer's "due" (284). But just before they are due to leave for Africa, Sally sees Averil in a restaurant, and that, nearly, is that.

The novel's last few pages describe Sally's visit to an ailing friend she hopes will decide for her about marrying. Miss Landison demurs but promises to leave Sally money if she will get a partnership in a motor firm (thus becoming a role model for single women) and help other people. She herself has "served" others to retain her "right" to reject "second best" and keep "the flower of love unchallenged in her heart" after her fiancé's (caddish) departure. Sally accepts the bargain, realizing that "since she would not give children to the race, could not . . . find her fulfillment in being the influence behind a man— . . . she must pay her footing otherwise among the company of lovers. Love and service went together inseparably." Understanding she is a "scapegoat," heartened by Miss Landison's suggestion that she may not be The Only One Of Her Kind, Sally wonders whether her "job is to teach some other unmated woman that she hasn't missed the greatest thing in the world [marriage and motherhood], if she's had a great friendship" (309–17).

We are left with a double message: it is all right not to have children if one serves other people, and lesbians don't have sex anyway. It probably was not fear of censorship that prompted Stevenson to write a "fiercely clean" novel, one also judged "sentimental and timid."[21] The *Times Literary Supplement* tellingly pronounced the novel's title "not its happiest feature. It is not the study of a statistically superfluous woman . . . but of one who is by her emotional constitution unfitted for a place in present-day society." (Shades of Mrs. Tweedie's new world!) "Rather fortunately," the review ends, "the author has not set out thoroughly the psychological implications in the story, which is left as a simple record of observed events. As such, it undoubtedly has weight" ("Surplus").

"Rather fortunately," eh? The nation certainly did fear an increase in lesbianism. As Sheila Jeffreys tells us, an amendment to the 1921 Age of Consent Bill to outlaw lesbian "acts" was quashed because, one opponent said, "It is a beastly subject, . . . better advertised by. . . this Clause than in any other way." Other Members of Parliament thought that such "moral weakness" heralded the "beginning of the nation's downfall"; the race would "decline," and married women might be lured away from their husbands; lesbianism sapped "the fundamental institutions of society" (111–14).[22]

Clearly the Establishment contemplated "superfluous" women with anxiety (or, perhaps more accurately, with horror and terror). Consequently, innumerable unmarried heterosexual women learned that when young they were worthless and, when middle-aged, headed for the madhouse. "Virgins," wrote Winifred Holtby in 1935, "are taught to pity themselves. From their childhood they learn to dread the fate of 'an old maid'. In more sophisticated circles they anticipate a nemesis of 'complexes'. Puritan morality taught unmarried women that the loss of virginity doomed them to the torments of Hell in the next world; twentieth-century morality teaches them that the retention of virginity dooms them to the horror of insanity in this one" (132).

The stories of such pitiful creatures could sympathetically be told if they committed themselves to service. In 1929 Dame Mary Scharlieb (surgeon, medical reformer, and one of Britain's first female magistrates) wrote a book called *The Bachelor Woman and Her Problems*. A mixture of common sense, Anglo-Catholic mysticism, and eugenicist fascism, it prescribes service to the community for secular "surplus" women. Dame Mary's message is that whereas "the motive [for work] with the mother was the welfare of her offspring, . . . the motive in the case of the unmarried woman must be the welfare of her race" (71). Rather sweetly recognizing that people often need "inspiration" to work, she approves what she calls "obsessive" or "absorbing" friendships between women. Such friendships had, of course, to be "pure."

Had Dame Mary's book not appeared five years after *Surplus*, I would have sworn that Stevenson had lifted chunks of it for her conclusion. Throughout the postwar period, though, "service" was an easy word to conjure with, as is evident in novels about advertising like Ethel Mannin's *Sounding Brass* (1926) and Dorothy Sayers's *Murder Must Advertise* (1933). Then as now, even advertising was rendered ethically acceptable by claiming dedication to community service.

Advertising aside, even lesbians like Stevenson's hero could avoid banishment if they undertook unselfish service. Like lesbians, though (who do it on purpose), thousands of heterosexual women were, as Holtby observed, "in a monogamous society . . . mathematically destined to remain unmarried" (131), and so barred from "the greatest thing in the world" (S. Stevenson, 317). The inherent troublesomeness of both types is remarkably dealt with by Dorothy Sayers in *Unnatural Death* (1927), one of her two novels with a female villain, this one a "serial" murderer of women. A mistress of disguise, Mary Whittaker "lives" two characters, using other personae when necessary. And she is a lesbian and a nurse—trained at the Royal Free Hospital, that hotbed of feminism. (The other nurse characters come from male doctors' clinics.) Misusing skills that should make her useful to the community (and the race), Mary kills by injecting air into her victims' veins. This is clearly very vile and female, and, if one wants to read it so, a monstrous usurpation of phallic power.[23] Lord Peter Wimsey, given the most "masculine" context Sayers can invent, realizes how death occurs by remembering how an air-lock in the petrol feed chokes an engine.

Sayers's ultimate perversion of womanhood, Mary finally hangs herself in prison during the solar eclipse. The sun/son—need we doubt it?—survives.[24] That is one banal way of banishing dangerous women. There are others. Mary's first victim, her great-aunt, lived prewar with a dearly loved friend who bred horses. Old retainers describe the couple as independent, huntin' types; a photograph shows that the horse-breeder had a "dour, weatherbeaten face, . . . handsome . . . with its large nose and straight, heavy eyebrows." Her companion was "smaller, plumper and more feminine" (119). Not coincidentally, the villain's description resembles the horse-breeder's; her devoted friend, whom she murders, is like the "more feminine" old lady.

Banishing lesbians to romantic friendship and the grave, or to criminal perversion of service and suicide by hanging, Sayers is comparably banal with regard to other "surplus" women. *Unnatural Death* introduces Miss Climpson, "thin, middle-aged . . . with a sharp sallow face and a very vivacious manner, . . . her iron-grey hair . . . dressed under a net, in the style fashionable in the reign of the late King Edward" (32). She works with other single women in what Peter calls his "Cattery," tracking down advertisers who lure young women to perils they wot not of. Peter sets her to discover the circumstances of the great-aunt's death: she must befriend gossipy village ladies and live "at the rate of about £800 a year"—sending Peter the bills. To Inspector Parker he explains her thus: " 'Miss Climpson . . . is a manifestation of the wasteful way in which this country is run. . . . Thousands of old maids, simply bursting with useful energy, forced by our stupid social system into hydros and hotels and communities and hostels and posts as companions, where their magnificent gossip-powers and units of inquisitiveness are allowed to dissipate themselves or even become harmful to the community' " (36). His "brilliant" idea is that Miss Climpson can ask questions a man couldn't,

"And so-called superfluity is agreeably and usefully disposed of. One of these days you will put up a statue to me, with an inscription:
'To the Man who Made
Thousands of Superfluous Women

Happy
without Injury to their Modesty
or Exertion to Himself.' " (37)[25]

Miss Climpson's "useful energy," intellectual resourcefulness, and physical bravery are crucial to solving the case. Her style, though, is constantly ridiculed: her letters, for example, are full of underlinings, digressions, and other "feminine" devices. One digression reminds Peter (and perhaps slow readers) of the dangers of girls' "pashes" on older women, referring him to Clemence Dane's "very clever book" on the subject (78). And it is her "pash" on Mary that gets Vera Findlater killed.[26]

Better than any 1920s novel I know, *Unnatural Death* belongs to the category of banality which constitutes "compulsory feudal service." The villainous lesbian acts out the fathers' fears in many (dis)guises, though she is less clever than the two men she tries to kill and fails to kill Miss Climpson (an eleventh-hour rescue by Peter, here). "Spinsterish" intelligence is harnessed by the ruling class, for only thus can it serve the community. (The other working-class "spinster" thus harnessed is Wimsey's butler, Bunter.) Weimar (soon-to-be-Nazi) Germany was competently working out a similar solution to the "surplus" problem (Bridenthal et al., 1–29),[27] but Sayers's particular enunciation of fascism has such a nice Oxford accent that readers must have felt ever so satisfied. Such a beautifully banal novel.

A Fourth Term

Whatever the "literary" value of these texts, the interest of those banned lies in their perfectly Shakespearean "obscenity," their rejection of the program of God's deputies, which decrees production of soldiers—woman's only true service; of those not banned, in their perfect embodiment of feudally useful "banal" solutions. Such things continue to be relevant to the ways we think and live.[28]

Twenty years after Allatini's *Despised and Rejected* identified the opposition to fascism's motherhood-for-militarism program, and with fascism more clearly named (and rampant), Virginia Woolf published *Three Guineas*. The day she finished correcting proofs she wrote in her diary, "Have committed myself. am afraid of nothing. Can do anything I like. No longer famous, no longer on a pedestal; no longer hawked in by societies: on my own, for ever. Thats my feeling: a sense of expansion, like putting on slippers" (Woolf, *Diary*, 5:136–37). Fifty years later, she would, I hope, forgive my hawking her in. To oppose war and the production of ammunition(s), she proposed a Society of Outsiders, whose members would observe "poverty, chastity, derision, and . . . freedom from unreal loyalties." It is not surprising that understanding how to further the 1928 "plan"— "birth-control, suicide, pacifism"—gave her a "sense of expansion." There is, of course, some danger in finding "exile" as comfortable as "putting on slippers," as several essays in this collection remind us. In 1988, however, as in 1918 and 1938, we still (repeatedly) know that we need a society of outsiders, of exiles, if you will. The programs of our interchangeable national leaders on both sides of the Atlantic force such conclusions on us. Now as then, it behooves us to write and read what is banished—including those un/reproductions that help us dismantle national equations of getting babies with making wars. We *can* play safe with the merely banal. But if we subscribe to the insiders' program, identified by the Little Mother's contention that "women are created for the purpose of giving life and men to take it," we deracinate ourselves, exile ourselves to the land of universal fascism—conscription and subscription to the most unreal loyalty of all.

Notes

I read a brief version of this essay for a Twentieth-Century English Literature session of the 1986 MLA. I am grateful to Mary Lynn Broe for editorial suggestions then and to Claire Culleton for provocative questions later. Claire Tylee has shared a great deal of work in progress, and I wish she were nearer to Texas than Malaga. I thank, a lot, Jane Marcus, window-smasher and ice-breaker, for always-legible marginal scribbles and for continuous support (and threats), and Ingeborg Majer O'Sickey for sharing lunchtime rituals and for keeping me honest.

1. "For the raising of a virile race, either of soldiers or of citizens it is essential that the attention of the mothers of the land should be mainly devoted to the three K's—Kinder, Kuche, Kirche" (Sir Frederick Maurice in 1903, quoted in Davin, 16). Thanks to Claire Tylee for bringing this and Anne Summers's "Militarism in Britain before the Great War" to my attention. And see Hammerton.

2. Hall Caine's *Our Girls* makes much of female munitions workers stuffing the "wombs" of shells. Claire Culleton explores equations of birthing with munitions-making in "Gender-Charged Munitions."

3. See also Marwick, *Deluge*, 36–37, 66; J. Stevenson, 72; Marwick, *Women*, 124; Blythe, 19; Williams, 247; Pankhurst, 269.

4. "From its first appearance [1916] this small book was kept out of England and France. But it did very well in the United States, until we entered the war" (La Motte, v [1934]). It was then suppressed. I am grateful to Claire Tylee for bringing the 1934 edition to my notice. The Bodley Head, which acquired Putnam's some twenty-six years ago, confirms that Putnam's did publish the title in 1916 (personal letter to me).

5. This was the usual charge brought against antiwar/antigovernment publications under DORA. Between first and second hearings, sales rose from 677 to 778 (*Times*, September 27, 1918, p. 3b; *ibid.*, October 11, 1918, p. 5d).

6. For an analysis of the pernicious influence of George Dangerfield's *The Strange Death of Liberal England* (1935), see Marcus "Introduction," 2–11.

7. For an excellent reading of *Despised and Rejected* as a pacifist novel, see Tylee.

8. In 1921 Mrs. "RGH" wrote Marie Stopes, "What I would like to know is how I can save having any more children as I think I have done my duty to my Country having had 13 children 9 boys and 4 girls and I have 6 boys alive now and a little girl who will be 3 year old in may. . . it do jest kill me to carry them in the shawl I have always got one in my arms and another clinging to my apron. . . . I was 19 when I married so you can see . . . I have not had much time for pleasure. . . . I am please to tell you I received one of those Willow plates from the News of the World for mothers of ten" (Hall, ed., *Dear Dr. Stopes*, 14).

9. Martha Vicinus—probably justifiably—reprimands Jeffreys for "simplifying history" ("Reformers," 6), but antagonism to nonmothers seems fairly well documented. Said Charlotte Haldane (*Motherhood and Its Enemies*): "Every woman who refuses motherhood is curtailing her psychological as well as her physiological development in a manner which may have serious consequences to herself" (quoted in Braybon, 222). Sex reformers' ideas horrified Mrs. Tweedie in 1917, when "state-sponsored" polygamy and promiscuity were suggested by Germans honest enough to say the Fatherland needed babies for work in "the next war in ten years' time" (Tweedie, 71–72).

10. Some DORA provisions were confirmed by the 1920 Emergency Powers Act, enabling the government to declare a state of emergency, make regulations, and set up courts; parliamentary consent facilitated monthly "renewal." Such "almost unlimited" powers were used chiefly to break strikes and control organized labor (J. Stevenson, 97; Mowat, 42, 318).

11. *Despised and Rejected* ends similarly: a "new humanity" is evolving from homosexuals, from whose suffering "will arise something great—something God-given: the human soul will complete itself" (349).

12. The "in/version" phrase is Jane Marcus's. My favorite *Well* story concerns an American producer who, told he could not film the novel because it was about lesbians, said, "All right; let's make 'em Austrians" (Mannin, *Confessions*, 178). If

Radclyffe Hall had had the sense to "make 'em Austrians" she would have been lauded for exposing all those pervertedly antimotherhood Germanic fiends.

13. Subsequent *Nation & Athenaeum* comment reiterates this point: "Sexual sins are almost the only ones seriously regarded. Men may perjure themselves, rob, or commit murder and these are but venial acts in comparison with any violation of the sex taboos" (1928:435); "We are told that certain writers put into literary form what small boys write on walls. . . . And, of course, it is only 'sex' that is wicked. War, murder, burglaries, hunting are all fit and decent subjects for the young. 'The Fifteen Decisive Battles of the World' is a Sunday School classic" (1928:838); "Why not start on those admittedly the most dangerous [books] to our present civilization—the murderous or the warlike . . . usually supplied to young people? Which have played the greatest havoc in the past, wars or illegitimate children?" (1929:199).

14. See my discussion in " 'Unutterable Putrefaction.' "

15. Garnett quoted in Partridge, 24; see also Bennett, 249, and MacCarthy, 140.

16. John Stevenson adds that in 1928 2.5 million men received war disability pensions (about 40 percent of those who had served); there were forty-eight special "shell-shock" hospitals and "over 600 *new* issues of artificial limbs" (94).

17. Of men aged twenty to twenty-four in 1914, over 30 percent were killed; of those aged thirteen to nineteen, over 28 percent (J. Stevenson, 94). Laver says that "general promiscuity . . . deprived [*grandes cocottes*] of their status and even . . . livelihood." He cites a Cole Porter lyric about a "busted, disgusted cocotte" whose territory is taken by "those damned Society women" (112).

18. "Flag-wagging" is J. B. Priestley's phrase: "The call [to enlist] was really little to do with 'King and Country' and flag-wagging and hip-hip-hurrah. It was a challenge to what we felt was our untested manhood" (quoted in Bailey, 194).

19. Jane Marcus provides a brilliant contextualized reading of Smith's *Not So Quiet . . .* in "Corpus/Corps/Corpse."

20. William Greg's oft-reprinted "Why Are Women Redundant?" (1862) wished five hundred thousand women "shipped across the Atlantic, or to the Antipodes" (52). See also Rebecca Saunders in this volume, and Hammerton.

21. "The book is absolutely, almost fiercely clean. In its way . . . it is unique" (Reid, 637). Cape's solicitors, who for the *Well* defense compiled a list of "lesbian literature," say *Surplus* is "sentimental and timid but the relation between the two women is obviously abnormal throughout" (Ernst Papers 238, Humanities Research Center, University of Texas at Austin).

22. Homosexual offenses (recorded) rose "threefold," 1921–38 (J. Stevenson, 375). Graves and Hodge claim that men were more "open," their "text-books" being Carpenter's *Intermediate Sex* and Ellis's *Psychology of Sex*. Lesbians "justified themselves . . . by pointing out that there were not enough men to go round . . . and that though the Act of 1880 penalized sodomy there was no definite illegality

to the female practice if not performed to the public scandal" (101). Goldring says that the shortage of men led to "numerous associations of . . . women with intellectual interests and no time . . . for the current forms of dissipation. Unless purposely paraded, such friendships aroused little curiosity or comment. . . . Growth of knowledge about sex psychology [however], seriously disturbed the conventional Tory aristocracy, whose favourite vices, although well-known to Continental observers, . . . had hitherto been concealed from the public gaze." Upper-class "sadism," the prevalence of flogging working-class children for minor offences, became objects of satire and criticism among middle-class intelligensia (228–29). In 1931, agreeing with Marie Stopes, Sheila Donnisthorpe's *Loveliest of Friends!*, in the purplest prose, damns lesbianism (having made it seem very nice and sexy) for destroying once "ordinary" wives.

23. Jane Marcus suggests that because in wartime only mothering and nursing are officially sanctioned as "womanly," postwar, nurses were potentially evil because they "knew too much." Mary's "misusing" her "instrument" is thus an allegory for misuse of womanhood. See also Marcus, "Asylums of Antaeus."

24. June 29, 1927, saw a total solar eclipse ("the first . . . visible in England for over 200 years," according to a note in Woolf's *Diary* 3:142).

25. Like William Greg, Peter (and Sayers?) considers "surplus" only unmarried and/or childless *middle-class* women.

26. Winifred Ashton ("Clemence Dane"), Sayers's friend, published *Regiment of Women* in 1917.

27. Thanks to Susan Post of Book-Woman in Austin for bringing *When Biology Became Destiny* to my attention.

28. Helen Cooper, Adrienne Munich, and Susan Squier's collection, *Arms and the Woman*, takes such "relevancy" much further, examining "the relationship between war and gender as figured in literature," and showing how "women's role in relation to war is . . . complex and often complicitous." In their essay, "Arms and the Woman: The Con[tra]ception of the War Text," the editors explore numerous Western literary varieties of the conventional—and inevitably, to the State, politically useful—"conjunction between the military and the amorous."

Works Cited

Allatini, Rose ("A. T. Fitzroy"). *Despised and Rejected.* 1918. Reprint. New York: Arno Press, 1975.

Bailey, Leslie. *BBC Scrapbooks.* Vol. 1: *1896–1914.* London: Allen and Unwin, 1966.

Bennett, Arnold. "A Censorship by All Means, But—." In *Arnold Bennett: The "Evening Standard" Years, 'Books and Persons,' 1926–1931*, edited with an Introduction by Andrew Mylett, 247–49. Hamden, Conn.: Archon Books, 1974.

Blythe, Ronald. *The Age of Illusion: England in the Twenties and Thirties, 1914–*

1940. London: Hamish Hamilton, 1963.

Braybon, Gail. *Women Workers in the First World War: The British Experience*. London: Croom Helm, 1983.

Brentford, Viscount (Sir William Joynson Hicks). *Do We Need a Censor?* London: Faber and Faber, 1929.

Bridenthal, Renate, Atina Grossman, and Marion Kaplan, eds. *When Biology Became Destiny: Women in Weimar and Nazi Germany*. New York: Monthly Review Press, 1984.

Brittain, Vera. *Radclyffe Hall: A Case of Obscenity?* New York: S. S. Barnes, 1969.

Caine, Hall. *Our Girls: Their Work for the War*. London: Hutchinson, 1917.

Cole, G. D. H., and Raymond Postgate. *The Common People, 1746–1946*. London: Methuen, 1946. Rev. ed. 1964.

Cooper, Helen, Adrienne Munich, and Susan M. Squier, eds. *Arms and the Woman: War, Gender, and Literary Representation*. Chapel Hill: University of North Carolina Press, 1989.

Culleton, Claire. "Gender-Charged Munitions: The Language of World War I Munitions Reports." *Women's Studies International Forum* 11, no. 2 (1988): 109–16.

Davin, Anna. "Imperialism and Motherhood in History." *History Workshop Journal* 5 (Spring 1978): 7–65.

Ernst, Morris. "Introduction." In Anne Lyon Haight, *Banned Books: Informal Notes on Some Books Banned for Various Reasons at Various Times and in Various Places*. 2d ed. New York: Bowker, 1955.

———. No. 338, Packet 1. Harry Ransom Humanities Research Center, University of Texas, Austin.

Forster, E. M., and Virginia Woolf. "The New Censorship." *Nation & Athenaeum*, September 8, 1928, p. 726.

Goldring, Douglas. *The Nineteen Twenties: A General Survey and Some Personal Memories*. 1945. Reprint. Folcroft, Pa.: Folcroft Library Editions, 1975.

Graves, Robert. *Goodbye to All That*. 1929. Reprint. New York: Doubleday, 1975.

Graves, Robert, and Alan Hodge. *The Long Week-End: A Social History of Great Britain, 1918–1939*. 2d ed. London: Faber and Faber, 1950.

Greg, William Rathbone. "Why Are Women Redundant?" In *Strong-Minded Women and Other Lost Voices from Nineteenth-Century England*, edited by Janet Horowitz Murray, 50–54. New York: Pantheon, 1982.

Haldane, Charlotte. *Motherhood and Its Enemies*. New York: Doubleday, 1927.

Hall, Radclyffe. *The Well of Loneliness*. 1928. Reprint. London: Virago, 1982.

Hall, Ruth. *Passionate Crusader: The Life of Marie Stopes*. New York: Harcourt Brace Jovanovich, 1977.

———, ed. *Dear Dr. Stopes*. 1978. Reprint. Harmondsworth, Middlesex: Penguin Books, 1981.

Hammerton, A. James. *Emigrant Gentlewomen: Genteel Poverty and Female Emigration, 1830–1914.* London: Croom Helm, 1979.

Holtby, Winifred. *Women and a Changing Civilization.* 1935. Reprint. Chicago: Academy, 1978.

Ingram, Angela. " 'Unutterable Putrefaction' and 'Foul Stuff': Two 'Obscene' Novels of the 1920's." *Women's Studies International Forum* 9 (1986): 341–54.

James, Norah. *I Lived in a Democracy.* London: Longmans, Green, 1939.

———. *Sleeveless Errand.* New York: Grosset and Dunlap, 1929.

Jeffreys, Sheila. *The Spinster and Her Enemies: Feminism and Sexuality, 1880–1930.* London: Pandora Press, 1985.

Kunitz, Stanley, and Howard Haycraft, eds. *Twentieth Century Authors.* New York: H. H. Wilson, 1942.

La Motte, Ellen N. *The Backwash of War: The Human Wreckage of the Battlefield as Witnessed by an American Hospital Nurse.* [1916]. Reprint. New York: Putnam, 1934.

Laver, James. *Between the Wars.* Boston: Houghton Mifflin, 1961.

MacCarthy, Desmond. "Obscenity and the Law." In *Experience.* London: Putnam, 1935. 140–48.

Mannin, Ethel. *Confessions and Impressions.* New York: Doubleday, 1930.

Marcus, Jane. "The Asylums of Antaeus: Women, War and Madness: Is There a Feminist Fetishism?" In *The Differences Within: Feminism and Critical Theory,* edited by Elizabeth Meese and Alice Parker, 49–81. Amsterdam: John Benjamins, 1989.

———. "Corpus/Corps/Corpse: Writing the Body in/at War." In Helen Zenna Smith, *Not So Quiet . . . : Stepdaughters of War.* 1930. Reprint. New York: Feminist Press, 1989.

———. "Introduction: Re-reading the Pankhursts and Women's Suffrage." In *Suffrage and the Pankhursts,* edited by Dale Spender and Candida Lacey, 1–17. London: Routledge & Kegan Paul, 1987.

Marwick, Arthur. *The Deluge: British Society and the First World War.* Boston: Little, Brown, 1965.

———. *Women at War, 1914–1918.* London: Fontana, 1977.

Mowat, Charles L. *Britain between the Wars, 1918–1940.* Chicago: University of Chicago Press, 1955.

Pankhurst, E. Sylvia. *The Home Front: A Mirror to Life in England during the World War.* London: Hutchinson, 1932.

Partridge, Eric. *The First Three Years: An Account and a Bibliography of the Scholartis Press.* London: Scholartis Press, 1930.

Playne, Caroline E. *The Pre-War Mind in Britain: An Historical Review.* London: George Allen & Unwin, 1928.

"Publisher of Pacifist Novel Fined." *The Times,* October 11, 1918, p. 5d.

Reid, Forrest. "The Feminine Note." *Nation & Athenaeum* 34 (February 2, 1924): 637.

St. John-Stevas, Norman. *Obscenity and the Law*. London: Secker and Warburg, 1956.

Sayers, Dorothy. *Unnatural Death*. 1927. Reprint. New York: Avon, 1964.

Scharlieb, Dame Mary. *The Bachelor Woman and Her Problems*. London: Williams & Norgate, 1929.

"Seized Novel Condemned." *The Times*, March 5, 1929, p. 13.

Stevenson, John. *British Society, 1914–1945*. Harmondsworth, Middlesex: Penguin, 1984.

Stevenson, Sylvia. *Surplus*. New York: D. Appleton, 1924.

Summers, Anne. "Militarism in Britain before the Great War." *History Workshop* 2 (1976): 108–23.

"Surplus." *Times Literary Supplement*, January 17, 1924, p. 39.

Tweedie, Mrs. Alec. *Women and Soldiers*. London: John Lane, The Bodley Head, 1918.

Tylee, Claire. *The Great War and Women's Consciousness*. London: Macmillan, forthcoming.

Vicinus, Martha. "Reformers and Radicals." *Women's Review of Books* 3 (September 12, 1986): 6.

Williams, John. *Home Fronts: Britain, France, and Germany, 1914–1918*. London: Constable, 1972.

Woolf, Virginia. *The Diary of Virginia Woolf*. Edited by Ann Olivier Bell assisted by Andrew McNeillie. Vols. 3, 5. New York: Harcourt Brace Jovanovich, 1980, 1984.

———. *Three Guineas*. New York: Harcourt, Brace and World, 1938.

Chapter 14

. . . .

Writing against the Grain

Sylvia Townsend Warner and the Spanish Civil War

Barbara Brothers

Sylvia Townsend Warner is an exile from the pages of literary history, her contributions unmarked even in Gilbert and Gubar's *Norton Anthology of Literature by Women*. Her politics labeled radical in the social text of the twentieth century and her poetic and fictional forms conservative in the Modernist canonical text, she is known by epithet—a *lady* communist, as Stephen Spender sarcastically dismissed her, and a *communist* writer who contributed to the *Left Review*, as those who purport to write the literary histories of the Spanish Civil War and the 1930s list her. Like other women writers of the 1930s denied authority in the arena of politics and war, she is denied authorship. Even apologists for the leftist writers of the 1930s view such women as dupes of the temporarily deceived. Ghettoized by the social text as *communist* and resegregated as *lady*, Warner is unnamed in twentieth-century literary history as well. Whatever social value is accorded to political commitment, such commitment is proclaimed by the academic, critical establishment, worshipers of the idol of Modernism, to be the antithesis of literary value. Like the adjective *woman*, *political* effaces the category *writer* to which the adjectives are applied.

I have limited this essay to Warner's contributions to the literature of the Spanish Civil War, though she published a significant body of literature from 1925 to 1978 informed by the issues of gender and class. Warner wrote short stories, poems, a novel—*After the Death of Don Juan* (1939)—and essays that depicted the people of Spain, the spirit of the republican struggle, the fascist invaders, and the British "gentlemen and their ladies" who supported the Nationalist side, actively or through nonintervention. Opposed to fascism and the institutional oppression of the poor, minorities, and women, she worked on behalf of the Loyalist cause, visited Spain twice during the war, and "wrote as much as anybody did about the war" (Cunningham, xxxii).

Literary histories of the Spanish Civil War proclaim themselves as part social history—the literature not real literature—and part literary history—a reinterpretation of the temporary aberrations of canonical writers and too-soon-dead soldier-poets. The "exclusionary politics" of the Modernist canon controls the script of literary history even when the subject is not aesthetics (see Celeste Schenck's essay in this volume). In the narrative of Spanish Civil War writing, women become emblem, bibliographic entry, or footnote, equivalent to their role in the social script as attendant—wife or sweetheart. Warner can be accommodated in neither role. Katharine Bail Hoskins, in *Today the Struggle* (1969), discusses nothing of what women wrote about the war and lists in the bibliography only two works by women, Jessica Mitford's *Hons and Rebels* and Virginia Woolf's "The Leaning Tower." Both are included only because they discuss male leftists of the 1930s. In Hoskins's "literary" history, Charlotte Haldane—novelist, journalist, and autobiographer of her political activities during the 1930s—is mentioned not by name but merely as the wife of Professor J. B. S. Haldane, a scientist; and in a bibliographic citation, Hoskins omits Nancy Cunard's name as editor of *Authors Take Sides*.

Nor do other authors of accounts of British and American writing about the Spanish Civil War afford Warner and the women writers of the decade a place in the narrative. John Muste, who takes his title *Say That We Saw Spain Die* (1966) from a poem by Edna St. Vincent Millay (*Harper's*, 1938), mentions nothing of the poem's substance or of the other five poems by Millay with which it was published. His bibliography cites novels, autobiographies, or collections of poetry by nine women writers, not one of whom receives any mention in the text. Only those women such as Margot Heinemann whom he can transform into mere emblems are discussed; Heinemann's poem about the death of her lover John Cornford is used as a particularly repugnant example of commitment to the leftist cause displacing personal affections. Dolores Ibarruri, La Pasionaria as she was known, is the "communist party's most popular *symbol* of the new Spain" (76; emphasis added). The substance and tone of the comments of Muste on Heinemann and Ibarruri, whom he makes representative of women writers, depict them as unnatural and ignorant; his characterization of them is similar to that vision of "bloodthirsty vampires" conjured up by male writers of World War I (see Marcus, "Asylums of Antaeus"). Though Valentine Cunningham does include selections by women in his 1986 Oxford anthology, *Spanish Front*, he marginalizes their contribution as effectively as Muste does in his book written twenty years earlier: he subsumes all but Warner's essay on the Writers' Congress in Madrid and a poem by Heinemann, the same one discussed by Muste, within the constricted ghetto "Women Writing Spain."[1]

Women who, like Warner, are or were radical in their politics suffer from double jeopardy. Not only are they writing against the grain (writing left), but they are also writing on a subject about which the general public thinks they are ignorant (writing politics). One reason women are thought to have no historical perspective is that they remain on the fringes of the "real" world of politics and political power. A woman, as Woolf points out in *Three Guineas*, thus has neither the experience to make her view credible in the eyes of the men who do nor the means to "enforce" (13) her opinion on them. Woolf lists the many ways in which a woman is or was marginalized on the issues of war and peace: she could not fight, not even in Spain "in defence of peace"; she could not use the "pressure of money" because she was not allowed to be a member of the stock exchange; the diplomatic service and the church were closed to her; and the press, civil service, and bar admitted her only if she pleased the men who controlled those institutions. Social practices, such as the codes of polite conversation and men's clubs, perpetuate the myth of women's political naiveté and ignorance. Since women are regarded as either credulous or querulous followers, bystanders, their opinions and activities can be dismissed.

In her address to the Royal Society of Arts in 1959, which echoes and expands Woolf's *A Room of One's Own* and *Three Guineas*, Warner argues that women are not taken seriously even as writers: "Supposing I had been a man, a gentleman novelist, would I have been asked to lecture on Men as Writers?" (378). Though women are writers, it is not commonly accepted that a woman "earns her living by her pen" ("Women as Writers," 385). That is, even if a woman is a writer, she is not that in the eyes of the world, which views a woman's writing as a pastime, incidental to her social role as wife, attendant, or an "educated man's sister," to use Woolf's phrase in *Three Guineas*. Thus we need not *attend* to the writing woman as to a man: women are to be waited upon but not listened to.

But women *are* writers, and they are witnesses to history. Like Woolf in *Three Guineas*, Warner emphasizes that the position of women in society often makes what they have to say different from what men *can* say. Because women have entered the world of writing through the "pantry window" ("Women as Writers," 383), not only writing literally on the kitchen table but also viewing life through that window, they have achieved what those running the castle have missed: "an ease and appreciativeness in low company" (384). Women do not lack a view of history; theirs is a different perspective.[2] That difference is expressed in both the substance and the form of Warner's writing—her choice of the "others" of society for her heroes and heroines and her rejection of "social realism as a vehicle," which Marcus emphasizes in her essay in this volume. Yet Warner is not a Modernist, for she is storyteller in Walter Benjamin's sense, valuing the tale, whether fantastic or real, for the lesson we might learn from it (Benjamin, "The Storyteller," in *Illuminations*).

Warner chose to be alien and critical. Temporarily she exiled herself by traveling to Spain, once in the service of the Spanish medical auxiliary and once to attend the Writers' Congress in Madrid. Permanently she set herself outside the accepted norms of her culture by opposing the politics and policies of her government and church and the conventions of her society. She chose not to marry but to live with and love a woman, Valentine Ackland. Though a member of the Church of England, she records that at the confirmation service her spirit rejected the complacent exclusionary allegiance and "sheepish conformity" that she perceived the institution to demand ("Young Sailor"). And she gave expression to her radical beliefs in seven novels, nine books of poetry, and more than ten volumes of short stories.

In her first book of poems, entitled *The Espalier* (1925) and published eight years before she joined the Communist party and began writing for the *Left Review*, Warner declared herself by choosing such subjects as a beggar wench and black American musicians as well as by writing a poem in celebration of Rosa Luxemburg, "I Bring Her a Flower." In the novels that preceded *Summer Will Show* (1936)—*Lolly Willowes* (1926), *Mr. Fortune's Maggot* (1927), and *The True Heart* (1929)—Warner had subtly attacked the institutions of marriage, the church, organized charity, and the stock exchange. She exposed the personal values and cultural hypocrisy that produced the oppression of the poor, women, and the unorthodox, the "others" of society. Set in 1848, *Summer Will Show* dramatizes the conversion of a married woman of the landed gentry in England to a communist and lover of a female Jewish radical in Paris.[3] Warner's heroine, who looks forward at the end of the novel to a new age, mirrors Warner's own hopes for a genderless, classless, raceless society of the future. *Summer Will Show* is an overt political fable like her novel on Spain that was to follow it. Mary McCarthy in a review in the *Nation* called it "the most sure-footed, sensitive, witty piece of prose . . . to have been informed by left-wing ideology."

In *After the Death of Don Juan*, Warner depicts the social and political turmoil that prevented the Spanish republic of 1931 from becoming stable enough to withstand the fascists within and outside Spain, manipulating the details of plot and character that she took from *Don Giovanni*. As in Warner's other novels, the "little" people are shown to be the victims of those whose gods are money and power. Her novel gives us an insight into the vision of left-wing activists. It is a clearer picture than Orwell's *Homage to Catalonia* or Hemingway's *For Whom the Bell Tolls* of the motivations of the various classes and factions of the society and government of Spain in the 1930s and of the conditions under which the Spanish people lived.

Warner dramatizes the difficulties the elected government of Spain faced in attempting to unite the various factions and to effect the educational and economic reforms needed to create a new life for the majority of the people of Spain: Don Saturno fails in his attempt to educate the villagers and free them from their illiterate dependence on the church, and his plans to irrigate the land are no more than paper proposals. Like the Spanish government, Saturno struggles against his own impracticality and lack of money as well as against the distrust of the villagers, a distrust that is fed by the church in the person of the sacristan Don Gil, who subtly plays upon their divided loyalties and suspicious natures. (The sacristan's name echoes that of Gil Robles, the leader of the Catholic Confederation of Autonomous Right Parties, which opposed the laic republic.)

One need only read a historical memoir such as Constancia de la Mora's *In Place of Splendor* to realize how well Warner has captured the mean-spiritedness of the Catholic church that held the peasants and women in bondage. Don Gil and the others like him who controlled the Spanish church behaved as if the kingdom of heaven belonged to the rich and powerful. His image of God is as a "tyrant": "the source and support of all fear, God like a heart eternally pumping fear into the universe, God in whose image and to whose glory man dresses himself in authority" (157). Gil makes himself over in his image of God. He treats his daughter-in-law as a servant and secures for her more wash than she can manage with her other chores so as to line his pockets with her meager earnings. He extends his control over the miller's daughter by encouraging her to filch from her father, Diono, the money Diono gives her for masses to stop their silkworms from dying.

Warner mocks the church through her portrayal of the two priests in her tale, both of whom are foolish and superstitious, hiding under tables from apparitions and exorcising evil spirits but unable to recognize evil or sin when confronted by either. She exposes the foolish and hypocritical romanticism that the church spawns through Dona Ana's simultaneous "pious" devotion to the church—Ana even has her priest travel with her—and her lustful physical passion for Don Juan, which provokes her on the journey. Dona Ana is haughty, proud, and poorly educated. Like the other aristocrats, she both uses and is used by the patriarchal institution. Warner's subtle but penetrating satire is beautifully illustrated by the scene in which Dona Ana, an "image of devotion, the image of penitence" (84), kneels before the altar. In an all-night vigil, Ana prays for the miraculous appearance of Don Juan. Even Dona Pilar, who must dutifully watch over her, knows her act is one neither of reason nor of piety. Warner's mocking commentary is delivered by Pilar, who, hearing the "desolate sexual cry" of a cat, thinks, " 'What a shameless animal!' " (85). Yet Ana arises after the morning mass feeling that, no Don Juan having appeared, she has "mismanaged" her "devotions" (89). She lacks the humility and understanding, neither of which the church assumed as its duty to teach her, to have even a moment's misgiving about what she was praying for—the chance to commit adultery. Don Gil, of course, cares not what she prays for, only that he has such a beautiful and high-born lady within: "For not on every night of the year does one keep watch over such a treasure, and hold the church key so powerfully" (88). To Don Gil, Dona Ana represents the means to an end. Through Gil and Ana, Warner portrays the values of the patriarchal church: devoted to power, the church, as Warner emphasizes in the novel and her essays on Spain, perpetuates illiteracy and superstition, thus enslaving women and the poor.

But the people of the village remember that, in the words of the Bible, it is the meek who are to inherit the earth, certainly Warner's view. A woman of the village identifies Dona Ana's real sin: "A most terrible sin, a most unusual sin, such a sin as no woman in this village has ever committed. She has married a husband who is young, rich, handsome, healthy, and kind" (64). In contrast to Gil's church of hierarchical "bullying," the men of the village fantasize about a church of thieves administered by a priest who is a captive servant of the people, reversing the church's subjugation of the many to the few, the peasants to the aristocrats, the women to the men.

Don Juan represents, of course, the fascists; he is both foreign invader and son of Spain, returning like a thief to his father's lands and his aristocratic brother's wife. The strength of class ties is illustrated by Don Ottavio's joining forces with Don Juan against Juan's father and the peasants of the village, their "common enemy," instead of challenging Don Juan to a duel (278). Earlier Don Saturno had reflected: "For the rich, quarrelling never so much among themselves, corrupting each other's wives, driving steel into each other's bellies, were as one in cheating the poor" (101). The soldiers Ottavio and Juan have summoned enter the village and massacre most of the inhabitants, the ending of the novel focusing on the July uprising of the army that marked the beginning of the Spanish Civil War.

The conflicting goals and programs of the various political parties of Spain during the years of the republic are portrayed well not only by the inhabitants of the castle but also by the villagers. Diego believes that Saturno's irrigating the land will bring social justice. His friend Ramon feels that "more than water is needed to wash away the castle. . . . For suppose the water is brought, it will still be theirs. They can turn it away if they choose. It will be another weapon in their hands, and we shall have put it there" (150–51). Ramon is a reflective but unheeded spokesman for the need for social revolution. The differing opinions of the workers and peasants about how to solve their problems represent those of the social-ists, communists, and anarchists and the numerous organizations that represented them and confuse us by their number and designation— POUM, UGT, FNTT, CNT. But their differences are forgotten as they die as brothers at the hands of the army in the conclusion of Warner's novel.

In her essay "Barcelona," written for the *Left Review* in December of 1936 following her first trip to Spain for the Republican Medical Services, Warner describes briefly what she learned of the July nineteenth uprising in that city and why it failed there. But the burned-out churches in Spain that were so useful as propaganda against the republican forces are the focus of Warner's essay. To those who decried the destruction of the sacred, Warner replied that the church in Spain was a despot. It physically abused the people by countenancing their extreme poverty. Its most griev-ous transgression, however, was spiritually despoiling them by inducing their illiteracy. The church had earned the hatred of the people: "It was a longer, a more universal resentment [than that against the power and wealth of the aristocrats] which stripped the walls and burned the pulpits and confessionals, and barred up the doors, a realisation that here, beyond the other strongholds of Fascism and capitalism, was the real stronghold of the oppressors." The Right claimed that both religious and artistic sensibilities should be offended by what were made to appear as barbarous acts of wanton destruction. In Warner's view, however, there were few such acts. She points out that the villas of the wealthy aristocrats were left unharmed, though like the churches they were stripped of the wealth stored not in banks but medievally in gold, jewels, and other possessions. She maintains that most of what was confiscated of artistic value was stored in museums. The churches were, however, scourged to rid the land of a "pestilence," the scars visible for Warner in the "animal fear" of a servant girl who stares in "abject terror," not at the men destroying a religious plaque but at the plaque itself: "She had had a religious upbring-ing, she could neither read nor write" (816).

Warner also points a finger at the Spanish church in "The Drought Breaks," a piece written for *Life and Letters Today* after she had attended the Writers' Congress in Madrid. (The other descriptive essays by Warner on her experience of the Writers' Congress are "What the Soldier Said" and "Harvest in 1937.") Her narrative focuses on a woman, Rafaela Perez, whose husband is shot by the Nationalists because he carries a trade union card, his blood and that of the other men of the village who supported the republic staining the outside walls of the church. Now the Reverend Mother has claimed Rafaela's three children and those of the other women whose husbands were killed: " 'Holy Church will not leave these innocents where they can be contaminated' " (Cunningham, 245). The mothers must contribute from their meager earnings to support the up-keep of these children in the "prison" of the church. Still believing in victory for republican forces, Warner ends her propagandistic story with their airplanes bringing the bombs to release the people. Warner's story is obviously aimed at countering the charges of the Right, but for those who suffered from such oppression, which indeed they did as is evident not just in Warner's and de la Mora's depiction of the church but in other historical accounts as well, the planes were "a greeting from life."

The need for a revolution to destroy the chains of illiteracy and poverty is the subject of the poems Warner first published in the *Left Review*. In "Some Make this Answer" the masters of death are "affable with church and state as with doxies." But the people no longer bow to those with a "gluttony to subdue," no longer "retreat" before the "thrust muzzle of flesh, master, or metal." Far more frightening than the "voltage of death" dispatched by such Jupiter-like beings are their suffering comrades, "the free and the fine wasted with cold and hunger, / Diseased, maddened, death-in-life-doomed, and the ten / Thousand this death can brag."

So, too, in "Red Front!" does Warner remind her comrades that the wine they drink was produced from vineyards whose soil has been "de-bauched" by the "blood" (255) of their fellows, the grape made wine by "vintaging politicians [who] led up the dance / And set to partners while economists pirouetted." Nor has the church, with "reddened hands and hems," spoken for them: "The priest and sages made merriment in their hymns, / Man in God's image, saying, man at man's bidding." The poem echoes with a sense of history—the French Revolution, the Paris uprising of 1848, and other attempts by the people to wrest control of their for-tunes. Its form is a variation of the ballade, the peroration addressed to the workers and the peasants. Interspersed between the stanzas of the envoi are stanzas of a variantly phrased marching refrain—"Comrade, are you cold enough, / . . . Comrade, are you mired enough, . . . / Comrade, are you grim enough, / . . . Comrade, have you bled enough" (256).[4]

The direct call for action in both of these poems by Warner offends the sensibilities of poetry readers taught to disdain didacticism and to distrust the poet's knowledge of anything but the "higher" truths concealed beneath the surface details of life. Yet the history and experience evoked by the surface details, her imagery and allusions, evoke the suffering and deprivation of the poor whom those in power in the government and in the church use to serve themselves. As Warner expresses the situation, revolution is necessary because the human costs of not fighting are greater than the price the people would pay through taking up arms and waging war to claim power over their own lives. Unlike so many of the poems written by left-wing activists in support of the Loyalist cause, Warner's do not romanticize or sentimentalize the soldier. Her poems are written in the context of suffering and unheroic battlefield conditions that the World War I poets, such as Wilfred Owen, pictured for those who remained at home. Evident in all her poems is her innate distrust of power and its ability to corrupt the human spirit.

Warner is neither naive nor a dogmatist. Her commitment is to her fellow human beings rather than to ideology. In "In this Midwinter," Warner uses the story of the birth of Christ to call upon men and women to reform themselves by accepting the responsibility of caring for a child. Warner tells the shepherds not to look for "lamb" or "saviour." Hers is not a tale of miraculous birth and rebirth. Rather, "comrade," we must love and cherish the child born this midnight as a "co-heir of earth" and "plight . . . our lantern's friendly assurance." Warner does not use the appellation in the particular sense of the Communist party member, for only "maybe" is Lenin savior.[5]

After her visits to Spain, Warner used the Spanish landscape to express the stark inner reality of life for the peasants and soldiers. "Benicasim," one of her four poems published in the *Left Review*, contrasts the seacoast and its villas, one of which was supported by the Spanish Medical Aid for the wounded of the Spanish People's Army, with the mountains through which the soldiers must pass:

Turn
(Turn not!) sight inland:

there, rigid as death and unforgiving, stand
the mountains—and close at hand.

In both time and space this "bright-painted landscape of Acheron," where
"in bleached cotton pyjamas, on rope-soled tread, / wander the risen-
from-the-dead," is "narrow." This poem and "Waiting at Cerbere," which
was first published in Spender's anthology *Poems for Spain* (1939), are the
only two of Warner's poems to be anthologized in collections of Spanish
Civil War verse, though Cunningham's *Penguin Book of Spanish Civil War
Verse* includes a number of her translations of Spanish writers' war poems.
Other poems set in Spain—"El Heroe," "Journey to Barcelona," "Port
Bou"—and poems that directly express Warner's political commitment to
communism, such as "Walking through the meadows," are included in
Warner's *Collected Poems*.

Warner's support for the Spanish republic took many forms and grew
out of her belief that the Spanish people had spoken and so should have a
government "chosen by them and true to them" and that the forces that
opposed their government were fascist, a movement infused by a spirit she
hated: "I am against Fascism, because Fascism is based upon mistrust of
human potentialities. Its tyranny is an expression of envy, its terrorism an
expression of fear" (statement given for *Authors Take Sides on the Spanish
Civil War*, in Cunningham, *Spanish Front*, 228). Like other leftists of the
1930s, Warner feared the growing fascist tide she perceived both abroad
and at home. Sir Oswald Mosley founded the British Union of Fascists in
1932, the year before Hitler became chancellor and the Reichstag Fire
Trials took place, events Warner claimed caused her to join the Communist party. Other events at home made Warner "agin [*sic*] the [British]
Government," though she goes on to observe that such "is not a suitable
frame of mind for a Communist for very long" ("Sylvia Townsend Warner
in Conversation," 35).

Why Warner and others like her were against the British government is
clear from the pages of *Left Review*. Over and over again those writers of
the 1930s who, like Warner, joined the Communist party repeated their
ideals—"democratic liberty, anti-Fascism, and peace" and a literature that
expressed the lives of those whose voices had not been heard (Day Lewis,
674).

Though Warner never considered herself an anarchist, she told Elizabeth Wade in 1936, "It [anarchy] ought to be the political theory of

heaven" (*Letters*, 42). In her view the Spanish and the people of Barcelona, in particular, were more anarchist than communist in spirit. Warner perceived that the problem with anarchism was that it lacked the necessary organization to effect change, and during the 1930s Warner could still believe that Marxist communism provided the plan by which people could take charge of their own destinies and be governed by policies that allowed the masses an opportunity for growth and expression. But communism was to become just another of the "taskmasters who enforced ignorance on [the people]" (*Letters*, 42), another patriarchal institution in its oppression of the many for the benefit of the few.

That the British government that signed the Non-Intervention Pact was not truly neutral—hypocritically supporting the rich and powerful while impeding the efforts of the working class who wished to aid the Spanish republican cause—is the point of Warner's story "With the Nationalists." Mr. Semple, "a business man upon a business errand," has no trouble securing a visa from his government, the same government that attempted to refuse visas for writers to attend the Madrid Congress because cultural reasons were suspect. The collusion of state, church, and business is depicted in the details of the journey of Mr. Semple, a shipping man. He secures help in making the right contacts from the senior partner of a firm that deals in church and table wines. He crosses the Spanish border from Portugal with a German businessman in a Mercedes-Benz driven by one of the British nonintervention observers: "Herr Beinlein exposed his project for opening, quite soon, an automobile works in Spain, . . . and though Mr. Semple did not go so far as to offer Herr Beinlein a donation towards this project, he thought about doing so; for as a patriot he could not be unaware of storm-clouds on Britain's horizon, and it seemed to him there was much to be said for placing a little nest-egg abroad" (*A Garland of Straw*, 125). That those who went to Spain to defeat the republic did so for economic exploitation and to play war games could not be clearer; the English business and German military social hour in the hotel in which no Spaniards are allowed breaks up when Semple "insults" two swarthy Italian generals by mistaking them for Spanish generals. Warner ends with an indictment of the Spanish church: a parade tomorrow of Moorish troops will end when the archbishop of Salamanca presents "them *all* with medals of the Sacred Heart" (130).

Like the other stories in *A Garland of Straw* (1943), "With the Nationalists" exposes the hatred and petty tyranny of fascism. That fascism, for Warner, is one man despising another man, one woman asserting her will over another woman, one human claiming superiority over another human is depicted in the opening story from which the volume takes its title. Miss Woodley hallucinates about the children she never had as she spends her days committed to a "home." Her sister had prevented her from marrying a man beneath her station—a man with madness in his family. Kitty visits Miss Woodley, "an insatiable ravening of triumph" upon her face. Warner leaves no question as to who is mad and to the irony of appearance and names.

Interspersing the stories of the Spanish Civil War among those with World War II as their setting, Warner makes the wars seem like one war with fascism, as those from the Left perceived might be the case. But their governments did not heed them, and the non-intervention agreement allowed the Germans free rein; Janet Flanner cites Hermann Göring's testifying at the Nuremburg trials to sending "his young fliers in rotation to Franco's war so that they could try their wings in a sort of rehearsal" (115).

Warner satirizes the contemporary scare of the "Red Menace" in two of the stories in *A Garland of Straw*. In "A Red Carnation," a young and innocent German soldier discovers not communist troops, which his government had portrayed as the enemy, nor the romantic Spain of his daydreams, but the stench and hatred of the poor. For Warner, poverty and ignorance were the real enemies not only of the Spanish people but of the young and working class of all nationalities. In another story, Warner depicts the English fear of the communists and the hypocrisy, smugness, ignorance, and power of the aristocrats in England who admired and curried favor with the German fascists. A mother writes to a friend to protest the schoolmistress's attempts to raise money for educational supplies for Spain: "I happened to discover that that Miss Hopgood was actually attempting to send *chemicals* to the Spanish Reds, passing them off as coloured inks and mathematical instruments for schools (as if people of that sort cared two-pence for education!) and it was all being got up as a tribute . . . to some Bolshevist schoolmaster" ("The Language of Flowers," in *A Garland of Straw*, 45). Instead, government officials and elected members of Parliament make arrangements to send flowers to be placed on the grave of the German governess of Queen Victoria as a "*simple*, peaceful gesture, recalling how much the two nations have in common" (46). Mendelssohn's grave was originally suggested because his Elijah was so popular, but, of course, he was "racially ineligible" (47).

The "racially ineligible," the economically disfranchised, and the others consigned to rap at the back door of the castle are Warner's subjects. Her view of history and of persons through the "pantry window" enabled her to challenge received opinion and to portray her characters as individuals and not stereotypes. Except for a few of the stories in *A Garland of Straw* in which her characters become mouthpieces for the ideas she is attacking or supporting, Warner's fictions of social protest are not marred by the perspective so often objected to in the leftist writers of the 1930s. Warner's view of history did not arise out of the guilt Virginia Woolf identified in "The Leaning Tower" and to which many admitted.[6] Nor was Warner an ideologue, turning as did W. H. Auden, Aldous Huxley, and others to some other "god" when that of communism and socialism failed. Although she issued a plea for "Art for Man's sake," literature with "an underlying morality, a resolute understanding and intolerance of social conditions" ("Underlying Morality"), the right subject or theme with no sense of art is only propaganda in Warner's view (see "Competition"). Warner treated her partisan choice of subjects and themes with ironic wit; she accepted human weakness but was intolerant of hypocrisy. She was not a sentimental romanticist. In content and form—her stories most often blend social realism and comic fantasy—she wrote against the grain. But the writers of social and literary history are uncomfortable with the idea that a woman should be taken seriously in matters of politics and social justice. Thus "critical fashion," as Arnold Rattenbury states, has either "mostly disguised this blatant fact [Warner's political commitment to the others of society] or blatantly ignored this author" (46).

Notes

I owe much to Jane Marcus, who, having heard about my interest in Sylvia Townsend Warner, spurred me on to learn more about Warner and the Spanish Civil War, and to William Greenway, who took time to read Warner, and to him, Bege Bowers, and Betty Greenway for responding to my essay. I thank also Hildegard Schnuttgen, reference librarian, for securing the books and essays I needed through interlibrary loan.

1. Jan Montefiore in *Feminism and Poetry* surveys the omission of women from literary-social histories and anthologies of the 1930s that purport to tell the story of those who wrote in that politically conscious decade (20–25).

2. For a fuller treatment of Warner's address and the ways it expands and "brings up to date the history of women writers," see Marcus, "Still Practice."

3. See my essay "*Summer Will Show.*"

4. Because "Red Front!" has not been reprinted, I have included the entire text of this long poem:

These are the last lees of a poor vintage
That now we cajole
From the echoing cask, tilting it with coward care.
Yet whether we spill or spare the wine runs ever to waste.
Listless it dribbles out, listless are the lips that taste,
And hollow the echo of the cask rumbles despair into the soul,
Being so like the rolling of tumbrils, the approaching slow footfall of a drum.

> *Comrade, are you cold enough,*
> *Lean enough, bold enough—*
> *Hush!—to march with us to-night*
> *Through the mist and through the blight?*
> *Dare you breathe the afterdamp?*
> *Can your cunning foot the swamp*
> *Where you tread on the dead?—*
> *Red! Red!*

Who would have thought the blood of our friends would taste so thin?
Would so soon lose body, would even before them greyed—
Had time kept troth—discolour, dwindle, and pine
Into a shallow cider tanged with tin?
Who could forecast this malady of the vine,
Or guess that a draught so heady in its beginning
Should peter out into verjuice, and a bouquet
Of metal and decay?—
And that we who toasted them then should sit here dumb,
Unjoyed, and yet athirst, and yet dreading the jolted cask, dismayed
To stir in the stumbling echo the rolling of tumbrils, the sullen footfall
    of a drum?

> *Comrade, are you mired enough,*
> *Sad enough, tired enough—*
> *Hush!—to march with us to-night*
> *Through the mist and through the blight?*
> *Can the knitted heart sustain*
> *The long Northeaster of In Vain,*
> *The whining, whining wind unbinding?—*
> *Red! Red!*

Too heavily, oh, too heavily dunged was the vineyard!
Too much blood was poured, too many brains spattered,

Too thickly among the vinestocks heaped the docketed dead.
Too fulsomely the chemicals were sprayed,
Too many shards of iron and too much lead
Among the blood and the bones and the brains were scattered.
So grossly dunged, so cumbered, the roots were wronged,
For round them the debauched soil thick-tongued
Kept mumbling ever of corruption, and extolling the unnumbered fatness yet
    to come.

Comrade, are you scarred enough,
Grimed enough, hard enough
Schooled in solitary fight—
Hush!—to join our march to-night?
Though ten thousand march unknown
Round you, dare you march alone
And not dread the bonded tread?—
    Red! Red!

This is the saddest wine that ever was pressed in France.
At the vintaging politicians led up the dance
And set to partners while economists pirouetted.
With reddened hands and hems
The priests and sages made merriment in their hymns,
Man in God's image, saying, man at man's bidding,
Tumbled and trampled, ruined with rain or summerlong heaped and bletted,
Have poured such virtue into this draught
That those who drink it hereafter shall never know misgiving.
But it was madness we quaffed.
Maniac mirth and boasting, bewilderment and idiot doubt.
The blood of the dead drunk in the land of the living
Intimidated our veins, and whether we laughed
Or wept at the feast, dull slumber and hollow waking came after.
And now the wine that we cannot do without runs out.
We meet to contest the lees, with suspicion and loathing
As beasts at a carcass assemble we meet here grudging and glum;
Yet company we must, we dare not come alone.
Dried are the lips that taste, and the hands that fumble
The spigot tremble lest the echoing cask abetted
By tap of bone reply with the rolling of tumbrils near by, the imminent footfall
    of a drum.

Comrade, are you grim enough,
Taut to fighting-trim enough—
Hark!—to march with us to-day

On the tall Bastille of Nay?
There it bulks to overawe,
Old as law and foul as law;
From its narrow eyes of fear
Sharp machine-gun-glances peer,
It shall see us closer yet—
Forward! Shout the foe well-met!
And the dint of dark confront—
  Red! Red! Red Front!

See the hoary blank facade
Twitch as though it were dismayed,
Hear the tattered cheer within
Those walls from our imprisoned kin.
Shout again, and it will fall!

Comrade, with the first footfall
Of our marching purpose here,
Through the blight and through the sneer,
The downfall of this place began.
Underground the rumour ran,
Jarring with rhythm resolute
The fortress at its sullen root.
When we were ten the echo told,
These rebels march a hundredfold;
Far-off we trudged, and under cloak
Of secret, but the echo spoke—
Knock! Knock! Knock! Knock!
Our march was muddied in the swamp,
We stifled in the afterdamp,
How far? we said—and as we said
Our far-away and footsore tread
Already to the work was sped.
The pick was busy on the rock.

Comrade, have you bled enough,
Are your wounds red enough?—
Comrade, are you vowed enough,
Braced enough, proud enough—
Hark! to march while bugles play,
Banners beckon, crowds hooray,
To salute of open day?
Can you brook the aftermath,
Can your prudence map the path

As you stand in a land
Where the boundaries are gone,
Where the towers are crumbled down?—
Can the knitted heart rebuff
The fawning South that sighs, Enough!—
The wheedling, wheedling wind impeding?—
Dare you in the million-throng
Strive as you alone were strong,
And the brunt of day confront?—
      Red! Red! Red Front!

5. The following is the complete text of "In this Midwinter," also never reprinted:

In this midwinter, shepherds, not a lamb possibly.
No green thing, green not even on wintercoat churchyard yews.
Air-borne, a poison-gas bomb let fall accidentally
On our uplands has blasted the penned pregnant ewes.
Foot-rot, lung-rot, womb-rot, not a lamb this year, shepherds.
Light not lantern on such an idle errand.

In this midnight, shepherds, not a saviour possibly.
No godling, God not even in turncoat mufti of doubt.
Man having rationalized destruction inalienably
Needs God no further. See, not a King is out.
War, famine, pestilence, not a saviour now, shepherds.
Light not lantern on such an idle errand.

In this midwinter, comrade, a child certainly
This midnight midwifes. Tougher than God or beast man yet
Envoy on envoy aims to persuade futurity.
To those new eyes we bear our lantern's well-met.
Not lamb nor Lenin, maybe, but to co-heir of earth, comrade,
Plight we darkling our lantern's friendly assurance.

6. Warner's "An English Fable" wittily protests the Public Order Act (passed to curb the violence in the East End from demonstrations provoked by Mosley's anti-Semitic marches): now the government could ignore the problem and go hunting, leaving the sheep and dogs to assemble somewhere else another day.

Works Cited

Benjamin, Walter. "The Storyteller." In *Illuminations*, edited by Hannah Arendt. New York: Schocken, 1969.

Brothers, Barbara. "*Summer Will Show*: The Historical Novel as Social Criticism." In *Women in History, Literature, and the Arts*, edited by Lorrayne Baird-Lange and Thomas Copeland, 262–73. Youngstown: Youngstown State University, 1989.

Cunard, Nancy, ed. *Authors Take Sides on the Spanish Civil War*. London: Left Review, 1937.

Cunningham, Valentine, ed. *Spanish Front: Writers on the Civil War*. New York: Oxford University Press, 1986.

Day Lewis, Cecil. "English Writers and a People's Front." *Left Review* 2 (October 1936): 671–74.

Flanner, Janet. *Uncollected Writings, 1932–1975*. Edited by Irving Drutman. New York: Harcourt, 1979.

Hoskins, Katharine Bail. *Today the Struggle: Literature and Politics in England during the Spanish Civil War*. Austin: University of Texas Press, 1969.

McCarthy, Mary. Review of *Summer Will Show*, by Sylvia Townsend Warner. *Nation*, August 15, 1936, p. 191.

Marcus, Jane. "The Asylums of Antaeus: Women, War and Madness." In *The Differences Within: Feminism and Critical Theory*, edited by Elizabeth Meese and Alice Parker, 49–81. Amsterdam: John Benjamins, 1989.

———. "Still Practice, A/Wrested Alphabet." *Tulsa Studies in Women's Literature* 3 (Spring–Fall 1984): 79–97.

Millay, Edna St. Vincent. "Say That We Saw Spain Die." *Harper's* 177 (October 1938): 449–52.

Montefiore, Jan. *Feminism and Poetry: Language, Experience, Identity in Women's Writing*. London: Pandora, 1987.

Mora, Constancia de la. *In Place of Splendor: The Autobiography of a Spanish Woman*. New York: Harcourt, 1939.

Muste, John. *Say That We Saw Spain Die: Literary Consequences of the Spanish Civil War*. Seattle: University of Washington Press, 1966.

Rattenbury, Arnold. "Plain Heart, Light Tether." *PN Review 23* 8 (1981–82): 46–48.

Warner, Sylvia Townsend. *After the Death of Don Juan*. New York: Viking, 1939.

———. "Barcelona." *Left Review* 2 (December 1936): 812–16.

———. "Benicasim." *Left Review* 3 (March 1938): 841.

———. *Collected Poems*. Edited by Claire Harman. Manchester, Eng.: Carcanet, 1982.

———. "Competition in Criticism." *Left Review* 2 (January 1936): 178–79.

———. "The Drought Breaks." *Life and Letters Today* 21 (Summer 1937). Re-

printed in *Spanish Front: Writers on the Civil War*, edited by Valentine
Cunninhgam, 244–47. New York: Oxford University Press, 1986.

―――. "An English Fable." *Left Review* 3 (August 1937): 406.

―――. *A Garland of Straw: Twenty-Eight Stories*. New York: Viking, 1943.

―――. "Harvest in 1937. In *Penguin Book of Spanish Civil War Verse*, edited by
Valentine Cunningham, 233–35. Harmondsworth: Penguin Books, 1980.

―――. "In this Midwinter." *Left Review* 1 (January 1935): 101.

―――. *Letters*. Edited by William Maxwell. New York: Viking, 1983.

―――. "Red Front!" *Left Review* 1 (April 1935): 255–57.

―――. "Some Make this Answer." *Left Review* 2 (February 1936): 214.

―――. *Summer Will Show*. New York: Viking, 1936.

―――. "Sylvia Townsend Warner in Conversation." With Val Warner and Michael Schmidt. *PN Review 23* 8 (1981–82): 35–37.

―――. "Underlying Morality." Review of *New Writing III*, ed. John Lehmann.
Left Review 3 (July 1937): 367–68.

―――. "We Are Gentlemen." Review of *Spanish Testament*, by Arthur Koestler.
Left Review 3 (January 1938): 745–47.

―――. "What the Soldier Said." *Time and Tide*, August 14, 1937. Reprinted in
Spanish Front: Writers on the Civil War, edited by Valentine Cunninhgam, 92–
94. New York: Oxford University Press, 1986.

―――. "Women as Writers: The Peter Le Neve Foster Lecture." *Journal of the
Royal Society of Arts* 107 (May 1959): 378–86.

―――. "The Young Sailor." In *Scenes of Childhood*, 90–95. New York: Viking,
1982.

Woolf, Virginia. "The Leaning Tower." In *Collected Essays II*, 162–81. London:
Hogarth Press, 1966.

―――. *A Room of One's Own*. New York: Harcourt, Brace and World, 1929.

―――. *Three Guineas*. New York: Harcourt, Brace and World, 1938.

Chapter 15

. . . .

Mystery Stories

The Speaking Subject in Exile

Ingeborg Majer O'Sickey

To work on language . . . to labour in the *materiality* of that which society regards as a means of contact and understanding, isn't that at the very outset to declare oneself a stranger to language?
—Julia Kristeva, *Récherches pour une sémanalyse*

I n Marguerite Yourcenar's 1939 novel *Coup de Grâce*, Sophie is murdered at the end of the story when her assassin—who is also the
narrator—shoots point-blank into her face. Her killer ends the novel
with the statement, "One is always trapped, somehow, in dealings with
women" (151). The "I" in Ingeborg Bachmann's novel *Malina* (1971) dies
at the end of the novel; she walks into a crack in the wall and disappears.
The novel ends with the indictment "It was murder" (356). Even though
the crimes seem fairly clear-cut, a feminist strategy could be constructed
to read *Coup de Grâce* and *Malina* as murder mystery stories in search of
clues about the victim, the murderer, his methods, and the anatomy of the
crime.[1]

Up to a certain point, Bachmann helps in the reader's search for clues:
through her character named I, Bachmann exposes symbolic language as
the weapon that murders I. I provides the evidence, and the reader indicts
her male alterego (Malina), the Father, and her lover Ivan.[2] The "trial"
takes the length of the book. We know that she is killed by the Father,
Malina, and by Ivan—"somehow" pushed into a crack in the wall.[3] Bachmann thematizes I's journey into linguistic exile and final disappearance
into the wall as a woman writer's retreat from the hostile land of symbolic
language into the terrain of the unconscious; she traces I's struggle in the
phallogocentric world of words in an explicitly political way. I "understands" Bachmann's theme and purpose. Nevertheless, I disappears into a
space in the wall. It is not I who tells us that her death was by murder. The
mystery, then, is not who did it but who narrates the end of the story, if not
I?

Although *Coup de Grâce* fits the description of "murder" story, it does
not at first seem to be a *mystery* murder story: Yourcenar's gripping account of a young man caught in the aftermath of the Bolshevik revolution
around 1918 in Kurland shows clearly that Erick von Lhomond, the man
who narrates this story, is Sophie's murderer. There appears to be no
cover-up; the novel seems to be his alibi, which he uses to say something
like "yes I did it, but she deserved it." Erick's retrospective is, as Yourcenar
says, an "interminable confession" (5). In Yourcenar's novel symbolic
language is not explicitly revealed as the murder weapon. Not Yourcenar,
not the narrator, and certainly not Sophie suggests explicitly that Sophie's
death was caused by any other means than the pistol. Not even the reader
is invited, as in Bachmann's narrative, to investigate the murder: Erick
makes his confession to himself. Nevertheless, the dissatisfied reader asks
who was really killed and what was the real motive for this murder?

The feminist strategy is to read the story backward and try to find the killer's motive, that is, to name the terms of Sophie's exile. When we do this we learn that the crime is not an act committed so much at the end of the novel when Erick shoots into Sophie's face in the twisted deed he calls a "coup de grâce," an honorable blow to an "equal," but, paradoxically, a slow, deliberate killing in the act of creation. Is there no more mystery, then? The motive is hatred of women. The method is linguistic erasure finished off with a blow in the face. But what of Sophie? Can we recuperate Sophie from Erick's narrative kill?[4]

Mystery and Symbolic Discourse

Discourse, whether verbal or visual, fictive or historical or speculative, is never unmediated, never free of interpretation, never innocent.
—Susan Rubin Suleiman, *The Female Body in Western Culture*

To answer the question whether the reader can recuperate Sophie from Erick's narrative kill, I will first talk about mystery, considering mystery and linguistic exile as analogous. There are two different ways to look at mystery. One, a reaction to Erick's authoritarian discourse, insists on indeterminacy where Erick claims perfect clarity, but only to propose an equally unassailable assertion about Sophie and the terms of her linguistic oppression; mystery is proposed in the conventional sense as a stage on the way toward resolution or solution. This move, paradoxically, turns the reader into Sophie's exiler even as she or he is trying to retrieve Sophie from Erick's construction of exile.

A second way to look at mystery is more nearly to read the story in a way that refuses resolution but opts for multiplicity of meaning, an indefinite continuation of the mystery. This reading, which valorizes mystery, also refuses a return from exile because such a return must be illusory. It is this second way that I propose as the feminist reading strategy for *Coup de Grâce* and *Malina*. Our exile from meaning, our condition of lack, is a permanent feature of our being as speaking subjects and can be alleviated or illuminated only through a double movement that recuperates meaning (understanding the buried life of the semiotic) by a voluntary loss of it: that is, an embrace of our linguistic exile. We come a little closer to understanding mystery by naming the politics that shape Sophie's and I's linguistic exile and acknowledging our exiled condition as permanent.

Women and the semiotic share in a banishment; suppressed by symbolic discourse, or, as Kristeva has called it, the "phenotext," the semiotic ("genotext") is marginalized.[5] As outsiders, women, like the semiotic, have the potential to subvert. Being alien and critical vis-à-vis symbolic language, then, is to embrace exile (recognizing one's position as a split speaking subject) and to subvert symbolic discourse by recuperating the semiotic.

It has often been said that alienation from ourselves as speaking subjects—linguistic exile—is a human condition, implying that gender does not play a role in the forms this exile takes.[6] But linguistic exile is different for women. Women are exiled from symbolic language that structures law and social conventions, among which perhaps the most significant are parental and marital relationships. For women, exile from language means exile not so much from use of it as from the power to structure and restructure it. My point is not, then, that women fight to gain the right to use symbolic language in the same way men do. Rather, a way must be found to peel away the encrustations that the symbolic has layered over the semiotic and to name the politics of the symbolic investment at the same time that the positional and provisional nature of the self as a speaking subject is recognized.

To accept symbolic language uncritically as law is, among other things, to accept the fiction of the transcendental ego. It is to pretend that the speaking subject exists as a unified consciousness that can act as such without cost to other subjects. To speak from this position is to ignore that there is a problem in language, that a gap exists between the sign and the referent. Such repression means that the speaking subject must pretend to have full access to knowledge, must pretend that her or his subjectivity is intact, that nothing is hidden, unnameable. To keep this fiction alive, the one has to objectify the other. The major strategy used by those who insist on a unified subjectivity based on a metaphysics of presence is to show the other as lacking in some way. This lack is variously described: Freud and his followers say that women lack because they do not have a penis; others have claimed that women lack because they "refuse" logic or the symbolic phallus. Derrida has demonstrated that whatever women lack has been declared privileged in Western thought, a phenomenon he has aptly called phallocentrism. Dichotomies have been invented to codify an absence— women are called and treated as the absent other by the fully present one—based on man/woman oppositions in which the right side of the dichotomy is said to be lacking (culture/nature, ratio/emotion, logos/body, and on and on).[7]

Of course, to speak at all, the writer must posit a unified consciousness. If the writer recognizes and subsequently undermines this fiction (on the level of genre, theme, and/or syntax[8]), she or he will not victimize subjects into objects, standing over characters (sentences, words, readers) as all-powerful dictator. Writing that takes account of the speaking subject as in process/on trial—disruptive writing—depends, I think, in large measure on awareness of the nature of language as oppressive.

It is significant that both novels in which women's linguistic exile and speechlessness are evoked so dramatically were written by women writers who chose to live in exile (Bachmann in Italy and Yourcenar in the United States). The crises of Bachmann's and Yourcenar's characters, their attempts and failures to signify, clearly reflect their authors' relationships to language in their dominant cultures—their conscious or unconscious experience of language as oppressive. Although I read both female characters' position in the masculinist culture as alienated, their authors have very different conceptions of what it means to be linguistically exiled.[9]

Exiling Writers—Exiled Writers

Art—this semiotization of the symbolic—thus represents the flow of jouissance into language. . . . Art specifies the means—the only means—that jouissance harbors for infiltrating that order. In cracking the socio-symbolic order, splitting it open, changing vocabulary, syntax, the word itself, and releasing them from the drives borne by vocalic or kinetic differences, jouissance works its way into the social and symbolic.

—Julia Kristeva, *Revolution in Poetic Language*

Julia Kristeva argues that male authors provide the best examples of exploding the myth of the unified subject and questioning established patterns of discourse; in *The Revolution in Poetic Language* (1974), she gives examples of semiotic ruptures into the symbolic pattern in texts by male authors (Artaud, Joyce, Lautréamont, Mallarmé). Women, says Kristeva, are too faithfully grammatical, too outside of culture to create these ruptures. Their situation within male discourse does not allow them to do much more than "purge themselves in reminiscences and desperate attempts to create an identity of self" (Marks and de Courtivron, 166). Obviously, Kristeva's position on women's writing is extremely problematic. No one will argue her point that in many women writers' texts mindfulness of ethics, attendance to social constraints, grammaticality, and so on are obvious features of the writing: Yourcenar's is one example of a colonized voice. One obvious counter would be to say that most texts by men are marked by adherence to ethics, social constraints, and the like, but that is not the point. The point is, rather, that it is inaccurate to insist that women writers have not and are not now writing texts that challenge the law of the symbolic. It makes more sense to say that women writers subvert "differently" rather than not at all. As Jane Marcus suggests ("Alibis"), "The woman writer's voice is not only dialogic, but triologic, and we may call women's writing a *triologue* or a triple-tongued discourse with her culture. She is already in exile by speaking *his* tongue, so further conditions of exile simply multiply the number of her 'veils' and complicate the problem of exegesis." Rather than claim that women writers do not subvert the symbolic order, it is more productive to read women writers' texts differently.[10]

Kristeva's statement that women are in some sense always already exiled and estranged in and from the culture they inhabit (Marks and de Courtivron, 138) is echoed by several writers in this volume. But though Kristeva argues that this estrangement prevents women writers from de-centering the frozen oppositions of man/woman "because they [women] tend to identify with power after having rejected it" (166), several essays here argue successfully against that evaluation. Bachmann's work is one example that may speak for many women writers who identify power and then reject it.

Kristeva's blind spots in this regard are disturbing. Kristeva—an exile from Bulgaria, living in France, and writing in the language of her exile—has chosen to join the center of one part of the French Left intellectual scene. I would speculate that apart from pragmatic considerations, such as her work as a practicing psychoanalyst and the desire to be accessible to readers within the so-called New Philosophy, working on male avant-garde writers in French is a "calculated political decision on her part," as Alice Jardine says ("Opaque Texts," 112). Kristeva's methods of inquiry and her choice of mostly male avant-garde writers for analysis have caused many feminist critics in the United States to be suspicious of her work.[11]

For her marginalization of women's texts and her problematic stance toward women she has been exiled from much of North American feminist criticism. My position is that Kristeva's work is too rich for us to banish into exile: substantial parts of it can be used profitably in discussing women's narratives. I believe that it is necessary to disagree with her stand on some very important issues, such as her Maria-idealization ("Stabat Mater")[12] and her rationalization of Céline's anti-Semitism (*Powers of Horror*),[13] but that these disagreements need not prevent a productive engagement with her work.

The Reader's Exile

Some readers look for themselves in whatever they read, and find just what they're looking for. What they touch changes not into gold as it did for Midas but into their own *substance*.
—Yourcenar, *With Open Eyes* (emphasis mine)

Now totality is precisely what we seem not to have in the modern, differentiated world, a world of displacements and metonymies more than of clear paradigms. Everybody hungers for totalization, for synthesizing by some means or other—synchronic analysis, archetypal patterning, etc.—our lived experience.
—Juliet Flower MacCannell, "Kristeva's Horror"

Erick von Lhomond, Sophie's murderer and the narrator in Yourcenar's *Coup de Grâce*, is a master at creating discourse based on the metaphysics of presence I mentioned earlier. He structures everyone's—especially Sophie's—experience by insisting that his code be considered the norm for behavior, feelings, and thought and in this way marginalizes her as other. He does this, as we know from Yourcenar's disturbing *apologia* in the preface to *Coup de Grâce*, with Yourcenar's complete approval. I's co-murderers in *Malina*—her father with the capital F, Malina, her alter ego, and Ivan, her lover—are masters at othering also; they want to silence I and impose their version of the world onto her reading and writing of the text. The difference is that whereas the I in *Malina* is given a voice with which to tell about her murder by the symbolic order, Yourcenar and her narrator claim military immunity from "civilian" crimes. Disguising Sophie's murder as a political story of war, they do not allow her to have a voice with which to express her struggle.

Yourcenar's denial that sexual politics structures Sophie's murder is congruent with Yourcenar's conception of women's position in society; nowhere do we find Bachmann's understanding of women's linguistic exile. Indeed, in self-disclosures, especially in the interviews collected under the title *With Open Eyes* (1984), Yourcenar emphatically rejects the idea of women's linguistic exile. "I am opposed to particularism, whether it is based on nationality, religion, or species. So don't count on me to support sexual particularism either," she says in response to her interviewer's questions about feminism. "A good woman," she continues, "is worth just as much as a good man and . . . an intelligent woman is worth just as much as an intelligent man" (221). These statements are important to the reader of *Coup de Grâce* because they show that Yourcenar's and Erick's treatment of Sophie is a collaborative erasure.

The first time I read *Coup de Grâce*—in October 1984 in Jane Marcus's seminar "Experimental Women Writers" at the University of Texas—I knew very little about Yourcenar except that she is a woman, a writer, Belgian from her mother's side, French from her father's, and that because of the outbreak of World War II she emigrated from France to the United States to live in Mount Desert, Maine.[14] Since then, I have read the collected interviews (which I privately renamed "With *Closed* Eyes") as well as her novels and essays, including her literary "debut," *Alexis* (1929; 1984 English translation), and her historical novels *Memoirs of Hadrian* (1954) and *The Abyss* (1976), which have established her reputation in the English-speaking world.

When I read *Coup de Grâce* in October 1984, I was excited about it as an incisive, revealing critique of the patriarchy. Specifically, I saw this text as a brilliant demonstration of the coding of women in the language of patriarchy as territory, geographical terrain. I saw Yourcenar's "coup" in her identification of symbolic language as the military man's in which an equation of woman/mother and country is made explicit and the connection between the military man's language and his misogynistic view and treatment of women is made manifest. Indeed, these connections are so explicit that we cannot miss them; Erick talks about Sophie as military men talk about conquering a country, mapping and measuring a geographical terrain, exploring, trading, populating, and discarding it. Here are some examples:

> I am glad that I kissed her lips one time, at least, and her wild hair. If she were to remain like a vast country subdued by me but never possessed, I was to remember, in any case, the exact taste of her very mouth that night, and the warmth of her living flesh. (76)

When he [Erick's confrère, Franz von Aland, who had fallen in love with Sophie] was alone with me he seemed always on the verge of offering some humble apology, such as excursionists make who have ventured upon a *private road*. (60; my emphasis)

[Shortly before he shoots Sophie] I felt pangs of something like regret, absurdly enough, for the children that this woman might have borne, who would have inherited her courage, and her eyes. (150)

I should have abandoned Sophie whether I wished to or not, much as a ruler abandons a province too far from his center. (92)

During this first reading I took on Sophie's voice, arguing with Erick, voicing my distrust of his narrative throughout. I objected to his description of Sophie's rape by a drunken soldier, which he calls "her tragic misadventure," "that affair," "the incident," "her mishap," "her first disaster" (28, 30, 112), and to his descriptions of Sophie as a domesticated animal one might own—"I would touch her firm arms across from me on the garden table, much as I might have patted a horse or a fine dog recently acquired" (35). I also objected to his racial stereotyping of "Mother" Loew, the Jewish moneylender, "fairly drowned in her own fat," "revolting obsequiousness blended ... with truly Biblical hospitality" (112, 113).

Erick's identity is rooted in his hatred for women, Jews, and the "lower" classes (personified by the Reds). His is the generation of "noblemen," who, caught in the borderline country between the two wars, became the backbone of the SS, putting into practice their hatred of Jews and women under the banner of fascism. Indeed, reading Erick's "confession" evokes the narratives of the Freikorpsmen examined in Klaus Theweleit's *Male Fantasies*. Theweleit has researched the connection between fascism and misogyny and states as one of his theses that the beginnings of Nazi ideology can be found in these men's violent hatred of women. In Theweleit's analyses of biographical and fictional narratives of Freikorpsmen—many of whom became key figures in the Nazi party—women are seen as aggressors or the (usually nameless) obstacles that stand between the men's execution of duty and fulfillment of destiny as soldiers. One sentence in Barbara Ehrenreich's introduction to *Male Fantasies* (xiii) captures Erick's conception of women perfectly: "In the Freikorpsman's life, there are three kinds of women: those who are absent, such as the wives and fiancées left behind, and generally unnamed and unnoted in the Frei-

korpsmen's most intimate diaries; the women who appear in the imagination and on the literal battlefront as 'white nurses,' chaste, upper-class
German women; and, finally, those who are his class enemies—the 'Red
women' whom he faces in angry mobs and sometimes even in single
combat." Sophie's "crime" is that she subverts and transgresses the categories Erick uses to define women: she does not remain chaste, does not
stay home, and defects "down" to the working class.

The second time I read *Coup de Grâce*, I read the preface to the novel. At
every turn Yourcenar's remarks in the preface directly contradict my reading of the "main" text. In the preface I was told that the narrator was not at
all the fascist I take him to be. I was told that if I thought so, I was a "naïve"
reader. I was told that Erick's racism must be excused because he is
upholding the tradition of his caste. I was told that Yourcenar, too, judges
Sophie the "loose," neurotic woman Erick at times says she is. I was told
that it is Sophie who is the violent one of the two. I was told that I was
foolish even to think in terms of victim and victimizer, that the designation
itself is pointless. And finally, I was told that I had been wrong to read
Coup de Grâce as a political novel. These passages follow:

> A naïve reader might make a sadist of Erick . . . or might see him
> merely as a brute in military brass, precisely forgetting that no brute
> would ever be haunted by recollections of having caused suffering.
> And such a reader would mistake for a *professional anti-Semite* this
> aristocrat whose habitual irony toward Jews is a matter of caste, but
> who reveals his admiration for the courage of the Jewish money-
> lender, and who elevates her son, Gregory Loew, to the heroic circle
> of friends and enemies already lost in death. . . .
> If, on the contrary, he gives first place in his narrative to Sophie,
> depicting her sympathetically even in her *errings and her tragic excesses*,
> it is not merely because the young girl's love flatters or reassures him;
> it is because his code obliges him to treat with respect that adversary
> that every woman becomes for a man whom she loves but who does
> not love her. . . .
> At the point where they now stand [the moment when he is about to
> shoot her] it matters little which of the two deals death to the other, or
> which one is the victim. . . . With regret for having to underline, in
> closing, what ought to be apparent, I should mention that *Coup de
> Grâce* does not aim at exalting or discrediting any one group or class,

any country or party. The very fact that I have deliberately given Erick von Lhomond a French name and French ancestors (perhaps in order to credit him with that sharp lucidity which is not a particularly German trait) precludes any interpretation of him as either an idealized portrait or a caricature of *one type of German officer* or aristocrat. It is for value as a human, not political, document (if it has value), that *Coup de Grâce* has been written and accordingly should be judged. (Preface, n.p.; my emphasis)

One must ask how the difference between being a "professional" and a "nonprofessional" anti-Semite exonerates Erick. This question still bothers those who are concerned about the whitewash of Kurt Waldheim. And how are we to distinguish between "habitual irony toward the Jews" and the policies of the Nazis, that is, the concrete enactment of such an attitude. Furthermore, how can we disassociate Erick, who not only fought the Bolsheviks in Kurland but "worked" for Franco and "others," from the politics of the day merely because his surname is French? As the narrator introducing Erick's retrospective says, "He had taken part in the various *movements* in Central Europe which culminated in the rise of Hitler, and had *turned up* in the Chaco and in Manchuria before serving under Franco in Spain" (4; my emphasis). However the preface and the narrative itself attempt to depoliticize Erick's career as a soldier, these explanations are curiously shallow: people do not just "turn up" in "movements" such as the ones that led to the rise of Hitler. Quite the contrary, as Theweleit has shown, German soldiers after World War I became political soldiers and "constituted one of the formative elements of Nazism"; they were given the honorary title of "First Soldiers of the Third Reich" (22, 23). It is, therefore, extremely difficult not to read *Coup de Grâce* as a political document that accounts for a certain fascist personality. Indeed, one does not need outside sources such as the narratives Theweleit discusses for confirmation of *Coup de Grâce* as a political story and for the evaluation of Erick as a fascist. Yourcenar herself tells us that her sources for *Coup de Grâce* were eyewitness accounts, ordinance maps, and magazines. To prove to her reader that her account is historically sound, she says about the reception of *Coup de Grâce* by the soldier circle that the "men who had fought in those Baltic wars have graciously volunteered to tell me that *Coup de Grâce* corresponds to their own memories of those years" (Preface, n.p.). I have no reason to doubt that the soldiers recognized their reality in *Coup de Grâce*: as I mentioned earlier, Erick's narrative uncannily resembles those texts of the Freikorpsmen Klaus Theweleit explores in *Male Fantasies*.

Yourcenar's hairsplitting about what does and does not make a fascist alerts the reader to her bad faith. This red herring, designed to involve the reader in a pattern of hairsplitting, invites a repetition of Yourcenar's trivialization of the horrors of fascism. It is therefore necessary to step back and reflect on the effect that Yourcenar's citation of testimony by former soldiers in the Baltic wars has on the novel as a whole. Yourcenar's hint at this gallantry, at quiet discussion of books, mystifies not only the historical reality of the Baltic war, covering over the counterrevolutionary and mercenary character of Yourcenar's informants with the word *men*, but the historical reality to which the novel belongs as well. (As though *men* could mean anything but *our men*, the soldiers who, with this word, become not a faction bent on destroying another faction but the *totality*. With the word *men* used to refer only to the counterrevolutionary forces, Yourcenar denies the revolutionaries human status.) In a sense, Yourcenar's story of aging soldiers (presumably now far removed from the conflict of the Baltic), with leisure to read and comment on her book, serves to situate the novel in a different historical frame (one could say an ahistorical one) from the 1939 publishing of the novel that would necessarily invite comparison with the novels of the Nazi mythologizers.

Coup without Grâce: Joining Exile

> In the society of males there would be no genius; genius lives through the existence of the feminine. It is true; the existence of the feminine guarantees the asexuality of the spiritual in the world. Where a work, an action, arises without knowledge of this existence, there arises something evil, dead.
> —Walter Benjamin, "Socrates"

Yourcenar's *apologia* for Erick forces a reading of the novel on several levels. The meaning of the main text seemed suddenly shot through with contradictions.[15] A dialogue occurs between the novel and its preface. It is in the center of this dialogue (which must take into account the woman writer's "triple-tongued discourse") between the preface, the novel, and my reading that I locate women's linguistic exile. Sophie's "second" exile is located there: thrown into exile by the narrator, she is recuperated by the feminist reader's arguments with Erick's portrait of her, only to be brutally abandoned by Yourcenar in the *apologia* for Erick in the preface. The life jacket she is thrown in the interpretive space that exists between the text(s) and the reader is constructed by the feminist reader's analysis of the anatomy of Erick's crimes. And there are other exiles—the revolutionaries, "Mother" Loew, her son, and finally, the reader, who must cut herself free of the author's demands that she share in Yourcenar's sexism and racism.

The symmetry is diabolical: just as Erick attempts to control Sophie's experience on his terms, Yourcenar attempts to control the reader's. Erick constructs a fictional Sophie who makes an "error in judgment" for which she must be killed; ostensibly, her "erring" happens at the moment when she defects to the Bolshevik's side. Sophie as Erick's *territory* has been lost to the Reds. The reader who analyzes Erick's narrative in political terms has also made an error in judgment; her reading must be killed. Our erring happens at the moment when meaning as Yourcenar's *territory* has been lost to the feminist reader.

But this is not the only "crime" Sophie and the reader commit. "Going over to the other side" also means that we refuse to accept Yourcenar's and Erick's logocentric position. When Sophie and the reader defect, we violate a rule that both Yourcenar and Erick insist upon. This rule is significantly also encoded in terms of territory; both posit a unified, transcendental ego whose boundaries are solid, inviolable. To allow us to go over to the other side both politically and psychically would mean the collapse of symbolic control (theirs); it would mean that other subjectivities (ours), other perspectives, would have to be acknowledged. Barricaded behind the wall that attempts to guard the unified ego, Yourcenar "forgets" that discourse, in its multidialogic nature between subjects in process/on trial, cannot be controlled. (One aspect of this impossibility to control discourse is, of course, that the text no longer belongs to the author.)[16]

When we look at Sophie's political and psychical "crime," Erick's statement, "I should have abandoned Sophie whether I wished to or not, much as a ruler abandons a province too far from his center" (92), reveals his fear of Sophie as the other as a fear of losing identity. Erick's remark hints at a recognition of *self* as territory: Sophie is a province in the larger country, Erick. It is possible that Erick has some repressed notion of the composite nature of his own personality, of its indebtedness to the other, who alone is capable of telling him what he looks like on the outside.

Bakhtin calls this relational and composite quality of the self "trans-gredience."[17] If such an intuition can be attributed to Erick, it would help explain why Sophie must be killed. If identity is intuited to lie elsewhere, the only way to control identity is to control the subjectivities that contrib-ute transgredient elements to the self. Erick does this by choosing as comrades those who can be depended upon to mirror a self compatible with his own sense of self (Conrad, Franz, and his soldier men). In constructing a distorted portrait of a woman (who is, not incidentally, in love with him), Erick constructs a perfect transgredient—until Sophie defects, that is. (Although we are at one point invited to read her defection as an admission by Erick that Sophie had convictions "which were, after all, the one thing she had of her own," her sexual/textual liberation from Erick is revoked immediately when he says that her political convictions come from "ideas that Gregory Loew had implanted in her"—48, 49.) After Sophie's defection Erick must silence her—she is now a threat to his view of himself precisely because her axiological perspective, her reality, is so different. She has taken her intimate knowledge of him—which in-cludes her knowledge of Erick's romantic attachment to her brother Con-rad—she has taken his "self" into alien and hostile territory. This is, I suggest, one of Erick's key motives for killing Sophie. In a sense, Erick becomes aware of being exiled from self by Sophie's action and must retrieve himself from exile not only by exiling Sophie linguistically (since by not letting her speak he can construct her view of him) but by *ingesting* her, by forcing her dangerous subjectivity to "live" only *in* him, only *within* the narrative he constructs.

In our arguments with Erick and Yourcenar, in the space of the preface and *Coup de Grâce*, the feminist reader can only guess at the "real" Sophie. But we can create a space of compassion and understanding for her linguistic exile in which we can look at Yourcenar's narrative and speculate on the reasons for her own colonized voice. We can see Sophie as the silent/silenced "I," who mysteriously disappears into the wall in Bach-mann's novel, and we can see Yourcenar as Malina, I's alter ego. The semiotic celebrated in *Malina* is suppressed in *Coup de Grâce*. But Your-cenar cannot barricade Sophie into a crack in the wall entirely; as subver-sive readers, we can, as Jean Rhys did when she retrieved Bertha Mason from the *Jane Eyre*ian attic in her novel *Wide Sargasso Sea*, give Sophie's murder a history.

Kinds of Death

A longing to cross borders arises in us. . . . Caught between borders we focus
our vision on the perfect, the impossible, the unreachable, whether that be in
love or freedom or in pure greatness. In the struggle of the impossible with the
possible lies the death of another possibility.
—Ingeborg Bachmann, *Werke*

Whereas Yourcenar gives no indication that as a woman and a woman
writer she feels at odds with the country of her birth or her culture,
Bachmann's narrative stands as a manifesto of the impossibility for a
woman writer to write the story that the (masculinist) world wants. History's complicity in women's linguistic exile is shown in her work as its
failure to acknowledge women's status as exiled speaking subjects. Bachmann's is a feminist aesthetics of retrieval and resistance in that she
recuperates the banished semiotic in her texts by naming the terms of the
woman's linguistic exile as political and by rejecting the narrative of history
as oppressive discourse and showing it as falsifying. Bachmann carried out
this aesthetic in her life as well. One of her rejections was to leave her
native Austria, an exile that liberated her. I use the word *liberated* ad-
visedly; I do not want to pass over the personal losses associated with the
deep understanding of one's own culture as profoundly alienating or to
gloss over the grief connected with the decision to leave that culture.
Nevertheless, I know from my own experience that distance from one's
own culture sets experiences of that culture into sharper relief. And when
exile is experienced, at least in part, as a liberation, it may be more
productive for women writers than for male writers who have left a culture
that they could at some point call their own.[18] Bertolt Brecht's, Thomas
Mann's, and Ernst Bloch's exiles in the United States come to mind.
Bachmann has said that she feels that she is able to recreate the pain, the
oppression, the sheer impossibility of being a woman in the dominant
culture better when at a distance from that culture (*Wahre Sätze*, 65).

Bachmann, Austrian by birth, chose Rome as her place of exile and
lived there from 1965 until she died tragically in a fire at the age of forty-
seven in 1973. Kristeva's formulation, that to work on language is to
declare oneself a stranger to language, is woven throughout Bachmann's
work. More than that, Bachmann has stated that she felt estranged from
her native language: "For me it has been very difficult to write in this
German language, because on the one hand, my relationship to Germany

is based on this language but my field of emotions and my experiences are from a different country. I'm from a small country, Austria, which has removed itself from history, yet carries with it an overwhelming and monstrous past" (63). German is also the language of the country that sent soldiers to Austria for the 1938 *Anschluss*, as Hitler called the Nazi invasion. *Anschluss*, literally translated, means to join to—as one train is joined to another train, it means to connect—as in the connection a traveler makes by transferring from one train to another. As with so many words coined in Hitler's Germany, *Anschluss* in no measure conveys the psychical violence through infiltration of thought or the physical violence experienced by those who were persecuted because of their political and/or racial identity; *Anschluss* does not give us a sense of the fear, the anguish, and the anger many Austrians experienced when German soldiers marched into their small country, nor does it even hint at the alienation Austrians resistant to Nazism felt toward those Austrians who welcomed Hitler's troops. In 1938 Austria's *Anschluss* began on March 13. The invasion into Bachmann's birthplace, Klagenfurt, irrevocably shattered and ruptured Bachmann's childhood. In her short story "Jugend in einer österreichischen Stadt" ("Youth in an Austrian city") Bachmann makes this rupture immediate and material in such a way that her reader can never again think of Bachmann without also visualizing her twelve years old in Klagenfurt in 1938. Neither can her reader ever again read or use the word *Anschluss* "innocently."[19]

The story is important in Bachmann's *oeuvre* also because it is here that she articulates for the first time the idea that fascism begins in the family. In an interview she said: "Fascism doesn't begin with the terrorism about which one can read in every newspaper. It begins in the relationship between one man and one woman. Fascism is the first thing in the relationship between a man and a woman and I have tried to say in this chapter [in *Malina*] that in this society there is always war" (*Wahre Sätze*, 144).[20] This conception of fascism, which can be found in all her fiction, is always problematized on the level of language and is intricately bound up with her understanding of women's exiled status in society and culture. In her short stories, especially in "Alles" ("Everything") and "Undine geht" ("Undine leaves") from the collection *Das dreissigste Jahr* (1961), Bachmann's insight into language as the male act of setting down of predicates, that is, the setting down of law and order, especially as these determine the terms of gender relations, finds its expression for the first time. From this very important articulation of language's role in structuring codes of male/

female relationships that results in women's homelessness, Bachmann began work in the mid-1960s on a novel cycle, initially to be titled *Todesarten* (*Kinds of Death*), in which she treats the connections between speech, speechlessness, and death. In *Malina*, the only completed novel of the cycle (*Der Falls Franza* and *Requiem für Fanny Goldmann* are fragments), the narrating "I" asks the question posed in one way or another throughout the *Todesarten*: "Who invented writing? What is writing? Is it something one owns? Who was it that first demanded that we be exiled from it? Allons-nous à l'Esprit? Are we of an inferior race?" (*Malina*, 334).

The Return to the *Chora*

There is no concept "I" that incorporates all the *I*'s that are uttered at every moment in the mouths of all speakers in the sense that there is a concept "tree" to which all the individual uses of *tree* refer. . . . Then, what does *I* refer to? To something very peculiar which is exclusively linguistic: *I* refers to the act of individual discourse in which it is pronounced, and by this it designates the speaker. . . . The reality is literally true that the basis of subjectivity is in the exercise of language.
—Emile Benveniste, *Problems in General Linguistics*

On one level, *Malina* is the story of the relationship between three people: I, Ivan, and Malina. I tells the story of her life with Malina and her love affair with Ivan. On another, much more illusive level, the novel tells the story of I's perception of these relationships. As Ellen Summerfield says, "It is not possible to decide where the moment of inception [of reality] is located, whether the psychical state creates and undermines the relationships or whether the relationships awaken (and realize) interior tendencies and possibilities to create the subjectivity anew. In the novel these two belong together and stand in a dialectical relationship to each other" (109). These diverse levels in the novel serve as more than mere vehicles to express a post-Modern sensibility; it is on this second, illusive level that linguistic exile is most forcefully evoked.

Even if Bachmann's narrator is not able to escape her linguistic exile, Bachmann translates her own linguistic exile into a new discursive space for the reader. Bachmann's crucial strategy in creating a new space lies in her splitting of character into the symbolic (Malina) and the semiotic (I) selves. That the two selves are not equally valued by society is made clear early on when I says about her relationship to her alter ego, Malina: "I was from the very start beneath him, and I must have known from the very beginning that he [Malina] would be my end" (14).[21]

I's erasure by her alter ego at the end of the novel is prefigured in I's narrative of her dreams, which fills the entire second chapter of the novel and is entitled "The Third Man."[22] I's dreams develop Bachmann's theme of I's—and women's—linguistic exile. Exile is made palpable in that I is able to recount but not analyze the dreams that tell of the terms of this exile. In this powerful chapter the connection of linguistic exile and fascism becomes clear as I recounts dreams in which the Father becomes alternately fascist in charge of gas chambers, inquisitor, opera director, censor of language, and book burner. The Father has torn out I's tongue so she cannot speak; he has burned her books so she cannot read; he has taken words away from her so she cannot write. I sees her self and experience as splintered, difficult to fit into sentences, into one perception. Her vision of herself as heterogeneous results in a dominance of genotext—in fragmentation of language, repetitions, silences. Malina, on the other hand, tries to force both selves and their experiences into an artificial whole. I comments several times in her narrative on Malina's attempts at symbolic control. She says, "it is Malina who doesn't let me tell it" (265); "I wanted to tell it, but I won't do it"; "you alone disturb my memory, you can take the stories over, from which big history is made" (335). It is clear that Malina has difficulties dealing with I's narrative, which in its disjointed, fragmented fashion is altogether too dangerous, too semiotic for him. As Allon White says, "Any modification in language, particularly infractions of syntactic laws, are a modification of the status of the subject . . . [that] destabilizes the relations of reason and calls into question the fixed boundaries of subject and object, cause and condition" (1). Malina cannot let I tell her story because her telling will endanger his carefully constructed metaphysics.

Bachmann's strategy of splitting her character into the semiotic and the symbolic goes beyond a psychological insight that is at least as old as Sigmund Freud. Her disruptions of the symbolic by destabilizing relations of reason and putting into question the fixed boundaries of male and female, of subject and object, become even more subversive by her choice of a female name for the male alter ego. By naming the male alter ego "Malina," Bachmann points out the female character's internalization of symbolic discourse and presents us with interruptures that we are invited to recognize as our own. She identifies I (the semiotic) as subordinated to

Malina (the symbolic) in Western culture and thus expands our insight into I's personal linguistic exile to a general understanding of women's linguistic exile. This understanding is created in several ways. First, Bachmann invites the reader to identify with Malina by creating the desire to solve the mystery of the split nature of the narrator. It is a *whole* subjectivity I want from the narrative, not a fragmented one. Second, Bachmann creates an identification between me and the narrator/character I. In this essay and in my notes about I all the verbs I use to describe I's actions, feelings, and thoughts disrupt the syntax of my narration of her experience. When the pronoun *I* is coupled with the third person verb form, symbolic control breaks down and the status of the subject becomes uncertain. This disruption happens at the moment when I interact with Bachmann's text.[23] I, the character/narrator "becomes" me not writing grammatical English. This disruption is based, as Emile Benveniste has shown, on the inherent vulnerability of an identity constructed through language. According to this view, we are subjects by virtue of a perpetually renewed identification with the first person pronoun, which refers not to our person but to an instance of discourse.

I's experiences begin to be mine, but, of course, not really. In this "not really" lies the brilliance of Bachmann's narrative; not a Hegelian synthesis but a Brechtian (or Marxian) "synthesis" takes place. Bachmann uses the name I as the *Verfremdungseffekt* (alienation effect) that keeps the reader from identifying with I in a seamless and unreflected transference, pointing out that I (the narrator) and I (the reader) can never be one because subjectivity is always in process/on trial. Perhaps in this impossibility of "fusion" Bachmann points out that the reader's inability to identify with a narrator named I is an instance of the degree to which the reader herself is alienated from what is, by definition, most intimate, the reader's "I-ness," her subjectivity. "My" identity suddenly comes to seem not "mine" but something constructed by the abstract rule system given in language. This alienation from the I may also serve Bachmann to make an essential point about accession to linguistic/social subjectivity: as Kristeva ("The Speaking Subject," 214–15) and others have shown, some sacrifice of *pre*-linguistic drives, bodily possibilities, and so on is always necessary. Accession to language is always simultaneously appropriation of a socially given subjectivity and alienation from a preverbal "self." The semiotic ruptures that are created by the subject-verb disagreement disrupt our notions of the unified speaking subject, alienating us from Malina's (and our own) desire for symbolic control and providing us with an opportunity to expand our understanding of the nature of our own linguistic exile. For the reader, then, I's disappearance into the wall has created a new space for experience; the verbal experience of the narrating I, divided into the female and the male halves, can become a reader's experience of linguistic alienation and stands in its form of duality as a divided experience, as a subversion of the discourse of the unified subject.

Murdered, I disappears into a crack in the wall. Malina, her male alter ego, remains. But he is not the one who narrates the end of I's story.[24] And this is where the mystery lies: who writes about I's disappearance into the wall, if not I? The mystery cannot be definitively solved for reasons I outlined at the beginning. To claim to solve the mystery would be to deny the subversive possibilities of I's narrative (and the semiotic); assimilated into the symbolic order by symbolic language, the semiotic would be tamed. We can only suggest some possible ways of reading. We might say that the crack in the wall into which she disappears is a metaphor for I's vagina,[25] that is, that I disappears into her vagina because her sexuality has been silenced by socially constructed versions. This reading recalls Cixous's statement in *La Jeune née* that "in censoring the body, breathing and speech are censured at one and the same time" (179). Perhaps I's murder can be seen as Bachmann's statement that I can no longer sustain the necessary collaboration with the symbolic once she has named the terms of her exile and exposed the modus operandi of the trinity (The Father, Ivan, and Malina).

I's death, her disappearance into the wall, then, must ultimately be seen as a displacement of the semiotic by the symbolic. Still, I's narrative has created a space for the reader which invites an understanding of the repression of the semiotic. I's disappearance into her "own" sexuality can thus be interpreted as her return into the *chora*:[26] residing in the wall of the womb, the semiotic, as a form of mystery, it has made itself unavailable to male (Malina's) rationality.

Notes

I especially wish to thank Jane Marcus for her critique on final versions of this essay and for her inspiring comments. I am also indebted to Douglas Anderson and Angela Ingram for valuable suggestions and editorial support. All translations from foreign-language sources are my own.

1. Vanderbeke (109–18) also reads *Malina* as a mystery murder story by tracing the different temporal levels of remembering the self by the narrating I.

2. I agree with Jane Marcus that the name "Ivan"—the Anglo-Saxon John and Germanic Hans—is Everyman and is on some levels allegorical. In Bachmann's short story "Undine geht" ("Undine leaves"), which precedes *Malina* by eight years, a similar device is used: Undine's polemical love declarations address *one* Hans and *all* Hanses.

3. The Father's violence in I's fatherdreams is not (as it has been read by some critics) the particularized violence of a biological father toward his daughter. Weigel (76) also treats the Father's violence in I's fatherdreams as the destructiveness that inheres in the law of the symbolic Father in the Lacanian sense.

4. I am grateful to Jane Marcus for suggesting that although another Sophie needs to be imagined when readers necessarily question Erick's portrayal of Sophie, the feminist reader must be careful not to fall into the trap of constructing a monolithic version of a woman figure.

5. The terminology *semiotic* and *symbolic* is Julia Kristeva's (*Revolution in Poetic Language*, 21–106). By *genotext* Kristeva means text dominated by the semiotic; by *phenotext* she means text dominated by the symbolic (see chapter 12 in *Revolution*).

6. An excellent example of the discussion of the speaking subject's alienation from the self as male is given by Lemaire (68): "The symbol is different from what it represents, this is its condition; thus if the subject who is called 'John' or who translates himself in discourse as 'I' saves himself through his nomination insofar as he inscribes himself in the circuit of exchange, he becomes, on the other hand, lost to himself, for any mediate relationship imposes a rupture of the inaugural continuity between self and self, self and other, self and the world." That her discussion of the symbolic source of individuation and of social identity as entailing the repression of that which does not "fit" does not differentiate on the basis of gender is in turn an enactment of the point I make above. John, as Every*man* stands for all.

7. It is significant that Bachmann's work, beginning with her story "Alles" ("Everything") prefigures and, at times, runs parallel to Derrida's identification of the oppressiveness inherent in oppositions based on the metaphysics of presence in *Of Grammatology*. In her novel *Malina* and the fragment *Der Fall Franza*, Bachmann thematizes the effect on women of logocentric thought inherent in the metaphysics of presence.

8. For a detailed discussion of this process, see Kristeva's chapter 5 in *Revolution in Poetic Language*. For a condensed argument, see Kristeva, "The Speaking Subject," 219.

9. In the context of my discussion of linguistic exile, it is important that I recognize that my identification of the terms of linguistic exile is not disinterested. See also Marcus's call to feminist critics for special sensitivity to self-interest as they discuss exiles ("Alibis").

10. Alice Jardine is one critic who recuperates Kristeva's notion of the semiotic's potential for social disruption for women writers such as Woolf and Wittig ("Pre-

Texts," 230–36). See also Marcus's identification of the semiotic modality in Djuna Barnes's *Nightwood* ("Laughing at Leviticus") and discussion of Virginia Woolf's use of the semiotic (*Virginia Woolf*). Makiko Minow-Pinkney's *Virginia Woolf and the Problem of the Subject* also makes use of Kristeva's idea of the semiotic.

11. One critic who frequently comments on Kristeva's methods is Gayatri Chakravorty Spivak. In "The Politics of Interpretations," she takes Kristeva to task especially for lacking "a political, historical, or cultural perspective on psychoanalysis as a movement" (278) in "Psychoanalysis and the Polis." In "French Feminism in an International Frame," Spivak accuses Kristeva of affinity with the very Sinophiles of the nineteenth century whom Kristeva criticizes in *About Chinese Women* and charges that Kristeva "prefers this misty past [matrilinear prehistory] to the present" (138).

12. Jane Marcus (review of *The Female Body in Western Culture*) points out the irony of Kristeva's criticism of women writers as colonized voices by comparing Kristeva's vision of women in "Stabat Mater" to Yourcenar's in *Coup de Grâce*.

13. Some responses to Kristeva's analysis of Céline's work in *Powers of Horror* follow: Juliet Flower MacCannell's fine review of *Powers of Horror* ("Kristeva's horror") begins with MacCannell's recognition of Kristeva's passionate involvement in the speaking subject and ends by charging: "Now it is not at all certain that the restaging of the fascist fantasy—and the analyst's mimetic identification . . .— will effect a cure at the *cultural* (written) level in the same manner as it might in the situation of analysis. What is certain, in fact, is that the transference can only go the other way, the wrong way: can writing love its reader? For Kristeva has clearly come to love deeply her analysand, Céline is the abject of desire" (347).

About Kristeva's treatment of Céline in *Powers of Horror*, Spivak ("Politics of Interpretations," 127) says sensibly, "Who is the excluded other that privileges interpretation? Not the writer, in this case Louis Ferdinand Céline, whose abject-transcending paranoia, otherwise known as *anti-Semitism*, the analyst-critic interprets for us through a somewhat positivist analysis of sentence structure" (my emphasis). Alice Jardine's discussion ("Opaque Texts") of Kristeva's ethics is revealing. On one hand, she criticizes Kristeva's choice of male authors' texts for analysis ("One may certainly criticize her lack of attention to women subjects and their texts—I certainly do," 110). On the other hand, she glosses over the problem of Kristeva's anti-Semitism in *Powers of Horror*: "As for exploring the intricacies of this new 'male condition,' [abjection] I will leave you to the text" (112).

Toril Moi, too, evades the issue: she faults Kristeva for her "alarming fascination with the libertarian possibilities of American-style late Capitalism" but adds, "much of her [Kristeva's] recent work, like *Pouvoirs de l'horreur* . . . could be valuably appropriated for feminism" (168).

14. Yourcenar's success in the English-speaking world rests on her favorite genre, the historical novel. This significant political fact resonates also in Your-

cenar's 1980 election to the prestigious Académie française and takes on double significance because she is the first woman to be included in this male club since its establishment 345 years ago.

15. Judith L. Johnston's insightful essay "Marguerite Yourcenar's Sexual Politics in Fiction," is a strong argument for reading *Coup de Grâce* as a political document. Johnston does not, however, address Yourcenar's colonized authorship and prefers simply to state that she disagrees with Yourcenar's revisions of the novel in the preface: "Though her preface to the 1981 translation denies any political value to this human document, the mutual bonding of authoritarian and submissive personalities portrayed in the love triangle of Erick, Sophie, and Conrad certainly derives from a political critique of her culture" (1).

16. Yourcenar's difficulty in letting go of her text is also evident in her collaboration in nearly all the translations of her books.

17. I am grateful to Douglas Anderson for suggesting this line of thought and for pointing out the relevance of Bakhtin's idea of the "transgredient" for an analysis of Erick's motives. For a detailed discussion of the Bakhtinian "transgredience," see Todorov, 95–96, 100–101.

18. Gabriele Kreis's *Frauen im Exil* (1984) is a fine discussion (the first in the German language) of women in exile from Nazi Germany. Some of the women she talked with are wives of famous men (Ernst Bloch, Leon Feuchtwanger); their status as exiles in the United States has never been the subject of any discussions.

19. A partial list of the words coined by the Nazis appears in Anti-Defamation League of B'nai B'rith, 109–10. The contrast between the literal translation and the real meaning shows the alienation from actual meaning that occurs in this kind of language use. In our own time, the language used in the United States to talk about Vietnam and the Vietnamese and, more recently, the language used in the Iran-Contra hearings is a chilly reminder that American English, too, hides violence in "neutral" terms. Some examples from the Holocaust include *Sonderaktionen*: special actions = special mission to kill Jews; *Endlösung*: final solution = the decision to kill all Jews; *Hilfsmittel*: auxiliary equipment = gas vans for murder; *Exekutivmassnahme*: executive measure = order for murder; *Ausschaltung*: elimination = murder of Jews; *Umsiedlung*: resettlement = order for murder; *Liquidiert*: liquidated = murdered.

20. Virginia Woolf's 1938 *Three Guineas* is, as far as I know, the first articulation of the inception of fascism in the family. It is likely that Bachmann read *Three Guineas*.

21. In a by now familiar move by a male critic, Helmut Heißenbüttel comments on I's death as the necessary death of a diseased part of the character I/Malina (25–26).

22. Angela Ingram's observation that there are striking similarities between I's ending and Harry Lime's first appearance in the Orson Welles movie *The Third*

Man is well taken. Bachmann's use of the title may well be an allusion to this movie. It may also refer to the Trinity composed of the Father, the Son, and the Holy Ghost.

23. H.D. similarly subverts the symbolic in *HERmione* in the play with the third person pronoun her/HER. In her fine essay "Palimpsest of Origins in H.D.'s Career" (esp. 64), Susan Stanford Friedman analyzes the effect of H.D.'s disruption of the symbolic in *HERmione* and points out that the relations of power are disturbed and relocated through language.

24. The semiotic and the symbolic modality in the production of language cannot be separated; their dialectical conflict constitutes the signifying process (see esp. chapter 10 in Kristeva, *Revolution*). The claim that it is Malina who makes the comment on I's death (as Heißenbüttel and Summerfield argue) must therefore be refuted.

25. I thank Jane Marcus for suggesting this line of thought.

26. For a brief explanation of Kristeva's use of the term *chora* see Roudiez in Kristeva, *Desire in Language*, 6: "The semiotic process relates to the *chora*, a term meaning 'receptacle,' which she borrowed from Plato, who describes it as 'an invisible and formless being which receives all things and in some mysterious way partakes of the intelligible and is most incomprehensible.'"

Works Cited

Anti-Defamation League of B'nai B'rith. "The Holocaust, 1933–1945." In *Teaching about the Holocaust and Genocide*, 109–10. Albany: State Education Department, 1985.

Bachmann, Ingeborg. *Das dreissigste Jahr*. Munich: Piper Verlag, 1961.

———. *Malina*. 1971. Edited by Christine Koschel, Inge von Weidenbaum, and Clemens Münster. Munich: Piper Verlag, 1978.

———. *Werke*. Edited by Christine Koschel, Inge von Weidenbaum, and Clemens Münster. Munich: Piper Verlag, 1978.

———. *Wir müssen wahre Satze finden. Gespräche und Interviews*. Edited by Christine Koschel and Inge von Weidenbaum. Munich: Piper Verlag, 1983.

Benveniste, Emile. *Problems in General Linguistics*. Translated by Mary Elizabeth Meek. Coral Gables: University of Miami Press, 1971.

Cixous, Hélène, and Catherine Clément. *La Jeune née*. Paris: Union Générale d'Éditions, 1975.

Derrida, Jacques. *Of Grammatology*. Translated by Gayatri Chakravorty Spivak. Baltimore: Johns Hopkins University Press, 1976.

Friedman, Susan Stanford. "Palimpsest of Origins in H.D.'s Career." *Poesis* 6 (1985): 64–66, 71.

Geary, Edward J., and Robert R. Nunn. *The Yourcenar Collection*. Brunswick, Maine: Bowdoin College, 1984.

Heißenbüttel, Helmut. "Über Ingeborg Bachmanns Roman '*Malina*.'" *Text + Kritik 6*. Munich: Richard Boorberg Verlag, 1971.

Höller, Hans. *Ingeborg Bachmann*. Frankfurt am Main: Athenäum Verlag, 1987.

Jardine, Alice. "Opaque Texts and Transparent Contexts: The Political Difference of Julia Kristeva." In *The Poetics of Gender*, edited by Carolyn J. Heilbrun and Nancy K. Miller, 109–23. New York: Columbia University Press, 1986.

———. "Pre-Texts for the Transatlantic Feminist." *Yale French Studies* 62 (1981): 220–36.

Johnston, Judith L. "Marguerite Yourcenar's Sexual Politics in Fiction 1939." Unpublished manuscript, Rider College, N.J.

Kreis, Gabriele. *Frauen im Exil*. Düsseldorf: Claasen Verlag, 1984.

Kristeva, Julia. *Desire in Language: A Semiotic Approach to Literature and Art*. Edited by Leon S. Roudiez. Translated by Thomas Gora, Alice Jardine, and Leon S. Roudiez. New York: Columbia University Press, 1980.

———. *Powers of Horror*. Translated by Leon S. Roudiez. New York: Columbia University Press, 1982.

———. *Récherches pour une sémanalyse*. Paris: Éditions du Seuil, 1969.

———. *Revolution in Poetic Language*. 1974. Translated by Margaret Waller. New York: Columbia University Press, 1984.

———. "The Speaking Subject." In *On Signs*, edited by Marshall Blonsky, 210–20. Baltimore: Johns Hopkins University Press, 1985.

Lemaire, Anika. *Jacques Lacan*. London: Routledge & Kegan Paul, 1977.

MacCannell, Juliet Flower. "Kristeva's horror." *Semiotica* 62 (Spring 1986): 325–55.

Marcus, Jane. "Alibis and Legends: The Ethics of Elsewhereness; Gender and Estrangement," in this volume.

———. "Laughing at Leviticus: *Nightwood* as Woman's Circus Epic." In *Silence and Power: A Reevaluation of Djuna Barnes*, edited by Mary Lynn Broe. Carbondale: Southern Illinois University Press, forthcoming.

———. Review of *The Female Body in Western Culture*, by Susan Rubin Suleiman. *Women's Review of Books* 4 (December 1986): 15–16.

———. *Virginia Woolf and the Languages of Patriarchy*. Bloomington: Indiana University Press, 1987.

Marks, Elaine, and Isabelle de Courtivron, eds. *New French Feminisms*. New York: Schocken Books, 1981.

Minow-Pinkney, Makiko. *Virginia Woolf and the Problem of the Subject*. New Brunswick: Rutgers University Press, 1987.

Moi, Toril. *Sexual/Textual Politics: Feminist Literary Theory*. London: Methuen, 1985.

Rosbo, Patrick de. *Entretiens radiophoniques avec Marguerite Yourcenar*. Paris: Mercure de France, 1972.

Spivak, Gayatri Chakravorty. "The Politics of Interpretations." In *In Other Worlds: Essays in Cultural Politics*, 118–33. New York: Methuen, 1987.

―――. "French Feminism in an International Frame." *Yale French Studies* 62 (1981): 154–84.

Suleiman, Susan Rubin, ed. *The Female Body in Western Culture*. Cambridge, Mass.: Harvard University Press, 1986.

Summerfield, Ellen. *Ingeborg Bachmann. Die Auflösung der Figur in ihrem Roman "Malina."* Bonn: Bouvier Verlag Herbert Grundmann, 1976.

Theweleit, Klaus. *Male Fantasies*. Translated by Stephen Conway, Erica Carter, and Chris Turner. Minneapolis: University of Minnesota Press, 1987.

Todorov, Tzvetan. *Mikhail Bakhtin: The Dialogic Principle*. Minneapolis: University of Minnesota Press, 1984.

Vanderbeke, Birgit. "Kein Recht auf Sprache? Der sprachlose Raum der Abwesenheit in *Malina*." In *Text + Kritik*, edited by Heinz Ludwig Arnold, 109–18. Munich: Text + Kritik, 1984.

Weigel, Sigrid. "Ein Ende mit der Schrift. Ein anderer Anfang." In *Text + Kritik*, edited by Heinz Ludwig Arnold, 58–92. Munich: Text + Kritik, 1984.

White, Allon. "L'éclatement du sujet: The Theoretical Work of Julia Kristeva." Stencilled Occasional Paper 49. Birmingham: University of Birmingham Centre for Contemporary Studies.

Yourcenar, Marguerite. *Alexis*. 1929. Translated by Walter Kaiser in collaboration with Yourcenar. New York: Farrar, Straus and Giroux, 1984.

―――. *A Coin in Nine Hands*. Translated by Dori Katz in collaboration with Yourcenar. New York: Farrar, Straus and Giroux, 1982.

―――. *Coup de Grâce*. 1939. Translated by Grace Frick in collaboration with Yourcenar. New York: Farrar, Straus and Giroux, 1981.

―――. *With Open Eyes*. Translated by Arthur Goldhammer. Boston: Beacon Press, 1984.

Chapter 16

. . . .

Exiled In and Exiled From

The Politics and Poetics of *Burger's Daughter*

Louise Yelin

I n a famous passage in *A Room of One's Own*, Virginia Woolf identifies
the position of women as simultaneously inside and outside patriarchal cultural hegemony: "If one is a woman one is often surprised by a
sudden splitting off of consciousness, say in walking down Whitehall,
when from being the natural inheritor of that civilisation, she becomes, on
the contrary, outside of it, alien and critical" (101). Woolf offers a way of
conceiving the question of women and exile. To be exiled is to be "outside
... alien and critical": on one hand, to be displaced by that culture
("outside" or exiled from); on the other, to be engaged in transforming/
displacing it ("alien and critical"). Paradoxically, the most disabling version of exile may be a consequence of women's position as inheritors of a
civilization, for a condition of their inheritance—their position "inside"—
is acquiescence in a cultural or political set that subordinates them, displaces them, or exiles them to the "outside." Woolf defines the stance of
much recent feminist criticism and theory—a stance that Joan Kelly identifies as the "doubled vision of feminist theory" and Rachel Blau DuPlessis calls the "both/and" vision of female Modernism and implicitly of
feminist criticism ("For the Etruscans"). But in this passage, at least,
Woolf's privileging of gender occludes other crucial aspects of the social/
cultural ensemble. What does it mean, for example, to be the inheritor of
the civilization symbolized (figured) by Whitehall? Surely not all women
can claim such an inheritance. To define feminism with reference to the
particular group of women Woolf sees as inside/outside "that civilisation"
yields an elitist, ethnocentric vision of both feminism and exile.

In this essay, I will examine Nadine Gordimer's *Burger's Daughter* as a
text that opens up—multiplies—the both/and vision of Woolf, Kelly, and
DuPlessis and of U.S.-European feminism in general. Gordimer writes
from a position both inside and outside the dominant European cultural
tradition ("Conversation," 30–31). Her frame of reference is defined by a
literary tradition that runs from Plato to Conrad and Proust and by her
situation in South Africa: she is a white, English-speaking woman actively
opposed to apartheid and its regime. For Gordimer, then, the African
context as well as the female one constitutes a version of exile in and
from—displacement from/of—the European cultural tradition. That is,
for Gordimer, the reality of apartheid mandates a politics of active opposition that inflects gender, exile, and feminism.[1]

In the first part of this essay I discuss the deployment of the both/and
vision in the narrative discourse of *Burger's Daughter*. Like any number of
novels, *Burger's Daughter* plays off a public/political narrative and a pri-

vate/personal one. But the way Gordimer does this, I suggest, destabilizes the opposition between the political and the personal. In the second part, I examine the novel's plot and argue that Gordimer revises the conventions of the female *bildungsroman* and thereby forces the reader to confront the cultural specificity of the values, codes, and genres of the dominant cultural tradition—European, bourgeois, patriarchal, and feminist. Thus I suggest that the politics and poetics of *Burger's Daughter* redefine the meaning of exile.

Destabilizing Narrative Discourse

The opening sequence of *Burger's Daughter* calls in question the nature of representation and, therefore, the status of its own narrative discourse. Even before the beginning, the status of the bourgeois self or subject— and its avatars, the subject of first-person narration and/or the protagonist of a ("the") novel—is thrown into relief by the epigraph from Claude Lévi-Strauss: "I am the place in which something has occurred." In this sentence, *I* occupies the place of the grammatical subject, but the sentence identifies *I* not as a person, a Cartesian subject of consciousness, but as a place, a site of activity. Because readers open the novel aware that it is about South Africa, the sentence invites us to identify I, the speaking subject, with (South) Africa, the place where something—the events that the novel describes?—occurs. Thus the epigraph evokes both the structuralist decentering of the subject and the poststructuralist displacement of humanism and with it of European ethnocentrism. This displacement, made from within European discourse about Africa, is itself displaced by the epigraph to part three, an epigraph spoken by as well as for South Africa, the slogan of the African National Congress, "Peace. Land. Bread." This sequence represents the post-Modern decentering of bourgeois subjectivity as part of a larger political project, which dislodges the imperial(ist) self and empowers formerly colonized "others" in and through the struggle against apartheid. The sequence of epigraphs, moreover, cautions us to read *Burger's Daughter* as a novel made from both inside and outside the European political and cultural hegemony that constitutes colonial others as other, from both inside and outside the liberation struggle in Africa.

This double perspective connects Gordimer with the stance of feminist theory and criticism, with feminism as it is at once part of and critical of—

inside and outside—the dominant cultural tradition. Gordimer's particular position as a white woman opposed to the white racist regime opens up or further multiplies the double perspective of U.S.-European feminism. This multiple perspective governs the way we read *Burger's Daughter* as the story of a particular woman in a particular family and also as the story of a place in which something occurs.

The opening sequence of *Burger's Daughter* calls in question the nature of representation and, therefore, the status of its own narration. The novel begins in 1962 with a group of people standing outside a prison waiting to bring parcels to those who are only later revealed as having been detained for participating in the struggle against the regime.[2] Among the group is the novel's protagonist, identified first as "a schoolgirl in a brown and yellow uniform" and subsequently as "Lionel Burger's daughter . . . fourteen years old, bringing an eiderdown quilt and hot-water bottle for her mother" and then given a name and a detailed description of her physical appearance (9–10). The three ways that Rosa Burger is designated in the opening sequence seem initially to be synonymous or complementary ways of describing the same person, but the three designations—schoolgirl, Lionel Burger's daughter, Rosa Burger—are hieroglyphs, signifiers of the relationship of the perceiver (narrator) and the persons/things described. How Rosa is seen depends on who is seeing her and from where, and who and where are not neutral terms but politically charged, like everything else in this novel about a country in which "society *is* the political situation" and "politics is character" (Gordimer, "A Writer in South Africa," 23).[3]

Throughout the novel, the terms that designate Rosa represent the different perspectives, the ideologically charged languages, of different groups in South African society.[4] The schoolgirl in uniform is the product of a journalistic view of the antiapartheid movement, one that purports to "humanize" it by packaging it for consumers of the mass media. (The novel as a whole works to defamiliarize this perspective and the view it produces of South Africa.) Lionel Burger's daughter is the object (person) seen by those Rosa calls the faithful, the activists in the struggle against apartheid and her parents' comrades in the South African Communist party. The faithful have their own narratives of the novel's events. One of these, an account of Rosa's participation in the movement, is given just after the opening sequence. In this account, party rhetoric appears as a hodgepodge of contending clichés that present Rosa as a heroine at once revolutionary and domestic: "Already she had taken on her mother's role in the household, giving loving support to her father, who was all too soon to be detained as well. On that day he had put others' plight before his own" (12). That white radicals in the antiapartheid struggle legitimate their movement with the rhetoric of bourgeois domesticity is a sign of the continuing hegemony of bourgeois-patriarchal ideology and, thus, of a contradiction that defines Rosa, especially for U.S. or European feminist readers, a contradiction between feminism (Rosa's liberation as a woman) and the struggle for justice in South Africa. The novel's treatment of this conflict distinguishes it from many recent novels written by women and suggests that female experience and indeed feminism are not universal but historically and geographically—politically—specific.

If the schoolgirl is the product of the mass media and Lionel Burger's daughter is Rosa as seen by the faithful, who gives us "Rosa Burger, about fourteen years old"? The obvious answer is the third-person narrator, but as Stephen Clingman points out (189–90), there are several third-person narrators. At least one of these presents events as if in a surveillance report for the government: one of the ways that *Burger's Daughter* calls narration in question is by linking it with spying and surveillance, with an organization of knowledge that is also an organization of power. Each narrator (narrative voice) represents a different perspective, point of view, position. Thus the third-person narration is the site of contending narratives, a place in which something—a contention of narratives—occurs. This narration and these contending narratives are also placed in dialogue with the narrative of Rosa herself.

Burger's Daughter plays off a third-person narration that attempts to name, capture, or represent—contain—a social totality against the more personal first-person narration of the protagonist.[5] Rosa's narrative emerges in part as a response to the question posed by the opening sequence, a question she also asks herself: "*When they saw me outside the prison, what did they see?*" (13). Rosa embraces narrative complexity and indeterminacy. She begins her story with a disclaimer: "I shall never know. It's all concocted. I saw—see—that profile in a hand-held mirror directed towards another mirror" (14). The two mirrors yield a series of reflections, each of which renders reality as representation. Each image in this series is like an element in a signifying chain; there is no absolute referent or transcendental signified, no original or authoritative master code.[6]

Rosa eschews not only the convention, whereby the author has authority over her (usually his) text, but also other versions of authority in first-person narration, in particular the idea that the narrating self can ever know the self-as-narrated or that the relationship between the self-as-narrated and the narrating self is one of continuity: "It's impossible to filter free of what I have learnt, felt, thought, the subjective presence of the schoolgirl. She's a stranger about whom some intimate facts are known to me, that's all" (14). Despite Rosa's repudiation of the idea that she is privy to her past self, her narration apparently privileges the personal, individual, private dimensions of experience. Thus she re-presents (reinterprets) the inaugural event of the novel: she tells us that she was carrying a hot water bottle because she was suffering "the leaden, dragging, wringing pain, . . . the peculiar fierce concentration of the body's forces in the menstruation of early puberty" (14–15). The hot water bottle now appears to signify menarche and therefore to inscribe *Burger's Daughter* in the subgenre of the female *bildungsroman*, where menarche so often encodes the protagonist's initiation into maturity, her subjection to the female destiny of anatomy and the constraints of the feminine gender. (I am thinking here of the "pungent suffering" that Jane Eyre experiences when her cousin John Reed throws a book at her and sends her to the Red Room [chapter 1]; of Catherine Earnshaw's wound when she is bitten by the dog Skulker as she escapes from Wuthering Heights and goes with Heathcliff to Thrushcross Grange, from which she emerges a "lady" [chapter 6]; and of Maggie Tulliver's encounter with Philip Wakem in the Red Deeps [*The Mill on the Floss*, Book V, chapter 1].)

But Rosa—or Gordimer or *Burger's Daughter*—also discredits this code, or at least treats it as lacking the special authority of a novelistic master code. For Rosa now says that she carried the hot water bottle to convey a message to her mother in jail: "*Dear Mom, Hope you are all right*. Then this innocently unsuitable tone became the perfect vehicle for the important thing I needed to convey. *Dad and I are fine and looking after everything. Lots of love from both*. She would know at once I was telling her my father had not been taken since she had gone" (16). This is the first and most innocuous of many instances in the novel when white antiapartheid activists use the language of domesticity or family values or romance—"private life"—as a cover for their political activities.[7] Indeed, the milestones of Rosa's life are not—or rather they are and are not—the developmental crises defined by psychoanalytic theories of personality but events in the modern history of South Africa. She is born on May 1, 1948, the year the first Afrikaner government took office (her birthdate, of course, identifies her with communism), and her life is punctuated by the treason trials during which her parents are imprisoned (1956–57), the Sharpeville massacre (1960), the banning and jailing of activists in the 1960s, and the movement sparked by the Soweto students' school boycott (1976–77). As a young woman, Rosa is "engaged" to activist Noel de Witt so that she can visit him in prison. A trip she takes during her subsequent affair with a Swede who is making a film about her father gives her the opportunity to smuggle a passport to a black comrade in a remote area. Throughout the novel, but especially in the opening sequence, the use of domesticity or the personal as a cover for political activity frames that ideological ensemble. The frame—irony—apparently distinguishes the self-conscious deployment of the personal/domestic from the unself-conscious rehearsal of domestic pieties, either in the annals of the faithful or the propaganda of the Afrikaner regime. But whether self-conscious or unself-conscious, ironic or straight, the deployment of domestic codes in *Burger's Daughter* makes it clear that private life—and its chief literary representation, the classic European novel?—is among other things a sign of white privilege.

The third-person narration is structured synchronically: each of the contending narratives signifies the stance of the observer(s) toward Rosa or the place where something occurs. Rosa's narrative is structured diachronically. It is divided into three sections (the three parts of the novel), which are distinguished by Rosa's narratees: in part one, her hippie lover; in part two, her father's first wife (her surrogate mother); in part three, her father himself. Like the multiple perspectives of the third-person narration, this structure implies that the narrating subject is not the only influence or authority over narrative discourse; unlike the organization of the third-person narration, it implies a plot, a sequence of development.

Difference and Plot: Rewriting the *Bildungsroman*

Rosa addresses her narrative first to her lover, next to her surrogate mother, and finally to her father. This sequence inscribes a movement toward the father; in other words, it rewrites the generic conventions of the *bildungsroman*, which tends to take its protagonist ever farther from her/his parents in her/his quest for whatever the novel or the culture she/he inhabits defines as maturity (Buckley, 17–19). As Elizabeth Abel et al. have noted (8), the ends of *bildung* and therefore of the *bildungsroman* are often gender-specific: autonomy (work) for men; marriage or romance or sexual fulfillment for women. Of course some novels—*To the Lighthouse*, for example, or Christina Stead's *The Man Who Loved Children*—

depart from these gender-marked norms in defining work or art, not love, as the object of women's quest. I argue here that *Burger's Daughter* revises even these female or feminist revisions of *bildung*, since Rosa's quest is defined primarily neither by love nor work but by political activity and it takes her toward as well as away from her father, and that this difference is among other things a sign or product of the African context of the novel, Gordimer's "responsibility toward the situation to which I was born" ("A Writer in South Africa," 22).[8]

If the inaugural event of the novel is Rosa's appearance outside the prison with a hot water bottle for (alternately) herself and her mother, its real plot motivator is the death in prison of Lionel Burger. Like the lives of so many novel protagonists, Rosa's early life is punctuated by a series of deaths: her brother's drowning, her mother's death, and her father's death, which—in a way that turns out to be spurious—sets her free. After Lionel dies, Rosa drifts away from the world of political action in which she has been involved and goes to live with her lover, an alienated, cynical, disaffected hippie named Conrad. In the schematic terms the novel simultaneously invites and refuses, Conrad represents the antithesis of the faithful, who defer all thoughts of present gratification for a future that may well be an illusion. Like the skeptical, deracinated characters in the novels of his namesake, Joseph Conrad, Gordimer's Conrad believes that he is without illusions and derides the activists' commitment to their cause.[9] When Conrad tells Rosa that she has grown up through other people, he means that she has never had an authentic emotional life. Among the "illusions" he punctures is Rosa's feeling for Noel de Witt, the "fiancé" she visited in prison, may have fallen in love with, and hoped to follow out of the country. But in undermining Rosa, Conrad serves the ends of the state, whether wittingly or not—again, like the characters of his namesake—and he therefore calls into question the idea of a personal realm untainted by politics. The entire first part of Rosa's narrative is a rejoinder to Conrad, a text whose pretext is his version of bourgeois individualism. At one point, Rosa answers Conrad by imagining her father's thoughts: "Lionel Burger probably saw in you the closed circuit of self; for him, such a life must be in need of a conduit toward meaning, which posited: outside self. That's where the tension that makes it possible to live lay, for him; between self and others; between the present and creation of something called the future" (86).

Are we to believe that because Rosa's response to Conrad is her version of Lionel's response she is not free, still subject to the authority of her father? (Consider Woolf's Lily Briscoe, who does not complete her painting until she dispatches Mr. and Mrs. Ramsay and sees things for herself.) On one hand, Rosa is not yet free, still mourning the deaths of her brother and parents; on the other hand, the outcome of the novel endorses Lionel's view—and Rosa's—and therefore calls in question the convention whereby freedom or maturity or development—*bildung*—is marked by the protagonist's superseding, transcending, or displacing paternal authority.

In other ways, too, Rosa's relationship with Conrad suggests the limits of private life. She uses it to separate herself from the faithful and their ongoing political activity. It is infantile and virtually incestuous: it repeats Rosa's relationship with Tony, the brother who drowns, and with "Baasie," a black boy who comes to live with the Burgers when his father is jailed and who is brought up as Rosa's brother. (When Rosa's parents are imprisoned in the 1957 treason trial, she goes to stay with relatives and "Baasie" is sent away.) In other words, private life or the personal, which is here portrayed as the working out of a repetition compulsion, is no more authentic than the political commitment of the faithful to a future they are trying to bring into being.

Eventually, Rosa does leave South Africa. After witnessing two events that her father's theories cannot account for—she observes a drunk die on a park bench and watches in horror as a black man viciously beats his donkey on a deserted road between a black "location" and Johannesburg—she feels politically impotent and attempts to "defect," to exile herself from "Lionel's country" (210). Rosa goes to the south of France to stay with Katya, Madame Bagnelli, her father's first wife. There, she falls in love with a married French academic named Bernard Chabalier. With Chabalier, Rosa seems for the first time to have an authentic emotional—sexual and personal—life, and she comes to believe that "it's possible to live within the ambit of a person, not a country. . . . There's nothing more private and personal than the life of a mistress, is there?" (302–4). Chabalier, then, represents romantic love as a version of personal liberation: his name, after all, has the same etymology as *chivalry* and *chevalier*. But in these echoes we can see (hear) the regressive undertones of romantic love, for the chivalric order is feudal, a step backward from the bourgeois order ironically named by Rosa's father, Lionel *Burger* (*Die Burger* is also the name of a leading Afrikaans newspaper) and from the socialist future represented by Rosa Luxemburg, for whom, along with his mother, Rosemarie Burger, Lionel Burger names his daughter.[10] (Significantly, we are never told definitively whether Rosa is named for either, neither, or both. Katya's friends call Rosa *Rose*, a name that identifies her with the object of the [male] romantic quest. Equally important, as a person named by the regime, Rosa is prohibited from participation in public life.) One could argue, of course, that the concept of progress which defines the bourgeois order as more advanced than the feudal order does not take women into account. Or, conversely, one could argue that romantic love is an ideology of male dominance, rendering women vassals subject to men.[11] Gordimer is not so much asserting one position or the other as suggesting the double-edged character of romantic love, as of other Western/European versions of personal liberation. This point is under-scored by the way the love affair of Rosa and Chabalier, the apotheosis of the personal, is punctuated by their discussion of languages—English, Afrikaans, French, the Langue d'Oc—as records of political struggle (267–75). The doubled-edgedness, the progression that is also a regres-sion is worked out not only for Rosa's sexual life but also in the way she is represented as a daughter in relation to two mothers.

Rosa's affair with Chabalier coincides with her visit with Katya, who takes her in and mothers her. In other words, Rosa's sexual awakening is enabled by her (re)discovery of her mother, a (re)discovery that, like her affair with Chabalier, is both a progression and a regression. That the (re)discovery of mother is more important than the love affair is implicit in the choice of Katya, not Chabalier, as the narratee in part two. Katya offers a contrast with Rosa's actual mother, Cathy Jansen Burger. Katya comes from an English-speaking family, whereas Cathy's family are Afri-kaners: Rosa's two mothers evoke the two mother tongues she tells Chabalier she grew up speaking (267). Mother tongues for Rosa, these languages are *lingue franche* for black South Africans (315). But language is not the main difference between the two mothers, for Cathy is a com-mitted activist and Katya resisted the discipline that tied the faithful together and eventually "defected" to Europe: thus she suggests the se-ductions of European culture, and her original name—she was born Colette Swan—evokes the two most important mothers in modern French literature. The allusions to Proust and Colette reinforce the identification of Katya with the idealized mother of the family romance or preoedipal fantasy (Garner et al., 20–24): Katya, fully realized in descriptions both by Rosa and by the third-person narrator, displaces the somewhat shadowy Cathy as a maternal presence. (There are two other fully realized maternal figures in the novel: Lionel, in Rosa's memory of snuggling up to his breast with "Baasie" and Tony as he taught them to swim, and Marisa Kgosana, a black activist whose maternal relationship with Rosa becomes one of sisterhood.) Thus, as in other modern novels about young women's loss of innocence (Elizabeth Bowen's *The Death of the Heart*, for example), Rosa's sexual awakening is associated with a return to mother. But the family romance is not the whole story, for though Katya represents the fantasy of the nurturing or sustaining mother, she is also limited in/by the individualism that defines her—a bohemian version more attractive than Conrad's or even Chabalier's, but one that is limiting nonetheless. And in this respect, Katya and all she stands for represent an interlude in Rosa's life, a stage in her development.

Under Katya's tutelage, and Bernard's, Rosa undergoes an aesthetic as well as a sexual awakening. Katya introduces her to modern art, for example, and one night she takes her to hear nightingales sing. Listening, the two women experience an ecstasy both like and unlike the one Keats describes in his "Ode to a Nightingale":

> Katya's breathing touched her as pine-needles did. All around the two women a kind of piercingly sweet ringing was on the limit of being audible. A new perception was picking up the utmost ring of waves whose centre must be unreachable ecstasy. The thrilling of the darkness intensified without coming closer. She gave a stir, questioning; the shape of Katya's face turned to stay her. The vibrating glass in which they were held shattered into song. The sensation of receiving the song kept changing; now it was a skyslope on which they planed, tipped, sailed, twirled to earth; then it was a breath stopped at the point of blackout and passing beyond it to a pitch hit, ravishingly, again, again, again. (261)

This passage, viscerally descriptive of female orgasm, epitomizes the way Gordimer evokes a *locus classicus* of European culture to point to the difference made by both the female and the African contexts. As a fable of literary production, Keats's ode suggests that the poet makes his poem as a way of recreating the solitary ecstasy he experiences in listening to the bird: "Away! Away! for I will fly to thee, / Not charioted by Bacchus and his pards, / But on the viewless wings of poesy." Keats's nightingale is both the occasion and the sign of the poet's affirmation of his vocation. The episode in *Burger's Daughter* has a different valence. The moment of ecstasy is sexual as well as aesthetic, not solitary but shared by a mother and daughter. Nor is this episode a fable of literary production: it is reported not by Rosa, who in any case does not write an ode, but by an omniscient narrator. And though it embraces both the aesthetic and the sexual/maternal dimensions of Rosa's relationship with Katya, it also marks what Rosa leaves behind when she leaves Katya: the maternal locus, Europe, the life of aesthetic pleasure.

Rosa does leave Katya. She goes to London, where she falls in with a group of South African exiles and soon encounters the man she knew as Baasie. The name, of course, means "little Boss" in Afrikaans, as he now reminds her when he tells her the name his father gave him, Zwelinzima, which in his language means "suffering land." In a late night phone call, Zwelinzima taunts her: "Whatever you whites touch, it's a take-over" (321). But the eventual result of this phone call is Rosa's return to South Africa: "I've heard all the black clichés before. I am aware that, like the ones the faithful use, they are an attempt to habituate ordinary communication to overwhelming meanings in human existence. They rap out the mechanical chunter of a telex; the message has to be picked up and read. They become enormous lies incarcerating enormous truths, still extant, somewhere" (328).

Rosa's response to Zwelinzima has at least a double significance. Rosa accepts the arbitrariness of language, the inability of language and especially politicized language to arrive at truth. But the instability that results from the dismantling of a master code does not lead her, like Conrad or Katya, to defect or remain in exile. Nor, conversely, does it make her believe that the rift between herself and Zwelinzima, suffering land, can be easily healed: although Gordimer flirts with allegory, she does not sink to sentimentalism. Rather, Rosa recognizes that "no one can defect" (332),[12] and the novel endorses this recognition. This passage occurs at the beginning of part three, which is headed by the ANC slogan and addressed by Rosa to Lionel Burger. The passage announces Rosa's re-commitment to political struggle, which leads her not only to resume her work as a physical therapist and reaffirm her relationship to her father but also to occupy his and her mother's place.

Burger's Daughter ends where it began, with a group waiting to bring parcels to the detained persons in prison. Rosa is now among those inside, detained for her participation in the movement now (1977) led by the Soweto students. (This movement began as a protest against instruction in Afrikaans.) Resistance is signaled, as before, in the use of domestic codes to convey messages among the faithful, both inside and outside the prison. A friend who visits Rosa remarks, "We joke a lot ... After all, why shouldn't family matters be funny? They're boring enough. You only realize how boring when you have to try to make them metaphors for something else" (360). But the friend does not have the last word: it is deleted by prison censors from a letter that Rosa sends to Katya: "There was a reference to a watermark of light that came into the cell at sundown every evening, reflected from some west-facing surface outside; something Lionel Burger had once mentioned. But the line had been deleted by the prison censor. Madame Bagnelli had never been able to make it out" (361). Rosa has taken her father's place; earlier, Lionel described the sun's appearance in prison only as the reflection of shadows (64). Moreover, Rosa's situation is like that of Plato's cave dweller who sees only shadows of images (*Republic*, Bk. VII). But here again, Gordimer at once recalls and recasts the European tradition: Rosa does not emerge like Plato's cave dweller into the light of truth, of pure forms, and in this respect the novel's ending apparently repudiates European cultural hegemony in the guise of the logocentrism symbolized by Plato. In addition, Gordimer subverts the hierarchical vision that underlies the cave analogy: while Plato's philosopher returns to the cave to educate those left in the darkness below,[13] Rosa's relationship with the other prisoners is one of equality, solidarity, and sorority. More important, the ending insists on the importance of the African context: it signals Gordimer's continuing opposition to apartheid, for the specific agent of her revision of European cultural traditions is, of course, the prison censor, whose action inscribes apartheid as absence. To this action, the novel is a counteraction that makes apartheid visible at least in its effects. In putting both these positions into play, *Burger's Daughter* partners a deconstructive poetics—a destabilizing of the discourses and especially the novelistic codes that inscribe European cultural hegemony—with a politics of opposition to apartheid and its regime.

This ending appears to assert that the African context takes primacy over the female one, that the exigency of abolishing apartheid overrides the concerns of gender, but it actually reenacts (reiterates) the novel's both/and vision and forces us once again to reconceive the meaning of exile. At the end of the novel, Rosa's position darkly echoes that of Woolf's walker down Whitehall. She has left Europe, and she is simultaneously inside and outside the "civilization" she inhabits, exiled in the prison (inside) and exiled from the Afrikaner regime against which she struggles, alien and critical, a victim and an opponent. Because Rosa is incarcerated in the prison where her father died, her exile in prison marks a (re)turn to her father that seems to exile her and with her the novel from a feminist tradition that conceives *bildung* as transcendence or displacement of paternal authority. But though the (re)turn to father appears to privilege the filial relationship that designates Rosa as Burger's daughter—her visitor reports, for example, that she looks like a little girl (360)—return is not identified with regression, for Rosa's life in prison is also governed by her sisterhood with her fellow prisoners. This experience of sisterhood—a sisterhood that transcends race—is made possible by Rosa's memory of "something sublime" in Lionel, the "sweet lucidity" and "elation" he shares with the black children in revolt against the regime (349). In other words, Rosa discovers herself in finding the father whose commitment to ending apartheid shapes her experience of sisterhood. *Burger's Daughter*, then, refuses a closure that privileges any one reading or reinstitutes a novelistic master code. Indeed, though the last scene finds Rosa occupying her father's place in prison, it ends not with Rosa or Lionel but with Katya, whose presence in the novel evokes the question of gender and especially gender and the personal as/and exile from Africa. Rosa, Lionel, Katya, censor: the refusal of closure here reinforces the both/and vision. That the last word, if there is a last word, belongs to Katya, who almost displaces Lionel in the narrative, suggests that although the struggle against apartheid takes precedence over sexual liberation or personal fulfillment, the issue of gender cannot be exiled from women's texts.

Notes

I thank my British Women Novelists class for provoking me to think about *Burger's Daughter*; Virginia Anderson, Mimi Doorga, Nasryne Matin, and Amy Tompkins of New Horizons Daycare Center for child care that freed me to think and write; Jean Herskovits for sharing with me her knowledge of African history; and Celeste Schenck, Deirdre David, Angela Ingram, Jane Marcus, Ronnie Scharfman, and Bob Stein for helpful comments on earlier versions of this essay and for encouragement that made me feel unlike an exile.

1. Gordimer notes in a 1982 interview that in South Africa color is the crucial issue. The interview ends at this point, and six months later it resumes with Gordimer asserting that when white oppression of blacks ceases, black women will fight against their oppression by black men ("Conversation," 20).

2. Gordimer assumes an audience familiar with South African history and not in need of having the particulars spelled out. The killing of blacks protesting at Sharpeville against the Pass Laws (1960) ended the possibility of change through nonviolent protest; subsequently, there was an increase in underground and armed

activity, including the founding of the armed wing of the ANC, Umkhonto we Sizwe, Spear of the Nation, and, concomitantly, an increase in the banning, detention, and imprisonment of opponents of the regime. The Communist party, banned in 1950, continued as an underground organization, its members banned and jailed. I thank Jean Herskovits for clarifying this chronology for me.

3. Joseph Lelyveld points out that South African whites literally arrange not to see blacks: the policy of forced resettlement of blacks in "homelands" or black locations ensures that apartheid is invisible to whites (7).

4. The model of narration I am relying on is the dialogical paradigm of Mikhail Bakhtin in "Discourse in the Novel" (261–63).

5. Boyers (72), Newman, Cooke, and Clingman all comment on the articulation of public and private in the novel.

6. Thus Gordimer's narrative style is secular in the sense intended by Said (16–42), a structure of affiliation not filiation.

7. According to Stephen Clingman (175), "the family" was a code name for the SACP when it was underground.

8. Barbara Harlow makes a similar point about Third World women's prison narratives, which, she argues (505), challenge the literary conventions of autobiography.

9. Susan Greenstein regards Conrad as a "debilitated version of his namesake" (234).

10. Rosa Luxemburg serves as a model for Rosa's commitment to political struggle in *Burger's Daughter*. Because Luxemburg defines a social democratic— that is, communist—politics that is not identical to Lenin's, Rosa Luxemburg also signifies the complicated relationship of South African communist opponents of apartheid to Soviet-inspired Communist parties and politics. Particularly germane to Lionel Burger's politics and the activism of South African communists (and Communists) generally is Luxemburg's notion that the particular program of "social democracy" is less important than the way that program is "interpreted in action" (Luxemburg, "Our Program," 380).

11. Feminist historians and theorists have argued the case both ways. For an interrogation of the concept of progress, see Kelly (both titles); for critiques of romantic love, see de Beauvoir and Rich. Rachel DuPlessis articulates the critique of romance with narrative theory in her notion of the romance plot as a trope for the sex/gender system (*Writing Beyond the Ending*, 5).

12. Here Rosa recalls Joseph Conrad's Marlow. For both, praxis—work for Marlow, political action for Rosa, narrative for both—compensates for the loss of meaning, for the fact that lies incarcerate truth, that meaning is not "inside like a kernel but outside, enveloping the tale which brought it out only as a glow brings out a haze" (Conrad, 68).

13. I thank Morris Kaplan for bringing this to my attention.

Works Cited

Abel, Elizabeth, Marianne Hirsch, and Elizabeth Langland. Introduction to *The Voyage In: Fictions of Female Development*, edited by Elizabeth Abel, Marianne Hirsch, and Elizabeth Langland, 3–19. Hanover, N.H.: University Press of New England, 1983.

Bakhtin, Mikhail M. "Discourse in the Novel." In *The Dialogic Imagination*, translated by Caryl Emerson and Michael Holquist, edited by Michael Holquist, 259–422. Austin: Texas University Press, 1981.

Beauvoir, Simone de. *The Second Sex*. Translated and edited by H. M. Parshley. New York: Bantam, 1961.

Boyers, Robert. "Public and Private: On *Burger's Daughter*." *Salmagundi* 62 (1984): 62–92.

Buckley, Jerome Hamilton. *Season of Youth: The Bildungsroman from Dickens to Golding*. Cambridge, Mass.: Harvard University Press, 1974.

Clingman, Stephen. *The Novels of Nadine Gordimer: History from the Inside*. London: Allen and Unwin, 1986.

Conrad, Joseph. *Heart of Darkness*. 1899. Reprint. New York: Signet, 1950.

Cooke, John. *The Novels of Nadine Gordimer: Private Lives/Public Landscapes*. Baton Rouge: Louisiana State University Press, 1985.

DuPlessis, Rachel Blau. *Writing Beyond the Ending: Narrative Strategies of Twentieth-Century Women Writers*. Bloomington: Indiana University Press, 1985.

DuPlessis, Rachel Blau, and Members of Workshop 9. "For the Etruscans: Sexual Difference and Artistic Production: The Debate over a Female Aesthetic." In *The Future of Difference*, edited by Hester Eisenstein and Alice Jardine, 128–56. Boston: Hall, 1980.

Garner, Shirley, Claire Kahane, and Madelon Sprengnether. Introduction to *The (M)other Tongue: Essays in Feminist Psychoanalytic Interpretation*, edited by Shirley Garner, Claire Kahane, and Madelon Sprengnether, 15–29. Ithaca: Cornell University Press, 1985.

Gordimer, Nadine. *Burger's Daughter*. New York: Penguin, 1980.

———. "A Conversation with Nadine Gordimer." *Salmagundi* 62 (1984): 3–31.

———. "A Writer in South Africa." *London Magazine* n.s., 5 (May 1965): 21–30.

Greenstein, Susan M. "Miranda's Story: Nadine Gordimer and the Literature of Empire." *Novel* 18 (1984–85): 227–42.

Harlow, Barbara. "From the Women's Prison: Third World Women's Narratives of Prison." *Feminist Studies* 12 (1986): 501–24.

Kelly, Joan. "Did Women Have a Renaissance?" In *Becoming Visible: Women in European History*, edited by Renate Bridenthal and Claudia Koonz, 137–64. Boston: Houghton Mifflin, 1977.

———. "The Doubled Vision of Feminist Theory: A Postscript to the Women and Power Conference." *Feminist Studies* 4 (1979): 216–27.

Lelyveld, Joseph. *Move Your Shadow: South Africa, Black and White*. New York: New York Times Books, 1985.

Luxemburg, Rosa. "Our Program and the Political Situation." In *Selected Political Writings of Rosa Luxemburg*, edited by Richard Howard, 377–408. New York: Monthly Review, 1971.

Nadine Gordimer: Politics and the Order of Art. Salmagundi 62 (1984).

Newman, Judie. "Prospero's Complex: Race and Sex in Nadine Gordimer's *Burger's Daughter.*" *Journal of Commonwealth Literature* 20 (1985): 81–99.

Rich, Adrienne. "Compulsory Heterosexuality and Lesbian Existence." In *Blood, Bread, and Poetry*, 23–75. New York: Norton, 1986.

Said, Edward W. "Secular Criticism." In *The World, the Text, and the Critic*, 16–42. Cambridge, Mass.: Harvard University Press, 1983.

Woolf, Virginia. *A Room of One's Own*. New York: Harcourt, Brace and World, 1929.

Questions of Multiculturalism

Sneja Gunew and Gayatri Chakravorty Spivak

T his discussion between Gunew and Chakravorty Spivak arose out of a desire to clarify the extent to which the project of post-colonialism and anti-imperialism was both distinct from and overlapping with the project of multicultural politics in Australia. Given the recent setbacks to the promotion of a multicultural Australia (where *all* Australians would eventually be seen as belonging to specific cultures), these are urgent questions.

SG: We might begin with the whole notion of authenticity—a question that keeps coming up in relation to the kind of writing that I am publicizing at the moment. I now refer to it as non-Anglo-Celtic rather than Migrant writing, since within Australia, *Migrant* connotes an inability to speak English. Thus it is the writing of non-Anglo-Celts but in English. The question that keeps rising in relation to this is the question of authenticity. And it takes various forms but I suppose one way of, in a sense, caricaturing it but, also, making it accessible is: "Aren't Patrick White's middle-Europeans or Beverley Farmer's Greeks just as authentic as the Greeks created by *ΠO*'s poetry or by Antigone Kefala?" In a sense, putting the question this way covers over, or makes invisible, other forms, other questions that could be posed, such as, "But why do these Anglo-Celts have access to publishing, to writing, to be part of Australian literature, and why are other writers like Kefala, Ania Walwicz, Rosa Cappiello, and others not seen as part of these cultural productions, why aren't they given a full measure of cultural franchise? In fact, in some senses, far from being invisible, the Migrant has always been constructed within Australian discursive formations, not just literature; and in literary forms the first such construction was Nino Culotta, who was an Irish journalist posing as an Italian, and wrote the most famous book for many, many decades about being an Italian immigrant trying to make it in Australia. And this book, I remember, was given to numerous immigrants as they arrived in Australia as some kind of explication of their status within the community, and is quite horrendous in all sorts of ways.

GCS: For me, the question "who should speak?" is less crucial than "who will listen?" "I will speak for myself as a Third World person" is an important position for political mobilization today. But the real demand is that, when I speak from that position, I should be listened to seriously; not with that kind of benevolent imperialism, really, which simply says that because I happen to be an Indian or whatever. . . . A hundred years ago it was impossible for me to speak, for the precise reason that makes it only too possible for me to speak in certain circles now. I see in that a kind of reversal, which is again a little suspicious. On the other hand, it is very important to hold on to it as a slogan in our time. The question of "speaking *as*" involves a distancing from oneself. The moment I have to think of the ways in which I will speak as an Indian, or as a feminist, the ways in which I will speak as a woman, what I am doing is trying to generalize myself, make myself a representative, trying to distance myself from some kind of inchoate speaking *as such*. There are many subject positions which one must inhabit, one is not just one thing. That is when a political consciousness comes in. So that in fact, for the person who does the "speaking as" something, it is a problem of distancing from one's self, whatever that self might be. But when the card-carrying listeners, the hegemonic people, the dominant people, talk about listening to someone "speaking as" something or the other, I think *there* one encounters a problem. When *they* want to hear an Indian speaking as an Indian, a Third World woman speaking as a Third World woman, they cover over the fact of the ignorance that they are allowed to possess, into a kind of homogenization.

SG: Yes, and they choose what parts they want to hear, and they choose what they then do with this material; and what seems to happen in very crude ways, within the context of multiculturalism, is that certain people are elevated very quickly to those who speak for *all* immigrants: in terms of funding, and in terms of the dissemination of their work, and so on. As a result, you don't hear about the rest, because "we have covered that," and those few token figures function as a very secure alibi. If you look at the proportion of, for example, multicultural, non-Anglo-Celtic artists who get funded by the Australian Council, they are a very small percentage, and often the same ones every year. Because it is, in fact, an incredible job to educate oneself to know just what is in the field, and who else is doing things. It requires a lot of labor; it is so much easier to have these recurrent token figures.

GCS: Proust in *A la recherche*, when someone is criticizing Francoise's French, writes: "What is French but bad Latin?" So from that point of view, one can't distinguish, you can't say that it is a French position or a Roman position. This is what he is pointing at—the moment you say "this is a white position," again you are homogenizing. I think there is safety in specificity rather than in those labels.

SG: This is what I was trying to refer to earlier when I was saying the question usually gets posed in the ways of asking: "Yes but aren't Patrick White's middle-Europeans authentic?" That is not the issue, because the whole *notion* of authenticity, of the authentic migrant experience, is one that comes to us constructed by hegemonic voices; and so, what one has to tease out is what is *not* there. One way of doing this (if one has knowledge from a particular culture), is to say: but look this is what is left out, this is what is covered over; this kind of construction is taking place, this kind of reading is being privileged or, these series of readings are being privileged; and then to ask, what readings are not privileged, what is not there, what questions can't be asked?

GCS: Subordinate people use this also; and we are not without a sense of irony: we use it. I talk a lot, right, and when I get very excited I interrupt people; and I am making a joke, but in fact it is never perceived as a joke unless I tell them. I will quite often say, "You know, in my culture it shows interest and respect if someone interrupts." And immediately there are these very pious faces, and people allow me to interrupt. It is not as if we don't perceive the homogenization; we exploit it, why not?

SG: So that what you have as one of the strategies of some of the writers that I work with, is that they play a kind of stage Migrant and poke fun at, and parody in all sorts of ways, these so-called authentic Migrant constructions. I am thinking here of the work of ΠΟ, the work of Ania Walwicz. . . .

GCS: In fact, tokenization goes with ghettoization. These days, I am constantly invited to things so that I will present the Third World point of view; when you are perceived as a token, you are also silenced in a certain way because, as you say, if you have been brought there it has been covered, they needn't worry about it anymore, you salve their conscience. In the United States, being an Indian also brings a certain very curious problem. Over the centuries we have had histories of, let's say, Indian indentured labor being taken to the Afro-Caribbean. After the change of regimes in certain African nations, Indians moved from Africa, then to Britain; then Indians in waves in the early 1960s, professional Indians, went to the United States as part of the brain-drain. These Indians who are spread out over the world, for different kinds of historical reasons, they are diasporic. . . .

SG: You could multiply this by the Greeks and the Italians in Australia, and numerous other ethnic groups who, for various reasons, have had to leave their original countries and move to other ones.

GCS: The Indian community in the United States is the only colored community that came in with the brain-drain. This is quite different from Indians and Pakistanis in Britain, and certainly very different from Indians of the Afro-Caribbean diaspora. And therefore we are used as an alibi because we don't share the same history of oppression with the local blacks, the East Asians, and the Hispanics; on the other hand, our skins are not white, and since most of us are postcolonials we were trained in the British way, so there is a certain sort of Anglomania in the United States, we can be used as affirmative action alibis.

SG: Yes, this happens to some extent, too, with Jewish immigrants, often refugees, who came at various stages to Australia. They, too, are used in that sense of affirmative action. For all sorts of reasons they have, some of them, come to very prominent positions and so they can be wheeled in very easily to say: "Of course this is not an Anglo establishment, a predominantly Anglo establishment—we've got x, y, z." So a similar kind of alibi operates. One of the things, though, that I wanted to hear you talk about more was a notion you brought up yesterday, about this idea of earning the right to criticize. As I understand it, this can be a trap that is provided by a certain kind of privilege that comes with being this sort of token who is constantly brought in. I wonder if you could say more about that.

GCS: It is a problem that is very close to my heart because I teach, after all, abroad. I will have in an undergraduate class, let's say, a young, white, male student, politically correct, who will say: "I am only a bourgeois white male, I can't speak." In that situation—it's peculiar, because I am in the position of power and their teacher and, on the other hand, I am not a bourgeois white male—I say to them: "Why not develop a certain degree of rage against the history that has written such an abject script for you that you are silenced?" Then you begin to investigate what it is that silences you, rather than take this very deterministic position—since my skin color is this, since my sex is this, I cannot speak. I call these things, as you know, somewhat derisively chromatism: basing everything on skin color, "I am white, I can't speak"; and genitalism: depending on what kind of genitals you have, you can or cannot speak in certain situations. From this position, then, I say you will of course not speak in the same way about the Third World material, but if you make it your task not only to learn what is going on there through language, through specific programs of study, but also at the same time through a *historical* critique of your position as the investigating person, then you will see that you have earned the right to criticize, and you will be heard. When you take the position of not doing your homework: "I will not criticize because of my accident of birth, the historical accident," that is a much more pernicious position. In one way you take a risk to criticize, of criticizing something which is *Other*—something you used to dominate. I say that you have to take a certain risk: to say "I won't criticize" is salving your conscience and allowing you not to do any homework. On the other hand, if you criticize having earned the right to do so, then you are indeed taking a risk and you will probably be made welcome, and can hope to be judged with respect.

SG: Perhaps the other side of the dilemma, though, is the sort of trap that people who are wheeled in as token figures speaking for those marginalized groups can fall into, denying their own privileged position. You were saying earlier, for example, that in a classroom situation you are the one with the power vis-à-vis the white Anglo-Saxon student. Similarly I think that one forgets when one speaks within very obviously privileged academic contexts about, say, immigrant groups within Australia, that one is also very much in danger of homogenizing, and of misrepresenting, and of not really following through those questions carefully enough; distinguishing carefully enough between those differences that one speaks "in the name of." That business of speaking "in the name of" is something about which I have a real phobia, and it is very difficult to think up strategies for undermining that.

GCS: And I don't think, really, that we will solve the problem today talking to each other; but, on the other hand, I think it has to be kept alive as a problem. It is not a solution, the idea of the disfranchised speaking for themselves, or the radical critics speaking for them; this question of representation, self-representation, representing others, is a problem. On the other hand, we cannot put it under the carpet with demands for authentic voices; we have to remind ourselves that, as we do this, we might be compounding the problem even as we are trying to solve it. And there has to be a persistent critique of what one is up to, so that it doesn't get all bogged down in this homogenization; constructing the Other simply as an object of knowledge, leaving out the real Others because of the ones who are getting access to public places because of these waves of benevolence and so on. I think as long as one remains aware that it is a very problematic field, there is some hope.

SG: Yes, and one of the strategies that one has learned from the Women's Movement, for example, is to make sure that you are constantly involved in political campaigns, that you are in touch with what is happening, that you are in touch with the very specific politics of trying to bring about certain reforms. So in a similar way, I suppose, one of the ways in the area of multiculturalism is to be very alert to what is happening with the various immigrant groups in terms of cultural politics. The things that are going on, the questions that are not being asked, what people are doing that has never been heard or seen—these are the issues.

GCS: Can you give me some specific examples of problems of cultural politics in the Australian context?

SG: Well, for example, I was walking along Glebe Road last week, and I looked in a shop window and suddenly saw, among the clothing (this was a tailor's shop), a poem hanging there. I walked in, and found a wonderful friend of mine, Nihat Ziyalan, who is a Turkish poet; and this is his way—one of the few ways that he can get heard—of making his work accessible to whoever is passing by. And people do apparently come in and talk to him about his work; but he certainly is not receiving any funding at the moment. Always there is this sense of voices in the wilderness that are never going to get heard, not through the regular channels, be it the Australia Council, be it SBS. In the case of the latter, the ethnic broadcasting television station, which is supposed to be serving multiculturalist Australia, in reality gets most of its programs from overseas, so it is Europe imported back into Australia, rather than seeing certain kinds of European or Asian or Middle Eastern groups within Australia and latching into those.

GCS: This is the real problem, isn't it? We are back to some extent where we started, the way one actually keeps talking about the same old things, that is, rather than look at the real problem of imperialism, to make it identical with the problems of immigrants; rather than look at the Third

World at large, to make everything identical with the problem at home. This is, in fact, simply the old attitudes disguised in one way or another. This is the real difficulty with cultural politics. If you go, as I do, to African Literature Association conventions, what you notice is that the black Americans (of course, when I generalize like this there are always notable exceptions), black Americans are much more interested in the question of any black tradition, whereas the continental Africans are much more interested in the problems that they and their colleagues are making for themselves, in the problems of the various African nations, in the problems existing between European language productions in Africa, and what is happening to African languages as it's all getting organized into philosophy, the discipline of literature, and so on and so forth. What you really mark is that it is the ones with United States passports who are trying to identify the problem of racism in the United States with what is happening in decolonized Africa.

SG: So again, that's the question of homogenization and that refusal of specificity.

GCS: Yes.

SG: And I think another thing that you have been referring to, that notion of a diaspora, that the diasporic cultures are quite different from the culture that they came from originally, and that sort of distinction—an elementary distinction, and also one, of course, that history teaches us is not made, and needs to be made.

GCS: You see these differences, in fact, you feel them in the details of your daily life, because actually the system is not so blind—it's the benevolent ones who become blind in this way. I'll tell you a little story. I was at the Commonwealth Institute in London in March, to discuss some films made by Black Independent Film-makers in London (a wonderful group of people, I was very pleased they asked me), and one of the points I made to them was in fact (I am a bit of a broken record on this issue), you are diasporic blacks in Britain, and you are connecting to the local lines of resistance in Britain, and you are therefore able to produce a certain idiom of resistance; but don't forget the Third World at large, where you won't be able to dissolve everything into black against white, as there is also black against black, brown against brown, and so on. These young men and women thought I was asking them to connect with some mystical ethnic origin because, of course, when they were brought into the places they inhabit, their sense of the old country was from the nostalgic longing toward customs, cooking, and so on and so forth, that they saw in their families. And so they were rebelling against what is basically a generational problem, and transforming it into a total ignoring of what is going on in the Third World at large. On the other hand, the system knows I am a resident alien in the United States; at that point I was actually lecturing in Canada, at the University of Alberta. I crossed from upstate New York into Toronto (I carry an Indian passport) with no problem because, of course, an Indian resident in the United States would not, the thinking goes, want to become an illegal immigrant in Canada. Two days later, I went to London, I did my program, and was returning back to Canada with the same passport, the same resident alien's visa in the United States, and I was supposed to take a plane from Heathrow on Sunday. Air Canada said to me: "We can't accept you." I said: "Why?" and she said: "You need a visa to go to Canada." I said: "Look here, I am the same person, the same passport. . . . " Indian cultural identity, right? But you become different. When it is from London, Indians can very well want to jump ship to Canada; I need a visa to travel from London to Canada on the same passport, but not from the United States. To cut a long story short, I was talking about a related problem to the black men and women who had made the films, and then it happened in my own life. In the end, I had to stay another day and telephone Canada and tell them that I could not give my seminar. I said to the woman finally before I left, in some bitterness: "Just let me tell you one small thing; don't say 'We can't accept you,' that sounds very bad from one human being to another; next time you should say: 'The regulations are against it'; then we are both victims." And the woman looked at me with such astonishment because, in Heathrow, a colored woman wearing a sari does not speak to a white woman like this. There, I was indeed speaking as an Indian, in that particular situation. So in those kinds of things, once you begin to look at the way regulations work, you will see the differences *are* made among different kinds of Third World peoples—but not when one is being benevolent.

SG: What is very much a question for me at the moment is that if you are constructed in one particular kind of language, what violence does it do to your subjectivity if one then has to move into another language and suppress whatever selves or subjectivities were constructed by the first. And of course, some people have to pass through this process several times. And a small gesture toward beginning to understand this would be to create a demand for multilingual anthologies within Australia. There is an incredible and disproportionate resistance to presenting the general Australian public with immigrant writing *in English* even, but to have it in conjunction with the reminder of these repressed languages seems to be another battle that still has to be fought.

GCS: One hears, for example, that some of the theoretical stuff that's produced, let's say, in France, is naturally accessible to people from Africa, from India, from these so-called "natural" places. If one looks at the history of post-Enlightenment theory, the major problem has been the problem of autobiography: how subjective structures can, in fact, give objective truth. During these same centuries, the Native Informant, who was found in these other places, his stuff was unquestioningly treated as the objective evidence for the founding of so-called sciences like ethnography, ethnolinguistics, comparative religion, and so on. So that, once again, the theoretical problems relate only to the person who knows. The person who *knows* has all of the problems of selfhood. The person who is *known*, somehow seems not to have a problematic self. These days, it is the same kind of agenda that is at work. Only the dominant self can be problematic; the self of the Other is authentic without a problem, naturally available to all kinds of complications. This is very frightening.

Note

This conversation was originally broadcast on Australian Broadcasting Commission Radio National on Saturday, August 30, 1986, in "The Minders," produced by Penny O'Donnell and Ed Brunetti.

The Contributors

SUSAN HARDY AIKEN is Associate Professor of English at the University of Arizona. Coeditor of *Changing Our Minds: Feminist Transformations of Knowledge* (State University of New York Press, forthcoming), she has published many essays and reviews on nineteenth- and twentieth-century literature and feminist criticism in such journals as *PMLA*, *Signs*, *Contemporary Literature*, *College English*, and *Scandinavian Studies*. She is at work on a study entitled "Isak Dinesen and the Engendering of Narrative."

SHARI BENSTOCK is Professor of English and Director of the Women's Studies Program at the University of Miami, Coral Gables. She is author of *Women of the Left Bank: Paris, 1900–1940* (1987), editor of *The Private Self: Theory and Practice in Women's Autobiographical Writings* (1988), and coeditor of *Coping with Joyce: Essays from the Copenhagen Symposium* (1989). She is author of *Textualizing the Feminine: Essays on the Limits of Genre* (University of Oklahoma Press, forthcoming).

MARY LYNN BROE is the Louise R. Noun Professor of Women's Studies and English at Grinnell College. She is author of *Protean Poetic: The Poetry of Sylvia Plath* (1980) and editor of *Silence and Power: A Reevaluation of Djuna Barnes* (Southern Illinois University Press, forthcoming). She has published articles on British and American women writers and feminist theory and is working with Frances McCullough on *Cold Comfort: The Selected Letters of Djuna Barnes* (Random House, forthcoming).

BARBARA BROTHERS is Professor and chairperson of English at Youngstown State University. Her publications include essays on Henry Green, Elizabeth Bowen, Barbara Pym, Sylvia Townsend Warner, and Margaret Kennedy. She is President of the College English Association, coeditor of the *CEA Critic*, on the editorial board of the *Barbara Pym Newsletter*, and a member of the MLA Delegate Assembly. She has served on the ADE executive committee and the Ohio Humanities Council. She is at work on an anthology of British women writers of the 1930s for the Feminist Press, on a history of women's writing of that period, and, with Bege Bowers, has coedited "The Novel of Manners: A Study of a Tradition."

KARIN (STEVENS) CONNELLY was born in Montana in 1939 and is now living in exile in the Middle West. Her work experience includes being a technical writer, Army Corps of Engineers; guest editor, *Mademoiselle* magazine; soft-prop maker, Guthrie Theatre; and teaching art in prisons, schools, and colleges. She is currently an instructor at Grinnell College in the Art Department and in the Writing Laboratory. She also works with women who are quilters and knitters and for 1988–89 has a Folk Arts Grant from the Iowa Arts Council to work with two Mesquakie women beadworkers to learn traditional Mesquakie beadworking techniques.

SUSAN STANFORD FRIEDMAN is Professor of English and Women's Studies at the University of Wisconsin-Madison. She is the author of *Psyche Reborn: The Emergence of H.D.*; coauthor of *A Woman's Guide to Therapy*; and author of articles on H.D., Adrienne Rich, childbirth, women's auto-biography, and feminist pedagogy. Current projects include a book on H.D.'s prose and an edition of the H.D.-Bryher correspondence about psychoanalysis.

ESTHER FUCHS is Associate Professor of Hebrew Language and Litera-ture at the University of Arizona at Tucson. Her publications include *Encounters with Israeli Authors* (1982); *No License to Die: Poetry and Fiction* (1983); *Cunning Innocence: On S. Y. Agnon's Irony* (1985); *Israeli Myth-ogynies: Women in Contemporary Hebrew Fiction* (1987); and *Sexual Politics in the Biblical Narrative* (Indiana University Press, forthcoming).

JUDITH KEGAN GARDINER is Professor of English and Women's Studies at the University of Illinois at Chicago. This essay relates to her book *Rhys, Stead, Lessing, and the Politics of Empathy* (1989). Her other publications include studies of Renaissance English literature, twentieth-century women writers, and literary theory. She is currently working on English women writers of the seventeenth century.

SNEJA GUNEW teaches at Deakin University, Victoria, in literary and women's studies. She is completing a book that examines the theoretical implications of non-Anglo-Celtic writing for Australian literature.

TRUDIER HARRIS is J. Carlyle Sitterson Professor of English at the University of North Carolina at Chapel Hill, where she teaches courses in Afro-American literature and folklore. Author of *From Mammies to Militants: Domestics in Black American Literature, Exorcising Blackness: Historical and Literary Lynching and Burning Rituals*, and *Black Women in the Fiction of James Baldwin*, she is also editor of three and coeditor of three of *The Dictionary of Literary Biography*'s six-volume series on Afro-American writers. She has published in numerous journals and contributed chapters to many books. In 1988 she received National Endowment for the Humanities support to complete her book on Toni Morrison's use of African, Afro-American, and other folk traditions.

ANGELA INGRAM is a resident alien who as an Associate Professor at Southwest Texas State University teaches in the English Department and in the Women's Studies program she helped invent. She has published work on Elizabethan-Jacobean drama, Virginia Woolf, and relatively obscure women's writing of the 1920s.

ANNETTE KOLODNY used part of the financial settlement from her Title VII suit to establish the Legal Fund of the Task Force on Discrimination within the National Women's Studies Association. Her essay "Dancing through the Minefield: Some Observations on the Theory, Practice and Politics of a Feminist Literary Criticism" won the 1979 Florence Howe Award for Feminist Criticism and has been widely reprinted. She publishes actively on feminist critical theory and American women writers, and she explored the cultural mythology of the American frontiers in *The Lay of the Land* (1975; reprinted 1984) and *The Land Before Her* (1984). She is Dean of the Faculty of Humanities at the University of Arizona in Tucson.

JANE MARCUS is Professor of English at City University of New York Graduate School and the City College of New York. She is, most recently, editor of *Virginia Woolf and Bloomsbury: A Centenary Celebration* (1987) and author of *Virginia Woolf and the Languages of Patriarchy* (1987) and of *Art and Anger* (1988).

BRADFORD K. MUDGE is Assistant Professor of English at the University of Colorado at Denver. He has published articles on Pope, Coleridge, Wordsworth, and Tennyson and is author of *Sara Coleridge, A Victorian Daughter: Her Life and Essays* (1989).

INGEBORG MAJER O'SICKEY, exiled by choice from West Germany since she was eighteen, has lived in England, Spain, Italy, and the United States. She has two children who are both alien and critically living in the United States. Her doctoral dissertation at the University of Texas at Austin was titled "Fascistic Discourse in the Narratives of Ingeborg Bachmann and Marguerite Yourcenar." A Faculty Fellow at Syracuse University, she is also an editor and translator and writes short fiction about the way women survive in patriarchal society.

HILARY RADNER is Assistant Professor in the Department of Communication and Theatre at the University of Notre Dame. She has most recently completed a study entitled "Shopping Around: Locating a Feminine Subject of Enunciation through Textual Practice," which focuses on feminine narrative as a cross-media phenomenon in print, film, and television.

SONIA SALDÍVAR-HULL is a graduate student at the University of Texas at Austin, where she is a Danforth Compton Fellow. She has presented numerous scholarly papers on contemporary Chicana writers and is a contributor to the *Longman Anthology of World Literature by Women* (1989). "Feminism on the Border: From Gender Politics to Geopolitics" will appear in *Chicano Literary Criticism in a Social Context* (Duke University Press, forthcoming).

REBECCA SAUNDERS teaches composition and expository writing and American literature at the University of Massachusetts, Boston, where she has also taught music. She has written on nineteenth-century novelists and on Doris Lessing. She is currently working on a study entitled "The Politics of Exile: Links between Feminism and Imperialism."

CELESTE M. SCHENCK is Ann Whitney Olin Junior Fellow at Barnard College. She is cofounder of Women Poets at Barnard, a series of readings and publications featuring the work of new poets, and general coeditor of Reading Women Writing, a series in feminist criticism published by Cornell University Press. She is author of *Mourning and Panegyric: The Poetics of Pastoral Ceremony* (1988), coeditor of *Life/Lines: Theorizing Women's*

Autobiography (1988), and author of *Corinna Sings: Women Poets and the Politics of Genre* (Cornell University Press, forthcoming).

GAYATRI CHAKRAVORTY SPIVAK is currently Andrew W. Mellon Professor of English and Director of the Program for the Study of Culture at the University of Pittsburgh. She has published extensively on topics relating to deconstruction, the critique of imperialism, and feminism-Marxism in Asia, Africa, Australia, Eastern and Western Europe, and the United States. In 1974 she published *Myself I Must Remake: Life and Poetry of W. B. Yeats* "in a deliberate response to a certain challenge articulated by the U.S. undergraduate movement in the sixties." In 1976 she published "what by many is considered a text of the other extreme": a translation with critical introduction of Jacques Derrida's *De la grammatologie*. Her most recent book is *In Other Worlds: Essays in Cultural Politics* (1988); her forthcoming book is entitled "Riding on the Hyphen: Deconstruction in the Service of Reading," one of whose objects of investigation is "the production of international feminism."

LOUISE YELIN is Assistant Professor of English at the State University of New York–Purchase, where she teaches the novel, nineteenth-century literature, and critical theory. She has written on Charles Dickens, Christina Stead, and feminist criticism and is currently at work on a book entitled "From the Margins of Empire," a study of colonial and post-colonial women writers in English.

Index

2345   3790